Windows® Game Programming For Dummies®

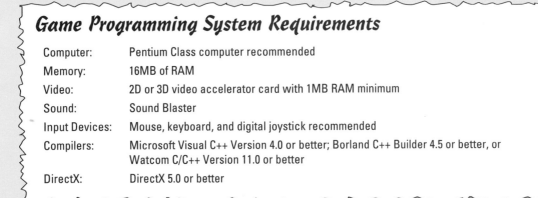

P9-DND-002

Game Programming System Requirements

Computer:	Pentium Class computer recommended
Memory:	16MB of RAM
Video:	2D or 3D video accelerator card with 1MB RAM minimum
Sound:	Sound Blaster
Input Devices:	Mouse, keyboard, and digital joystick recommended
Compilers:	Microsoft Visual C++ Version 4.0 or better; Borland C++ Builder 4.5 or better, or Watcom C/C++ Version 11.0 or better
DirectX:	DirectX 5.0 or better

Main Components of DirectX

DirectDraw	The rendering component
DirectSound	The digital sound component
DirectInput	The input device component
DirectSetup	Used to install the run-time for DirectX
DirectPlay	The networking component
Direct3D	The 3D rendering component

Files Needed to Compile Most DirectX Programs

`DDRAW.LIB|H`	The main DirectDraw import library and header
`DSOUND.LIB|H`	The main DirectSound import library and header
`DINPUT.LIB|H`	The main DirectInput import library and header
`WINMM.LIB`	Windows Multimedia Library

...For Dummies®: Bestselling Book Series for Beginners

Game Engine Library Files

GPDUMB1.CPP|H	Part I of the game engine main source files
GPDUMB2.CPP|H	Part II of the game engine main source files

The Most Important DirectX Data Structures

```
LPDIRECTDRAW            // the main DirectDraw object
LPDIRECTDRAWSURFACE     // a DirectDraw surface
LPDIRECTDRAWPALETTE     // a DirectDraw palette
LPDIRECTDRAWCLIPPER     // a DirectDraw clipper
PALETTEENTRY            // a single RGBF palette entry
HRESULT                 // general DirectX result
DDSURFACEDESC           // a DirectDraw surface description
DDSCAPS                 // DirectDraw surface capabilities struct
LPDIRECTSOUND           // main DirectSound object
DSBUFFERDESC            // DirectSound description
DSCAPS                  // DirectSound capabilities struct
DSBCAPS                 // DirectSound buffer caps
LPDIRECTSOUNDBUFFER     // a general sound buffer
LPDIRECTINPUT           // main DirectInput object
LPDIRECTINPUTDEVICE     // general input device
LPDIRECTINPUTDEVICE2    // second generation input device
UCHAR char[256]         // keyboard state table
DIMOUSESTATE            // mouse data record
DIJOYSTATE              // joystick data record
```

The Microsoft DirectX Web Site URL

www.microsoft.com/directx/default.asp

...For Dummies®: Bestselling Book Series for Beginners

TM

References for the Rest of Us!®

BESTSELLING BOOK SERIES

Are you intimidated and confused by computers? Do you find that traditional manuals are overloaded with technical details you'll never use? Do your friends and family always call you to fix simple problems on their PCs? Then the ...*For Dummies*® computer book series from IDG Books Worldwide is for you.

...*For Dummies* books are written for those frustrated computer users who know they aren't really dumb but find that PC hardware, software, and indeed the unique vocabulary of computing make them feel helpless. ...*For Dummies* books use a lighthearted approach, a down-to-earth style, and even cartoons and humorous icons to dispel computer novices' fears and build their confidence. Lighthearted but not lightweight, these books are a perfect survival guide for anyone forced to use a computer.

> *"I like my copy so much I told friends; now they bought copies."*
>
> — Irene C., Orwell, Ohio

> *"Quick, concise, nontechnical, and humorous."*
>
> — Jay A., Elburn, Illinois

> *"Thanks, I needed this book. Now I can sleep at night."*
>
> — Robin F., British Columbia, Canada

Already, millions of satisfied readers agree. They have made ...*For Dummies* books the #1 introductory level computer book series and have written asking for more. So, if you're looking for the most fun and easy way to learn about computers, look to ...*For Dummies* books to give you a helping hand.

IDG BOOKS WORLDWIDE®

1/99

WINDOWS®
GAME PROGRAMMING
FOR
DUMMIES®

by André LaMothe

Foreword by Steve Smith

Manuel Núñez
Amazon.Com Aug. 2000

IDG
BOOKS
WORLDWIDE

IDG Books Worldwide, Inc.
An International Data Group Company

Foster City, CA ♦ Chicago, IL ♦ Indianapolis, IN ♦ New York, NY

Windows® Game Programming For Dummies®

Published by
IDG Books Worldwide, Inc.
An International Data Group Company
919 E. Hillsdale Blvd.
Suite 400
Foster City, CA 94404
www.idgbooks.com (IDG Books Worldwide Web site)
www.dummies.com (Dummies Press Web site)

Library of Congress Catalog Card No.: 98-70130

ISBN: 0-7645-0337-5

Printed in the United States of America

10 9 8 7 6 5 4 3

1B/QU/RR/ZZ/IN

Distributed in the United States by IDG Books Worldwide, Inc.

Distributed by CDG Books Canada Inc. for Canada; by Transworld Publishers Limited in the United Kingdom; by IDG Norge Books for Norway; by IDG Sweden Books for Sweden; by IDG Books Australia Publishing Corporation Pty. Ltd. for Australia and New Zealand; by TransQuest Publishers Pte Ltd. for Singapore, Malaysia, Thailand, Indonesia, and Hong Kong; by Gotop Information Inc. for Taiwan; by ICG Muse, Inc. for Japan; by Intersoft for South Africa; by Eyrolles for France; by International Thomson Publishing for Germany, Austria and Switzerland; by Distribuidora Cuspide for Argentina; by LR International for Brazil; by Galileo Libros for Chile; by Ediciones ZETA S.C.R. Ltda. for Peru; by WS Computer Publishing Corporation, Inc., for the Philippines; by Contemporanea de Ediciones for Venezuela; by Express Computer Distributors for the Caribbean and West Indies; by Micronesia Media Distributor, Inc. for Micronesia; by Chips Computadoras S.A. de C.V. for Mexico; by Editorial Norma de Panama S.A. for Panama; by American Bookshops for Finland.

For general information on IDG Books Worldwide's books in the U.S., please call our Consumer Customer Service department at 800-762-2974. For reseller information, including discounts and premium sales, please call our Reseller Customer Service department at 800-434-3422.

For information on where to purchase IDG Books Worldwide's books outside the U.S., please contact our International Sales department at 317-596-5530 or fax 317-596-5692.

For consumer information on foreign language translations, please contact our Customer Service department at 1-800-434-3422, fax 317-596-5692, or e-mail rights@idgbooks.com.

For information on licensing foreign or domestic rights, please phone +1-650-655-3109.

For sales inquiries and special prices for bulk quantities, please contact our Sales department at 650-655-3200 or write to the address above.

For information on using IDG Books Worldwide's books in the classroom or for ordering examination copies, please contact our Educational Sales department at 800-434-2086 or fax 317-596-5499.

For press review copies, author interviews, or other publicity information, please contact our Public Relations department at 650-655-3000 or fax 650-655-3299.

For authorization to photocopy items for corporate, personal, or educational use, please contact Copyright Clearance Center, 222 Rosewood Drive, Danvers, MA 01923, or fax 978-750-4470.

 is a registered trademark or trademark under exclusive license to IDG Books Worldwide, Inc. from International Data Group, Inc. in the United States and/or other countries.

About the Author

André LaMothe holds degrees in mathematics, computer science, and electrical engineering. He is the author of the best-selling books *Tricks of the Game Programming Gurus, Teach Yourself Game Programming in 21 Days,* and the *Black Art of 3D Game Programming*. André has also written numerous articles in *Game Developer, Byte, Software Developer,* and *Circuit Cellar*. He is currently the CEO of Xtreme Games LLC, where he is designing the next generation of 3D graphics engines. You can get in touch with him via e-mail at ceo@xgames3d.com, or visit him at his Web site — www.xgames3d.com.

ABOUT IDG BOOKS WORLDWIDE

Welcome to the world of IDG Books Worldwide.

IDG Books Worldwide, Inc., is a subsidiary of International Data Group, the world's largest publisher of computer-related information and the leading global provider of information services on information technology. IDG was founded more than 30 years ago by Patrick J. McGovern and now employs more than 9,000 people worldwide. IDG publishes more than 290 computer publications in over 75 countries. More than 90 million people read one or more IDG publications each month.

Launched in 1990, IDG Books Worldwide is today the #1 publisher of best-selling computer books in the United States. We are proud to have received eight awards from the Computer Press Association in recognition of editorial excellence and three from Computer Currents' First Annual Readers' Choice Awards. Our best-selling ...*For Dummies*® series has more than 50 million copies in print with translations in 31 languages. IDG Books Worldwide, through a joint venture with IDG's Hi-Tech Beijing, became the first U.S. publisher to publish a computer book in the People's Republic of China. In record time, IDG Books Worldwide has become the first choice for millions of readers around the world who want to learn how to better manage their businesses.

Our mission is simple: Every one of our books is designed to bring extra value and skill-building instructions to the reader. Our books are written by experts who understand and care about our readers. The knowledge base of our editorial staff comes from years of experience in publishing, education, and journalism — experience we use to produce books to carry us into the new millennium. In short, we care about books, so we attract the best people. We devote special attention to details such as audience, interior design, use of icons, and illustrations. And because we use an efficient process of authoring, editing, and desktop publishing our books electronically, we can spend more time ensuring superior content and less time on the technicalities of making books.

You can count on our commitment to deliver high-quality books at competitive prices on topics you want to read about. At IDG Books Worldwide, we continue in the IDG tradition of delivering quality for more than 30 years. You'll find no better book on a subject than one from IDG Books Worldwide.

John Kilcullen
Chairman and CEO
IDG Books Worldwide, Inc.

Steven Berkowitz
President and Publisher
IDG Books Worldwide, Inc.

IDG is the world's leading IT media, research and exposition company. Founded in 1964, IDG had 1997 revenues of $2.05 billion and has more than 9,000 employees worldwide. IDG offers the widest range of media options that reach IT buyers in 75 countries representing 95% of worldwide IT spending. IDG's diverse product and services portfolio spans six key areas including print publishing, online publishing, expositions and conferences, market research, education and training, and global marketing services. More than 90 million people read one or more of IDG's 290 magazines and newspapers, including IDG's leading global brands — Computerworld, PC World, Network World, Macworld and the Channel World family of publications. IDG Books Worldwide is one of the fastest-growing computer book publishers in the world, with more than 700 titles in 36 languages. The "...For Dummies®" series alone has more than 50 million copies in print. IDG offers online users the largest network of technology-specific Web sites around the world through IDG.net (http://www.idg.net), which comprises more than 225 targeted Web sites in 55 countries worldwide. International Data Corporation (IDC) is the world's largest provider of information technology data, analysis and consulting, with research centers in over 41 countries and more than 400 research analysts worldwide. IDG World Expo is a leading producer of more than 168 globally branded conferences and expositions in 35 countries including E3 (Electronic Entertainment Expo), Macworld Expo, ComNet, Windows World Expo, ICE (Internet Commerce Expo), Agenda, DEMO, and Spotlight. IDG's training subsidiary, ExecuTrain, is the world's largest computer training company, with more than 230 locations worldwide and 785 training courses. IDG Marketing Services helps industry-leading IT companies build international brand recognition by developing global integrated marketing programs via IDG's print, online and exposition products worldwide. Further information about the company can be found at www.idg.com. 1/24/99

Dedication

I dedicate this book to all the people who never give up. Our time will come. . . .

Author's Acknowledgments

The acknowledgments are the hardest thing to write for any book. It's amazing how many people are involved in creating a published book. Here it goes:

First, I want to thank all the people at IDG who put up with such an eccentric author! Thanks to Robert Wallace, the project editor, for being my voice at IDG and making all my "artistic" changes happen; Jill Pisoni for getting this project through all the scrutiny; Darlene Wong for taking care of business; and the permission and media experts Heather Dismore and Joyce Pepple for making the CD something special.

Also, I want to thank Todd Masten (tmasten@ns.net) for letting me use his incredible music in the games and demos, Jarrod Davis for tech editing the book and not hurting my feelings, my cousin Dennis Duarte for legal advice, Michael Perone for getting me those hard-to-find programs, and Mark Bell for talking me into writing *Underworld* — but I'm still right about everything else, Mark!

Next I want to thank the DirectX team at Microsoft, the Microsoft Games Evangelist Steve Smith for doing the foreword to this book and helping with DirectX permission, and Audra Gaines-Mulkern, the DirectX project manager, for really getting the right people in touch with the right people and for allowing us to add the very latest DirectX software to the CD for this book — thanks!

Finally, I want to thank my mom and dad for putting up with my 2.5 second phone conversations and for my complaining when I'm writing. And last and most importantly, thanks to my very special friend Jennifer Jane for keeping me from blowing a blood vessel from the pressure. See, I fixed the door, speaker, and headlight!

Publisher's Acknowledgments

We're proud of this book; please register your comments through our IDG Books Worldwide Online Registration Form located at http://my2cents.dummies.com.

Some of the people who helped bring this book to market include the following:

Acquisitions, Development, and Editorial

Project Editor: Robert H. Wallace

Acquisitions Editor: Jill Pisoni, Senior Acquisitions Editor

Media Development Manager: Joyce Pepple

Permissions Editor: Heather Heath Dismore

Copy Editors: Diane L. Giangrossi; Susan Diane Smith, Senior Copy Editor; Wendy Hatch

Technical Editor: Jarrod Davis

Editorial Manager: Colleen Rainsberger

Editorial Assistants: Donna Love, Darren Meiss

Production

Project Coordinator: Sherry Gomoll

Layout and Graphics: Steve Arany, Cameron Booker, Lou Boudreau, Linda M. Boyer, J. Tyler Connor, Todd Klemme, Angela F. Hunckler, Anna Rohrer, Brent Savage, Anne M. Sipahimalani, Deirdre Smith, Kate Snell

Proofreaders: Kelli Botta, Vickie Broyles, Michelle Croninger, Joel K. Draper, Rachel Garvey, Henry Lazarek, Carrie Voorhis, Janet M. Withers

Indexer: Sherry Massey

Special Help

Joell Smith, Associate Technical Editor; Publications Services, Inc.; Stephanie Koutek, Proof Editor

General and Administrative

IDG Books Worldwide, Inc.: John Kilcullen, CEO; Steven Berkowitz, President and Publisher

IDG Books Technology Publishing Group: Richard Swadley, Senior Vice President and Publisher; Walter Bruce III, Vice President and Associate Publisher; Joseph Wikert, Associate Publisher; Mary Bednarek, Branded Product Development Director; Mary Corder, Editorial Director; Barry Pruett, Publishing Manager; Michelle Baxter, Publishing Manager

IDG Books Consumer Publishing Group: Roland Elgey, Senior Vice President and Publisher; Kathleen A. Welton, Vice President and Publisher; Kevin Thornton, Acquisitions Manager; Kristin A. Cocks, Editorial Director

IDG Books Internet Publishing Group: Brenda McLaughlin, Senior Vice President and Publisher; Diane Graves Steele, Vice President and Associate Publisher; Sofia Marchant, Online Marketing Manager

IDG Books Production for Dummies Press: Debbie Stailey, Associate Director of Production; Cindy L. Phipps, Manager of Project Coordination, Production Proofreading, and Indexing; Tony Augsburger, Manager of Prepress, Reprints, and Systems; Laura Carpenter, Production Control Manager; Shelley Lea, Supervisor of Graphics and Design; Debbie J. Gates, Production Systems Specialist; Robert Springer, Supervisor of Proofreading; Kathie Schutte, Production Supervisor

Dummies Packaging and Book Design: Patty Page, Manager, Promotions Marketing

◆

The publisher would like to give special thanks to Patrick J. McGovern, without whom this book would not have been possible.

◆

Contents at a Glance

Cartoons at a Glance

By Rich Tennant

The 5th Wave — By Rich Tennant

"Kevin here heads our Windows software development team. Right now he's working on a spreadsheet program that's sort of a combination of Lotus 1-2-3 and FrankenWolf."

page 7

The 5th Wave — By Rich Tennant

Re-al Game Pro-gram-mers

Oh wow!

WINDO-TECH

Real Game Programmers do their best work between 1 and 5 a.m.

page 133

The 5th Wave — By Rich Tennant

HELP? 911

"...and you say a giant has your mother and father locked in a dungeon? And your sister's being held hostage in a tower? You just sit tight, Davey — a SWAT team is on its way."

page 291

The 5th Wave — By Rich Tennant

DOYNK SOFTWARE

"It's been reported that we went a little crazy trying to bring this game to market on time..."

page 389

The 5th Wave — By Rich Tennant

SOFTWARE CENTER GAMES FIN

"YOU KNOW THAT GUY WHO BOUGHT ALL THAT SOFTWARE? HIS CHECK HAS A WARRANTY THAT SAYS IT'S TENDERED AS IS AND HAS NO FITNESS FOR ANY PARTICULAR PURPOSE INCLUDING, BUT NOT LIMITED TO, CASHING."

page 423

Fax: 978-546-7747 • E-mail: the5wave@tiac.net

Table of Contents

Part III: The Rest of the Puzzle: Sound, Input, and Setup 291

Chapter 13: Making Noise with DirectSound 293

Foreword

●●●

*T*he multimedia and computer-games industry has grown incredibly in recent years. When I got hold of my first computer back in 1982, 64K of RAM was considered huge (if not excessive). Consequently, games had limits on the size, complexity, and graphical detail which they could obtain. Limits were also imposed by the speed of the processors used in the early machines. As a result, games were fun to play, but they left a lot to be desired by way of realism.

This situation slowly changed, as is so often the case. Better hardware was constantly being developed. My beloved first computer became obsolete and was relegated to the attic to gather dust (and it's probably still there, now that I think about it). Slowly but surely, game technology has advanced and improved. And, over time, as hardware got better, so too did the games designed to run on it. And everyone was happy. . . .

Then along comes the IBM Personal Computer (PC) and its clones. For the longest time, this platform was not the best one for games. Anyone who has ever used a green-screen monochrome or CGA display understands what I mean here. And as for that internal PC speaker: Ouch!

After an age in which the PC had all the multimedia potential of a dead tree, *things* started to happen. Interesting things. Cool things! IBM invented the VGA card, and suddenly game programmers were given the incredible 320 x 200 resolution, 256-color mode to play with (and the more canny programmers found the undocumented 320 x 240, 256-color Mode X). Cool animation techniques like page flipping became available, and game programming got pretty good.

And then came SVGA — bigger, meaner, and faster than VGA. Loads of hardware manufacturers started building their own particular SVGA cards and adding their own custom features and their own ways of doing graphics. Of course, the cards all had backwards compatibility with the older VGA chipsets, so providing that you used modes like 320 x 200 with 256 colors, or 640 x 480 with 16 colors, you were fine. Anything higher (like 640 x 480 with 256 colors) and you had to start writing to specific hardware.

The field of audio for multimedia applications was pretty much the same as video hardware at this point. Some wonderful sound hardware was coming out on the market, but each unit worked in its own way. To support them all, you had to write code that was specific to each. Not much fun.

This situation never changed, and graphics and audio hardware continued —
and still continues — to diversify as more and more innovations and im-
provements are made. In the past, this made for a wealth of choices to the
consumer, but was a real headache to the poor programmer who has to deal
with all the variations and changes in hardware if he or she wants to use the
coolest features. Of course, Windows (meaning Windows 3.1 and, later,
Windows 95) used hardware-specific drivers to access hardware. But who
would dream of using the Windows Graphic Device Interface to write high-
performance graphics-based games?

Here at Microsoft, a few people started to wonder whether using the cool
hardware independence that Windows programming provided for performance multimedia (games) was possible. What was needed, the Microsoft
folks decided, was an SDK (Software Development Kit) to allow access to
hardware, without the need for the programmer to worry about the specifics
of how the hardware actually works. We needed functionality to provide for
audio, input devices, 2D and 3D graphics, and networking (as applied to
multiuser gaming, anyhow).

And so, DirectX was born — the Windows 95 (and Windows NT) games SDK.
Within DirectX you find DirectSound (for audio), DirectDraw (for 2D graphics), Direct3D (for 3D hardware acceleration), DirectInput (for joysticks,
mice, and other input devices) and DirectPlay (for multiplayer networking).

From the beginning, the whole philosophy behind DirectX has been to
provide as thin a layer as possible between the games programmer (who
wants to write screamingly fast code) and the hardware. Rather than get in
the way and slow things down, DirectX instead provides standardized
access to hardware-specific features. This access in many cases actually
makes game elements run faster than they would without access to the
hardware; for example, drawing sprites using the hardware blitter is much
faster than drawing sprites using your own code. Also, in the case of
DirectDraw and those wonderful SVGA cards, we now have access to all
sorts of new resolutions at all sorts of bit-depths, like 640 x 480, 512 x 384,
800 x 600 and even 1,024 x 768 — all in 8-, 16-, 24-, or 32-bit color.

Writing cool games is hard. Extremely hard. DirectX doesn't really make
writing game code a whole lot easier. But it does remove the need to write
hardware-specific code, which is both difficult and time consuming, and it
allows the programmer to concentrate on writing better games.

I can't think of a better place to start investigating the world of DirectX
programming than *Windows Game Programming For Dummies*. André
LaMothe has consistently written some of the best books I've ever read
on computer games programming. André's titles include *Tricks of the Game
Programming Gurus, Teach Yourself Game Programming in 21 Days, The Game*

Programming Starter Kit, and my personal favorite, *The Black Art of 3D Game Programming* — which was the first book ever to provide a good explanation of BSP technology (as used by many of the 3D walkthrough games on the market) as well as a working engine and tools to support it.

On top of the technical content (which is excellent), André's writing style is fun and easy-going, making this book a truly rare experience: an enjoyable technical read. Not only will you find out a lot about game programming from this book, but you'll have a great time doing it.

I would heartily recommend this book to anyone thinking about developing games or performance multimedia for the PC, whether that person is serious or just curious. I really can't think of a better place to start!

Steve Smith, Games Technology Evangelist for Microsoft Corporation

Introduction

● ●

*W*elcome to *Windows Game Programming For Dummies*. You're about to embark on the coolest, most excellent journey of all time! You can find out exactly what makes a video game tick. Furthermore, you're going to write games using the latest, greatest technology from Microsoft code-named: DirectX. Yes, Microsoft made something really cool, and DirectX Versions 5.0+ actually work!

I know that understanding game programming would seem to take a lifetime, but I think that I have found a way to mash it all into this little yellow-and-black book. Granted, in doing so I may have caused a worm-hole somewhere — but hey, no pain, no gain. So read the book cover to cover, and you'll be able to rattle off sentences like, "I used a transparency-encoded sprite blitter for the foreground animation and DMAed the virtual buffer into the display."

Who Are You?

Game programming is a weird science, and to do it, you must be a weird scientist and a nerd deluxe. Those are the first prerequisites. I mean, what kind of person sits in front of a computer for up to 130 hours a week and stares at the screen? But at the same time, game programming is incredibly rewarding and opens up doorways to worlds that you create. So you need to be totally open-minded and totally obsessed with making games. Those are the most important qualities. Anyone can master the technical stuff, but you must realize that making a game involves about a billion details.

Now that you have the point about the nutty professor syndrome, I want to tell you what you are getting into.

> ✔ You need to be able to program in C with a dash of C++. I'm not talking about being a compiler designer or anything, but that is the language in this book. You actually use a C++ compiler, but the amount of C++ specific code you need is almost `NULL`, so don't trip if you're not part of the `object.oriented.bandwagon()`. If you want additional information on C++, check out *Visual C++ 6 For Dummies,* by Michael Hyman and Bob Arnson (published by IDG Books Worldwide, Inc.).

✔ You need to be familiar with Windows 95 and DOS, at least. Knowledge of Windows 98/NT would be cool, but only if you are going to work in them. If you can get around and feel comfortable with running multiple applications at the same time, you'll be fine.

✔ You need to have a rudimentary knowledge of tensor analysis, vector calculus, and Newtonian physics.

Just kidding! If you can add, multiply, and maybe square a number or two, that's all the math skills you require. But knowing advanced mathematics doesn't hurt — especially for 3D game programming.

In a nutshell, you simply need to know how to program in C and have the desire to explore game programming. This book takes care of the rest.

About This Book

This book is probably unlike any other ...*For Dummies* book around. It integrates Windows programming, DirectX, game programming, music, art, artificial intelligence, and a lot more. Game programming is a fierce subject to master, and is absolutely nonlinear. It's totally parallel; you need to know everything to know anything. So even though this book has great value as a reference, it's mostly a manual for beginners on the subject of game programming.

On the other hand (and I have eight of them), if you're a DOS game programmer who is interested in making the switch to Windows and DirectX, this book will be of great value. I include only the important parts of DirectX and Windows game programming in a form that enables you to very quickly get up and running in the Windows/DirectX platform. To find these important parts, I had to read every single sentence in every single DirectX SDK release, so you didn't have to. I still have nightmares. . . .

You may be asking: "What kind of games will I be able to write when I finish this book?" The answer really depends on you, but in general, you should be able to write just about any 2D game you can think of as long as you can put in the time to finish it. You're not going to walk away writing *Quake,* but you will be able to make games like *Space Invaders, Defender, Pac Man, Raptor,* and *Commander Keen.* If you want to write *Quake,* then you better put aside the next five years of your life and get a really comfortable computer chair!

Conventions Used in This Book

Most of the conventions that I use in the text are pretty standard programming fare, so you've seen them. Nevertheless, I included this section, just in case aliens kidnapped you and made you program on Titan and in Fortran for the past 20 years. Here's what I do to make life easier for both of us:

 ✔ **Code:** Code elements such as functions appear in my running text as follows: GetDC. In most instances, the code blocks that I use for examples fill up several lines, like this:

```
// set cooperation level
lpdd->SetCooperativeLevel(hwnd, DDSCL_ALLOWREBOOT |
        DDSCL_ALLOWMODEX |DDSCL_FULLSCREEN |
        DDSCL_EXCLUSIVE );
```

 ✔ **Screen resolution shorthand:** In general, I use two different conventions to write screen resolution: (Width x Height x Total_Colors) and (Width x Height x Bits_Per_Pixel). Therefore, 320 x 240 x 256 is the same as 320 x 240 x 8; likewise, 640 x 480 x 65536 is the same as 640 x 480 x 16. Sometimes one form is more convenient than the other, depending on the context.

 ✔ **Hungarian notation:** As per the convention used by Microsoft, I use Hungarian notation to denote how a programming element is used in code. For example, the *lp* in lpdd shows that this element is a 32-bit pointer to something. I cover Hungarian notation in more detail in Chapter 3.

About Windows 95/98/NT and DirectX 5.0+

I wrote this book using Windows 95/98/NT along with both the Microsoft compilers: Visual C++ 4.0 and 5.0. For DirectX, I used versions 3.0, 5.0, 6.0 and 6.1. In general, the C/C++ compilers and DirectX are all at a sufficient level of sophistication, meaning that newer releases and versions will all work very similarly.

One factor that makes DirectX so cool is that DirectX 1.0 applications will still work with DirectX 5.0 and so on. This flexibility is because DirectX is based on the Component Object Model (COM), which you can read about in Chapter 7. So don't worry if you have DirectX 6.0; the techniques you use in this book are applicable. Moreover, this book presents the basic functionality of Windows and DirectX, so the newer versions with cooler stuff won't make that much of a difference to you.

About Game Programming

Well, here's where I give you my pitch. Game programming is the best. I can't think of anything that I would rather do than make games. Games are the ultimate form of art — they're little universes that other people can experience. And as a game programmer, you can create entire worlds that you can experience yourself, or have your friends experience.

After you're finished with this book, how a computer game works will no longer be a mystery. You will know exactly how to make one. Who knows; maybe you will make the next *Doom, Quake,* or *Myst.*

Finally, there's nothing like seeing all your friends addicted to playing one of your games — well, maybe if they each pay you $20 bucks for it!

How This Book Is Organized

This book contains six parts. Each part contains material that, I believe, should go together.

> ✔ **Part I: Getting Familiar with Windows Programming:** In this part, you set up your game programming workstation. This process includes setting up your compiler, installing DirectX, and getting ready to program and run the demos. After your system is ready to go, I introduce all the components that make up a game and explain how they relate to each other. The remaining chapters of this part focus on Windows 95 programming and building software to make game programming easier in this environment.

✔ **Part II: Jacking In with DirectX:** In this part, you find out about DirectX, which is one of the most advanced technologies ever created for game making. You explore how and why DirectX works, along with its relationship to COM and the Windows 95 API (Win32). After being introduced, it's time to dance; you can work with DirectDraw (the 2D rendering component of DirectX) until you are a nice shade of blue (R=0,G=0,B=255). Finally, you use all the information in this part to build a set of functions. These functions are part of a library that you make as the book proceeds; you use the library to make games.

✔ **Part III: The Rest of the Puzzle: Sound, Input, and Setup:** In this part, you explore the remaining parts of DirectX (well, at least the interesting ones) such as DirectSound, DirectInput, DirectSetup, and finally AutoPlay. After your brain is fried with this new information, you can put the final touches on the game library by adding the new functionality of these DirectX subsystems.

✔ **Part IV: The Glue of Games:** In this part, it's time to stop playing games and start making them! You find out about the internals of game programming that you use to control the physics of the game world you create. Also, I take everything covered in previous parts and create a real video game called *Underworld.* Finally, you find out how to create your own game company empire; that is, how the heck you sell those games!

✔ **Part V: The Part of Tens:** Part V contains the traditional Part of Tens; maybe in this book it should be the Part of 00001010s! These chapters offer lists of ten or more helpful insights on important programming issues. I include chapters on the ten basic rules of game design, the ten biggest mistakes game programmers make, and the ten best game programming resources on the Web.

Icons Used in This Book

It's a tradition for *...For Dummies* books to use special icons in the margins of the text to help bring your attention to various situations, traps, and pitfalls — to generally help illuminate your trek through the perilous waters of technology. Here are the icons this book uses:

This icon denotes helpful tips, tricks, and good restaurants.

Be careful when this icon is present; the operation you are about to perform can have serious consequences if you don't heed the warning in this paragraph.

When you see this icon, be aware that some C++ stuff is coming up.

This icon lets you know that the section is really technical, and you should make sure that you really want to be tortured by this information.

Pay attention to this icon: The information in the section it marks is really cool, and you should stop to think about the coolness of it.

You should remember the concept in text marked by this icon because that concept is important.

This icon tells you that the paragraph contains information about files or programs found on the CD that comes with this book.

Part I
Getting Familiar with Windows Programming

The 5th Wave — By Rich Tennant

"Kevin here heads our Windows software development team. Right now he's working on a spreadsheet program that's sort of a combination of Lotus 1-2-3 and FrankenWolf."

In this part . . .

*I*n this part, you find out about what it takes to create a video game and how to set things up. You also dive into the wonderful world of Windows programming — and yes, everything you heard about Windows programming is true! But I'm going to make it as easy as possible and just show you what you need to know to make games that work with Windows. If you're a DOS programmer, you'll be happy to see that you can practically do what you've always done . . . but in 32 bits!

I cover Windows basics, the Graphics Device Interface, input, multimedia, and, of course, using the compiler. Follow the steps in this entire part, and you'll create a complete Windows shell that can be used under Windows 95, Windows 98, or even Windows NT.

Chapter 1

Setting Up for Windows 95/98/NT Game Programming

* *

In This Chapter

▶ Putting your workstation together

▶ Getting DirectX installed

▶ Working with your compiler

▶ Using game programming tools

* *

*I*n this chapter, I start off with just a few details on what the heck you're going to be doing. In addition, I want you to know what hardware and software you need to actually compile the demos (if you want to change them) and use the Windows code I provide on the CD.

Designing the Ultimate Game Programming Workstation

If you were to walk into any reasonably profitable game company, you would think that you had entered a movie studio. You would find a lot of really weird-looking cubicles with all kinds of paraphernalia strewn about, not to mention the weird-looking people. But mostly, you would see computers — a lot of them.

The basic tool of the game programmer is the computer; it's as simple as that. The more powerful your computer, the better. Playing games is one thing and requires one type of computer system, but writing them is another and requires a much different, and more advanced, computer. When you develop games, you're going to run a number of applications at the same time, and you're going to do a lot of compiling and tweaking of code. Hence, here's a list of system requirements:

- A Pentium computer running at 100 MHz or more
- Windows 95, 98, or NT
- 16MB of internal RAM with a 1GB hard drive
- A Sound Blaster-compatible sound card
- A good mouse — very important
- A joystick — preferably a new digital model
- The largest monitor possible (you're going to be staring at it a lot, so the bigger the better — at least 15 inches or more)
- A printer to print out code for review
- A 2X or better CD-ROM drive

Of course, if you don't have all the items on this list, don't worry; you'll probably get along fine. But game development is taxing on your computer, so having some serious hardware is nice. To give you an idea of a professional development system, here's the setup I use to write 3D games:

- Pentium II at 300 MHz
- 256MB of RAM
- 9.0GB SCSI hard drive
- 24X CD-ROM
- Windows 95, Windows 98, and Windows NT
- Sound Blaster Awe 64 Gold sound card
- Force-feedback digital joystick
- 21-inch multisync monitor
- Secondary monochrome monitor for debugging
- HP 850 color printer

You also need networking, removable media storage devices, scanners, a 3D sound system, a graphics tablet, and whatever other gadgets that are appropriate for your development.

Installing DirectX and the SDK

Installing DirectX is simple. Just find the folder labeled DIRECTX\ on the CD that comes with this book. Open the directory and read the README.TXT file. It describes how to install DirectX and the DirectX SDK. Basically, you can run the Setup or Install program, and it loads DirectX run-time and the SDK into a directory — usually called DXSDK\ — onto your hard drive. You see, DirectX consists of two components: the run-time files and the SDK (Software Development Kit). You need both because you want to run DirectX applications and write them yourself.

If you already have the DirectX 5.0 or better run-time and SDK on your system, you don't need to install it again. But if you don't, make sure that you install DirectX or else nothing will work.

After you finish installing DirectX, take a look around all the directories and get to know the location of the libraries, include files, help, and samples, in case you need them — which you will. I suggest that you drag the SDK Help system onto your desktop so you can query it anytime you need to. Also, when you start compiling programs, you need to know the paths to the .LIB files and the .H files for the SDK so make sure that you know the locations of these files. They're both in the SDK\ directory under LIB\ and INCLUDES\.

All the material and concepts from this book are compatible with all future versions of DirectX, so keep an eye out at the Microsoft DirectX Web site for updates to DirectX: www.microsoft.com/directx/default.asp. Also, I include the new DirectMedia Run-Time within the directory DIRECTX\. DirectMedia is built on top of the DirectX foundation objects and allows you to view Web pages with full animation.

Setting Up Your C/C++ Compiler

After you have your hardware together and DirectX is loaded on your computer, you must consider the rest of your software. The most important piece of software is your compiler, because you use it to compile your game programs — and the code from this book. I suggest that you use Microsoft Visual C++ Version 4.0 or better. Microsoft compilers generate really good Windows code. I admit that Watcom does a better job for DOS 32, but in my opinion, Visual C++ is the best for Windows development.

You can pick up a standard Microsoft Visual C++ compiler for about $99 from your local software store, so I suggest that route; it's the path of least resistance. On the other hand, if you're a Borland kind of person, I suggest Version 5.0 or greater.

Whichever compiler you select, you need to know how to operate it. Visual compilers are quite complex and probably not something you're just going to figure out as you go. I suggest that you read the user manual just a bit so that you are comfortable with creating projects, compiling console applications, and compiling Windows Win32 applications.

If you have never programmed Windows before, don't worry; I explain the basics in Chapters 2 through 6. But you need to know your way around the compiler, so I suggest that you figure out at least how to compile a DOS-like console program before diving into this book. Usually, the user manual or quick start for any compiler shows you how to create a simple project and make a Hello World program.

The reason why this knowledge is so important is that nothing is more frustrating than getting compiler and linker errors that can be solved with nothing more than a click of the mouse — if you just know the correct click! So take some time to explore your compiler — you'll be glad you did.

As you compile all the projects for this book, keep in mind that you are programming Win32 applications by using the DirectX libraries. That means you must always select the Win32 application for your target, and you must include the DirectX libraries in your project as required. Here are the libraries that you need from DirectX, which you can find in the \SDK folder of the installation:

- ✔ DDRAW.LIB: DirectDraw
- ✔ DINPUT.LIB: DirectInput
- ✔ DSOUND.LIB: DirectSound

You're also going to use the Windows Multimedia Library (WINMM.LIB) from time to time, which should be in one of your C/C++ compiler's library directories.

In addition to the library files, you need the headers, which are also in the SDK\ subdirectory of the DirectX SDK main installation:

- ✔ DDRAW.H: DirectDraw
- ✔ DINPUT.H: DirectInput
- ✔ DSOUND.H: DirectSound

I remind you about the libraries and headers as you go through the book, so if you're a bit confused, don't panic.

Of course, to compile any of the programs on the CD, you may want to copy the source code and files from the CD to your hard drive. I suggest that you simply drag the entire WGPSRC\ directory from the CD to your hard drive. This directory contains a directory for each chapter of the book so that you can easily find the source code and files you need.

If you are using Microsoft Visual C++ 6.0, you will need to make a minor change to all the Windows programs on the CD-ROM. Visual C++ 6.0 doesn't perform implicit casts anymore on some types, therefore, during the initialization of the Windows Class it throws up. There is a line in every program that looks like this:

```
wndclass.hbrBackground=GetStockObject(BLACK_BRUSH);
```

Change to this:

```
wndclass.hbrBackground= (HBRUSH)GetStockObject(BLACK_BRUSH);
```

Using Multimedia Tools

All right, you have DirectX installed, the compiler is ready to go, but something is missing. Of course, you need support software such as paint programs, 3D modelers, sound editors, and anything else you think that you will need.

Luckily for you, we talked a number of people into letting us put demos or shareware versions of their software on the CD (actually, Heather Dismore at IDG did — thanks, Heather). So you can get started right away with nothing more than the CD that comes with this book. But take a quick look at the purpose of each of these programs.

Paint programs

An artist uses a paint program to create the bitmap objects for a game. I got the killer paint program named Paint Shop Pro 4.12 by Jasc Systems for this book. This is one of my favorite paint programs. You can use this software to draw all your bitmaps and animations for your games.

Now, I know that not everyone's an artist — that means you, Joel — so I have placed a number of bitmap files with all kinds of cool textures, explosions, and creatures from my art archives for you to use. The files are within the folder named ARTWORK\ within the directory \SOURCE on the CD.

3D modelers

Programs called *3D modelers* enable you to create full 3D objects and then render them as bitmaps. This technique gives you images that are photorealistic. The cool thing about using 3D modelers is that you can easily create multiple views of an object, and you can make changes to your objects very quickly. If you're not an artist, I suggest that you try the modeler because it makes everyone look skilled.

On the CD, you can find Caligari TrueSpace III, the best modeler I have ever seen in its price range. I used it to create over 800 objects for my last game, so I can attest to its value.

Sound programs

The final piece of software that you're going to need is a sound editor — something to record and process digital sounds with. Luckily, you don't have to be a musician to work with sound effects or to record them, but you do need access to sound effects and/or you need to have (or know someone with) a good voice.

To help you out with raw material, I have placed on the CD a library of sounds that I created for you to use in your games. The library is in the directory SOUNDS\. In addition, I include just about the best sound editor in the business: Sound Forge XP. This program is amazing and will do far more sound processing and algorithmic effects than you'll ever need. I'm still trying to figure this baby out!

That's my speech, so lock and load and let's rock!

Chapter 2

Exploring the Basics of Video Game Design

A video game is more than the sum of its pieces; a game has a synergy that, after the game is complete, makes it something unique. To create this synergy takes a lot of technical know-how, as well as a sense of design and art. Basically, you need to be a da Vinci and an Einstein all in one. In this chapter, you find some of the high-level concepts of video game design as well as some of the low-level concepts, such as real-time programming techniques and proper data structure usage.

A Long Time Ago, in a Galaxy Far, Far, Away

Video games have been around as long as computers have. Most computer historians would agree that the first computer games, usually text-based adventure or military-simulation games, were made for UNIX mainframes in the '60s and '70s. The revolution in games for personal computers came in the late '70s with the advent of the Atari 800 and Apple II personal computers, which were the first computers to have good color, decent sound, and reasonable graphics power. Game programmers wrote Atari and Apple games in BASIC or pure *machine language,* which is the native binary language used by the computer's CPU (Central Processing Unit).

The Atari 800 and Apple II reigned supreme for game programmers and game players — until 1984. That year, the IBM Personal Computer (called a *PC*), which had never been seen as a good gaming platform, started selling very well in the personal computer marketplace. Also, the 80286 processor arrived on the market, and the EGA (Enhanced Graphics Adapter) card was available, with the VGA (Video Graphics Array) card on its way. The IBM PC now had some hardware that could be used by programmers to make good games.

Even so, the PC was still nowhere near what was generally considered to be a game machine, but because the IBM PC was so popular and in such common use, many game programmers started writing games for the PC. In the latter part of the 1980s, the 80386 processor, the VGA card, and the Sound Blaster sound card became available to PC gamers. At this point, the IBM PC was starting to push heavily into the game market. Although the PC still had crude video hardware compared to other, more game-centric 16-bit machines (such as the Atari ST and the Amiga 500), so many PCs were in the marketplace at the time that making games for the token game machines was akin to corporate suicide. And some companies didn't get the message early enough; about a zillion companies that kept making software for the Atari and Amiga are now long-forgotten empires.

By 1990, few programmers wrote a game for any platform other than the PC. But many programmers weren't happy with the performance of the PC. The early IBM PC was a nightmare to write games for. You had to be a computer genius to get any performance out of the machine, and you had to know programming information that simply wasn't documented.

And then one day in 1991, id Software, Inc. released the fastest 3D game ever for the IBM PC and compatibles. The groundbreaking game was *Wolfenstein 3D;* see Figure 2-1 for an example. Even though a couple of million copies of this game were sold, the public didn't know too much about *Wolfenstein 3D* because it was sold using the *shareware* technique — no big ad campaigns or other promotions — so this technological marvel was played only by the gamers of the world, and the public generally didn't have a clue.

Figure 2-1:
A screen
shot of
*Wolfenstein
3D.*

The significance of *Wolfenstein 3D* is greater than any other computer game (even *Doom*), but most people didn't realize that at the time. Game programmers blew it off even though *Wolfenstein 3D* was faster and more impressive than any other game. Basically, that game was a single step away from *Doom*. The technology used for making *Wolfenstein 3D* was very different from the *Doom* technology, but it was in the same ballpark — and that was the key. If anyone else but id Software had realized this fact, then *Doom* may not have been the first game to change and redefine the PC game market.

So id Software released *Doom* in 1993; see Figure 2-2 for a screen shot of the game that changed computer gaming forever. *Doom* was fast, looked good, had great graphics and a dependable game engine, had good sound effects, and was wicked fun. And *Doom* set the tempo for game programming for the years to follow.

Figure 2-2:
A screen
shot of
Doom.

Since the release of *Doom,* the game programming society has realized that the PC can do almost anything game-wise. The hardware and software manufacturers have built on this supposition and, today, the top-of-the-line gaming PC is a 266 MHz, 3D-accelerated, wave-table synthesized, 32-bit game platform that is nothing short of a dream machine. Coupled with the new Microsoft DirectX technology, the PC can do almost anything a gamer would want.

Although the heyday of computer game programming is over, the *Star Trek* era of game programming is here. Now gaming is a multibillion-dollar industry that will continue to grow and move into new markets. Wouldn't you be happy if some of the billions moved into your bank account?

I could go on and on with stories of the Silicon Valley game empire, but the preceding version lays the foundation for you. I think that you can imagine all the cool things that happened!

Video Game Design

The basic sequence of game design is as follows:

- ✔ Come up with an idea for a game.
- ✔ Create storyboards and rough sketches of your game world, the main characters, and the action.
- ✔ List the details of your game and take into consideration everything about the game "universe."
- ✔ Finally, put these concepts all together into a design document, something like a movie script that contains everything about your game.

The following subsections detail these steps.

Developing an idea

Before you write a game, you need an idea — a story, something to start with. You need to brainstorm and come up with an idea for a game, and the idea should be loosely based on something that has at least a fleeting resemblance to a story. Then you need to come up with the goals of the game. Ask yourself questions such as "What will the player do?" and "How will the player do it?"

Maybe you're wondering, "Where do I get ideas for games?" Well, I don't have any magical formula for you, but here are some places that I like to look:

- ✔ **Other games:** Don't copy another game, of course, but improving and taking a new perspective within the game is fine.
- ✔ **Movies and videos:** Watch as many sci-fi movies as possible and see if you can come up with a game based on some of their ideas and content. Of course, you need to get permission from the filmmaker if you use any characters or story lines from those movies.
- ✔ **Real-life games:** You can take a game such as hockey and make a computer version of it, or make a futuristic version of it.
- ✔ **Dreams and nightmares:** This technique is a gold mine; in your mind, you can try anything out. Go to sleep thinking about games, demons, monsters, or whatever, and hopefully you will have a killer dream that gives you an idea for a game. (Sounds silly, but take a look at *Doom* and *Quake;* I don't think that these ideas came from children's books!)

After you have your game ideas, then you need to outline the story.

Storyboarding

One of the best ways to see a game is to *storyboard* it, or create a number of drawings that show the levels of the game or the different scenes and goals. Each storyboard should include a paragraph or two to describe what is going on. Figure 2-3 depicts a basic storyboard for an imaginary shoot-'em-up game. As you can see, the storyboard has six slides; each slide represents a different level of the game, and the final slide is the goal. Notice that the storyboards are sketched and messy. Storyboard sketches are used only for brainstorming and for getting down on paper the general flow of the game. (Mine is messy because I drew this figure while I was playing *Fury III*.)

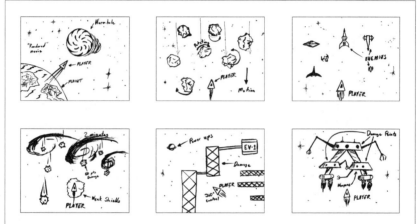

Figure 2-3:
A typical
game
storyboard.

Considering the details

After you create storyboards, then you need to write the details of the game design. This stage is where the process gets complex. You need to think of every possible detail and write something about it, because when you make your game, you are a god — well, at least a demigod. If you don't program a detail, it's not going to happen.

You need to figure out all the rules and the structure of the game. For example, here's a list of questions to consider:

- ✔ What can the game character do? Can he or she fly, swim, and teleport?
- ✔ How many different enemies will the hero fight?
- ✔ What kind of weapons are available?
- ✔ How does the player get rejuvenated?

✔ Can more than one player play at once? If so, what are the ramifications of this?

✔ Will the game's perspective be a side view, top view, or first-person and full-3D view?

✔ What kind of sound track? Rock, rap, techno?

✔ What is the personality of the main character?

These examples are just some of the details you need to think about. The key here is to create the characters, rules, laws, and goals of your game universe in as much detail as possible, which is necessary because you're going to generate the artificial universe they will all exist in. The more detail you include, the better the game will be.

Constructing a design document

After you have all the storyboards and details of the game written down, then you need to create a *design document*. The goal of the document is to record all your ideas in a format that resembles a movie script. Creating the document is a housekeeping step, but it gives you another chance to change your mind, see whether some rule or event is totally stupid, or add another game element.

The result of developing the design document is that your imaginary world becomes more vivid in your mind. When you start talking to yourself about the stuff that is happening in your game, when your imaginary world is so thick with texture and so alive with detail that you can see it, then writing a game around it is much easier, because you aren't making things up as you go. Having a clear picture of a game's world is one of the most important issues in game design.

The universe you create must be coherent; it must be well thought out, just like the universe we live in. If your game universe is coherent, the players will lose themselves in it; they will experience a momentary suspension of disbelief. When this happens, players become immersed in your world and really have fun. On the other hand, if you come up with a half-baked idea and then wing it as you go, you will end up with a game that looks like it was put together without any thought or planning. You won't pull the players into your world, and they won't play your game!

After you have a design document in hand, you are in a far better position to create a solid game. As you work on the game, you won't be tempted to impulsively add elements that are inappropriate or out of place in your game's world.

Don't misunderstand. Changing and adding to your design is acceptable, but make sure that all the elements work well together. If players aren't distracted by inconsistencies in your game's universe, they can be fully involved with the characters and situations.

Puzzles That Rock!

Before I talk about more technical issues, I need to be diligent in my responsibility to future game programmers by helping to stop the madness. "What madness?" you ask. The madness of games that have no puzzles in them! Although creating games without puzzles is much easier, games with them are going to do much better in the marketplace, simply because people enjoy thinking a little even while they're blowing things up!

Most games are pretty mindless, and the games that make you really think are often too difficult to really enjoy. To create a stand-out game, you must find a middle ground, which means putting puzzles in games when and where they are needed so that something other than carnage and destruction is the goal.

Honestly, all games have puzzles; the puzzles may not be obvious, but they're there. For example, *MYST* is obviously a big puzzle, but games such as *Duke Nukem* and *Doom* also have puzzles. The puzzles are in the form of hidden switches, of patterns or sequences, and of certain equipment that must be used in specific ways. The beauty of these puzzles is that they are woven into the game so cleanly, you don't even realize that you're solving a puzzle.

When you design your game, create puzzles around your game play so that the player has to think a bit. At the same time, try to design puzzles that aren't obvious. For example, suppose that you create a side-scrolling game and the player has to get across a gap between two cliffs. The first thing the player tries to do is make the character jump across. This effort fails, and the character falls to her death. The player realizes that getting across the gap must be possible, so she starts looking for a solution. The player might try pushing on the rocks that form a wall or jumping up and down in various locations hoping to activate a hidden switch. Eventually the player goes back to the cliff, looks at the other side, and finally notices a blinking red light. The player fires her weapon at the blinking red light and presto! A bridge lowers and the puzzle is solved.

The preceding example is a reasonable puzzle that's part of the game. Having a switch on the other side of the cliff that, when activated, engages the bridge is consistent with the game's logic. The player just had to figure out how to activate it. Of course, you could make the task easier by labeling the blinking light, but you get the idea of how puzzles should work.

Now I want to provide an example of a bad puzzle. Imagine the same scenario, but this time when the player gets to the bridge, the game stops and the player is presented with a math problem! Granted, in some games, a math problem is appropriate, but this obviously isn't one of them. A math problem has nothing to do with the game, ruins the experience, and pulls the player out of the illusion. So make your puzzles part of the game, not inconsistent add-ons to the game. Your goal is to make a good puzzle, but also the right kind of puzzle.

The following lists some basic puzzle types. Think about which one would fit well in your game:

- ✔ **Simple switches and patterns.** These kinds of puzzles are composed of either a single control or a series of controls that must be latched on/off or in some pattern. This puzzle is common in 3D, first-person games.

- ✔ **Temporal sequences.** This kind of puzzle has something to do with time, or more importantly time running out. You must start, stop, or do something on a clock.

- ✔ **Unorthodox usage of objects.** These types of puzzles are the result of a great game design. The player can use an object for a purpose that the designer may not have intended. For example, the player might be able to turn his weapon on overload and use it as a bomb to blow open a door.

- ✔ **Constructing a solution.** Puzzles of this type are usually complex to set up, but can be very rewarding to the player. The player must construct a solution from pieces or objects in the game. For example, she descends a mountain with a parachute made out of a sheet and rope.

- ✔ **Actual word puzzles and riddles.** These kinds of puzzles are usually presented to the player as actual text or audio, and the player must give the correct solution.

- ✔ **Passcodes.** Players must provide information to solve these puzzles, such as numbers, passwords, sequences of symbols, and so on. These kinds of puzzles are good to stop the player from moving on to another level without obtaining all the important pieces he will need to solve the game.

- ✔ **Cause and effect.** These puzzles are based on forcing the player to think, "What if I do this? Then this might happen, causing that, which would lead to *that* . . ." and so on. For example, the cliff scenario earlier in this section was a cause-and-effect puzzle. The player shot the control panel with her blaster, which caused the control panel to lower the bridge.

- ✔ **Random puzzles.** These puzzles have no obvious solution; the player simply has to guess the right answer. For example, the player is faced with three doors, but only one is the way out. The player could possibly have to try all three doors. If you use this kind of puzzle, try not to punish the player too much for an incorrect selection, because the player didn't have any information to base a good selection on.

Never include puzzles that take a rocket scientist to figure out. You're not going to impress the player; you'll just make him mad. And he will think that your game is silly and not fun to play.

Elements of the Game

A professional video game can be anywhere from 7,500–500,000 lines of code. For example, the *Tetris* game requires about 7,500 lines, and *Doom* needs about 200,000 (including all the tools). Even though they both look different and are light-years from each other technologically, these programs have relatively the same elements and structure.

Games have some special properties. The first is that a game is a *real-time* application, which means that the game reacts as you change the input and that everything seems to happen at the same time. For example, you can fire, move, and watch things blow up all at the same time. The game doesn't stop, do an explosion, play a sound, let you move, and then fire; all the action happens at the same time — at least it seems that way.

A game uses special programming techniques to accomplish these feats. In short, a game is a *multitasking* application, in which each task is a part of the game. However, PC games have been around since the days of DOS, so this multitasking has been and usually is implemented by the game programmers, not the operating system (OS). (Such multitasking is not as difficult to implement as you may think.)

Basically, a game is nothing more than an infinite loop that processes all the objects in the game and then draws the next frame of animation. Figure 2-4 illustrates a typical game loop as a flow chart. Here are the sections in detail:

✔ **Section 1:** In this section, the game starts up and initializes all its variables. Here the program sets up data structures, allocates memory, locks resources, and loads graphics and sound files.

✔ **Section 2:** Typically, the game enters into a main menu loop. Here the player can select game options and control the overall game experience. This section is usually a single function that loops indefinitely until the player starts a new game (entering the main loop) or exits back to the OS.

✔ **Section 3:** After the player has started a game, the program activates the main game loop. This point is the top of the game loop, where the game logic is reset for the next frame. Here is also where the video

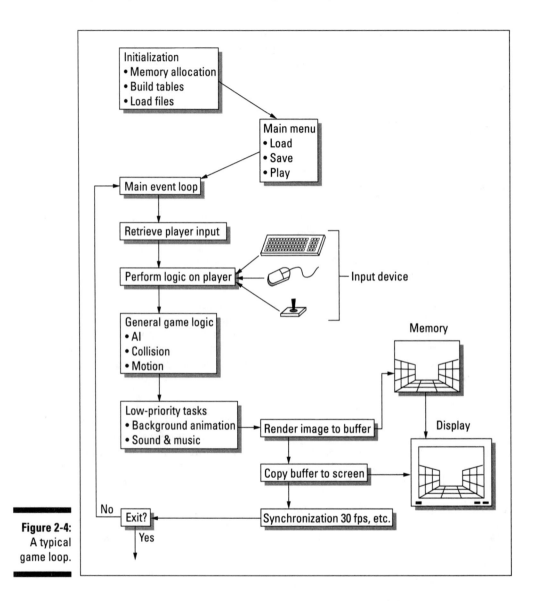

Figure 2-4:
A typical
game loop.

display is cleared and/or objects for the next frame of animation are drawn. (A video game creates the illusion of motion by redrawing the video screen in rapid succession — usually 15–60 times a second.)

✔ **Section 4:** At this point, the program retrieves the player's input.

✔ **Section 5:** Based on the players input, the program performs the player's logic. This process involves moving the player, firing weapons, and testing for collisions.

✔ **Section 6:** Based on the player's actions, the program executes the internal game logic. The program processes all the artificial intelligence, moves all the objects, performs collision detection, and so on.

✔ **Section 7:** At this point, the program has processed all the player logic and all the objects, so now it handles low-priority tasks. It performs background animation, music, sound processing, and any program-based housekeeping chores (such as garbage collection).

✔ **Section 8:** The current animation frame is ready to be rendered, so the program draws the player's character and all the objects to an invisible section of memory (usually called a *double* or *virtual* buffer).

✔ **Section 9:** The program renders the off-screen video image representing the next frame to the visible display.

✔ **Section 10:** The final stage of the game loop pipeline is the synchronization step. Here, the main loop locks the game to a specific frame rate, so that the game runs at a consistent rate on all machines. The program accomplishes this task with a delay or through other timing techniques.

✔ **Section 11:** This is the exit section. The game is over, and it's time to clean up. In this section, you release all resources, reset things to the way you found them (just like Mom taught you), and exit back to the OS.

Wow! That seems like a long process. Well, it is, and it isn't. If you write the game carefully and in modules, then this sequence works out great. However, if you spaghetti-code the main loop, then you'll definitely wish you stayed in bed the day that you have to fit everything.

Now before I move on, I want to bring some key issues to your attention. The first thing is that there are a lot of brands on the market that are as tasty as the real thing. (Now, would any programming book be complete without a reference to *Real Genius?*)

Secondly, the game loop outlined earlier in this section is just a model; you don't have to do things in exactly the same order or have as many steps. As long as the end results are the same, the approach you use doesn't matter. For example, you may decide to do all the logic processing first, and then get the player input, and then render the next frame. My point is this: Because the game loop is running at around 30 fps (frames per second), the order in which you do the middle stuff isn't important — as long as you do it.

Game Loops

In this section, I give you an example of a fairly simple game loop, so you can see the actual structure. Because this chapter up to this point doesn't discuss any graphics programming or information on Windows or DirectX,

I decided to create a *console application,* which you can do by simply choosing to create a console application instead of a Win32 application when you create a new project with your C/C++ compiler.

Normally, console applications are used to experiment and do pure-text applications that are devoid of graphics. However, if you look through the Win32 SDK documentation long enough, you find out that you can print text in any color and position on the console output window. I was able to create a crude graphics system that allowed me to draw character graphics — which was enough power to make the demo.

Don't underestimate the power of console applications. You can use them to access all the resources of the computer just as you can with a standard Win32 application — including all the memory and 32-bit addressing!

To keep the demo simple, I created a little ship and a vertically scrolling star field. Don't worry if you don't understand the graphics calls to control the console; just focus on the `main()` function and the high-level details. The name of the program is `PROG2_1.CPP`, and you can find both the source and executable on the CD-ROM. The controls for the ship are

A — Move left.

S — Move right.

Q — Quit.

Here's the code:

```
// INCLUDES ////////////////////////////////////////////////
#include <stdio.h>
#include <stdlib.h>
#include <ctype.h>
#include <conio.h>
#include <windows.h>
#include <time.h>
// DEFINES /////////////////////////////////////////////////
#define MAX_X        77  // maximum x position for player
#define SCROLL_POS   24  // the point that scrolling occurs
// PROTOTYPES //////////////////////////////////////////////
void Init_Graphics(void);
inline void Set_Color(int fcolor, int bcolor);
inline void Draw_String(int x,int y, char *string);
// GLOBALS /////////////////////////////////////////////////
CONSOLE_SCREEN_BUFFER_INFO con_info;   // holds screen info
HANDLE hconsole;          // handle to console
int   game_running = 1; // state of game, 0=done, 1=run
```

```
// FUNCTIONS ///////////////////////////////////////////////
void Init_Graphics(void)
{
// this function initializes the console graphics engine
COORD console_size = {80,25}; // size of console
// seed the random number generator with time
srand((unsigned)time(NULL));
// open i/o channel to console screen
hconsole=CreateFile("CONOUT$",GENERIC_WRITE | GENERIC_READ,
        FILE_SHARE_READ | FILE_SHARE_WRITE,
        OL, OPEN_EXISTING, FILE_ATTRIBUTE_NORMAL, OL);
// make sure we are in 80x25
SetConsoleScreenBufferSize(hconsole,console_size);
// get details for console screen
GetConsoleScreenBufferInfo(hconsole,&con_info);
} // end Init_Graphics
///////////////////////////////////////////////////////////
inline void Set_Color(int fcolor, int bcolor=0)
{
// this function sets the color of the console output
SetConsoleTextAttribute(hconsole,(WORD)((bcolor << 4) |
                        fcolor));
} // Set_Color
///////////////////////////////////////////////////////////
inline void Draw_String(int x,int y, char *string)
{
// this function draws a string at the given x,y
COORD cursor_pos; // used to pass coords
// set printing position
cursor_pos.X = x;
cursor_pos.Y = y;
SetConsoleCursorPosition(hconsole,cursor_pos);
// print the string in current color
printf("%s",string);
} // end Draw_String
///////////////////////////////////////////////////////////
inline void Clear_Screen(void)
{
// this function clears the screen
// set color to white on black
Set_Color(15,0);
// clear the screen
for (int index=0; index<=25; index++)
    Draw_String(0, SCROLL_POS,"\n");
} // end Clear_Screen
```

(continued)

(continued)

```
// MAIN GAME LOOP ///////////////////////////////////////////////
void main(void)
{
char key;               // player input data
int  player_x = 40;  // player's x position
// SECTION: initialization
// set up the console text graphics system
Init_Graphics();
// clear the screen
Clear_Screen();
// SECTION: main event loop, this is where all the action
// takes place, the general loop is erase-move-draw
while(game_running)
    {
    // SECTION: erase all the objects or clear screen
    // nothing to erase in our case

    // SECTION: get player input
    if (kbhit())
       {
       // get keyboard data, and filter it
       key = toupper(getch());
       // is player trying to exit, if so exit
       if (key=='Q' || key==27)
          game_running = 0;
       // is player moving left
       if (key=='A')
          player_x--;
       // is player moving right
       if (key=='S')
          player_x++;
       } // end if
    // SECTION: game logic and further processing
    // make sure player stays on screen
    if (++player_x > MAX_X)
       player_x=MAX_X;
    if (--player_x < 0)
       player_x=0;
    // SECTION: draw everything
    // draw next star at random position
    Set_Color(15,0);
    Draw_String(rand()%80, SCROLL_POS,".\n");
    // draw player
    Set_Color(rand()%15,0);
    Draw_String(player_x,0,"<-*->");
    Draw_String(0,0,"");
```

```
      // SECTION: synchronize to a constant frame rate
      Sleep(40);
      } // end while
// SECTION: shutdown and bail
Clear_Screen();
printf("\nG A M E   O V E R \n\n");
} // end main
```

Take a look at the `main()` function. First, the function initializes the console graphics and clears the screen, and then the program starts the main event loop. Notice that the program uses the control variable `game_running` as an exit flag from the main loop. In general, you should track the current state of the game in a variable or set of variables; this practice makes it easy to switch from one code section to another. Anyway, the program enters the main event loop and then queries the keyboard via `kbhit()` and `getch()`; if the user presses a key, then the position of the player is updated on-screen.

The next section of the main event loop does the general logic processing. In this case, the function doesn't do much more than make sure that the ship doesn't move off the screen (which is 80 characters wide and 25 characters tall). After the program performs the collision test, it starts the main rendering section and draws the player and stars. (Actually, the program draws only one new star per frame, but the screen scrolls.) Finally, the function utilizes a time delay to slow down the game, so that it isn't just a blur to the user, and the loop continues forever — well, at least until you press ESC or Q.

If you want to, you can spend some time tweaking this simple demo until you feel comfortable with the concepts of real-time and game loops.

State Machines and Automatons

About 90 percent of game programming is graphics and sound programming, and the other 90 percent is logic programming — and no, the total of those percentages doesn't equal 100 percent. By using solid programming techniques and software structures, you can write a 100,000-line game without too much trouble.

Begin your study of solid programming techniques with one of the most basic software constructs: the *finite state machine* or *FSM*. An FSM is an abstract machine that you model with software (or hardware). Take a look at Figure 2-5. The FSM changes from state to state based on its current state and the input that it receives.

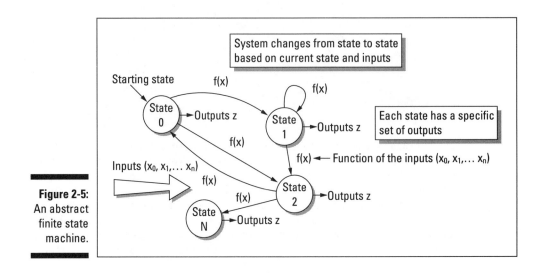

Figure 2-5:
An abstract
finite state
machine.

An FSM's input can be from counters, logic functions, or from other FSMs. So the FSM works by looking at its current state, its inputs, and the rules about when it can change states; after this analysis, the FSM then performs the right action. This self-analysis happens each cycle of time or each frame in the case of a video game.

Most functions and objects that you create in a video game are FSMs. For example, suppose that you want a little green light to blink on the player's control interface. This action is perfect for an FSM. The light has only two states: ON and OFF. Furthermore, the input to switch between states is *time*. So after every second, you may want to toggle the state of the light FSM. (Figure 2-6 shows an example of this FSM.)

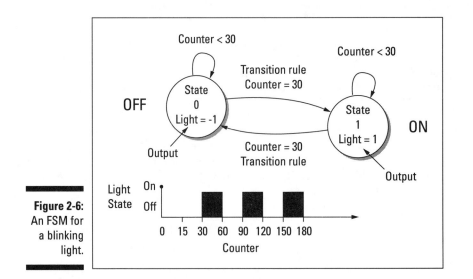

Figure 2-6:
An FSM for
a blinking
light.

The following listing shows how you can code the FSM for a blinking light:

```
int light_state = -1; // state of light, this is global
int Light_Object(void)
{
// this function will toggle the state of the light once
// every 30 frames; assume 30 fps
static int counter = 0; // this keeps track of the internal state
// test whether it's time for a state change
if (++counter >= 30)
   {
   // reset counter
   counter=0;
   // toggle light state
   light_state=-light_state;
   } // end if
} // end Light_Object
```

If you're a C++ programmer, you may notice that a finite state machine emulates some of the functionality of a *C++ object.*

The `Light_Object()` function remembers information that can be used to control something else. In this case, the counter is used as the *state control* to change the state of a global variable. Use the function by just making a call to it in your main event loop, perhaps like this:

```
while(game_running)
    {
    // erase
    // move
    // logic
    Light_Object();
    // draw
    Draw_Light(light_state);
    } // end while
```

Of course, to make this code fully functional, you need the rest of the event loop logic, and you need to write `Draw_Light()`, but you get the point; the `Light_Object()` function can now be thought of as an entity that is self-contained and runs *asynchronously* or without supervision from other control logic.

Now you probably have a "come on, give me something hard" look on your face. Okay, for the next example, how about a more complex FSM that can be used to drive a computer-controlled tank? Assume that the tank has these five states:

  ✔ State 0 — Northbound

  ✔ State 1 — Westbound

  ✔ State 2 — Southbound

  ✔ State 3 — Eastbound

  ✔ State 4 — Stationary

The tank can be in any of these states at any time. The rules to make state changes are as follows:

  ✔ If the tank hits an obstacle, then the tank makes a left-hand turn, or counterclockwise.

  ✔ If the tank is in any state for more than 1,000 cycles, then a random state is chosen. Figure 2-7 depicts the state and transition rules of the tank FSM.

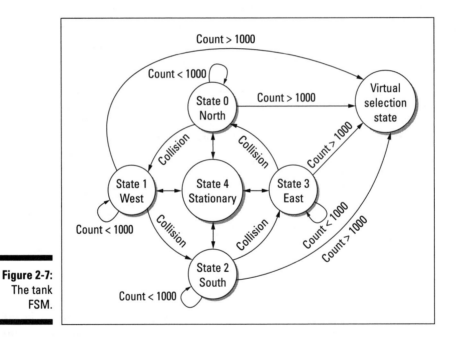

Figure 2-7:
The tank
FSM.

The following software FSM models the tank:

```
#define TANK_NORTHBOUND    0
#define TANK_WESTBOUND     1
#define TANK_SOUTHBOUND    2
#define TANK_EASTBOUND     3
#define TANK_STATIONARY    4
int tank_state = TANK_NORTHBOUND;
```

```
void Tank_Object(void)
{
static int counter = 0; // counts frames and, at count of
                        // 1000, selects a random state
// test for state transition collision rule
if (Tank_Collision())
   {
   // turn tank counter clockwise
   if (++tank_state > TANK_EASTBOUND)
      tank_state = TANK_NORTHBOUND;
   } // end if
// test for state transition 1000 cycle rule
if (++counter >= 1000)
   {
   // reset counter
   counter=0;
   // select new random state
   tank_state = rand()%(TANK_STATIONARY+1);
} // end Tank_Object
```

The function Tank_Object() is a software implementation of the tank FSM specification. The function has five states, follows the rules, and is very simple. One reason that the function is so clean is the clever selection of state values; the values are in numerical order such that 0, 1, 2, and 3 are in counterclockwise order. This organization makes the state transitions trivial because the function only has to add 1 to the current state for the tank to make a left turn after hitting an obstacle.

Notice that the function remembers its internal state, which is encoded in the variable *counter*. Furthermore, the function modifies the global tank state. Note also that an FSM can be totally self-contained, even though the above code does not reflect that. I just used a global variable to contain the state, so that other functions could "see" the state of the tank. You may or may not want to do this, but that choice is up to you and the situation.

To make a finite state machine, first you create a set of states that an object or process can be in. Then you create a set of rules to make transitions from one state to the next. Finally, you implement the FSM with a well-thought-out function or set of functions. The results are autonomous, self-contained objects that perform their tasks without outside forces like other objects or the main event loop watching over them.

The autonomy of video game objects and processes is one of the most important aspects of writing game software. You must try to make each object and process as self-sustaining and self-contained as possible. In the real world, if you put a rock and a dog in the same room, the rock doesn't ask the dog for help being a rock; the rock knows how to be a rock, and the dog knows how to be a dog.

Now take a look at a more realistic game loop that itself is an FSM. In fact, a game is itself an object that contains many objects. Therefore, you should make the main event loop an FSM, so that the game can switch states by itself.

In general, a game can be in about a half-dozen major states. A game can be initializing, running, in the main menu, shutting down, and so forth. You can create a main loop that contains each of these states and then allows state transitions to be made from state to state. Doing so allows a clean delineation of each state that the main loop is in and makes it easier to program the main loop. For example, take a look at the set of states below:

```
#define GAME_STATE_INIT
#define GAME_STATE_MENU
#define GAME_STATE_START
#define GAME_STATE_RUN
#define GAME_STATE_SHUTDOWN
#define GAME_STATE_EXIT
```

Now pick up these states and write a main loop that takes them into consideration. Look at Figure 2-8 to see the FSM graphically.

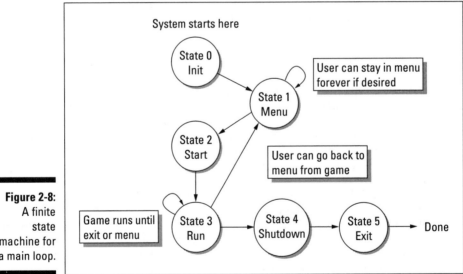

Figure 2-8: A finite state machine for a main loop.

The code that implements the FSM for a main loop follows:

```
int game_state = GAME_STATE_INIT; // start the game off in this state
void main(void)
{
```

```
// enter main event loop
while(game_state!=GAME_STATE_EXIT)
    {
    // what state are we in? (could use if's, too)
    switch (game_state)
         {
         case GAME_STATE_INIT:
             {
             // perform initializations
             Init_Game();

             // swtich states to main menu
             game_state = GAME_STATE_MENU;
             } break;
         case GAME_STATE_MENU:
             {
             // in this section, you would call the
             // menu function; it would return
             // the new state of the game (start,
             // exit)
             game_state = Main_Menu();
             } break;
         case GAME_STATE_START:
             {
             // this state is used to get ready to run
             // the game; you would call any last
             // minute functions and then switch to
             // the running state
             Startup_Work();
             game_state = GAME_STATE_RUN;
             } break;
         case GAME_STATE_RUN:
             {
             // in this state you would run the game;
             // you might put the entire game loop
             // right here, or call a function
             // from this state (the game can usually
             // only go to the menu state)
             game_state = Run_Game();
             } break;
         case GAME_STATE_SHUTDOWN:
             {
             // this is the end of the road; if the
             // game gets to this state, then it
             // releases all resources and switches to
```

(continued)

(continued)

```
                    // the exit state
                    Do_Cleanup();
                    // exit game
                    game_state = GAME_STATE_EXIT;
                    } break;
              default:break;
              } // end switch
        } // end while
} // end main
```

Isn't that cool! This software structure is going to be the model that you'll most often follow as you write games. Sure, you may use more or fewer states or different logic controls, but the structure remains the same.

Algorithms, Data Structures, and Optimization

If you go to Chapter 3 next, you'll enter into the abyss of Windows programming. Before that happens, I want to give you a few tips on the use of algorithms and data structures in game programming.

Game programming is cutting-edge, high-speed, seat-of-the-pants programming. Game programmers can't always do things the cleanest, most traditional way. So check out this list of tips, rules, and philosophies for game programmers:

✔ You *can* use global variables — just don't use them if you don't have to.

✔ Never use a GOTO statement unless you absolutely must; in most cases, you can find a better way to do the operation.

✔ If you don't know how much memory a variable or other element is going to take, then allocate an array of records on the fly, but avoid linked lists and trees if you can. (I discuss helpful tips regarding choosing data structures for games in Bonus Chapter 24 on the CD, in case you're interested.) Keep your data structures as simple as possible.

✔ Make most of your data types into 32-bit data types; don't try to save memory by using 8- or 16-bit data types. Speed is of the utmost importance, and 32-bit data is much faster on 32-bit processors.

✔ Don't pass a lot of variables to functions; put them in a structure and pass a pointer.

✔ Use long, clear variable names; a little extra typing will save you a lot of headaches.

✔ Try to think of everything as an object, and try to minimize the communication between one object and another. (In other words, don't make code dependent on other, unrelated code.)

✔ Use modular programming techniques, which means use header files, defines, and typedefs.

✔ Always initialize all your variables.

✔ Try not to use floating-point mathematics. Integers are faster.

✔ Put comments all throughout your code. A comment on each line of code is best.

✔ Don't optimize your code as you write it. Program efficiently, but optimize later.

✔ A good algorithm is worth thousands of lines of assembly language. If some procedure is slow, first see if you can find a better way of doing it before resorting to assembly language.

✔ Keep a good supply of caffeinated drinks around at all times.

✔ Use *inline* functions for small functions that are called a lot.

✔ Program defensively. From the very beginning, create some kind of error system that generates an error log for each function. Turn it on and off with conditional compilation; for example:

```
#ifdef ERROR_ON
// do error processing
#endif
```

✔ Minimize the use of complex C/C++ functions. If you can write the code that does what you need, then do so. The C/C++ libraries are fast, but they aren't that fast!

✔ If you need to allocate small arrays of data and you know that they will never be larger than 16–256 elements, then make the arrays into static arrays. You don't need to add the complexity of memory allocation and deallocation for such small data items.

✔ If you prefer to use C++ objects and classes, then do so — but don't get class-happy and create class after class. Keep your classes simple and concrete. Remember — the best programs have no class.

Chapter 3

The Nuts and Bolts of Windows 95/98/NT Programming

● ●

In This Chapter

▶ Exploring the history of Windows

▶ Multitasking makes Windows special

▶ Understanding the basics of Windows Programming

▶ Recognizing the elements of Hungarian notation

▶ Creating a simple Windows application

▶ Identifying the parts of a Windows application

● ●

*T*his chapter introduces the Windows environment and programming in Windows. If you have no experience in programming within Windows, you'll note that a lot of information is presented here, so take your time and make sure that you understand all the concepts. I build on these basics in later chapters.

The History of Windows — A Programmer's Perspective

Windows is an important reason why computing has made leaps and bounds in the last few years. Humans don't think in terms of text; we think in terms of pictures. Bill Gates knew this, as did Steve Jobs when he developed the Apple Macintosh, which was the first real windows-based computing environment available to the public. (Actually, windows technology was originally invented by the Xerox Palo Alto Research Center [or PARC] many years before, but the company didn't fully capitalize on the idea.)

Eventually, Microsoft developed a graphical, windows-based operating system for the booming IBM personal computer market. Microsoft Windows 1.0 was released in 1985; it barely worked, looked bad, and simply needed too much computing power for the 8086 machines of the day. Version 2.0 came out a bit later, and it was a little better; you could write programs such as calculators to work on it, but the equivalent DOS versions used less memory and were about 10 times faster.

Then Windows 3.0 was released in 1990, and it really worked! It was what Windows 1.0 should have been if that program hadn't been limited by the state of PC technology at the time. Windows 3.0 was still a DOS application (it ran on top of DOS), but it did support multitasking (sort of) and a lot of applications became available for it.

Window 3.1 came out in 1992. It was fast, it looked better, and it was the last nail in the coffin of DOS for business applications. Windows 3.1 was alluring to programmers. It had multimedia support for audio and video, and made the PC into a real multimedia and business computer that rivaled small workstations. For all that, however, Windows 3.1 was still a 16-bit program running on a 32-bit computer. At the time, the 486DX processor was already available and the Pentium was on the horizon, so the world was ready for 32-bit computing.

In late 1995, Windows 95 was released — and it was killer! It had remnants of Windows 3.1 here and there, and it contained some 16-bit code, but the interface was intuitive, the kernel supported real multitasking and multithreading, and the program had network support, multimedia, and much more. Most importantly, Windows 95 is a 32-bit operating system from the programmer's point of view. For the first time in Windows history, writing a Windows application was fairly easy.

Now Windows 98 is on the horizon. Windows 98 is a cleaned-up version of Windows 95 that uses a lot of new technologies (such as ActiveX, COM, DCOM, and dynamic HTML), and it uses some of the Windows NT advances. From the programmer's perspective, however, Windows 95, Windows 98, and Windows NT are the same. Properly written applications for Windows 95 run on Windows 98 and Windows NT, because all three operating systems use the Win32 library — the basis for all Windows programs.

The one technology that makes it possible to write game programs that work for all three is *DirectX*. DirectX has been around for a few years, though in embryonic form. But now a DirectX 32-bit game is just as fast and probably faster than a 32-bit DOS game. I never thought I would say that — well, at least without getting paid to!

Windows 95, Windows 98, and Windows NT are all the same as far as game programmers are concerned. You can take an application that you have written for Windows 95 and it will run unchanged on computers using Windows 98 or NT, as long as they are running with DirectX installed. And that's really cool.

Multitasking, Multithreading, and Multiple Personalities

The big deal about the Windows operating system is its ability to *multitask.* Multitasking allows more than one application to execute at the same time. Theoretically, writing a multitasking operating system isn't that difficult, but getting it to actually work reliably *is* difficult — which is why Windows has taken so long to evolve.

DOS is a single-tasking operating system. Only one program can run at a time. You can implement crude multitasking with DOS by using interrupts, but for the most part only one big application is going to control the entire computer's resources. This situation is fine for games, but DOS just isn't sufficient for a workstation or business computer. Multitasking allows many applications that have nothing to do with each other to run at the same time. The hardware is better utilized, which means that you can get more work done and spend less time working and more time playing games — and that should be your primary goal.

If you're a DOS programmer, you will find that Windows programming really isn't that different — can you see my nose growing? Windows takes care of running multiple applications, and you don't; writing multitasking applications is almost the same as writing non-multitasking, DOS-like applications. Remember that the computer has only one video screen, one sound card, and so on, which means that — when your program requests a resource that's in use — the program may need to wait for the resource. So keep resource sharing in mind as you program. (I explain this process in the next chapter.)

Windows is also cool in that it supports *multithreading.* Multithreading can be thought of as many little processes within a single application. Figure 3-1 depicts a multitasking operating system versus an operating system that also offers multithreading. With a multitasking operating system, you can run a game, a word processor, and a paint program all at once. All these programs are called *programs, processes,* or *tasks.* However, if an operating system supports multithreading, then within each of these programs other even smaller *threads* of execution can start. For example, the word processor could have one thread to handle input, while another is saving to the disk, while yet another is doing a spell-check on a document.

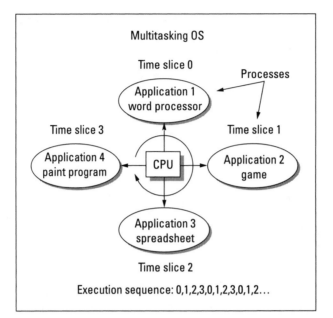

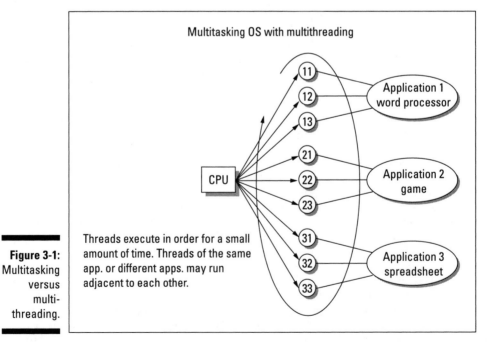

Figure 3-1:
Multitasking
versus
multi-
threading.

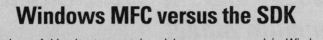

Windows MFC versus the SDK

The last few sections of this chapter contain the quickest Windows programming crash course in history, but this sidebar discusses some important acronyms that may baffle you: *MFC* and *SDK*. MFC stands for Microsoft Foundation Classes, and SDK stands for Software Development Kit.

In the beginning, programmers used only the SDK to create programs for Windows. The SDK consists of a number of libraries, headers, and an API (Application Programming Interface) to write Windows programs. On the other hand, the MFC is a set of C++ classes built on the SDK to make programming Windows applications easier.

Programming with the MFC is easier, right? Don't believe it!

I have programmed in Windows for a long time, and I can say that MFC doesn't make programming any easier. The SDK is bad enough, but MFC is like watching the movie *Ishtar;* it's horrible!

Truthfully, Windows is so complex that a high-level layer was needed to hide the low-level guts of the Windows API, and that is why MFC came to be. But learning MFC means learning yet another API. And learning another API is too much to ask for life-forms that live on average less than 100 years. So for Windows programming in this book, I use the simpler SDK. It is easy to understand, works on all machines, is supported by more compilers, and is based on C rather than C++.

Now multitasking and multithreading aren't free and they don't make a computer run faster. They are an abstraction. A computer with one microprocessor can still only execute one instruction stream at a time, so a multitasking operating system isn't going to make things faster. But if you have two processors or more, then a multitasking operating system will allow the tasks to run on each processor and they will run faster than if they were run on a single processor system.

In reality, depending on their architecture, certain single processors can execute more than one instruction. The Pentium processor can execute two instructions at once (one in the U pipe and one in the V pipe), whereas the Power PC and Pentium II can execute up to five. The number of instructions a processor can execute depends for the most part on how many *execution units* the processor has and the size of its *instruction pipeline*.

So why do game programmers care about multitasking and multithreading? Well, multithreading is more important than the multitasking. Multithreading enables you to write a game that is a single application with a number of subprocesses (threads) that can work without your supervision. All programmers like the idea of *automatons* (self-sustaining objects) that do the job and don't need help. Multithreading solves this problem nicely. Unfortunately, multithreading is fairly advanced, so you'll have to research it on your own. You are going to do things the old-fashioned way in this book!

Windows 95 and the Event-Based Programming Model

Writing a Windows application can be easy or difficult, depending on how much Windows stuff you need to do. Writing a word processor requires a great deal of knowledge about Windows; but to write a game under DirectX, you need to know very little. This section and the remaining sections of the book give you the short version of Windows programming and cover the basics of what you need to know.

As shown in Figure 3-2, Windows is an *event-based* operating system, which means that a main loop that repeats indefinitely processes messages as they come in. A *message* is a signal from Windows, another application, or the user, that instructs your application about something that has happened. For example:

- **Windowing event:** When the user resizes a window, Windows sends a message to the application about how the window has been resized.

- **Keyboard event:** When the user presses a key, a key-press message is sent to the application, allowing it to process the information and perform the appropriate action (such as popping up a menu).

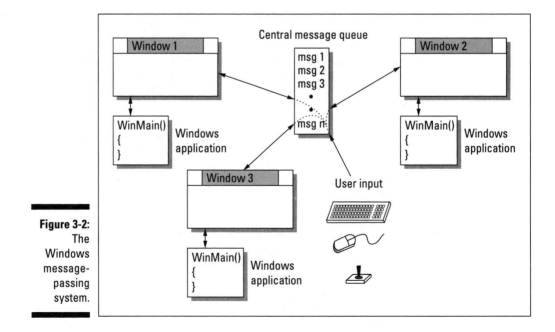

Figure 3-2:
The
Windows
message-
passing
system.

> ✔ **Drawing event:** If another window is drawn over your application's window and the contents of your window must be redrawn, a repaint message is sent to your application.

Everything in Windows is a message. As you can see from Figure 3-2, a Windows program spends its life processing messages and returning to the main loop. To create a working Windows program, you must process important messages when they occur, which satisfies the operating system and keeps things running correctly. But when your program isn't processing a Windows message, then it's free to do whatever you want. This is how you sneak video game logic and rendering into a Windows application.

Of course, creating a working Windows application involves a lot of details, but in essence all a program does is process messages. Your program can do any other tasks as long as it does its housekeeping. After you get a working Windows program shell up and running, you can literally cut and paste the code to create other applications. (In this book, for example, you do this with just about every Windows game application you make.)

Hungarian Notation for Those Who Like Excessive Typing

A discussion of Hungarian notation is important enough for an entire section, because this notation is one reason why Microsoft code looks so alien.

This Hungarian dude at Microsoft — Charles Simonyi — was charged with creating a set of conventions for all Microsoft programmers to follow when writing code, so that other programs could tell the types of variable names (whether something was a constant, a class, a typedef, a pointer, and so on). The results of Simonyi's work were called *Hungarian notation*, which is a set of naming rules that are religiously followed by all Microsofties; hence, all code written by Microsoft follows this format. So you must know how to read Hungarian notation, or you'll continually wonder why everything looks so cryptic. The code examples (other than API prototypes) in this book don't use too much of this notation, but knowing it is good. Table 3-1 contains the original specification.

Table 3-1	Hungarian Notation Specification
Prefix	*Data Type (Base Type)*
c	char
by	BYTE (unsigned char)
n	short or int (refers to a number)
i	int
x, y	short (used as *x*-coordinate or *y*-coordinate)
cx, cy	short (used as *x* or *y; c* stands for *count*)
b	BOOL (int)
w	UINT (unsigned int) or WORD (unsigned word)
l	LONG (long)
dw	DWORD (unsigned long)
fn	function
s	string
sz,str	string terminated by 0 byte
lp	32-bit long pointer
h	handle
msg	message

Variable naming

Nearly all the Hungarian notation prefixes in Table 3-1 are self-explanatory. You may be wondering about the "handle" prefix: *h. Handles* are 32-bit integers or references to other objects. Handles are used in the notation rather than 32-bit integers because Microsoft never promised not to change handles to a different data type, so as long as you always use handles, you won't have a problem.

Most variables in Microsoft code use a prefix followed by the variable name itself. Furthermore, each variable name has the first letter of each subname capitalized. The following lists some examples:

✔ szName: A *NULL* terminated string

✔ dwHitList: A *WORD;* notice the capital H and L

✔ lpData: A 32-bit pointer to something

✔ lpwData: A 32-bit pointer to a *WORD*

Sometimes a lowercase *g* followed by an underscore (_) signifies that a variable is global, such as: g_lTime, which is a global variable that is a *LONG*.

Function naming

Functions are named using an uppercase per-word style without any underscores between words. Here are some examples:

```
WORD IsFull(void);
int LoadBitmap(void);
BOOL IsRunning(void);
```

Types & Constants

Typdefs and constants are in all uppercase. The naming conventions for these are a little looser with underscore characters; here are some examples:

```
typedef unsigned char UCHAR;
typedef int BOOL;
#define MAX_BRAINS 100
```

Classes

Classes are named the same way functions are, that is, with the first word of multiword names capitalized. However, all classes have the prefix *C*. Here is an example:

```
class CPoint
{
public:
    CPoint(void);
    ~CPoint();
private:
    int x,y;
};
```

A (Very) Simple Windows Program

If you understand how to read the alien language of Hungarian notation in Windows, then you're ready to create a simple Windows program. I am totally against tradition, so I made up a new, more Generation X-style of first program instead of the standard Hello, World program. Actually, I show the code for two programs; one prints the message by using standard console C code, and the other does so in a full, working Windows application.

From this point onward in the chapter, I show you a lot of material: functions, flags, variables, types, and so forth. In most cases, I only show a subset or partial list of examples, so make sure that you call up your Windows Win32 SDK help files for a more detailed version of anything that isn't clear. The help systems of most C/C++ compilers are amazingly complete.

What's up, world! — Old-school style

Creating a program that prints out "What's up, world" in standard console C is pretty easy. Here's the code:

```
// PROG3_1.CPP - what's up standard version
#include <stdio.h>

// main entry point for all standard DOS/console programs
void main(void)
{
printf("\nWhat's up, world!");
} // end main
```

This program will work on just about any computer that has a C/C++ compiler. Just type in the code, compile, and run (or check the CD-ROM for the code itself). After that, somewhere on your console, you should see:

```
What's up, world!
C:\
```

What's up, world! — Windows style

Writing a Windows application that opens up a real window takes a few pages of code, but you can get something on the screen a lot quicker if you use the API to create a window for you. The following demo shows you how to create a working Windows application. Don't worry too much about the WinMain() and the message API call; just gaze in amazement at the results. I get to the details in the next section.

The source code for the following program can be found on the CD-ROM that came with this book.

```
// PROG3_2.CPP - A simple message box
#define WIN32_LEAN_AND_MEAN
#include <windows.h>
#include <windowsx.h>

// main entry point for all windows programs
int WINAPI WinMain(HINSTANCE hinstance,
                   HINSTANCE hprevinstance,
                   LPSTR lpcmdline,
                   int ncmdshow)
{
// call message box API
MessageBox(NULL, "What's up, world!",
                 "My First Windows Program",MB_OK);

// exit program
return(0);
} // end WinMain
```

If everything worked, you should see on your screen a message box that looks like the one shown in Figure 3-3.

Figure 3-3:
PROG3_2.CPP
in action.

If you're interested in the parameters of the MessageBox() function, here's its prototype:

```
int MessageBox(
HWND     hWnd,       // handle of parent window
LPCTSTR  lpText,     // pointer to message string
LPCTSTR  lpCaption,  // pointer to title string
UINT     uType);     // style of message box
```

If you're having trouble getting the Windows program to compile, refer to Chapter 1. All you need to do is create a new project, specify a Win32 application, add the source file (which is on the CD) to the project, and compile. And if that doesn't work, try a hammer and a blowtorch!

The Parts of a Real Windows Application

Now's the time to get technical and review all the components of a complete Windows application. You won't need to know all this stuff inside and out, but you should take a look at it at least once, so that you can appreciate what DirectX does for you.

You must take a number of items into consideration when you write a real Windows application:

- ✔ Win32 libraries
- ✔ Include files
- ✔ WinMain() entry point
- ✔ Windows class
- ✔ Registering the windows class
- ✔ Creating a window
- ✔ Showing the window
- ✔ Event loop
- ✔ Event handler

The following sections take a look at each of these in detail.

The Win32 libraries

The Windows programming API is composed of a number of static libraries and *DLLs* (Dynamic Link Libraries) that are loaded as needed by the application. Fortunately for you, when you create a Windows Win32 application, the compiler takes care of including all the libraries for you, so you don't have to worry about that task.

The only time that you have to explicitly add libraries to your application is if the libraries aren't part of the default library set for a Win32 application. For example, if you want to use the multimedia extensions to Windows, then you need to add WINMM.LIB library to your project. This file should be within the /LIB directory of your particular compiler's file system.

In addition, when you create DirectX applications, you will add the DirectX libraries to your application. But for now, just make sure to check the Win32 application in your application project's target application.

The include files

A number of Windows include files must be included in your application to access the entire API; however, someone at Microsoft was nice enough to put all these includes into a single include file named WINDOWS.H. All you have to do is include this file in your application and all the Windows headers will be included for you.

The message box demo in the previous section, "A (Very) Simple Windows Program," has another include file and a define. The other include was WINDOWSX.H. This header includes a number of useful macros, so always include it in your programs. Finally, the line #defineWIN32_LEAN_AND_MEAN forces various options in the WINDOWS.H file to be taken, so you need to include this in your program, too.

Begin every Windows program with the following:

```
#define WIN32_LEAN_AND_MEAN
#include <windows.h>
#include <windowsx.h>
```

After the Windows includes, you need to include all the headers that your program needs, such as STDIO.H, MATH.H, and so on.

Da WinMain() man

As shown in the sample Windows program in the last section, the name of the main entry point is WinMain() rather than the standard main() found in a normal C or C++ program. WinMain() is the entry point for all Windows applications and is analogous to main() in C or C++ programs, with the addition of some new parameters. Here's the prototype of WinMain():

```
int WINAPI WinMain(HINSTANCE hinstance,
                   HINSTANCE hprevinstance,
                   LPSTR lpcmdline,
                   int ncmdshow);
```

Notice that the function is declared with the type WINAPI, which makes sure that the function uses the *PASCAL* calling convention and is 32-bit. You must remember to declare WinMain() exactly this way, or else the parameters may get passed incorrectly.

The first parameter `hinstance` is the handle of the application instance; think of this as a unique id of the application. The second parameter `hprevinstance` is obsolete, but it used to be the handle of the preceding instance. The parameter `lpcmdline` is a pointer to the command line parameters. It is similar to the argument list `*argv[]` in a non-Windows `main()`, but is a single string rather than an array of them and is missing the executable's name. For example, the command line:

```
APP1.EXE FILE1.BMP FILE2.BMP
```

would look like this in the standard C/C++ `main(int argc, char **argv)`:

```
arvg[0] = "APP1.EXE"
argv[1] = "FILE1.BMP"
argv[2] = "FILE2.BMP"
```

However, in `WinMain()`, the same command line would look like:

```
lpcmdline = "FILE1.BMP FILE2.BMP"
```

Notice that the entire command line is a single string rather than parsed out into substrings, as in the C/C++ standard `main()`.

Moving on, the last parameter of `WinMain()` is `ncmdshow`. This integer value directs your application in the way that the window initially should be shown. Typically, this value will be `SW_SHOWNORMAL`. Some other popular options are shown in Table 3-2.

Table 3-2	**Window Startup Codes for** ncmdshow
Value	*Meaning*
SW_SHOW	Shows the window in its default size and position
SW_SHOWNORMAL	Shows the window in its default size and position
SW_SHOWMAXIMIZED	Shows the window in a maximized state
SW_SHOWMINIMIZED	Shows the window in a minimized state

The Windows class

I said in the Introduction to this book that you would use very little C++, but the concepts of C++ are ingrained in the design of Windows (which is a good thing). Each object in Windows *is a window*. Yes, everything is a window — even buttons, scroll bars, text boxes, and so forth. This abstraction was absolutely necessary to make an operating system as complex as Windows work. Otherwise, a million different types of objects would exist in Windows, and if you think that Windows programming is complicated now. . . .

Each object in Windows is a type of window derived from a base window class or type. To create your own window, you must create a window class. A *window class* describes your particular window's properties. After you define a Windows class, you can create as many windows with that class as you wish. Here is the structure of a Windows class:

```
typedef struct _WNDCLASS
{
UINT     style;          // style flags
WNDPROC  lpfnWndProc;    // pointer to event handler
int      cbClsExtra;     // extra bytes
int      cbWndExtra;     // extra bytes
HANDLE   hInstance;      // handle of instance
HICON    hIcon;          // handle to icon
HCURSOR  hCursor;        // handle to cursor
HBRUSH   hbrBackground;  // handle to background brush
LPCTSTR  lpszMenuName;   // name of menu
LPCTSTR  lpszClassName;  // name of class
} WNDCLASS;

WNDCLASS wndclass; // a declaration of a window class
```

The style field is used to define the general flags or properties of the window class. This field controls conditions such as how the window looks, whether it is resizable, who is responsible for redrawing it, what kind of messages it can process, and so on. Most of the time, you can fill the style field like this:

```
wndclass.style = CS_DBLCLKS | CS_OWNDC |
                 CS_HREDRAW | CS_VREDRAW;
```

Too many flags exist to list them all, but these are the standards. They instruct Windows to send messages on any window resizing, and on double-clicks of the mouse buttons. In addition, the CS_OWNDC flag gives the window its own *device context,* which speeds up the process of painting to the window.

The lpfnWndProc field is a function pointer that points to the event handler function. This function is going to process all the messages from Windows. I cover the details of the event handler a little later, in the subsection "The event handler"; but in general, you assign lpfnWndProc the address of your event handler like this:

```
wndclass.lpfnWndProc = WindowProc;
```

Where `WindowProc()` is a function that you write and has the following prototype:

```
LRESULT CALLBACK WindowProc(HWND hWnd, // the window
                    UINT msg,       // the message itself
                    WPARAM wParam, // more info on message
                    LPARAM lParam);// more info on message
```

The next two fields, `cbClsExtra` and `cbWndExtra`, were a good idea by Microsoft, but no one ever seems to use them. They direct Windows to save extra space for data in either the windows class or the window itself. They are unused because most programmers prefer storing information in a *container* class by creating a type or class that contains the windows class and put the data separately as another field or record. Set them to 0.

```
wndclass.cbClsExtra = 0;
wndclass.cbWndExtra = 0;
```

The next field `hInstance` is used to store the instance of the application; this is simply set to the `WinMain()`'s `hinstance` parameter like this:

```
wndclass.hInstance = hinstance; // from winmain
```

The next two fields are similar, so handle them at the same time. `hIcon` is the handle of the icon you wish displayed when the application is minimized or viewed as a shortcut or link, and `hCursor` is a handle to the cursor you want your application's pointer to be. Both of these items can be loaded as resources from content that you have created, or you can simply use some of the built-in defaults. The latter is the approach you use here.

You need two functions: `LoadIcon()` and `LoadCursor()`. These load into your program an icon and cursor, respectively, given an id. Use them like this:

```
wndclass.hIcon   = LoadIcon(NULL,  IDI_APPLICATION);
wndclass.hCursor = LoadCursor(NULL, IDC_ARROW);
```

This code loads the standard application icon and the standard-shaped arrow for the cursor. Some other options are shown in Table 3-3.

Table 3-3	A Listing of Useful Cursor and Icon Values
Value	*Meaning*
Icon Constants	
IDI_APPLICATION	Default application icon
IDI_ASTERISK	Asterisk
IDI_EXCLAMATION	Exclamation point
IDI_HAND	Hand-shaped icon
IDI_QUESTION	Question mark

Value	Meaning
Cursor Constants	
IDC_ARROW	Standard arrow
IDC_CROSS	Crosshair
IDC_IBEAM	Text I-beam
IDC_NO	Slashed circle
IDC_WAIT	Hourglass

Alrighty then, almost done! The next field is hbrBackground, and it's the handle to the background brush. Defining graphical terms is a little premature, but what the heck — Windows uses what are called *brushes* and *pens* to draw. A window must have a brush assigned to it to draw the background with. Usually, it's white or black. In addition, brushes may be bitmaps.

Therefore, you need to assign hbrBackground a handle to a valid brush — one you create or one of the systems defaults. Again, I take the easy way out and use a system default. Here's how you do it:

```
wndclass.hbrBackground= (HBRUSH)GetStockObject(BLACK_BRUSH);
```

This code assigns a black brush to the window, so it will have an amazingly black background. Table 3-4 contains a list of other popular stock brushes.

If you are using Microsoft Visual C++ 6.0, you will need to make a minor change to all the Windows programs on the CD-ROM. Visual C++ 6.0 doesn't perform implicit casts anymore on some types, therefore, during the initialization of the Windows Class it throws up. There is a line in every program that looks like this:

```
wndclass.hbrBackground=GetStockObject(BLACK_BRUSH);
```

Change to this:

```
wndclass.hbrBackground= (HBRUSH)GetStockObject(BLACK_BRUSH);
```

Table 3-4	Windows Default Stock Brushes
Value	Meaning
BLACK_BRUSH	Black brush
DKGRAY_BRUSH	Dark gray brush
GRAY_BRUSH	Gray brush
LTGRAY_BRUSH	Light gray brush
WHITE_BRUSH	White brush

Next is the `lpszMenuName` field, which is the name of the resource for the menu that you attach to your window. Menus are a bit complicated, so I cover them in more detail in Chapter 4; for now, just set the menu field to `NULL`.

```
wndclass.lpszMenuName= NULL;
```

Last but not least is the `lpszClassName` field, which is the name that you wish to refer to your new window class. I usually call it something like `"WINCLASS1"`; if I create another windows class, I call it `"WINCLASS2"`; and so on.

```
wndclass.lpszClassName = "WINCLASS1";
```

That's all there is to filling in a `WNDCLASS` data structure. Now you are ready to register it with Windows.

Registering the Windows class

After you create a window class, the next step is to *register* the class. Registration lets Windows know about your window class and enables you to create windows with the class by using only the ASCII name of the class. This approach was done with `"WINCLASS1"` in the example found in the earlier section, "A (Very) Simple Windows Program." Here is the prototype for registering a window class:

```
ATOM RegisterClass(CONST WNDCLASS *lpWndClass);
```

Note that `lpWndClass` is a pointer to your new window class. If the function is successful, it returns an `ATOM` that is non-zero; if a problem occurs, the function returns `0`.

What the heck's an `ATOM`, you ask? Don't jump out of your seat! An *ATOM* is an integer that references an internal string database that Windows keeps. But don't worry, because you only need to test the results of the function rather than use the results. So to register your window class `wndclass`, do the following:

```
if (RegisterClass(&wndclass)==0)
   {
   // error
   } // end if
```

Now you can create windows to your heart's content with the new window class.

Creating a window

To create a window in Windows, you need a single function call with about 11 parameters. Here is the prototype for `CreateWindow()`:

```
HWND CreateWindow(
  LPCTSTR  lpClassName,  // pointer to class name (string)
  LPCTSTR  lpWindowName,    // pointer to window title (string)
  DWORD    dwStyle,      // windows style flags
  int      x,            // horizontal position of window
  int      y,            // vertical position of window
  int      nWidth,       // width of window
  int      nHeight,      // height of window
  HWND     hWndParent,   // handle to parent (usually NULL)
  HMENU    hMenu,        // handle to menu (usually NULL)
  HANDLE   hInstance,    // handle to application instance
  LPVOID   lpParam       // pointer to startup creation data
  );                     // don't worry about it (NULL)
```

If you've read this chapter from the beginning to this point, you should be able to make a pretty good guess about the function of these parameters:

- ✔ `lpClassName` is the window class name that you registered before making a call to `CreateWindow()`.

- ✔ `lpWindowName` is a string such as "My Window" that goes on the title bar of the window.

- ✔ *x* **and** *y* are the screen position to open the window at.

- ✔ `nWidth` **and** `nHeight` is the size of the window in pixels.

- ✔ `hWndParent` is the handle of the parent window; in your case, this will always be `NULL`.

- ✔ `hMenu` is the handle of the window menu, which will also be `NULL` because any menu attachment is done at the window-class-registration stage.

- ✔ `lParam` is an advanced feature, so just set it to `NULL`.

Did I forget anything? Yup! I forgot the `dwStyle` parameter, which is yet another flags value that enables you to control the properties of the window by using the logical OR function (which, for shorthand, most programmers call *logically ORing*) to connect various property flags. Table 3-5 contains a subset of the most important window flags that you might use.

Table 3-5	Window Creation Style Flags (Key Flags are in Bold)
Value	*Meaning*
WS_OVERLAPPED	Creates an overlapped window. An overlapped window has a title bar and a border.
WS_OVERLAPPEDWINDOW	Creates an overlapped window with all the controls and a system menu useful for standard Windows applications.
WS_POPUP	Creates a plain pop-up window. This flag is the simplest and is what I use for all the DirectX applications in this book.
WS_POPUPWINDOW	Creates a pop-up window with a border and a system menu.
WS_VISIBLE	Creates a window that is initially visible; with this style a call to ShowWindow() is not needed.
WS_VSCROLL	Creates a window that has a vertical scroll bar.
WS_HSCROLL	Creates a window that has a horizontal scroll bar.
WS_MAXIMIZE	Creates a window that is initially maximized.
WS_MINIMIZE	Creates a window that is initially minimized.

Finally, notice that the CreateWindow() function returns a HWND, which is a handle to a window that will be non-NULL if the call was successful. Furthermore, the window handle will be needed as a parameter for a number of calls in the future, so saving the HWND value in a global variable is a good idea. The following shows how to create a standard window at position (100,100) with size (320,200):

```
// define global to save window handle in
HWND main_window_handle = NULL;

main_window_handle =
  CreateWindow("WNDCLASS1",   // preregistered class
          "My First Window", // title of window
          WS_OVERLAPPEDWINDOW | WS_VISIBLE, // flags
          100,100,   // position
          320,200,   // size
          NULL,      // handle to parent
          NULL,      // handle to menu
          hinstance,       // instance from WinMain
          NULL);
```

Also, you should test the result `main_window_handle` to make sure that it's non-`NULL` and that the window was created successfully.

If you don't want to tell Windows the position and size of your window, you can request default values with the flag `CW_USEDEFAULT`. Here's how:

```
main_window_handle =
  CreateWindow("WNDCLASS1",        // preregistered class
              "My First Window", // title of window
              WS_OVERLAPPEDWINDOW | WS_VISIBLE, // flags
              CW_USEDEFAULT,CW_USEDEFAULT,    // position
              CW_USEDEFAULT,CW_USEDEFAULT,    // size
              NULL,       // handle to parent
              NULL,       // handle to menu
              hinstance,        // instance from WinMain
              NULL);
```

The window will pop up on-screen with an arbitrary size and position.

Show me the window!

After you create a window, you need to display it. Displaying a window is a bit of a misnomer; the window in the example will be displayed immediately after creation because the `WS_VISIBLE` style was used as one of the style flags. However, if you don't set this flag, or if you want the window to open up in a slightly different way, make a call to `ShowWindow()`. Furthermore, `ShowWindow()`can also be used to hide a window. Here's the prototype:

```
BOOL ShowWindow(HWND  hWnd,        // handle of window
                int  nCmdShow); // show state of window
```

`hWnd` is the handle of the window, which is `main_window_handle` in the case of the example. Set `nCmdShow` to the way you want the window shown. If the function is successful, it returns `TRUE`; if not, it returns `FALSE`. Table 3-6 contains an abridged list of show commands.

Table 3-6	Commands for `ShowWindow()`
Value	*Meaning*
SW_SHOW	Activates the window and displays it in its current size and position.
SW_HIDE	Hides the window.

(continued)

Table 3-6 (continued)

Value	Meaning
SW_RESTORE	Activates and displays the window from either a minimized or maximized state.
SW_MAXIMIZE	Maximizes the specified window.
SW_MINIMIZE	Minimizes the specified window.
SW_SHOWMAXIMIZED	Activates the window and displays it as a maximized window.
SW_SHOWMINIMIZED	Activates the window and displays it as a minimized window.

In addition to ShowWindow(), you can instruct the window to refresh or repaint itself with a call to UpdateWindow(), which has this prototype:

```
BOOL UpdateWindow(HWND  hWnd);
```

Here, hWnd is the handle to the window. The function returns TRUE if successful and FALSE otherwise. Here is an example of how you could use ShowWindow() and UpdateWindow():

```
// register window class...
// create window...
// now show and update window
ShowWindow(main_window_handle,SW_SHOW);
UpdateWindow(main_window_handle);
```

If you followed the chapter from the beginning, you've seen the details of creating a window class, registering it, creating a window, and displaying it. That's everything! Now you can find out how to build an event loop and event handler. So take a closer look at WinMain() in the next section.

WinMain() and the event loop

WinMain() is the entry point for all Windows applications and usually contains the window creation code for the application's window, along with the main event loop. The *main event loop* is a simple loop that retrieves the messages record from the message queue, performs a filtering or translation, and then dispatches the message to the event handler. And of course when the main event loop isn't processing messages, it's free to perform any other kind of processing — such as game logic. (See Figure 3-4.)

Don't confuse the main event loop with the event handler. The main event loop is part of WinMain() and dispatches messages to the event handler.

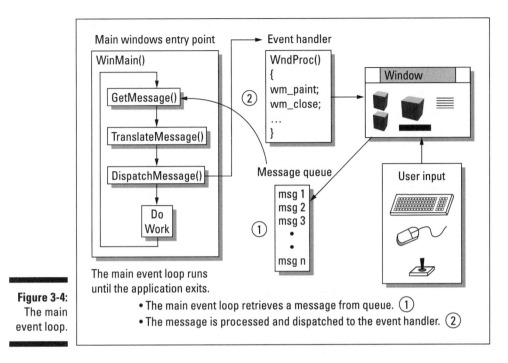

Figure 3-4:
The main
event loop.

The main event loop runs
until the application exits.
• The main event loop retrieves a message from queue. ①
• The message is processed and dispatched to the event handler. ②

The MSG-type record that contains each message is shown here:

```
typedef struct tagMSG
{
HWND    hwnd;       // window the message was sent to
UINT    message;  // the message id
WPARAM  wParam;   // further info about the message
LPARAM  lParam;   // further info about the message
DWORD   time;     // time of the message event
POINT   pt;       // contains the mouse state when
} MSG;            // the message occurred
```

The fields are all self-explanatory. In general, *message* contains the event id, and *wParam* and *lParam* further qualify and subclass the event.

Writing an event loop is easy; in fact, I wonder why Microsoft didn't hide the whole thing in a single function. You need three main functions to write an event loop. Here are the prototypes and a description of each:

```
BOOL GetMessage(LPMSG lpMsg,  // ptr to message structure
                HWND  hWnd,    // handle of window
                UINT wMsgFilterMin,  // first message
                UINT wMsgFilterMax); // last message
```

GetMessage() does nothing more than retrieve a message from the message queue. If the queue is empty, then GetMessage() waits for a message.

```
BOOL TranslateMessage(
          CONST MSG *lpMsg); // ptr to message structure
```

TranslateMessage() function is fairly advanced and is used to *translate* or convert accelerator commands (such as Ctrl+A) into more basic events. Use it, but don't worry about it.

```
LONG DispatchMessage(
          CONST MSG *lpmsg); // ptr to message structure
```

DispatchMessage() is the last function in most event loops and is the one that does the work. DispatchMessage() sends the MSG structure that GetMessage() retrieved and TranslateMessage() translated to the event handler for processing — which I still need to cover in detail. I know, I know! The next section, "The event handler," discusses that very issue.

You can write a main event loop in many ways, but a couple of methods have become very popular. Here is the first method, which is used in most windows applications that perform most of their work as a result of events:

```
MSG msg; // holds the message

// enter in the main event loop
while(GetMessage(&msg,NULL,0,0))
    {
    // translate the accelerator keys
    TranslateMessage(&msg);

    // send the message to the event handler
    DispatchMessage(&msg);
    } // end while
```

This method's problem is that it will wait in GetMessage() until a message to process shows up in the message queue. This delay won't work for a game, because the main loop must continually process game logic and render the next graphics frame. Thus, you need a more real-time method.

It's possible to detect whether a message is waiting in the queue and then process it only when there is a message. By using the PeekMessage() function technique, you can create an event loop that checks for a message and — if there is one — it processes it, otherwise the loop falls through to the real-time code. Here is an example of that method:

```
MSG msg; // holds the message

// loop until there is a WM_QUIT message
while(1)
    {
    // is there a message?
    if (PeekMessage(&msg,NULL,0,0,PM_REMOVE))
        {
        // test if this is a quit
        if (msg.message == WM_QUIT)
            break;

        // translate any accelerator keys
        TranslateMessage(&msg);

        // send the message to the window proc
        DispatchMessage(&msg);
        } // end if message

    // main game processing goes here

    } // end while
```

This loop works by first testing whether a message is in the event queue with the PeekMessage(&msg,NULL,0,0,PM_REMOVE) call. This call instructs Windows to test for a message in the queue; if a message is there, then it is removed from the queue and the function returns TRUE. Otherwise, the function returns FALSE.

If a message is in the queue, then the message is tested to see if it's a WM_QUIT (you have to do this manually); if so, the loop is exited. If not, the standard TranslateMessage() and DispatchMessage() functions are called, and the message is processed. After DispatchMessage() returns, the loop falls through and processes the main game logic. Using this structure, you're guaranteed that the main game logic is executed each cycle, regardless of whether a message is processed.

The event handler

The event handler, or WinProc, is a function that you must write to handle all the messages that you are interested in handling. (Why does that sentence sound circular to me?) Windows can send dozens of different kinds of messages, but you only have to handle the ones that you are interested in. Messages that you don't process are handled by the Windows default message handler, named DefWindowProc(). Now how's that for an original name?

In the earlier subsection "Classes," I talk about the prototype of the message handler and describe how you assign its address when you create a window class. Now you can look at the details of the message handler and then write one that has the bare-minimum message-handling capability. First, take a look at the prototype WindowProc function in detail:

```
LRESULT CALLBACK WindowProc(HWND hWnd, // the window
                    UINT msg,        // the message itself
                    WPARAM wParam,  // more info on message
                    LPARAM lParam);// more info on message
```

Notice the weird declaration return type and modifier LRESULT CALLBACK. Because Windows is an event-based, message-passing operating system, it includes a lot of *callback* functions, or functions that you supply to Windows that are called by Windows when an event occurs. In this way, Windows can communicate with your application in a clean fashion instead of the application having to poll for everything. LRESULT is basically a 32-bit integer, but that may change, so play it safe and use the predefined type.

Callbacks take a little getting used to, but after a while you realize that they are pretty cool. You have probably used them before in your code, but called them "hooks" or maybe a more technical name such as "things." Take a more detailed look at the event handler's parameters:

✔ hWnd: The handle of the window that sends the message; usually this is the only window in your application. However, this value is needed because many windows functions need a window handle as a parameter.

✔ msg: *Not* a standard MSG; it is simply a code or id of the window message that is being processed. Table 3-7 contains a list of common windows messages — and this list is by no means complete.

✔ wParam: Further qualifies the message; it may be a number, an id, a subclass, or such.

✔ lParam: Further qualifies the message; it, too, can be a number, an id, a subclass, or whatever.

Everything you do in the event handler is based on the values of these parameters.

Table 3-7	Important Windows Messages
Value	*Meaning*
WM_ACTIVATE	Sent when a window is activated or becomes the focus
WM_CLOSE	Sent when a window is closed
WM_CREATE	Sent when a window is first created

Value	Meaning
WM_DESTROY	Sent when a window is about to be destroyed
WM_MOVE	Sent when a window has been moved
WM_MOUSEMOVE	Sent when the mouse has been moved
WM_KEYUP	Sent when a key is released
WM_KEYDOWN	Sent when a key is pressed
WM_TIMER	Sent when a timer event occurs
WM_USER	Enables you to send messages
WM_PAINT	Sent when a window needs repainting
WM_QUIT	Sent when a Windows application is finally terminating
WM_SIZE	Sent when a window has changed size

Now take a look at a bare-bones event handler and its contents. I have heavily commented it, so you can see how each event is handled.

```
LRESULT CALLBACK WindowProc(HWND hwnd,
                    UINT msg,
                    WPARAM wparam,
                    LPARAM lparam)
{
// this function will handle all messages sent to your
// window

HDC hdc;        // device context used for graphics
PAINTSTRUCT ps; // also used for graphics

// find out what the message was
switch(msg)
    {
    case WM_CREATE:
        {
        // this message is sent when the window is
        // first created, so do your initialization here

        // return to event loop
        return(0);
        } break;

    case WM_PAINT:
        {
        // this message is very important; it is
```

(continued)

(continued)

```
                // sent when your window needs repainting
                // remember: Windows doesn't know what you
                // want in your window, so in this example
                // we simply tell Windows that we painted
                // window, so that it won't keep sending

                // get the graphics device context
                hdc = BeginPaint(hwnd,&ps);

                // make GDI graphics calls here

                // release the graphics device context
                EndPaint(hwnd,&ps);

                // return to event loop
                return(0);
                } break;

        case WM_DESTROY:
            {
                // this message is sent when the window is to
                // be destroyed; when this happens, you must
                // post a quit message to the event queue,
                // which sends a WM_QUIT to the message queue
                PostQuitMessage(0);

                // return to event loop
                return(0);
                } break;

        default: break;
        } // end switch

// let windows handle anything you didn't
return(DefWindowProc(hwnd, msg, wparam, lparam));
} // end WindowProc
```

That's all there is to it. The preceding handler will suffice to create a working Windows program — though granted, it won't do much.

This chapter discusses the basics of programming in Windows, primarily from the game programmer's point of view. The next chapter discusses event handlers in more detail, and is a good follow-up chapter if you need to know more about how to handle the really *big* events.

Chapter 4

How to Handle Big Events

● ●

In This Chapter

▶ Building a Windows program

▶ Handling events

▶ Controlling input

● ●

*I*n this chapter, I talk about handling events in Windows. Remember, Windows is an event-based operating system; instead of asking it questions about what's happening, it tells us!

When you create a game in Windows, you want to write your programs to take Windows *messaging* into consideration. Windows is just like your hypochondriac Uncle Ted; if you sit in front of either one long enough, they'll both tell you everything you never wanted to know about themselves. But you can't make a good game program in Windows without listening to it complain, so get used to it — just like you did with Uncle Ted.

Also in this chapter, I discuss the basics of controlling input directly from Windows, without using any of the convenient functionality of DirectX. Though mostly you'll control input from devices such as the keyboard or joystick by using DirectInput (which I discuss in Chapter 14), you need to understand the Windows device functions to create basic programs such as the ones discussed in this chapter.

Your First Real Windows Program

In Chapter 3, I show you how to build a very basic Windows program. If you read that chapter and made that little program, or if that information was just too basic for you and you want to spend your time on the meatier code blocks, then you're ready for this section.

Aren't you dying to create a *real* Windows program? I know I am. The following is a complete Windows program that creates a 320 x 200 window, places it on the screen, and allows you to move it around.

```c
// INCLUDES ///////////////////////////////////////////////
#define WIN32_LEAN_AND_MEAN
#include <windows.h>
#include <windowsx.h>
#include <stdio.h>
#include <math.h>
// DEFINES ////////////////////////////////////////////////
// defines for windows
#define WINDOW_CLASS_NAME "WINCLASS1"
// GLOBALS ////////////////////////////////////////////////
HWND main_window_handle = NULL; // save the window handle
// FUNCTIONS //////////////////////////////////////////////
LRESULT CALLBACK WindowProc(HWND hwnd,
                       UINT msg, WPARAM wparam, LPARAM lparam)
{
// this is the main message handler of the system
PAINTSTRUCT ps; // used in WM_PAINT
HDC         hdc;       // handle to a device context
// find out what the message is
switch(msg)
    {
    case WM_CREATE: // called when window created
         {
         // do initialization stuff here
         return(0);
         } break;
    case WM_PAINT: // called when window needs painting
         {
         // simply validate the window
         hdc = BeginPaint(hwnd,&ps);
         EndPaint(hwnd,&ps);
         return(0);
         } break;
    case WM_DESTROY: // called when window is killed
         {
         // kill the application
         PostQuitMessage(0);
         return(0);
         } break;
    default:break;
    } // end switch
// process any messages that you didn't take care of
return (DefWindowProc(hwnd, msg, wparam, lparam));
} // end WinProc
```

```
// WINMAIN /////////////////////////////////////////////////
int WINAPI WinMain(   HINSTANCE hinstance,
                      HINSTANCE hprevinstance,
                      LPSTR lpcmdline,
                      int ncmdshow)
{
WNDCLASS winclass;   // this will hold the class you create
HWND    hwnd;  // generic window handle
MSG  msg;        // generic message
// first, fill in the window class structure
winclass.style = CS_DBLCLKS | CS_OWNDC |
                 CS_HREDRAW | CS_VREDRAW;
winclass.lpfnWndProc    = WindowProc;
winclass.cbClsExtra     = 0;
winclass.cbWndExtra     = 0;
winclass.hInstance      = hinstance;
winclass.hIcon          = LoadIcon(NULL,IDI_APPLICATION);
winclass.hCursor        = LoadCursor(NULL, IDC_ARROW);
winclass.hbrBackground = GetStockObject(BLACK_BRUSH);
winclass.lpszMenuName  = NULL;
winclass.lpszClassName = WINDOW_CLASS_NAME;
// register the window class
if (!RegisterClass(&winclass))
   return(0);
// create the window
if (!(hwnd = CreateWindow(WINDOW_CLASS_NAME,    // class
     "Hello Dave",                  // title
     WS_OVERLAPPEDWINDOW | WS_VISIBLE, // flags
     0,0,      // x,y
     320,200,  // width, height
     NULL,     // handle to parent
     NULL,     // handle to menu
     hinstance,// instance
     NULL)))   // creation parameters
return(0);
// save the window handle in a global
main_window_handle = hwnd;
// enter main event loop
while(1)
    {
    if (PeekMessage(&msg,NULL,0,0,PM_REMOVE))
    {
   // test whether this is a quit
      if (msg.message == WM_QUIT) break;
```

(continued)

(continued)

```
        // translate any accelerator keys
        TranslateMessage(&msg);
        // send the message to the window proc
        DispatchMessage(&msg);
        } // end if
    // main game processing goes here
    } // end while
// return to Windows like this
return(msg.wParam);
} // end WinMain
```

To create an executable that uses the code listed here, all you need is the source file PROG4_1.CPP, which is on the CD-ROM that came with this book. Create a new Win32 project, add the source file, and build the executable.

When you run PROG4_1.EXE, you see something like Figure 4-1. The window should have the title "Hello Dave," be 320 x 200, and positioned at (0,0) — which is the upper-left corner of your screen. If you want to, you can experiment with the program by changing the code. For example, with just a few keystrokes to change existing or add new code, you can do the following:

✔ Change the position and size of the window

✔ Change the window's title

✔ Change the window flags in both the class and the CreateWindow() call

✔ Change the background color of the window

✔ Change the icon and cursor of the window

✔ Put up a message box when the window is created, moved, or sized (if you're feeling brave)

Figure 4-1:
Your first
real
Windows
program.

_Hello Dave

Windows-Style Event Handling

In the previous section, I show you code that contains a complete event handler and the basic messages that it handles: WM_CREATE, WM_PAINT, and WM_DESTROY. This section goes into a bit more detail on how you go about writing message handlers.

First off, keep the basic switch structure that was used in the code list PROG4_1.CPP in the event loops. To add a new event handler section, just add another case statement to the main switch statement and do whatever you want to do in response to the message. For example, if you want to respond to the WM_SIZE message, then add a *case* statement such as this:

```
case WM_SIZE:
    {
    // the width and height of window are stored in the
    // high part and low part of lParam; use macros
    // LOWORD and HIWORD to extract
    // width window of client area
    int width = LOWORD(lParam);
    // height of window client area
    int height = HIWORD(lParam);
    // do whatever with the width and height
    // inform windows that you have processed the message
    return(0);
    } break;
```

With C++, you don't have to declare global or local variables at the beginning of the function; you can assign a variable almost anywhere in the body of the code (a technique known as defining variables *on the fly*).

Many messages can be sent, as shown in Table 3-7 (refer to Chapter 3). In general, look up the details of the message in your favorite Windows API or with the C/C++ compiler Help system. In most cases, extra information is contained within wParam and lParam of the message that you need to take into consideration (as shown in this section's code example). You see more examples when you access the input devices later in this chapter, in the section "Input! Input! I Want Input!"

Of course, knowing what messages to respond to and how to respond to them isn't that simple, but because you are going to be writing games, your programs won't need to handle many Windows messages. In fact, after I cover all this preliminary Windows in Chapters 1 through 5, I provide you with a game console "shell" in Chapter 6 that insulates you from the Windows aspect of Windows programming so that you can focus on writing the game logic and graphics. But you should at least have a general understanding of what Windows is doing before putting an interface layer on top of the Windows event loop.

Understanding the WM_PAINT message and GDI

The function of the WM_CREATE and WM_DESTROY messages are obvious enough — they create a window and destroy it, respectively — but the WM_PAINT message deserves further explanation. WM_PAINT is sent whenever your window needs *repainting*. Repainting occurs whenever the window's size is changed, the window is moved, another window is drawn on top of your window — whenever the graphical content of your window is messed up or changed.

Windows has no clue about how to draw the contents of your window (the *client area*) and thus sends a WM_PAINT message to your program to tell it that it should repaint your window. On the other hand, Windows does know how to draw the window itself — the border, the menu, and the controls — so you don't have to worry about that stuff. You just worry about the client area.

You *can* paint the entire window, including the border, menu, and controls, but most programmers don't need this kind of control. However, you can create a new window type that had a different look (maybe something in 3D or something similar to UNIX Motif) in this manner.

Unfortunately, anything having to do with graphics has to do with *GDI* — the *Graphics Device Interface*. GDI is the API that you had to go through to perform graphics with Windows (at least until DirectX came to be). So to repaint your window, you must know something about GDI. I discuss GDI in detail in the next chapter, but I cover the basics right here.

GDI is a set of data structures, types, and functions that enable you to draw graphics. GDI is cool in that it is *device independent,* which means that — as a Windows programmer — you don't need to know the resolution or number of colors for the computer that your application is running on. GDI does the best in all situations, and that flexibility is good. By the same token, however, if you tell GDI to do something, it may not do exactly what you ask — which is bad in game programming.

Get the most use out of GDI. Use DirectX for rendering the game itself, but use GDI for the main menu, installation, and other nongraphically intensive parts of the game.

To communicate with GDI, you must have a *Graphics Device Context,* or GDC. A GDC is a data structure (or pointer to one) that contains information such as the resolution, memory, number of colors, and so on, about the graphics card on the computer. To draw graphics, you need to send the GDC (or a handle) as a parameter to most of the graphics functions for them to work.

With regard to graphics, Windows has this system called the Graphics Device Interface or GDI. And to draw with it, you must define in your program a graphics context that describes the actual hardware. Then you can make calls to GDI functions — and Windows has a lot of them!

Taking into consideration everything I discuss in this section about Windows graphics, check out the main event handler and the WM_PAINT section of PROG4_1.CPP (the code for which is listed in the earlier section, "Your First Real Windows Program"):

```
case WM_PAINT: // called when window needs painting
    {
    // validate the window
    hdc = BeginPaint(hwnd,&ps);
    EndPaint(hwnd,&ps);
    return(0);
    } break;
```

When the WM_PAINT case is entered, a handle to the current graphics device context is retrieved. This process is done with BeginPaint(). You can use the handle hdc to draw anything that you want; but in this case, nothing is drawn. The EndPaint() calls tell Windows that your program is finished painting and also tell Windows that something needed repainting, and the program handled it. If you didn't include a BeginPaint()..EndPaint() pair, then Windows would keep sending WM_PAINT messages even if the window didn't need painting. Windows would think that you didn't get the message in the first place.

Take a look at the two data types from the same example:

```
PAINTSTRUCT ps; // used in WM_PAINT
HDC         hdc;    // handle to a device context
```

Windows stores the position of a window, as well as other information about it that may be needed to repaint it, in the PAINTSTRUCT ps variable. And HDC hdc is a handle to a graphics device context that Windows must give your program so that the program can draw with it.

If you want to draw graphics within another message, you can get a graphics device context in many ways. The most common way is like this:

```
// get device context from Windows
hdc = GetDC(hwnd);
// do graphics
// give device context back to Windows
ReleaseDC(hwnd, hdc);
```

In this code snippet, hdc is the handle to the graphics device context and hwnd is the window handle. In Chapter 5, I cover all the gruesome details about GDI, but for now just let the basics sink in.

Sending your own messages

Perhaps you're wondering whether you can send a window message and trick Windows into doing something yourself instead of in response to events. For example, suppose that you want to close a window, kill your application, cause a repaint, and so on. These tasks can be done in a number of ways, but the simplest is with PostMessage() or SendMessage(). PostMessage() sends a message to the message queue for processing without any special urgency and returns to the caller. SendMessage(), on the other hand, sends a message directly to the window event handler, bypassing the event queue and returning after the message has been processed. Take a look at Figure 4-2 to see this process graphically.

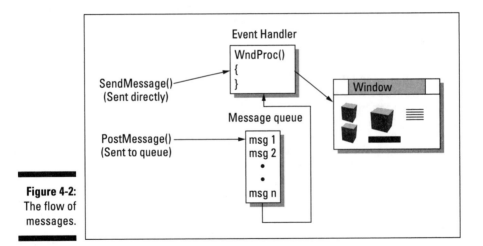

Figure 4-2:
The flow of
messages.

The prototypes of SendMessage() and PostMessage() are both the same except for the return values:

```
LRESULT SendMessage(
    HWND    hWnd,     // handle of destination window
    UINT    Msg,      // message to send
    WPARAM  wParam,   // first message parameter
    LPARAM  lParam);  // second message parameter
```

```
BOOL PostMessage(
    HWND    hWnd,      // handle of destination window
    UINT    Msg,       // message to post
    WPARAM  wParam,    // first message parameter
    LPARAM  lParam);   // second message parameter
```

You just send the window handle, the message, the wParam, the lParam, and that's it. For example, if you want to send a WM_PAINT message, then you do something like the following:

```
SendMessage(hwnd, WM_PAINT,0,0);
```

Note that you can send your own messages! Windows has a special message just for you that enables you to send your very own message to your window. It is called WM_USER. To send a message of this type, just do the following:

```
SendMessage(hwnd, WM_USER,data_1, data_2);
```

And to process WM_USER in the main event handler, add this case statement:

```
case WM_USER: // a user message
    {
    // data_1 will be in wparam
    // data_2 will be in lparam
    } break;
```

You can do whatever you want with the WM_USER message; just make sure to cast wParam and lParam before using them, or you may get an error or warning from your compiler.

Input! Input! I Want Input!

DirectInput was first released with DirectX Version 3.0, and by Version 5.0 it became really solid. DirectInput supports keyboard, mouse, and joystick with one uniform interface. However, basic mouse, keyboard, and joystick support in DirectInput is a bit complicated to set up, so for now I want to show you the old-fashioned Windows Win32 way of getting input from these devices.

The Win32 way of getting input means using messages and events, and doing so is a bit dramatic if you just want to see whether the player pressed the enter key. Anyway, the techniques outlined in the following subsections are good for building demos and examples. At this point in the discussion, you just want to know how to get some input into your code, so the method doesn't have to be the fastest or cleanest way. Furthermore, you need to know how to "talk" to the keyboard and mouse, so that if you aren't using DirectX, you can still make a Windows application that can get input.

The keyboard

The keyboard is probably the most complex input device available for the PC. The keyboard actually has a small microcontroller chip in it that controls the complex business of detecting key presses, controlling repeat rates, illuminating indicator lights, converting data into a serial stream, and so on. One of the main goals for the designers of the Windows keyboard input system was to minimize the complexity of obtaining input from the keyboard.

To accomplish this goal, a number of abstractions and generalizations had to be made. Because many different kinds of keyboards are available, identifying exactly what keys are on a particular keyboard is difficult. In addition, different keyboards may send different codes for a specific key. So some standards were made.

The first standard is called the AT 101 standard, which dictated that a generic IBM PC keyboard should have 101 keys. Furthermore, each key has a specific 8-bit scan code assigned to it. So if you create a keyboard, you had better follow the standard. You can add to the standard, but you must include at least the basic implementation of the AT 101 keyboard.

Cool. So how does it work? When a key is pressed on the keyboard, the keyboard sends a specific scan code. Unfortunately, scan codes have nothing to do with ASCII codes. *ASCII* stands for American Standard Code for Information Interchange and is what most programmers use when referring to characters on a keyboard. (For example, the letter *A* is ASCII 65.) Scan codes are arbitrary for the most part and were created by counting off the keys on the keyboard and assigning a number to each of them.

The designers of Windows knew that translating scan codes into ASCII codes all the time would be a pain, so those designers created functions to convert between the two code protocols. In addition, Windows uses what are *virtual key codes*, which are similar to scan codes, but are Windows-specific, defined in a header file, and guaranteed never to change. So most of the time you use the virtual key code or the ASCII code in your programs, but seldom do you use the scan code, because it is keyboard specific. There are a lot of virtual key codes, so I can't show them all to you, but Table 4-1 contains the most useful for a game programmer. Also, even though the table shows integer values for each virtual key code, you should use the defined symbol.

Table 4-1	A Partial List of Virtual Key Codes	
Symbol	*Value (Hex)*	*Meaning*
VK_BACK	08	Backspace key
VK_TAB	09	Tab key
VK_RETURN	0D	Enter key

Symbol	Value (Hex)	Meaning
VK_SHIFT	10	Shift key
VK_CONTROL	11	Ctrl key
VK_PAUSE	13	Pause key
VK_ESCAPE	1B	Esc key
VK_SPACE	20	Spacebar
VK_PRIOR	21	Page Up key
VK_NEXT	22	Page Down key
VK_END	23	End key
VK_HOME	24	Home key
VK_LEFT	25	← (left-arrow) key
VK_UP	26	↑ (up-arrow) key
VK_RIGHT	27	→ (right-arrow) key
VK_INSERT	2D	Insert key
VK_DELETE	2E	Delete key
VK_HELP	2F	Help key
VK_0–VK_9	30–39	0–9 keys
VK_A–VK_Z	41–5A	A–Z keys
VK_F1–VK_F12	70–7B	F1–F12 keys

In most games, the keyboard is used like a bunch of buttons rather than keys that relate to characters. As a game programmer, most of the time you can get away with virtual codes in your program rather than translating to an actual character (such as *A* or *d*) because the keys *A* and *d* may mean "turn left" and "arm torpedoes." My point is that — to programmers — keys are just buttons with letters on them.

Windows has three main messages that it sends for keyboard events. Here they are, along with the data values for wParam and lParam:

- ✔ **WM_CHAR:** The highest level keyboard message and is sent when a key is pressed or when a key is held and starts repeating. This message contains the ASCII code and key-data state.
- ✔ wParam: Contains ASCII character code.
- ✔ lParam: Contains bit-encoded key-data.
- ✔ **WM_KEYDOWN:** This message is lower level than WM_CHAR and is sent when a key is down. The message contains the virtual-key code and key-data state.

✔ wParam: Contains virtual-key code.

✔ lParam: Contains bit encoded key-data.

✔ WM_KEYUP: Similar to WM_KEYDOWN, but sent the instant a key is released.

✔ wParam: Contains virtual-key code.

✔ lParam: Contains bit encoded key-data.

Table 4-2 contains the bit encoding for the key-data bits that are returned with each message. (That was a mouthful!)

Table 4-2	Bit Encoded Key-Data for WM_CHAR, WM_KEYUP, and WM_KEYDOWN
Bits	*Description*
0–15	Contains the repeat count.
16–23	Contains the scan code. This value depends on the original equipment manufacturer (OEM) of the keyboard.
24	Boolean; indicates whether the key is an extended key, such as the right-hand Alt and Ctrl keys that appear on enhanced keyboards.
25–28	Reserved.
29	Boolean; indicates whether the Alt key is down.
30	Boolean, the last state; indicates whether the current key was the same as the last.
31	Boolean; indicates the transition state of the key. A value of 1 means that the key is being pressed, and 0 means that it is being released.

With all that in mind, take a look at how to use the messages. Here is how to add a case statement in the main event handler for the WM_CHAR message:

```
case WM_CHAR:
    {
    // get the ascii code and data bits
    int ascii_code = (int)wparam;
    int key_bits   = (int)lparam;
    // do whatever...
    // tell windows that you processed the message
    return(0);
    } break;
```

And to process the WM_KEYDOWN message, do the following:

```
case WM_KEYDOWN:
    {
    // get virtual key code and data bits
    int virtual_code = (int)wparam;
    int key_bits     = (int)lparam;
    // I usually switch on the virtual_key code
    switch(virtual_code)
        {
        case VK_RIGHT:{ } break;
        case VK_LEFT: { } break;
        // ...
        default: break;
        } // end switch
    // tell Windows that you processed the message
    return(0);
    } break;
```

Of course, you can use whichever technique you wish to test for all the keys, but I like using a switch statement as shown here.

That's all there is to reading the keyboard. Just put a messages handler in for the keyboard messages and then process the message.

A clever way to bypass the entire message-passing system to retrieve keyboard input is by using the GetAsyncKeyState() function. GetAsyncKeyState() takes the virtual key code and returns back a WORD that indicates whether the key is pressed. Using this function, you can completely forget about the Windows messages. Furthermore, you can put the call anywhere you wish. Here are some macros I wrote around the function:

```
#define KEY_DOWN(vk_code) ((GetAsyncKeyState(vk_code) & 0x8000) ? 1 : 0)
#define KEY_UP(vk_code)   ((GetAsyncKeyState(vk_code) & 0x8000) ? 0 : 1)
```

Due to the margin constraints of this book, part of the macro definition may take up two or more lines. As a rule, you must make sure that any macro definitions are always on a single line. Otherwise, the compiler errors out — and you have a bad day in general.

Use the macros like this:

```
if (KEY_DOWN(VK_ESCAPE))
   // exit
else
if (KEY_DOWN(VK_SPACE)) // fire weapons
if (KEY_UP(VK_ENTER)) // disengage shields
```

The mouse

If the keyboard is the most complex input device, then the mouse must be the most useful. Without the mouse or similar pointing device, Windows wouldn't exist. (Actually, you can navigate Windows without a mouse, but it is extremely difficult.) Anyway, the mouse is a little more straightforward than the keyboard. You can do two things with the mouse — move it and click its buttons — so Windows supports a message for each of these events.

The message WM_MOUSEMOVE is sent when the mouse moves. Not only does the message contain the (x,y) position of the mouse relative to the upper-left corner of the window, but it contains the state of the buttons. Figure 4-3 shows how the mouse coordinates are mapped.

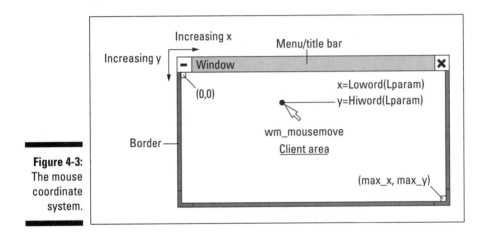

Figure 4-3:
The mouse
coordinate
system.

Here are the details of WM_MOUSEMOVE:

- ✔ wParam: Contains the button flags as shown in Table 4-3.

- ✔ lParam: The LOWORD contains the x position and the HIWORD contains the y position of the mouse cursor.

Table 4-3	The Mouse Button Constants
Value	*Description*
MK_LBUTTON	Set if the left mouse button is down.
MK_MBUTTON	Set if the middle mouse button is down.
MK_RBUTTON	Set if the right mouse button is down.
MK_CONTROL	Set if the CTRL key is down.
MK_SHIFT	Set if the SHIFT key is down.

And here is how you would process a WM_MOUSEMOVE message in the main event handler:

```
case WM_MOUSEMOVE:
     {
     // extract x,y and buttons
     int mouse_x = (int)LOWORD(lParam);
     int mouse_y = (int)HIWORD(lParam);
     int buttons = (int)wParam;
     // process data, for example
     // is the user pressing the left mouse button?
     if (buttons & MK_LBUTTON) // do something...
     } break;
```

Simple, huh? This stuff is just too darn easy!

Now if you want to test only for the mouse buttons being pressed, but without the mouse being moved, Windows has a number of messages for this purpose. See Table 4-4.

Table 4-4	General Mouse Button Events
Message	**Meaning**
WM_LBUTTONDBLCLK	The left mouse button was double-clicked.
WM_LBUTTONDOWN	The left mouse button was pressed.
WM_LBUTTONUP	The left mouse button was released.
WM_MBUTTONDBLCLK	The middle mouse button was double-clicked.
WM_MBUTTONDOWN	The middle mouse button was pressed.
WM_MBUTTONUP	The middle mouse button was released.
WM_RBUTTONDBLCLK	The right mouse button was double-clicked.
WM_RBUTTONDOWN	The right mouse button was pressed.
WM_RBUTTONUP	The right mouse button was released.

The button messages are just as simple; just write a message handler that tests for them, and wParam and lParam have the same meaning as they do for WM_MOUSEMOVE. For example, to test for a left-button double-click, do the following:

```
case WM_LBUTTONDBLCLK:
     {
     // extract x,y and buttons
     int mouse_x = (int)LOWORD(lParam);
```

(continued)

(continued)

```
int mouse_y = (int)HIWORD(lParam);
// do something intelligent
// tell windows you handled it
return(0);
} // break;
```

I don't have enough room to put the code for a complete demo on using the mouse and keyboard, but the CD-ROM with this book contains a program called `PROG4_2.CPP` that contains a complete example of coding for the mouse and keyboard. And the program even has graphics. Check it out!

The joystick

You can actually communicate with the joystick using the Windows multimedia library without DirectInput, but because you are going to use DirectInput in game programming, I see no need to torture you with it. The Windows Multimedia joystick interface is complicated and obsolete, so writing any real code would be a waste — and I'm running out of room in this book!

However, if you must absolutely know about it, the functions you should research are listed next.

This function is used to acquire the joystick:

```
MMRESULT joySetCapture(HWND hwnd,
                       UINT uJoyID,
                       UINT uPeriod,
                       BOOL fChanged);
```

This function is used to retrieve the capabilities of the joystick:

```
MMRESULT joyGetDevCaps(UINT uJoyID,
                       LPJOYCAPS pjc,
                       UINT cbjc);
```

This function is used to set the sensitivity of the joystick:

```
MMRESULT joySetThreshold(UINT uJoyID, UINT uThreshold);
```

This function is used to query the joystick state:

```
MMRESULT joyGetPosEx(UINT uJoyID, LPJOYINFOEX pji);
```

Chapter 5

Putting Windows GDI to Work: Drawing Text and Graphics

· ·

In This Chapter

▶ Working with the WM_PAINT message

▶ Examining the GDI drawing surfaces

▶ Rendering text

▶ Using pens, brushes, and bitmaps

▶ Drawing shapes

· ·

*T*he Windows GDI (Graphics Device Interface) functions are responsible for all graphics rendering. GDI not only supports graphics on the display screen but is also responsible for printing on the printer. This chapter focuses on some of the most important GDI capabilities: color, text, shapes, and bitmapped images. See Chapter 4 for an introduction to GDI. And if, after this briefing on GDI, you want a little taste of sound and music under Windows, check out Chapters 6 and 13.

To Paint or Not to Paint?

You are responsible for painting your window's client area — that is, everything inside the window (not the window title bar and controls, which Windows takes care of).

Painting involves two important concepts:

> ✔ **Validating:** Whenever you (or Windows) disturbs the client area of
> your window, Windows sends a WM_PAINT message to your application.
> Your program must let Windows know that your program has handled
> the message; this process of informing Windows is referred to as
> *validating* the rectangle (the area to be painted).

> ✔ **Defining the rectangle that needs to be painted:** You don't want to paint areas that don't need to be painted, so pay attention to the *invalid rectangle,* which is the area that needs repainting and which is encapsuled in data structures along with the WM_PAINT message.

You have two methods of processing the WM_PAINT message, each with an advantage and a disadvantage regarding the preceding concepts, to choose from in repainting the client area:

> ✔ BeginPaint()..EndPaint(). *Advantage:* This function pair does the necessary validating automatically, without requiring any additional lines of code. *Disadvantage:* The rcPaint field, which is the invalid rectangle, is also the *clipping* rectangle for your window. You can't draw anything beyond the clipping window — meaning that, if you desire to do any painting in portions of the client area that are not invalidated, you must redefine rcPaint to gain access to the remaining client area.
>
> ✔ GetDC()..ReleaseDC(). *Advantage:* The drawing surface returned has a clipping rectangle that is the entire client area, so you don't have to worry about redefining the invalid rectangle every time you repaint the client area. *Disadvantage:* You need to validate the invalid rectangle yourself with a call to ValidateRect(); otherwise, Windows continues to send WM_PAINT messages to your application. However, if you just want to paint in your window when not servicing a WM_PAINT message, then *GetDC()* is the best way.

The following sections detail these functions' differences and show you the code you need to use for each function.

BeginPaint ()

Windows sends the WM_PAINT message to your window any time the client area is disturbed by another application. You must process this message in winproc, your program's main event handler, and repaint the client area using code like this:

```
PAINTSTRUCT ps; // a Windows paint structure
HDC hdc;        // handle to graphics device context

case WM_PAINT:
    {
    // obtain handle to device context
    hdc = BeginPaint(hwnd, &ps);

    // paint client area
```

```
// release handle and validate window
EndPaint(hwnd, &ps);
// always tell Windows that you processed the message
return(0);
} break;
```

Perhaps at this point, you don't know how to use the GDI functions to do the actual painting part, but don't worry about that for now; I get to that subject later in the chapter, in the section "Drawing Shapes." What's important is that, when the call is made to BeginPaint(), two things happen: A handle to the current graphics device context is returned, and the fields of ps are filled in, which is the following structure:

```
typedef struct tagPAINTSTRUCT {
    HDC  hdc;      // handle to device context
    BOOL fErase;   // flags whether app should redraw background
    RECT rcPaint;              // clipping rectangle
    BOOL fRestore;             // reserved
    BOOL fIncUpdate;           // reserved
    BYTE rgbReserved[32];  // reserved
} PAINTSTRUCT;
```

When BeginPaint() returns, this structure is filled in. The hdc field is the handle to the graphics device context, which is the same as the value returned from BeginPaint().

The fErase field is a bit interesting. Normally, your program checks to see whether this field is TRUE; if so, your program is also responsible for repainting the background. However, if you give your window class a non-NULL background brush, Windows repaints the background for you. You don't need to worry about this bit, because you already set the background brush with this code in the class definition:

```
wndclass.hbrBackground  = GetStockObject(BLACK_BRUSH);
```

So that problem is handled, but the next field in the typedef struct, the rcPaint field, needs a bit of attention. The field is a RECT structure that contains the four points of a rectangle; here's its definition:

```
typedef struct _RECT {
    LONG left;   // leftmost edge of the RECT
    LONG top;    // topmost edge of the RECT
    LONG right;  // rightmost edge of the RECT
    LONG bottom; // bottom-most edge of the RECT
} RECT;
```

The problem with using this structure returned by Windows is that the `rcPaint` rectangle indicates the *invalid* rectangle. The invalid rectangle is the only area that needs repainting. Take a look at Figure 5-1, which depicts a window that needs repainting, but in this case, only part of the window's client area needs to be repainted. This portion is the part that will be sent in `rcPaint`. Therefore, look at `rcPaint` before repainting your window's client area so you don't paint parts of the client area that you don't need to.

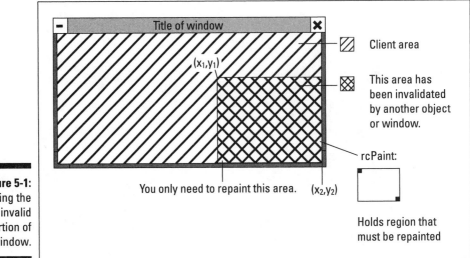

Figure 5-1:
Painting the invalid portion of a window.

So what? You may think that you can save yourself the trouble of drawing a portion of the window and repaint the entire window contents on every `WM_PAINT` message, regardless of the rectangle defined in `rcPaint`. "Maybe this method is a little inefficient," you think, "but it would work." Unfortunately, it doesn't work. Not only is `rcPaint` the invalid rectangle, but it is also the *clipping* rectangle for your window, which means that anything you try to draw beyond the clipping rectangle won't be drawn. That's a bummer, especially if you want to redraw the entire client area.

Fortunately, Windows offers another function to handle those situations: `GetDC()`. This function saves you from having to worry about defining `rcPaint` because, with `GetDC()`, the clipping rectangle is the entire client area. Check out the next subsection for more on this function.

So why use `BeginPaint()..EndPaint()` in the `WM_PAINT` message rather than `GetDC()..ReleaseDC()`, which apparently is a lot less of a headache? The answer is that `GetDC()..ReleaseDC()` does not validate the invalid rectangle — which is necessary, otherwise Windows keeps sending paint messages. Boy, that had to sound confusing!

Every time a WM_PAINT message is sent by Windows, your program must *validate* the rectangle. (I explain validating in the introduction to this section.) The BeginPaint()..EndPaint() pair does this validating automatically, so your program can just call that pair, and Windows believes that the program repainted the client area of the window, whether it did or not.

How do you draw into any part of the client area when processing WM_PAINT and the rcPaint rectangle contains a rectangle smaller than the window's entire client area? Simple. Use the InvalidateRect() function, which invalidates a rectangle. Here's its prototype:

```
BOOL InvalidateRect(
    HWND hWnd,             // handle of window to invalidate
    CONST RECT *lpRect,    // ptr to rect area to invalidate
    BOOL bErase);          // erase flag for BeginPaint()
```

You send the window and a pointer to the RECT structure that you want to validate or invalidate. If you always want to process the entire client area, use NULL for lpRect. The bErase parameter works like this: If you set it to TRUE, then when the next call to BeginPaint() is made, the background is redrawn with the current brush — if there is one; if not, the default brush is used. Otherwise, if you set bErase to FALSE, on the next call to BeginPaint(), Windows doesn't touch the background, regardless of whether you've set a background brush. Keeping Windows from touching your background gives you a little more control over your window.

Keep in mind that when Windows fills in the background on your window, the contents are always destroyed.

If you want to use BeginPaint()..EndPaint() in your WM_PAINT handler but want the entire window client area to be invalidated, then simply invalidate it yourself! Here's how:

```
case WM_PAINT:
    {
    // invalidate the whole window
    InvalidateRect(hwnd,NULL,TRUE);

    // start painting
    hdc = BeginPaint(hwnd,&ps);

    // do graphics here

    // stop painting
    EndPaint(hwnd, &ps);

    return(0);
    } break;
```

Or if you don't want to do any graphics yourself, you can do this:

```
case WM_PAINT:
    {
    // validate whole window; basically ignore message
    ValidateRect(hwnd,NULL);
    return(0);
    } break;
```

GetDC()

GetDC() saves you from having to worry about defining rcPaint because with GetDC(), the clipping rectangle is the entire client area. Now, the graphics context you get from a call to GetDC() differs from the one you get from BeginPaint() (detailed in the preceding section). In the case of GetDC(), the clipping rectangle is the entire client area, so you don't have to worry about the valid client area being smaller than the window, as you do with BeginPaint().

GetDC()..ReleaseDC() does not validate the invalid rectangle, as does BeginPaint()..EndPaint(). Validating the invalid rectangle, which involves having your program tell Windows that the WM_PAINT message Windows sent has been handled, is necessary; otherwise Windows keeps sending paint messages.

So how do you validate the client area if you use GetDC()..ReleaseDC()? Just use the ValidateRect() function, which is used to validate a rectangle and trick Windows (I like to trick Windows as much as possible; it makes me feel powerful). Here's the prototype:

```
BOOL ValidateRect(
    HWND hWnd,              // handle of window
    CONST RECT *lpRect);   // pointer to
                           // RECT area to validate
```

Pretty simple, eh? You send the window and a pointer to the RECT structure that you want to validate or invalidate. If you always want to process the entire client area, use NULL for lpRect.

Keep in mind that, when Windows fills in the background on your window, the contents are always destroyed.

If you use GetDC()..ReleaseDC() in the WM_PAINT message, you can validate the window by doing something like this:

```
case WM_PAINT:
    {
    // get the device context from Windows
    hdc = GetDC(hwnd);

    // do graphics here

    // release the device context to Windows
    ReleaseDC(hwnd,hdc);

    // validate the window
    ValidateRect(hwnd, NULL);

    return(0);
    } break;
```

If you're using GetDC() from a part of your code that isn't in WM_PAINT, you don't have to worry about validating the window, because you aren't processing a WM_PAINT message.

You can draw on your window at any time using GetDC()..ReleaseDC(); however, you have to be careful when processing the WM_PAINT message, because you must validate the window manually. The goals are to repaint the window and tell Windows that you did so, to keep Windows from sending WM_PAINT messages to your program.

Display-Surface Fundamentals

Before you get into all the drawing functions of GDI, here are some concepts to understand:

- **Resolution:** Number of pixels on the display. Common resolutions are 640 x 480, 800 x 600, and 1,024 x 768.
- **Color Depth:** Defines the number of bits per color you can use, determined by the amount of available memory on the video card. Usually, video cards have a color depth of 8, 16, or 24 bits per pixel (bpp), which means that 1, 2, or 3 bytes per pixel, respectively, are needed to determine the color of each pixel. Table 5-1 illustrates the number of colors associated with various bit depths (including some weird ones).
- **Color Space:** Means the actual number of colors available based on the color depth. For example, 8 bits gives you 256 colors, and 16 bits gives you 65,536 colors.

Table 5-1	Number of Colors for Each Bit Depth
Color Depth **(in Bits per Pixel [bpp])**	**Color Space** **(Number of Colors)**
1	2 (monochrome)
8	256 (palletized modes)
15	16,000 (Hi-Color)
16	65,536 (Full Hi-Color)
24	16.7 million (True Color)
32	4.2 billion (Ultra True Color)

Most video cards use 2 bytes per pixel for 15-bit or 16-bit color modes and 4 bytes per pixel for 24-bit or 32-bit color modes so that all pixels are WORD- or QUAD-byte aligned. This arrangement helps with display memory access and rasterization speed.

Don't get *bits* per pixel (bpp) and *bytes* per pixel confused. Many times both are abbreviated by bpp, so you have to use the context of the definition to make sense of it. For example, 24 bpp is definitely referring to bits per pixel, whereas 3 bpp is referring to bytes per pixel, because 3 bits per pixel makes no sense.

Table 5-2 contains a list of various video modes and color depths along with their memory requirements. As you can see, the high-resolution modes with a lot of color can quickly eat up memory. Also, this table illustrates a point of video game programming: The logic of a game is complex enough, but having to pump so much video data out per frame is extremely taxing on any computer. For that reason, you seldom see 3D games that are in high resolution.

Note: The modes marked by an asterisk in the table (Mode X) are not supported by Windows GDI, but they are supported by DirectX. They're commonly used for DOS games and are extremely fast.

Table 5-2	Video Modes Memory Requirements		
Resolution	**Memory (in Bytes)**		
	8 bpp	**16 bpp**	**24/32 bpp**
320 x 200*	64,000	NA	NA
320 x 240*	76,800	NA	NA
640 x 480	307,200	614,400	1,228,800
800 x 600	480,000	960,000	1,920,000

Resolution	Memory (in Bytes)		
	8 bpp	16 bpp	24/32 bpp
1,024 x 768	786,432	1,572,864	3,145,728
1,200 x 1,024	1,228,800	2,457,600	4,915,200
1,600 x 1,200	1,920,000	3,840,000	7,680,000

As you can see from the table, a 2MB video card handles most resolutions and color depths, whereas a 1MB card can barely handle 800 x 600 in Hi-Color (16 bpp). Anyway, one more area of confusion exists with color on the PC, and that is between RGB modes and palletized modes. The next section takes a look at those modes.

RGB modes

Whenever the display card is put into a video mode that requires more than 8 bpp, the mode is said to be a pure *RGB* (Red, Green, Blue) mode. An equal number of bits is used to represent red, green, and blue. Figure 5-2 illustrates the bit encoding for 15-, 16-, 24-, and 32-bit color modes. As you can see from the figure, you just place the value of Red, Green, and Blue into each component, and the pixel is defined. Moreover, in RGB modes, video display memory itself is filled with RGB data words, so you have a one-to-one correlation between each pixel and the RGB values it encodes.

Palletized modes

The palletized video modes use a form of *color indirection,* which requires some explanation: In the palletized modes, 8 bits (1 byte) represent each pixel; therefore, you have a total of 256 different colors or values per pixel. The designers of the VGA could have decided to use RGB encoding and set aside 2 bits for red, green, and blue, leaving the remaining bits for intensity. (And actually, they did! EGA monitors supported this type of mode, but that's another story.) Anyway, each pixel can have 256 different values, so how can you correlate these values to color if the pixel data or descriptor isn't RGB encoded? The answer is with a *Color Look Up Table,* or *CLUT.* The VGA card and its descendants all have at least a 256-color lookup table, with each of the 256 entries having 8 bits for red, green, and blue. So each pixel has 24 bits — a True Color entry for each element in the lookup table.

The term *True Color* refers to 24-bit color. It's just a name because programmers got sick of saying "16-bit color," "24-bit color," and "32-bit color!"

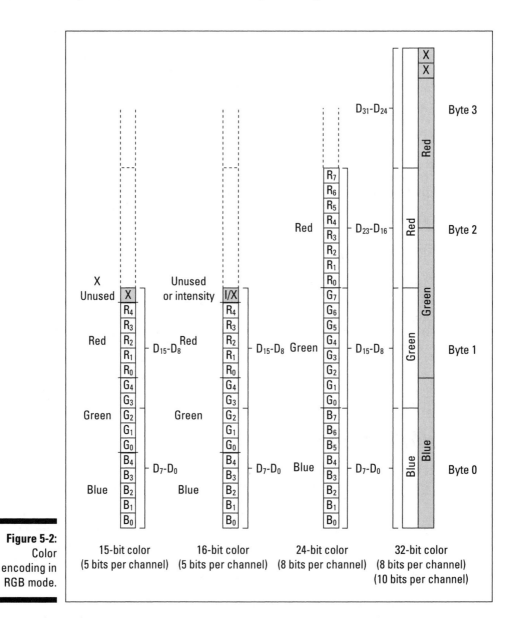

Figure 5-2: Color encoding in RGB mode.

You initialize each entry of the lookup table with the RGB values you want. When you place a pixel on the screen, the value of the pixel is not the actual color but an index into the CLUT and is used to look up the RGB values of the color in the CLUT. As the video hardware renders the display, the hardware's DAC (Digital to Analog Converter) continually performs this color lookup for each pixel on the screen and sends the resulting RGB values to the monitor for display.

In many video cards, only 6 bits of each 8-bit RGB component are used to generate the final color; thus, you have a total of 2^{18} (262,144) colors instead of 2^{24} (16.7 million). You can always write 8 bits into each component, but the upper 2 bits will be discarded on video cards with 6 bits-per-component.

Think of the color palette like 256 buckets of paint. You fill each bucket with a different paint and give it a number; then when you plot pixels on the screen, you paint with numbers. That's how the palletized modes work. Normally, palletized modes are found in low resolutions, such as 320 x 200 and 320 x 240, but not necessarily. If you are programming in Windows, the minimum resolution is 640 x 480; furthermore, some cards only have enough memory for 256 colors, so you will end up using a 256-color palletized mode.

Also, when you run Windows in 256-color mode, you can definitely see the visual degradation. In 256-color mode, you don't have a whole lot of colors to work with — and worse yet, Windows steals about 20 of them so that it can draw windows and controls in a uniform manner. Suddenly, only 236 colors are left to applications to be redefined. And this limitation has an even more limiting caveat: Each application can't define its own 236 colors — all applications have to share the same 236 colors. This problem is why 256-color applications, especially games, look so bad. It's fine for a single game to run full screen and use 256 colors, but when Windows applications have to share a meager 256 colors, things get ugly fast.

Windows color management

If you read the previous sections on RGB and palletized modes, you must think that Windows is really hard to work in with respect to color. However, that's not entirely true. Windows insulates the programmer from all this palette stuff for the most part. In Windows, programmers always request 24-bit RGB colors, regardless of the video mode. (Of course, a good programmer figures out the video capabilities and then optimizes the code for the number of colors available, but doing so isn't necessary.)

Windows uses two primary data structures for color objects:

- COLORREF: A simple 4-byte structure consisting of a red, a green, and a blue component; use it when you want to create colors on the fly.
- PALETTEENTRY: A more complex 4-byte structure used to create palettes that includes a flags component in addition to the standard RGB components.

Here's the definition for `COLORREF`:

```
typedef struct tagCOLORREF {
    BYTE bRed;    // red component
    BYTE bGreen;  // green component
    BYTE bBlue;   // blue component
    BYTE bDummy;  // always 0
} COLORREF;
```

A `COLORREF` must be 32 bits (4 bytes), and the last byte must be 0.

And here's the definition for `PALETTEENTRY`:

```
typedef struct tagPALETTEENTRY {
    BYTE peRed;    // red component
    BYTE peGreen;  // green component
    BYTE peBlue;   // blue component
    BYTE peFlags;  // control flags set to PC_NOCOLLAPSE
} PALETTEENTRY;
```

The first three bytes of a `PALETTEENTRY` are similar to a `COLORREF`, but the two structures differ in the last byte, which is used for a control flag in the case of a `PALETTEENTRY`. The three values `peFlags` can have are

- ✔ **PC_NOCOLLAPSE:** This flag setting, which you would normally use, indicates that the color is not to be compressed, collapsed, or otherwise messed with by Windows.

- ✔ **PC_RESERVED:** This flag indicates that this color may be used for animation and hence may change, so Windows shouldn't count on the RGB values staying the same for long.

- ✔ **PC_EXPLICIT:** This flag is used for advanced hardware indirection; don't use it.

In general, to create colors as parameters or to be used as an assignment, use `COLORREF`s; to create palettes and use more advanced features, use `PALETTEENTRY`s because they have more information. Finally, to create a `COLORREF`, manually shift the bits of the desired Red, Green, and Blue, or use the `RGB()` macro like this:

```
// to create white
COLORREF white = RGB(255,255,255);

// to create pure red
COLORREF red = RGB(255,0,0);
```

For the remaining discussions on color, I assume that your Windows environment has 16-bit color or better. If not, all the code will still work; it just won't look as good. If you're using a lower bit depth, Windows approximates the color you're requesting with the closest match in the palette.

In the chapters on DirectX color management (Chapters 8 through 11), you find out how to totally take control of the palette in low-color modes. You'll know exactly what is going on with color, and other applications using your color space won't be a concern.

The Windows Printing Press

The text-rendering system of Windows is extremely complex and well beyond the scope of this book. In this section, I give you the very basics of printing and changing the text color, and that's about it. In reality, about the only thing you need to do with text is possibly draw some hi-scores or print out basic informational text on the game display.

DirectX has no support for fonts or text, so to print words, you have to code the text yourself, creating your own text system (with multiple proportional fonts, if you want it to look good), or use GDI. Although GDI is much slower than DirectX, GDI can be used to draw text in your DirectX applications.

For the majority of the examples that follow, be aware that you can put the code anywhere in your Windows application as long as you have a valid graphics device context.

Two kinds of fonts exist: *fixed pitch* and *proportional pitch*. Figure 5-3 shows the difference between a fixed-pitch font and a proportional-pitch font. The pitch has to do with the width of a character. In a fixed-pitch font, all characters are the same width — not that an *i* is stretched out to be as wide as a *w*, but the amount of space an *i* takes up is equal to the amount of space a *w* takes up, even if the space is mostly empty. Fixed-pitch fonts are great for programmers because you can easily compute the exact amount of space a character string will take up; however, these fonts are bad for users because fixed-pitch fonts are ugly.

Proportional-pitch fonts are much better on the eyes; the characters flow together based on what width the character needs rather than on a fixed amount. Determining the amount of space a particular character string in a proportional-pitch font will take up is more complex and can't be done with simple math; calls must be made to Windows. However, as you see in the subsection "Retrieving the TEXTMETRICs," the Windows calls aren't too bad. For now, go to the next section to see how to print some text.

Figure 5-3:
Fixed-pitch
versus
proportional-
pitch fonts.

> **Proportional Fonts Are Nice**
>
> Fixed Pitch Fonts Are Ugly

Printing text

You can choose from two ways to print text:

- ✔ TextOut(): The simplest method, with no formatting or processing ability. This function simply prints out a static string.

- ✔ DrawText(): The most complex method, which gives you much more control — justification, clipping, and so forth. I don't use this function in this book, but I do give you the prototype later in this section.

Take a look at TextOut() first:

```
BOOL TextOut(
    HDC hdc,            // handle of device context
    int nXStart,        // x-coordinate of starting position
    int nYStart,        // y-coordinate of starting position
    LPCTSTR lpString,   // address of string to print
    int cbString);      // number of characters in string
```

The prototype is simple enough to understand; you send the handle of the graphics device context, the position to print at (in client coordinates), the string to print, and the string's length. The only bummer about TextOut() is that it has no formatting or processing capability like printf() does; TextOut() simply prints out a static string. Hence, if you want to print variables or use formatting, you must use sprintf() to create the string.

Here's an example using TextOut() that prints out the value of a running counter in the window client area at (0,0):

```
char buffer[80];          // used to build up strings
static int counter = 0;   // used to count
case WM_PAINT:
    {
    // start painting
    hdc = BeginPaint(hwnd,&ps);
    // create the output string and get its length
    int length =
```

```
sprintf(buffer,"The Count is %d   ",(int)counter++);
// print the text
TextOut(hdc,0,0,buffer,length);
// end painting
EndPaint(hwnd,&ps);
return(0);
} break;
```

The one problem with this example is that the text prints only when a WM_PAINT message is sent (program PROG5_1.CPP on the CD illustrates this point). To see the value of the counter change, generate WM_PAINT messages by using the resize control to resize the window.

If you want the message to print out each cycle, you can place the text-printing code in the real-time portion of the main event loop, right after the main message processing. Program PROG5_2.CPP on the CD illustrates this technique, and here is an excerpt from that program's WinMain() showing the important code addition:

```
// enter main event loop
while(1)
    {
    if (PeekMessage(&msg,NULL,0,0,PM_REMOVE))
    {
    // test whether the message is WM_QUIT
    if (msg.message == WM_QUIT)
            break;
     // translate any accelerator keys
      TranslateMessage(&msg);
      // send the message to the window proc
      DispatchMessage(&msg);
      } // end if
      // main game processing goes here
    // get the graphics device context
    hdc = GetDC(hwnd);
    // create the output string and get its length
    int length =
    sprintf(buffer,"The Count is %d   ",(int)counter++);
    // print the text
    TextOut(hdc,0,0,buffer,length);
    // release the device context
    ReleaseDC(hwnd,hdc);
    } // end while
```

The second method to print text is with the `DrawText()` function, which is a little more complex than `TextOut()` but gives you much more control (such as justification, clipping, and so forth). I don't use this function in the book, but here is the prototype, for reference:

```
int DrawText(
    HDC      hDC,            // handle to device context
    LPCTSTR  lpString,       // pointer to string to draw
    int      nCount,         // string length
    LPRECT   lpRect,         // clipping rectangle
    UINT     uFormat);       // formatting flags
```

Refer to the C/C++ help of your compiler or your favorite reference for the definitions of all the flags and further details.

Color me bad

If you run either of the programs referenced in the preceding section, you notice that the text is an ugly color on top of another ugly color. In essence, the text's background doesn't match the black background of the window, so you see character blocks.

This shared ugliness brings up a couple of concepts I need to discuss before I talk about how to set the color of text:

- ✔ **Foreground and background:** Each text character has a foreground and a background. The foreground is the character itself, and the background is the block that the character is within.

- ✔ **Transparency:** Setting the text background to transparent makes the text look like it was drawn rather than stamped; usually the preferred method of printing a character string.

- ✔ **Opaque (without transparency):** Makes the characters' background color occlude everything under them.

So, to get ready to print you need to perform these three steps:

- ✔ Set the transparency mode of the text.
- ✔ Set the foreground color of the text.
- ✔ Set the background color of the text.

`SetBkMode()` takes care of the first step, and here's its prototype:

```
int SetBkMode(
    HDC hdc,          // handle of device context
    int iBkMode);     // flag specifying background mode
```

In this prototype, hdc is the device context, and iBkMode is the background mode, which has a value of TRANSPARENT or OPAQUE.

Now that you can select the background mode, the following two functions are used to select the foreground and background color of text:

```
COLORREF SetTextColor(
        HDC     hdc,      // handle of device context
        COLORREF crColor); // text color


COLORREF SetBkColor(
        HDC hdc,          // handle of device context
        COLORREF crColor); // background color
```

SetTextColor() is used to set the color of the text itself, and SetBkColor() is used to set the color of the background under the text (and the background color of other GDI objects also). Both functions take the device context along with the color as parameters. What's interesting about the functions is that both return values return the current colors before you changed them.

Any GDI context that you retrieve or create has a default set of objects, color, fonts, and so forth attached to it, and if you change any of them, save the old ones and restore the old values after you're done using them. So if you change the text color, restore the old color after you're done drawing.

The term for making changes to the device context is *selection*. When you change anything, you are selecting the element (for example, the text color) into the device context. And when you change it back, you are *deselecting* the element from the device context. Hey, I didn't make this stuff up!

To accomplish this save-change-use-restore cycle, most GDI functions return the old value that you're changing. SetTextColor() and SetBkColor() are no different. The following example prints out red text and blue text in the two background modes: transparent and opaque.

```
COLORREF old_text_color,
        old_back_color; // save the old colors
// get the device context
hdc = GetDC(hwnd);
// set transparency mode
SetBkMode(hdc,TRANSPARENT);
// set colors and save old
old_text_color = SetTextColor(hdc,RGB(255,0,0));
old_back_color = SetBkColor(hdc,RGB(0,0,0));
// print the text
TextOut(hdc,0,0,"I'm the red text!",strlen("I'm the red text!"));
```

(continued)

(continued)

```
// switch background mode to opaque
SetBkMode(hdc,OPAQUE);
// change text color; no need to save old color
SetTextColor(hdc,hdc,RGB(0,0,255));
// print the text
TextOut(hdc,0,0,"I'm the blue text!",strlen("I'm the blue text!"));
// restore the old colors
SetTextColor(hdc,old_text_color);
SetBkColor(hdc,old_back_color);
// release dc back
ReleaseDC(hwnd, hdc);
```

The example is a bit generic; you're probably already comfortable with the details of where to put the code. In any case, the code first sets the background mode and colors and then prints out. At the end, it restores the old colors. However, in general, you don't need to save and restore values unless you want to; it's just a safety precaution to protect you from using a device context that has been accidentally modified.

If you want to see an example of the previous code, look at PROG5_3.CPP on the CD. The program prints text in random positions and colors.

Retrieving the TEXTMETRICs

As I mention in the introduction to the earlier section, "The Windows Printing Press," Windows uses a proportional-pitch font; hence, determining the exact width and height of a text string is difficult because you don't know how the characters will print out next to each other. This problem, along with a few others, is part of the motivation for determining various properties and information about the currently selected font.

The properties of the current font are referred to as the TEXTMETRIC. This data structure holds all the information that you would ever want to know about a font. Here is its prototype (I placed an asterisk by each field that has value; as far as the rest of the fields go, take a look at the Win SDK Help):

```
typedef struct tagTEXTMETRIC {
  LONG tmHeight;   // * the height of the font
  LONG tmAscent;   // the ascent of the font
  LONG tmDescent;  // the descent of the font
  LONG tmInternalLeading; // the internal leading
  LONG tmExternalLeading; // the external leading
  LONG tmAveCharWidth;    // * the average width
  LONG tmMaxCharWidth;    // * the maximum width
  LONG tmWeight;          // the weight of the font
```

```
    LONG tmOverhang;        // the overhang of the font
    LONG tmDigitizedAspectX; // the average x-aspect ratio
    LONG tmDigitizedAspectY; // the average y-aspect ratio
    BCHAR tmFirstChar;    // * first character font defines
    BCHAR tmLastChar;     // * last character font defines
    BCHAR tmDefaultChar; // used when desired char not in set
    BCHAR tmBreakChar;    // the break character
    BYTE tmItalic;        // is this an italic font
    BYTE tmUnderlined;    // is this an underlined font
    BYTE tmStruckOut;     // is this a strikeout font
    BYTE tmPitchAndFamily;//family and technology
    BYTE tmCharSet; // what is the character set
} TEXTMETRIC;
```

To retrieve the TEXTMETRIC information, you use the GetTextMetrics()
function to fill in a TEXTMETRIC structure, and then access the fields that
interest you. Here's the prototype:

```
BOOL GetTextMetrics(
        HDC           hdc,    // handle of device context
        LPTEXTMETRIC lptm); //  ptr to text metrics struct
```

What are little letters made of?

The following figure illustrates some of the terms of printing that you may never use unless you
get a job at a print shop.

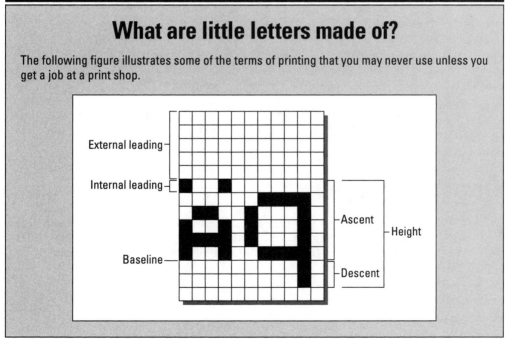

(continued)

(continued)

Here is a quick synopsis of the various parts of a character font:

✔ **Height:** The total height in pixels of the character

✔ **Baseline:** A reference point, usually the bottom of an uppercase character

✔ **Ascent:** The number of pixels from the baseline to the top of where an accent mark may be

✔ **Descent:** The number of pixels from the baseline to the bottom of lowercase extensions

✔ **Internal leading:** The number of pixels to allow for accent marks

✔ **External leading:** The number of pixels to allow for other characters above the character, so that they don't run on top of each other

I know: These terms sound a little strange. They're centuries old, so be grateful they're not in Greek or Latin! At least you have a better idea of some issues involved in designing a font.

Here's an example:

```
TEXTMETRIC tm; // holds the data
// get the textmetrics
GetTextMetrics(hdc,&tm);
// use tm data to center a string given the horizontal
// width of screen is WINDOW_WIDTH
int x_pos = WINDOW_WIDTH - strlen("Center This String")*tm.tmAveCharWidth/2;
// print the text at the centered position
TextOut(hdc,x_pos,0,"Center This String",
        strlen("Center This String"));
```

Text is boring, isn't it? Most game programmers use only a couple of hand-drawn bitmapped fonts throughout a program and don't worry about text.

Drawing Shapes

GDI has an extremely complex and diverse graphics engine. The engine isn't the fastest in the world, but it has almost no limits as to what it can render in 2D. Here's a list of the basic object primitives that GDI can handle:

✔ Points

✔ Lines

✔ Circles and ellipses

✔ Curves

✔ Polygons

✔ Bitmaps

✔ Metafiles (kind of like digitized recordings of other, more basic commands — like a list of instructions that can be played back)

The only object primitives that I cover in this section are points, lines, rectangles, and circles and ellipses. The other primitives work similarly, so use these basic types as examples of where you start with the others. To draw any of these GDI primitives, you need to set up a couple of things. GDI uses the analogy of a painter when drawing; instead of just drawing a line, GDI draws a line with a specific *pen*, and GDI fills any solid region with a *brush*. Pens draw the outlines of objects, and brushes fill in the interiors.

Penmanship with GDI

A *pen* in GDI is an object that is used to draw an outline object, such as a line, curve, or unfilled rectangle. A pen has two properties:

✔ **Color:** A standard RGB color

✔ **Style:** The way the line will be drawn — solid, dashed, and so on

To draw an object, you must first create a pen to draw with. Sounds easy! The basic pen data structure is called an HPEN, and to define a pen, do this:

```
HPEN pen_1; // a handle to a pen
```

Now, as written, pen_1 is useless; it's a handle to a pen that doesn't exist. You must now assign it to a valid pen that you create. To create a pen, you can use a stock object, or you can create a pen yourself from scratch. Use GetStockObject() to help define a window class. Here is another example of using it, this time to request a white pen:

```
pen_1 = GetStockObject(WHITE_PEN);
```

That code works great, but you don't have a million choices for stock objects; you only have about half a dozen. A better approach is to create your own pen, which you do with CreatePen(); here's its prototype:

```
HPEN CreatePen(int fnPenStyle, // pen style
               int nWidth,      // pen width
               COLORREF crColor);    // pen color
```

You supply the style of the pen, the logical width of the pen (set to 0 for a 1-pixel-thick pen), and the desired color, and CreatePen() creates the pen and returns a handle to it. If CreatePen() can't create the pen due to low resources, NULL is returned. Table 5-3 contains a list of all the pen styles.

Table 5-3	**Pen Styles for** CreatePen()	
Style	*Description*	*Example*
PS_SOLID	Pen is solid.	_____
PS_DASH	Pen is dashed.	_ _ _ _ _ _ _
PS_DOT	Pen is dotted.	. . . .
PS_DASHDOT	Pen has alternating dashes and dots.	_._._._._._._
PS_DASHDOTDOT	Pen has alternating dashes and double dots.	_.._.._.._.._..
PS_NULL	Pen is invisible.	<think Claude Rains>

Here is how you create three solid pens of red, green, and blue:

```
HPEN red_pen   = CreatePen(PS_SOLID, 0, RGB(255,0,0));
HPEN green_pen = CreatePen(PS_SOLID, 0, RGB(0,255,0));
HPEN blue_pen  = CreatePen(PS_SOLID, 0, RGB(0,0,255));
```

If you are a C programmer, notice that I am creating and defining variables at the same time, which C++ allows you to do, but not C.

That's all there is to creating pens. To use a pen, select it into the device context by using the SelectObject() function, which takes the device context and the object to be selected into the context. Here's the prototype:

```
HGDIOBJ SelectObject(HDC  hdc, // handle of device context
          HGDIOBJ hgdiobj); // handle of object
```

An HGDIOBJ is a generic data type that can handle pens, brushes, bitmaps, and so on. Here is how to select the red pen into the device context:

```
// select the red pen in and save old one
HPEN old_pen = SelectObject(hdc, red_pen);

// code to draw with the pen goes here
```

It's that simple. Finally, after you're done with your pens, you must delete them with DeleteObject(), like this:

```
// delete all the objects
// which is usually done at end of program in WM_DESTROY
DeleteObject(red_pen);
DeleteObject(green_pen);
DeleteObject(blue_pen);
```

Again, DeleteObject() takes any GDI handle, so you can send it a number of different object types. You see this function throughout the book.

The right brush for the right job

Brushes are used to fill the interior of objects that are drawn. You can create solid brushes, patterned brushes, or brushes that are bitmap images. The handle to a brush is HBRUSH, and, just as you do with pens, you can load a brush by using GetStockObject(), like this:

```
HBRUSH brush_1; // a brush
hbrush = GetStockObject(hdc, WHITE_BRUSH);
```

Brush patterns

Of course, the selection of brushes is even more limited than the selection of pens, so you will want to create your own. Just like a pen, a brush needs a color. But unlike a pen, a brush doesn't exactly have a style; a brush has a *pattern,* which is a bitmap image that the brush uses to paint or fill with. You can request GDI to create a pattern for you, or you can supply one via a bitmap. Or you can just make your brush a solid color — which in most cases is what you want to do anyway. Here's how you create a solid-blue brush:

```
HBRUSH blue_brush = CreateSolidBrush(RGB(0,0,255));
```

CreateSolidBrush() takes a single parameter — the color — and returns a handle to the generated brush. If you want to create a brush with a pre-defined pattern, you can use CreateHatchBrush(); here's its prototype:

```
HBRUSH CreateHatchBrush(int      fnStyle, // hatch style
                        COLORREF clrref);// color value
```

This function takes a pattern selector along with the desired color and creates a brush. Table 5-4 contains a list of patterns that can be requested.

Table 5-4	Patterns for CreateHatchBrush()
Value	**Pattern**
HS_BDIAGONAL	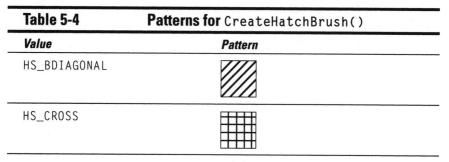
HS_CROSS	

(continued)

Table 5-4 *(continued)*

Value	Pattern
HS_DIAGCROSS	
HS_FDIAGONAL	
HS_HORIZONTAL	
HS_VERTICAL	

Here is how to create a green brush with a 45-degree crosshatch pattern:

```
HBRUSH green_cross_brush = CreateHatchBrush(HS_DIAGCROSS,RGB(0,255,0));
```

One final way that you can create a brush is with a bitmap. I discuss bitmaps in more detail in Chapter 6. For now, here are the basics on bitmap brushes. You can create a patterned bitmap brush with an 8 x 8 bitmap as the brush pattern. The call is as follows, where hBitmap is a handle to a bitmap that you have created or loaded:

```
HBRUSH bitmap_brush = CreatePatternBrush(hBitmap);
```

If you're just foaming at the mouth to try bitmapped brushes, here's a quick way to do it: Create a bitmap resource using your development studio and add it to your project; then use the LoadBitmap() function to load the bitmap in and get a handle to it. You can then pass the handle to CreatePatternBrush(), and presto! A bitmapped brush.

Selecting and deselecting a brush

After creating a brush (using whatever technique makes you happy), you must select it into the graphics context by using SelectObject(), like this:

```
HBRUSH blue_brush = CreateSolidBrush(RGB(0,0,255));
HBRUSH old_brush = SelectObject(hdc, blue_brush);
```

And when your application terminates, you must first deselect the brush, and then you can delete it. So the sequence is something like this:

```
// deselect brush by restoring original
SelectObject(hdc, old_brush);

// now delete the blue brush
DeleteObject(blue_brush);
```

If you try to delete a brush that is currently selected into the device context, Windows crashes — don't call me, because I told you so!

Plotting pixels

Plotting pixels is the simplest operation that any graphics system can perform. If you can plot a single pixel, you can create a game engine to rival the one in *Quake*. Figure 5-4 shows the standard default coordinate system that all the graphics primitives are based on. The origin (0,0) is in the upper-left corner of the window client area, and the positive x-axis is to the right; the positive y-axis is downward. This setup is similar to quadrant I of a standard Cartesian coordinate system, except that the y-axis is inverted.

Windows has a number of coordinate-mapping modes to change the orientation of the coordinate system, but the default is one unit per pixel and looks like a standard x-y coordinate with the y-axis inverted.

The function used to plot pixels doesn't need a pen or a brush:

```
COLORREF SetPixel(HDC hdc, // handle of device context
                  int X,   // x-coordinate of pixel
                  int Y,   // y-coordinate of pixel
                  COLORREF crColor); // pixel color
```

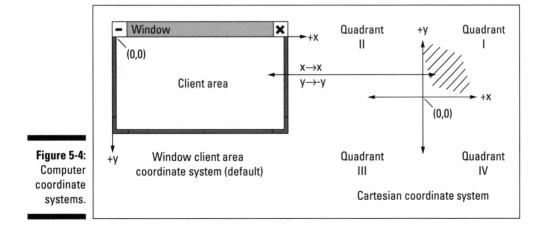

Figure 5-4: Computer coordinate systems.

The function returns the actual color that the pixel was plotted with (which is important when your video card doesn't have enough color depth and Windows uses a closest match). Here is an example use of the function:

```
// plot a pixel at 50,60 in pure white
SetPixel(hdc, 50,60, RGB(255,255,255));
```

Program PROG5_4.CPP on the CD illustrates SetPixel() in use. It plots randomly positioned pixels with random colors.

Laying down lines

You could write your own line-drawing function, but luckily for you, Windows already has one! You have a number of ways to implement a line function, but GDI opted to use the *line-to* method. With this method, instead of giving the line function a starting point and an ending point each time, you tell it where to draw to in relation to the previous position. So the first thing you need to do to draw a line is set the starting point, which you do by using MoveToEx(); here's its prototype:

```
BOOL MoveToEx(
      HDC hdc,  // handle of device context
      int X, // x-coordinate of new current position
      int Y, // y-coordinate of new current position
      LPPOINT lpPoint); // address of old current position
```

The parameters are obvious, except for the last: lpPoint. This parameter is used to hold the last position of the cursor before you change its position with the call. In most cases, you can set this parameter to NULL unless you want to know that last cursor position. Anyway, the function is used to position the line-drawing cursor. So if you want to draw a line starting at position (10,20), code something like

```
MoveToEx(hdc, 10,20,NULL);
```

Understand that this code doesn't draw anything; it simply positions an invisible cursor. To actually draw the line, call LineTo(), as follows:

```
BOOL LineTo(HDC hdc, // device context handle
          int nXEnd,        // x-coordinate of end point
          int nYEnd); // y-coordinate of end point
```

So to draw a line from (10,20) to, say, (50,100), do this:

```
MoveToEx(hdc, 10,20,NULL);
LineTo(hdc, 50, 100);
```

But what color and style is the line? I am assuming that a pen has been defined and selected into the graphics device context. **Remember:** All outlines are drawn with the current pen.

Here's the complete example:

```
// create the pen
HPEN green_pen = CreatePen(PS_SOLID, 0, RGB(0,255,0));
// select it into the context
SelectObject(hdc, green_pen);
// draw the line
MoveToEx(hdc, 10,20,NULL);
LineTo(hdc, 50, 100);
```

Of course, you may want to save the old pen, and you do want to delete the pen object when your application ends — I'm just reminding you!

Now what if you want to draw two lines, one connected to the other? You could make two separate calls to MoveToEx() and LineTo(), but you don't need to. All you need to do is use MoveToEx() to position the initial point; then you can call LineTo() as many times as you want, and it keeps connecting the dots. For example, to draw a triangle containing the points (100,100), (150,150), and (50,150):

```
// start the triangle
MoveToEx(hdc, 100,100,NULL);
LineTo(hdc, 150, 150);
LineTo(hdc,50,150);
// close the triangle
LineTo(hdc, 100, 100);
```

Program PROG5_5.CPP on the CD is an example of drawing lines.

Getting boxed in with rectangles

You can draw any polygon with a collection of lines; however, GDI has a number of primitives, so you don't have to write your own rectangle and polygon functions. Take a look at the most basic rectangle function:

```
BOOL Rectangle(
    HDC hdc,             // handle of device context
    int nLeftRect,       // x-coordinate of upper-left corner
    int nTopRect,        // y-coordinate of upper-left corner
    int nRightRect,      // x-coordinate of lower-right corner
    int nBottomRect);// y-coordinate of lower-right corner
```

This function draws a solid rectangle with the current pen and brush. This example draws a 50-x-50-pixel square with its upper-left corner at (10,10):

```
Rectangle(hdc, 10,10,60,60);
```

A couple more functions may be of interest. They use a RECT structure to hold the coordinates instead of explicitly listing the coordinates:

```
// creates a filled rectangle
int FillRect(HDC hDC, // handle of device context
    CONST RECT *lprc, // ptr to rectangle
    HBRUSH hbr);        // handle of brush to use

// creates an outlined rectangle
int FrameRect(HDC hDC, // handle of device context
    CONST RECT *lprc,  // ptr to rectangle
    HBRUSH hbr);        // handle of brush
```

Both functions take a handle to a device context, a pointer to a RECT structure, and a handle to a brush — which is cool. You can thus avoid selecting a brush into the graphics context. Here is how you draw an outlined rectangle:

```
static RECT rect = {100,100,200,200}; // cool trick!
// define brush
HBRUSH brush = CreateSolidBrush(RGB(0,0,255)
// draw it
FrameRect(hdc, &rect, brush);
// delete the brush when you're done
DeleteObject(brush);
```

A couple of neat things: First, I defined the coordinates of the rectangle while I created the RECT structure, and second, you don't have to select the brush into the device context — it's a parameter of the function. For an example of drawing rectangles, look at PROG5_6.CPP on the CD. The program draws random, colored rectangles, both filled and wireframe.

I can't emphasize enough the importance of using the DeleteObject() function after you're done with an object. If you create a number of pens and/or brushes, delete them when your program exits; otherwise, you may get a resource leak. Also, you can create only so many pens and brushes at one time. If your program creates many brushes or pens during run-time, keep deleting the old ones so that you don't run out of resources.

Going crazy with circles and ellipses

Now's the time for circles and ellipses. I'm sure you know what a circle is, but you may be a little rusty on ellipses. They're like ovals, or squished circles. Figure 5-5 shows a circle and an ellipse and the formulas for them.

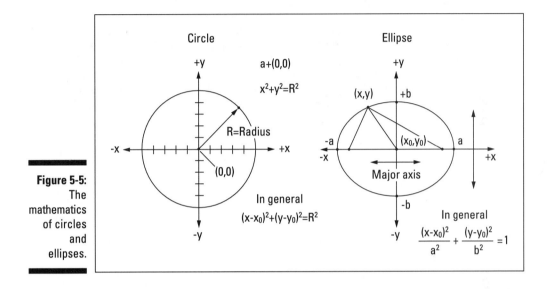

Figure 5-5:
The
mathematics
of circles
and
ellipses.

Because a circle is a special case of an ellipse — that is, one where the major and minor axes are equal — you really only need to be able to draw an ellipse. The function to do that is called, surprisingly, `Ellipse()`; here it is:

```
BOOL Ellipse(HDC hdc, // handle to device context
int nLeftRect,   // x of bounding rect's upper-left corner
int nTopRect,    // y of bounding rect's upper-left corner
int nRightRect,  // x of bounding rect's lower-right corner
int nBottomRect);// y of bounding rect's lower-right corner
```

Give the function the bounding rectangle of the ellipse. The function draws the outline of the ellipse in the current pen and fills it with the current brush. To draw a circle at (100,100) with a radius of 10 (diameter of 20), do this:

```
Ellipse(hdc, 90,90,110,110);
```

And if you want to draw an ellipse with a major-axis width of 100 and a minor-axis height of 60, centered at (100,100):

```
Ellipse(hdc, 100 - 50, 100 - 30, 100 + 50, 100 + 30);
```

Of course, you must select a pen and brush into the graphics device context; are you tired of my reminding you?

Windows has a great deal of support for curved objects because one of the goals of Windows was to be able to render business and scientific data on-screen. Before you write any graphics function yourself, look through the GDI API — chances are that Windows can already do it for you!

As a final example of drawing primitives, I decided to do something a little dramatic; a bouncing-ball demo — wow! Program PROG5_7.CPP on the CD is a demo that draws a bouncing ball on-screen, using the Ellipse() function. Take a close look at the program because it performs rudimentary animation. Also, for a change, I decided to create all the drawing objects in the WM_CREATE message and to destroy them in the WM_DESTROY message.

Chapter 6

Wrapping Up Windows Programming

*I*f you've been reading this book from cover to cover and have been diligently following along with the text, then give yourself a hand because the hard part is over! If not, then get ready to enjoy this chapter's discussions on some Windows programming basics: timers, menus, menu messages, and sound. All these minor topics are important to creating complete Windows applications as well as to game programming.

At the end of this chapter, I also show you how to use what I cover in this chapter (and some bits from Chapters 1 through 5) to create the WinX game console. You use this console to write games much like you would DOS games, but with all the resources of 32-bit programming and the Windows operating system.

Timing Is Everything

In game programming, you often want to perform a specific task at timed intervals. For example, you may want to play a heartbeat sound every second, or poll input devices every 100 milliseconds, or decrease the player's health every 5 seconds, and so on. Or perhaps you want to time how long something happens — to optimize some code, perhaps, or to force a specific section of code to wait a specific amount of time. Hence, you need to be able to respond at timed intervals and to count how long something takes.

You can write low-level code and timing software to accomplish these types of functions. However, writing timing software is rather difficult, and making sure it works on every machine from a 386 to a Pentium II isn't that easy. The solution is to use the built-in timing and counting ability that Windows comes with. Here's what Windows provides:

- ✔ **Low-accuracy Windows timer events:** Sent to your application in the form of a WM_TIMER message to inform you that something must be done. This method works great, but the basic Windows timers aren't that accurate — they can be plus or minus milliseconds.

- ✔ **High-accuracy Windows multimedia timer events:** Much more accurate than low-accuracy Windows timer events. Instead of sending WM_TIMER messages, Windows calls a callback function that you supply to process your timing task.

- ✔ **Medium-accuracy counting:** A built-in clock that you can query when you want to count how many milliseconds have transpired from one point to another, or to create a delay. Alas, this clock isn't that accurate, either, but it's close enough for government work.

If you're an assembly-language programmer, you can use a Pentium-only instruction *RDTSC* (Read Direct from Time Stamp Counter), which is a 64-bit CPU clock-cycle-accurate timer. Most assemblers don't support it, but you can create the instruction yourself by writing the op code bytes (0 x 0F31) directly into the code space. Refer to your favorite assembly-language manual or Intel Pentium documents for more information.

The following sections show you how to use the basic low-accuracy timer and how to set up a delay loop with the built-in clock.

Time for timers

You can create as many timers as you want, all with different time delays. To create a timer, you make a Windows API call with an id that you want the timer referred to as. Then Windows creates the timer and starts sending your event handler WM_TIMER messages along with the timer id in wParam when the timer delay is up; see Figure 6-1, which shows the timing loop. To create a timer, use the SetTimer() function:

```
UINT SetTimer(HWND hWnd,          // handle of window
              UINT nIDEvent,// timer ID
              UINT uElapse, // time delay in microseconds
        TIMERPROC lpTimerFunc); // address of callback
```

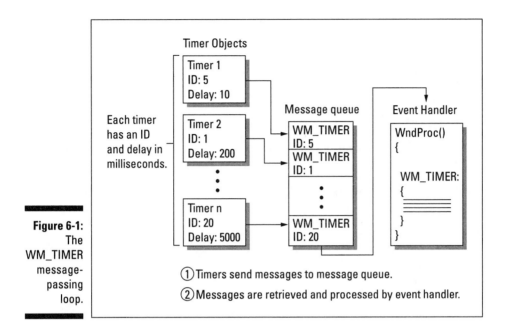

Figure 6-1: The WM_TIMER message-passing loop.

Timer Objects

Each timer has an ID and delay in milliseconds.

Timer 1
ID: 5
Delay: 10

Timer 2
ID: 1
Delay: 200

Timer n
ID: 20
Delay: 5000

Message queue

WM_TIMER
ID: 5

WM_TIMER
ID: 1

WM_TIMER
ID: 20

Event Handler

WndProc()
{

WM_TIMER:
{

}
}

① Timers send messages to message queue.

② Messages are retrieved and processed by event handler.

To create a timer, you send

- ✔ The window handle.
- ✔ A non-zero id.
- ✔ The delay in milliseconds.
- ✔ A pointer to a timer callback function.

However, you don't use the callback, so always set it to NULL. If the function is successful, it returns the id that you sent; otherwise, it returns 0. You need this id to kill the timer after you're done with it. And of course, the id is needed to determine what timer sent the WM_TIMER message in your event handler if you have more than one timer. Here's an example that creates two timers, one with a one-second delay and the other with a three-second delay:

```
// the timer IDs (totally arbitrary)
#define TIMER_ID1_SEC  1 // id of one-second timer
#define TIMER_ID3_SEC  2 // id of three-second timer

case WM_CREATE:
    {
    // create one-second timer
SetTimer(hwnd, TIMER_ID1_SEC, 1000,NULL);
```

(continued)

(continued)

```
        // create three-second timer
        SetTimer(hwnd, TIMER_ID3_SEC, 3000,NULL);

        // exit event handler
        return(0);
        } break;
```

Not much to it. Of course, you may want to check the return value to make sure that it's non-zero and that the timer was actually created.

Here's how you process the `WM_TIMER` message:

```
case WM_TIMER:
    {
    // timer event is present; determine which timer fired
    switch(wparam)
        {
        case TIMER_ID1_SEC:
            {
            // more code for first timed item
            } break;

        case TIMER_ID3_SEC:
            {

            // more code for second timed item
            } break;

        // test for other IDs; other code you require

        default:break;

        } // end switch
} break;
```

Timers take up resources, so don't let them sit around and run — kill the timers after you're done using them or kill them in the `WM_DESTROY` message. To kill a timer, use the `KillTimer()` function, which takes the window handle and the id of the timer to kill. Here's how you kill the timers in the preceding example:

```
KillTimer(hwnd,TIMER_ID1_SEC);
KillTimer(hwnd,TIMER_ID3_SEC);
```

Program `PROG6_1.CPP` on the CD is an example that creates two timers, just like the example here; it prints text in response to one timer and beeps in response to the other.

Count on Windows

Creating a counter in Windows is much simpler than using the timers. All you have to do is query the current, millisecond-accurate time and perform a comparison with your start time. The function that retrieves a millisecond timer is `GetTickCount()`. Here's an example that waits 100 ms:

```
// next line gets the current value
DWORD frame_start_time = GetTickCount();

//your code goes here

// now make sure that you have waited 100 milliseconds
while(GetTickCount() - frame_start_time < 100);
```

`GetTickCount()` is relative: You must compute differences in time, not absolute time, because `GetTickCount()` can't be reset to 0.

What's on the Menu?

Just about every window has a menu. In fact, an application may have a main menu along with a number of pop-up menus (press the right mouse button anywhere in Windows to see a pop-up menu). I just cover creating the main menu that most windows have, but these techniques are applicable to pop-up menus, floating menus, and so on.

A word about Windows resources

Before I delve into the steps of creating a menu, here's a little background on *resources,* which you can think of as a database of media and information that you create and attach to your program. A Windows-based application can have a number of resources appended to the end of the .EXE file that can be loaded at run-time. Resources are a nice way to add data to your application without having to write a lot of support code yourself.

Here's a small list of the kinds of resources that you can add to your application:

- ✔ Strings
- ✔ Menus
- ✔ Dialog boxes
- ✔ Bitmaps
- ✔ Icons
- ✔ Sounds

Moreover, most C/C++ compilers come with resource editors that help you create and add resources to your application in a drag-and-drop fashion. The resources are described in a resource file with an .RC extension and then later compiled into a .RES binary file with a resource compiler (RC.EXE, RCPP.EXE). However, this step is usually invisible if you're using a development studio such as Microsoft Visual C++ or Borland C++ Builder.

Of course, you don't have to use resources if you don't want to; you can load everything off disks in separate files, or generate things on the fly, but using resources is a cool way to create your programs.

Menu, please

To create a menu for your window, you have a number of steps to follow:

1. **Create a Windows Resource Script (.RC) with the menu definition in it.**

2. **Create a header file (.H) to include in your application and to contain the various constants defining your menu items.**

3. **Add the Resource Script to your project.**

4. **Include the resource header in your C++ file along with the other .H files.**

5. **Write code to load the menu into your application and attach the menu to your window.**

6. **Write code to process the WM_COMMAND menu-selection messages, which are sent when a menu item is selected.**

7. **Compile your application along with the Resource Script into a single executable file.**

Figure 6-2 is a graphical representation of the process, to help show the interconnections. The following subsections take a look at the steps in more detail.

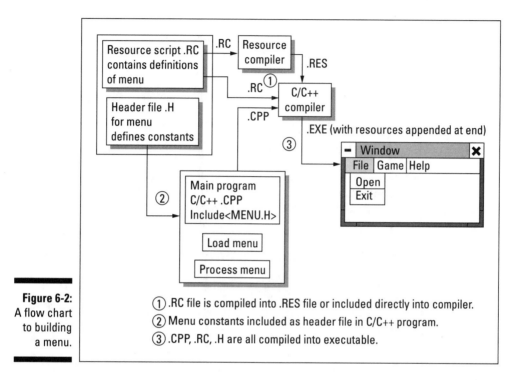

Figure 6-2:
A flow chart
to building
a menu.

Creating a resource script and a header file

A menu is like a little program that describes the menu items along with the menu selections for each item. In addition, a menu can have submenus within it, making menus hierarchical by nature. The language in which you must describe Windows menus is based on C and Pascal and is very simple, with just a few commands to learn. You can use the built-in compiler tools to create menus, but look at the old-fashioned way first.

Every compiler creates menus differently (for that matter, nearly every version of every compiler does, too). I include the "old-fashioned way" because it's impossible to talk about a method for creating menus that is useful for every compiler.

To create an .RC file, you must use a pure ASCII text editor, such as the editor you use to write your C/C++ code in. Within the file, you create the menu. Here is the format of a menu (code keywords are in bold):

```
MENU_NAME MENU DISCARDABLE
BEGIN
//menu definition goes in here
END
```

Although it's missing a great deal, that code is the shell of a menu. The first string is the name of the menu and is followed by MENU DISCARDABLE, which indicates to Windows that a menu definition follows and the data can be unloaded. Then within the BEGIN..END pair, you create the menu.

The next example creates a menu that has two main selections:

- ✔ File, which has three items: Open, Close, and Exit
- ✔ Help, which has just one item: About

Figure 6-3 shows the structure of the menu. You create an .RC file with the following contents (call it MYMENU.RC). All the keywords are in bold so that you can differentiate them from the stuff you control.

```
MYMENU MENU DISCARDABLE
BEGIN
    POPUP "File"
    BEGIN
        MENUITEM "Open",     1000
        MENUITEM "Close",    1001
        MENUITEM "Exit",     1002
    END

    POPUP "Help"
    BEGIN
        MENUITEM "About",    2000
    END
END
```

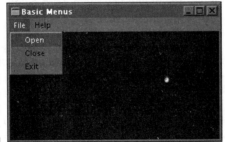

Figure 6-3:
Sample
menu
structure.

The first thing to notice is the hierarchy. The name of the menu is MYMENU, and this menu consists of two pop-up menus named File and Help. Then within File, the menu items are defined with the MENUITEM command along with an integer id associated with each. This integer id is the value that Windows will send to your application when the menu item is selected. The ids can be anything you want, but they must be less than 0 x 7FFFF.

The best strategy for selecting menu-item ids is to use multiples of 100 or 1,000 for each top-level menu and then increment by 1 for each menu item within each top-level menu. For example, your menu may have four items on it with ids 100, 101, 102, and 103.

Now of course, you can add as many items as you want to each menu selection, have as many top-level menus as you want (as long as they fit on the screen), and do plenty of other things to each menu item, such as gray it out or put in lines or breaks. (Check the Windows documentation for more on how to program those elements.) The only option I want to show you is the use of the ampersand symbol: &, which you place inside a menu item's name, just before the character that you want to make an Alt shortcut for accessing that menu.

For example, if you want the *x* in Exit to be a hot key, define it like this:

```
MENUITEM "E&xit",    1002
```

When the menu item is displayed, you don't see the ampersand. Instead, you see an underline under the *x,* denoting that it's a hot key.

When you add a header file to your .RC resource, your application doesn't have to use hard-coded numbers; in essence, you #define all the ids in the .RC file so that you can use them instead of numbers — a very programmer-friendly approach. Hence, continuing with the example, you create an .H header like this:

```
// MYMENU.H, header with menu ids
// Notice the clean naming I used for the ids; you
// can very quickly figure out the menu, submenu, and item

#define ID_MYMENU_FILE_OPEN   1000
#define ID_MYMENU_FILE_CLOSE  1001
#define ID_MYMENU_FILE_EXIT   1002
#define ID_MYMENU_HELP_ABOUT  2000
```

Then you include the header in your .RC file and use names for your ids instead of hard-coded constants, like this:

```
#include "MYMENU.H"

MYMENU MENU DISCARDABLE
BEGIN
    POPUP "File"
```

(continued)

(continued)

```
    BEGIN
        MENUITEM "Open",       ID_MYMENU_FILE_OPEN
        MENUITEM "Close",      ID_MYMENU_FILE_CLOSE
        MENUITEM "Exit",       ID_MYMENU_FILE_EXIT
    END


    POPUP "Help"
    BEGIN
        MENUITEM "About",      ID_MYMENU_HELP_ABOUT
    END
END
```

Adding the resources to your application

To load the .RC file to your application, simply add the file into your project, and the compiler does the rest. Just make sure that the header file is within reach of your compiler. Of course, you can perform the entire process described in the preceding section totally with the compiler's resource editor, which creates the .RC file along with the .H file, and you can use the artificially generated files instead. However, the mechanics differ for each compiler, so you need to refer to your particular compiler's documentation for details.

Loading the menu and attaching it to your window

After creating your menu resource file and header file, you're ready for business. Of course, you must include the menu header file in your C++ file so that it will have access to the id references; then you're all set. Now, to actually load the menu into your application at run-time, you have three choices, which are detailed in this subsection.

The first way is to define the menu when you create your Windows class:

```
// set menu name to the ASCII name of your menu
winclass.lpszMenuName = "MYMENU";
```

The second way is to leave this variable NULL and simply load and attach your menu when you create the main window, by using the LoadMenu() function, which is capable of loading a menu resource from your .EXE. Here's how you use it when creating the window to load the menu (the code in bold is the only line change from the standard CreateWindow() call used elsewhere in this section):

```
// create the window
CreateWindow(WINDOW_CLASS_NAME,         // class
    "Basic Menus",                      // title
    WS_OVERLAPPEDWINDOW | WS_VISIBLE,   // flags
```

```
0,0,                             // x,y
WINDOW_WIDTH,                    // width
WINDOW_HEIGHT,                   // height
NULL,                           // handle to parent
LoadMenu(hinstance, "MYMENU"),  // handle to menu
hinstance,                      // instance
NULL);                          // creation parameters
```

Normally, LoadMenu would be NULL, but you can attach a menu by sending CreateWindow() a menu handle — HMENU. LoadMenu() does just this: It takes the instance of the application along with the menu name and returns a menu handle object HMENU, which is then passed to CreateWindow(). Presto — you have a menu on your window.

The last way to attach a menu is to attach it after the initial window creation. In fact, with this technique, you can change the menu on the fly and change menus as much as you want as long as they're in the resource file. You do it first by getting the handle to your menu with LoadMenu(); then by attaching the menu to your window with SetMenu(). Here's an example:

```
// load the menu from resource and get handle to it
HMENU hmymenu = LoadMenu(hinstance, "MYMENU");

// attach the menu to the window and save old
SetMenu(hwnd, hmymenu);
```

The ASCII name you use to refer to the menu that you create is contained in the .RC file and can be anything you want. I've been using MYMENU, but it could as well be MAIN_MENU_1, or anything else. However, this name has nothing to do with the name Windows displays for the menu and menu items; that information is specified in the menu definition.

Processing the WM_COMMAND message

So you made your menu, loaded it in, and attached it, but it doesn't do anything! Well, as with all Windows constructs, a menu event sends a message, and the message is called WM_COMMAND. All you need to do to process menu item selections is add WM_COMMAND to your event handler and then switch on wParam, which contains the menu-item id.

For example, if you create a window with the MYMENU menu and then the user chooses the File⇨Close menu item, a WM_COMMAND message is sent with the value ID_MYMENU_FILE_CLOSE, which is equal to the value we set it at — in this case, 1001, which is the integer id that the code in the previous sections established. That's all there is to it. Here's an example of the message handler to process the example menu used in the previous sections:

```
// process menu messages
case WM_COMMAND:
    {
    // what menu item?
    switch(wparam)
        {
        case ID_MYMENU_FILE_OPEN:
            { } break;
        case ID_MYMENU_FILE_CLOSE:
            { } break;
        case ID_MYMENU_FILE_EXIT:
            { } break;
        case ID_MYMENU_HELP_ABOUT:
            { } break;
        default: break;
        } // end switch
    } break;
```

As an example of a complete menu-capable program, PROG6_2.CPP on the CD loads the MYMENU resource and then allows you to click each of the menu items. When you click an item, a message is displayed. Be sure to check out the code for File⇨Exit and Help⇨About. If you want to create this application yourself, remember to include the MYMENU.RC resource file as part of your project.

If you don't like using a string name for your menu, assign in your header an id number to the menu name itself; then in your Windows code, use MAKEINTRESOURCE(MYMENU) every place that you would use MYMENU. Now MYMENU is no longer a string but a simple numerical constant.

Play It Again, Sam: Sound and Music

The sound portion of this book focuses on DirectSound (see Chapter 13), and I don't want to bore you with the limited sound capabilities of Windows (well, limited compared to DirectSound). But the following tricks enable you to load and play sounds very quickly, which can be useful when you're experimenting with sounds and want to hear some audible feedback, or simply want to make some noise without using DirectSound.

The very powerful function named PlaySound() can load and play a sound from disk or as a resource. Here's this function's prototype:

```
BOOL PlaySound(
        LPCSTR pszSound, // string identifying sound
        HMODULE hmod,    // executable module to play from
        DWORD fdwSound); // sound flags
```

These parameters may seem a little abstract, but here's the deal:

- ✔ pszSound: Pointer to a string that's a filename on disk, or to a .WAV file resource that's part of your application

- ✔ hmod: Context-sensitive; depends on the flag settings

- ✔ fdsSound: Flags parameter; indicates how pszSound should be interpreted (filename or resource identifier), along with the properties of how to play the sound

Table 6-1 contains a partial list of the flags that can be logically joined using OR (commonly shortened to "logically ORed together") to create fdwSound.

Table 6-1	List of Control Flags for PlaySound()
Value	**Meaning**
SND_FILENAME	The pszSound parameter is a filename; in this case, hmod is NULL.
SND_RESOURCE	The pszSound parameter is a resource identifier; in this case, hmod must identify the instance that contains the resource.
SND_LOOP	The sound plays repeatedly until PlaySound() is called again with the pszSound parameter set to NULL. You must also specify the SND_ASYNC flag to indicate an asynchronous sound event.
SND_NOWAIT	If the sound driver is busy, the driver returns immediately without playing the sound.
SND_SYNC	PlaySound() returns after the sound event completes.
SND_ASYNC	PlaySound() returns immediately after starting the sound.

To use the PlaySound() function, you must include MMSYSTEM.H and insert the library WINMM.LIB into your application project. WINMM.LIB can be found within the \LIB subfolder of your compiler installation.

Playing a .WAV file from a disk is easy. You can start a .WAV and continue processing, wait for it to complete, or play it in a loop. Here are some examples:

- ✔ To play a .WAV asynchronously from disk:

```
PlaySound("SOUND.WAV",NULL,SND_FILENAME | SND_ASYNC);
```

To play a .WAV from a file in loop mode:

```
PlaySound("SOUND.WAV",NULL,SND_FILENAME | SND_ASYNC | SND_LOOP);
```

Of course, the file `SOUND.WAV` must be on the disk in the folder of your application, but you get the idea. To play a sound that's a resource, simply use the resource name. Here are the same examples, using a resource:

To play a .WAV asynchronously from a resource (where `SOUND_WAV` is the integer id of the `.WAV` resource):

```
PlaySound(MAKEINTRESOURCE(SOUND_WAV),hinstance,SND_RESOURCE | SND_ASYNC);
```

To play a `.WAV` from a resource in loop mode:

```
PlaySound(MAKEINTRESOURCE(SOUND_WAV),hinstance, SND_RESOURCE | SND_ASYNC |
          SND_LOOP);
```

As an example of using `PlaySound()`, `PROG6_3.CPP` on the CD contains a menu-driven program that you use to select from a number of sound effects on the main menu and then play each one. Also, be sure to include `PROG6_3.RC` if you want to compile this yourself; otherwise, you'll be without a menu!

The 411 on Windows 95: Getting Information

Windows is an extremely complex system, with many settings, configurations, and capabilities for each individual computer; hence, the Windows API has a number of functions to retrieve information about the computer and environment. Covering these functions in their entirety would require a whole chapter, so I just point you in the right direction and show you a few of my favorite information functions. (That's kinda sad, huh? I have "favorite functions." . . .)

The Win32 API has about 150 to 200 `Get` functions — one for just about anything you may want to know about the PC or Windows itself. Here's a sample list of some helpful information functions:

- `GetCommandLine()`: Command-line info
- `GetCurrentProcess()`: Information about a running-application process
- `GetCurrentTime()`: The current time
- `GetExceptionCode()`: The last exception code (error)

  ✔ GetFileAttributes(): The attributes of a file

  ✔ GetSystemMetrics(): Information about various Windows settings

The only function that I cover in any detail is the last —
GetSystemMetrics(). This function is very useful because it can request
many different types of information based on the command you send it, so
it's like a hundred functions in one! Here's its prototype:

```
int GetSystemMetrics(
        int nIndex);  // ID of system metric to retrieve
```

Table 6-2 contains a partial list of system metric information ids that you
can request. You simply call the function with one of the ids, and the return
value is the information.

Table 6-2   Useful Information ids for GetSystemMetrics()

Value	*Meaning*
SM_CMOUSEBUTTONS	Number of mouse buttons, or zero if no mouse is installed
SM_CXBORDER SM_CYBORDER	Width and height of window border
SM_CXSCREEN SM_CYSCREEN	Width and height of screen
SM_CXMIN	Minimum width of window
SM_CYMIN	Minimum height of window
SM_SLOWMACHINE	TRUE if the computer has a slow processor; FALSE otherwise

I gotta have more memory, man!

I don't mention memory management much because you don't have to worry about it in Windows 95, Windows 98, or Windows NT. In the old days of Windows programming, memory allocation was a major problem; you had to access memory with special functions, lock it, and so forth. It was a mess. But with the most recent versions of Windows, you can use standard C/C++ memory-management functions, such as malloc() and free() (used in C) and new and delete (used in C++).

The reason Windows 95, Windows 98, and Windows NT don't have memory-management problems is that each application executes in its own virtual address space of 4GB (or more). This feat is made possible by the memory management of Windows and the new hardware memory management that Intel has provided on its 486 and later processors.

And the cool thing about Windows is that it has a virtual memory manager, which means that in many cases you can allocate more RAM memory than is available on the machine!

Handling files without getting paper cuts

I want to quickly mention the functions that deal with file I/O under Windows. True, you can use a number of file I/O functions within Windows. But you don't *have* to use them. I prefer using the standard C/C++ file and stream I/O functions. However, don't try to use the DOS low-level functions — they don't work!

For performance reasons related to caching and the Windows file system, use block-based file I/O, such as `lread()`, rather than byte-based I/O, such as `fgetc()`. You can pretty much use all your old DOS-based file I/O techniques and libraries that you've used in the past. On the other hand, Windows does have a rich and robust set of file I/O functions; if you're going to do anything serious, you should at least check them out in the Windows SDK Help.

The WinX Game Console

If you've followed the book from the beginning of Chapter 1 to this point, you should be a Windows-programming demigod. Actually, Windows is one of the most complex programming environments in history, and becoming a master takes years. However, you know the fundamentals, and I'm sure that you can write a complete Windows application with menus, graphics, and sounds.

The first five chapters and the preceding sections of this chapter relate directly to the basics of Windows programming. This section goes a step beyond the basics to the core element that every Windows game programmer needs: a Windows game console, which is the programming equivalent of a wrapper shell around Windows and `WinMain` that insulates in many ways your game from Windows commands. The game programming you do later in the book uses this console, so that as you use DirectX to control all graphics, sound, and input, you'll hardly notice that you're programming in Windows.

As you can see from all the demo programs on the CD for this chapter and preceding chapters, Windows-based applications contain a lot of redundant code. You always have to create a Windows class, register it, open a window, write an event handler, and so on. These operations change very little from application to application. The only thing that changes, really, is how messages are processed and what messages are processed.

So you should be able to make a template and then work from it to create a full Windows application. When I created all the demos for this book, that's exactly what I did. I took the first working Windows program, stripped it, made the next demo from it, and repeated this process over and over. Now I go one step further and create a Windows-based game-console shell — which I named *WinX* — that hides all the details of Windows under its abstraction.

The goal is to create games that run under Windows and use DirectX. However, because you don't need any Windows stuff for your games, you don't have to closely interface your game code to the Windows minimal application. So you create a working Windows application template that creates an empty window without any output. The application processes only the most basic messages, but it does work. Then you create a few functions and call them from the `WinMain()` function. And from your point of view, the new shell functions will be called by Windows (similar to a DOS C/C++ `main()` function), and you can put all the game code in them, which totally insulates you from the details of programming in Windows.

Of course, if you want to add more code or message processing to the Windows portion of your program, you can, but you don't have to. Take a look at Figure 6-4, which depicts the software architecture of the WinX game console. In essence, it's nothing more than three functions located strategically within a minimal Windows program. The three functions are

```
int Game_Init(void *parms=NULL);
int Game_Shutdown(void *parms=NULL);
int Game_Main(void *parms=NULL);
```

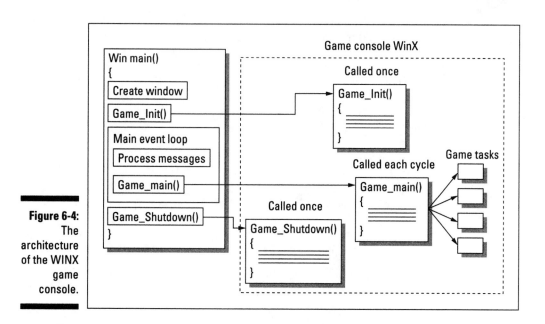

Figure 6-4: The architecture of the WINX game console.

You should notice the slightly weird prototypes with initialization. Actually, this is called *default parameters* in C++. C++ allows you to assign a default value to your parameters, so you don't have to type them during function calls. Referring to the three functions: You don't need to assign anything to parms; you can simply call the function(s) without any parameters. For example, a call like Game_Init() assigns parms NULL by default. Or if you like, you can send a parameter like this: Game_Init(&x); in this case, parms is equal to the address of *x*.

Game_Init() is called once after all the Windows initialization has been completed. That's where you do all your initialization. Game_Shutdown() is called after the application has killed all the Windows stuff and is ready to exit. That's where you put all your shutdown and resource-deallocation code. Finally, Game_Main() is like the main() of a standard C program; it's called in the main event loop whenever Windows isn't processing a message. Within this function goes the entire game, just like it would in a C program's main(). The only difference is that Game_Main() can't loop infinitely; you must process one cycle and then exit the function, but that's not a big deal.

On the CD, you can find the complete source for the game console. The code for the game shell is called WINX.CPP. If you run WINX.EXE, you see nothing more than a 320 x 200 window without any menus.

I use WINX.CPP as the code starting point for all the demos in the remaining chapters of this book.

The following is the main event section for the WinX console. The only thing that has changed from any of the other demos is the main event loop of WinMain() and the addition of the game-console function call. Here's the new stuff in WinMain() (I put the new calls in bold so that you can see exactly where they are):

```
// perform all game-console-specific initialization
Game_Init();

// enter main event loop
while(1)
    {
    if (PeekMessage(&msg,NULL,0,0,PM_REMOVE))
       {
       // test whether this is a quit
       if (msg.message == WM_QUIT)
           break;

       // translate any accelerator keys
       TranslateMessage(&msg);
```

```
            // send the message to the window proc
            DispatchMessage(&msg);
            } // end if

     // main game processing goes here
     Game_Main();

     } // end while

// shut down game and release all resources
Game_Shutdown();

// return to Windows
return(msg.wParam);
```

And here are the game-console functions themselves:

```
int Game_Init(void *parms)
{
// do all initialization for your game in this function

// your code goes here

// return success
return(1);
} // end Game_Init

/////////////////////////////////////////////////////////////

int Game_Shutdown(void *parms)
{
// shut down your game and release all resources
// that you allocated in this function

// your code goes here

// return success
return(1);
} // end Game_Shutdown

/////////////////////////////////////////////////////////////

int Game_Main(void *parms)
{
```

(continued)

(continued)

```
// this is the workhorse of your game; it will be called
// continuously in real-time, like main() in C;
// all the calls for your game go here!

// your code goes here

// return success
return(1);
} // end Game_Main
```

Are you starting to see the coolness yet? Using this shell technology, everything is taken care of for you, and your three functions, including Game_Main(), are called by Windows. Within them, you put the meat of your code, which is based on DirectX, not Windows.

Anyway, that's it for Windows.

To show you a demo of using the technology, I've created a simple drawing program, called DRAW.CPP, that uses the shell as a starting point. Use the arrow keys to move the brush around, and press C to change colors and ESC to exit. I used GDI instead of DirectX for the graphics because I haven't discussed DirectX yet in this book; but read on (if you haven't already), and you won't be DirectX-free for long!

Part II
Jacking In with DirectX

The 5th Wave · By Rich Tennant

Re·al Game Pro·gram·mers

MONDO-TECH

OH WOW!

Real Game Programmers do their best work between 1 and 5 a.m.

In this part . . .

After you get Windows under your belt, you're ready to get to the good stuff — DirectX. First, you discover the Component Object Model (or COM), which is what DirectX is based on. Then I talk about all the graphical aspects of DirectX; mostly, I stick to DirectDraw because it's the largest of all the DirectX components. Get the hang of DirectDraw, and then you can go step-by-step through the construction of the first part of the GPDUMB game engine.

Finally, to showcase all that's covered in this part, I put together a game, called *Star Ferret*, that's based on the game engine. Feel free to experiment with this first example of a real Windows game.

Chapter 7

The Architecture of DirectX and the Dreaded COM

In This Chapter

▶ Seeing how all the pieces fit together

▶ Introducing COM — Component Object Model

▶ Understanding the architecture of DirectX and its interfaces

▶ Writing DirectX applications

*G*DI, the Windows Graphics Device Interface (see Chapter 5), is much too slow for creating real-time action games. Sure, you can write an adventure game, or a card game, but that's about it. That's why DirectX was created: to give the PC programmer the tools necessary to write *real* games — like what Figure 7-1 shows — and other multimedia applications that rival the performance of DOS32 applications. And that's the goal of this book: to show you how to write games that run under Windows without using GDI.

DirectX fulfills the dream of a low-level API that's integrated smoothly with Windows and the Win32 API. By using DirectX, you can access video, audio, input devices, and networking capabilities without writing one line of GDI or using the standard Win32 libraries. And if you use DirectX to work with any of these systems, you won't conflict with GDI, Windows, or Win32.

This chapter is more of a primer on concepts and terms than anything else. For DirectX to work, a number of subsystems, such as COM and the Win32 API, have to communicate with each other. In addition, DirectX has more components than just DirectDraw. You need to know a little about all these aspects of using DirectX so that you can understand how they all fit together.

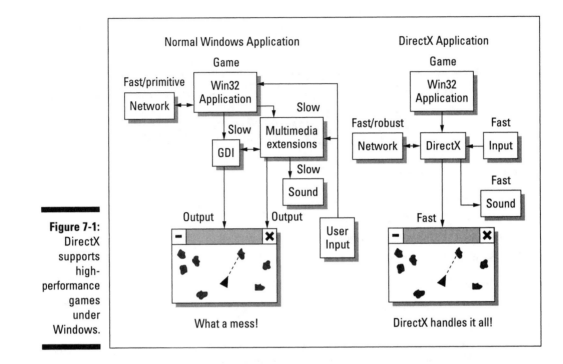

Figure 7-1:
DirectX
supports
high-
performance
games
under
Windows.

DirectX Fundamentals

Windows is a shared, cooperative, multitasking operating system, which means that all applications have to share such resources as the mouse, the video display, the sound card, and so on. Video games by their very nature break this rule. A game usually takes over everything, and because of games' need for high performance, you typically run only one game at a time.

DirectX gives you a shortcut to the hardware without going through normal Windows channels, as shown in Figure 7-2. DirectX is a set of Dynamic Link Libraries (.DLLs), and low-level device drivers that have the ability to control all aspects of the PC without much help from GDI or the standard Win32 library. And to create a DirectX application, all you need are the header files, the DirectX libraries, and the .DLLs on your machine. So you can think of DirectX as an add-on library that has all these capabilities.

.DLLs are the basis for much of Windows. They allow software libraries to be loaded on demand and to be shared by other applications. In addition, .DLLs can be upgraded and replaced without recompiling or breaking the applications that use them, as long as the .DLLs continue to implement the functionality of the older versions.

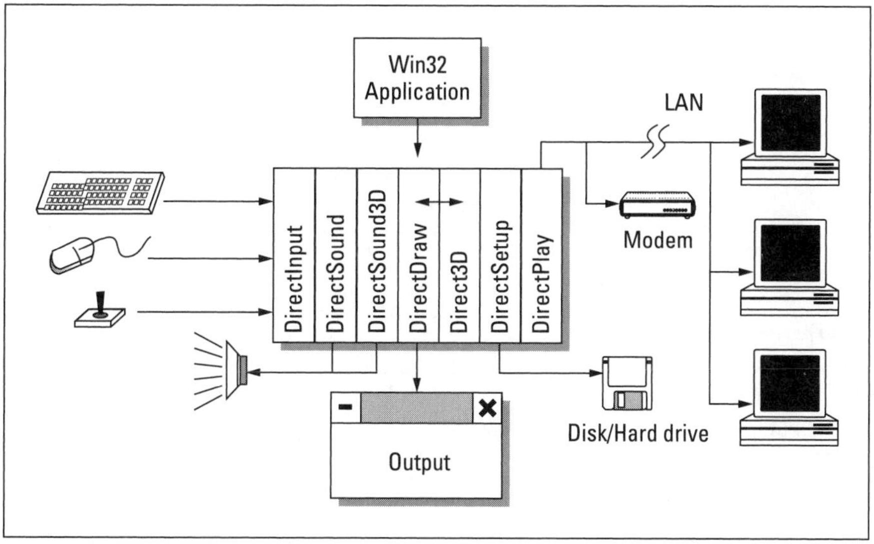

Figure 7-2:
An over-
view of
DirectX and
the system
components.

However, DirectX is much more than just libraries. It's a set of standards and philosophies that other software and hardware manufacturers are following. Just about every software company has written DirectX applications, and just about every hardware manufacturer has written DirectX drivers for their hardware. The result is a massive infrastructure that you can count on being there now and in the future.

To make the magical DirectX technology work, Microsoft had to come up with some new techniques and conventions to make DirectX very robust. In other words, a game written for DirectX 1.0 should be able to run on a computer with DirectX 3.0 or 6.0 installed. In addition, Microsoft knew that a technology like DirectX would get out of hand very quickly if it was written without a great deal of foresight and planning. What was needed was a way of writing software that was object oriented, upgradable, capable of working with multiple languages, and black box – like to the programmer. Sound impossible? The answer is *Component Object Model* — COM.

What the heck is COM?

COM — Component Object Model — is a technology invented a few years back as nothing more than a magazine article (I lost the article) that described a set of programming techniques to create component software, much like computer chips. Let me explain: The cool thing about using digital computer chips, as Figure 7-3 shows, is that each chip has a set of inputs and outputs. When you're designing with digital chips, you don't care what's inside the chip, whether it be silicon or little elves. All you care about is that if you follow the rules of the chip's interface, the chip works.

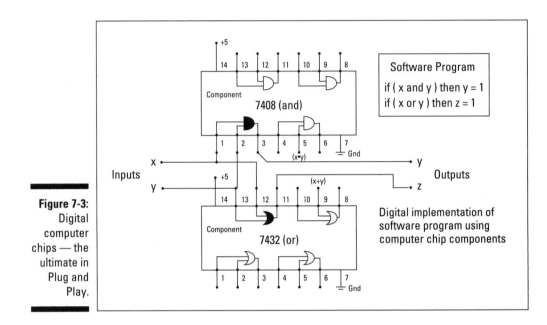

Figure 7-3:
Digital
computer
chips — the
ultimate in
Plug and
Play.

Furthermore, if you connect the output of one chip to another, and as long as the inputs and outputs are in the right format (the same logic system and voltages), the chips work together. This analogy is the basis for component software and COM. The idea of COM is to create software components that are like computer chips, or Lego blocks, that you can just plug in together. As long as you follow the rules, they work. (COM was actually the basis for *OLE* — object linking and embedding.)

This stuff is great in theory, but software is generally messy. The following discussion tells you just what you need to know, focusing on the Microsoft version of COM.

COM is a set of techniques and conventions to create reusable software components that work with any language and have the feel of computer chips or Lego blocks (but you can't play with them). The main advantage is that COM objects are interchangeable and upgradable without recompilation.

Suppose that a software engineer creates an application that uses a specific COM object. She ships the application along with the COM object (which is usually implemented in a .DLL), and the user loads the application on his machine and uses it.

Then the software engineer decides that she wants to add some more capabilities to the application but doesn't want to reship the entire product. With COM, she doesn't need to reship the whole thing. The new COM object that implements the changes is downloaded by the user, and presto — the application uses it! This situation is possible because COM objects are loaded dynamically by the client application that uses them, so you can create an application that has a number of COM objects and then later replace them with newer, more updated COM objects, as Figure 7-4 shows.

The following discussion is heavy with C++ jargon. Try to follow along, but don't worry if it sounds like Klingon — most programming does the first time around!

So that's what COM does for you, but how exactly do you make a COM object? That question has a very long answer, but let me give you a general idea of one way to make it: A COM object is really a C++ class that contains a number of interface classes. These interface classes are pure and virtual and must be implemented in a container class. Each interface class contains the functions that the COM object supports, so a COM object can have one or more interfaces that you communicate with and call functions through. Take a look at Figure 7-5 to see the relationship between the COM object and the interfaces it contains.

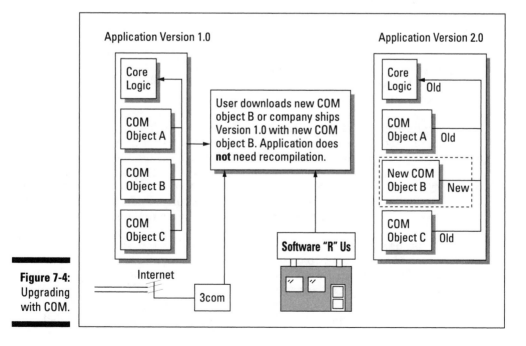

Figure 7-4:
Upgrading with COM.

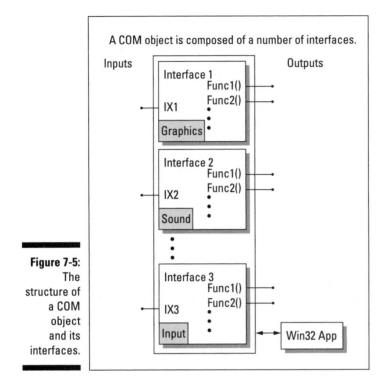

A COM object is composed of a number of interfaces.

Inputs   Outputs

Interface 1
          Func1()
IX1   Func2()
            .
Graphics   .

Interface 2
          Func1()
IX2   Func2()
            .
Sound   .

Interface 3
          Func1()
IX3   Func2()
            .
Input   .   Win32 App

Figure 7-5:
The
structure of
a COM
object
and its
interfaces.

One interface may contain methods to draw objects, another interface may contain methods to make sounds, and so on. But each interface is a pure virtual class that you only create a template for in its definition; you wait to implement the interfaces until defining the component itself.

You have many ways to implement a bunch of interface classes and then contain them all in a container class, but the COM specification dictates exactly how you must do this implementation and containing. In addition, the COM specs explain exactly how a client application can talk to a COM object, how to create a COM object, how to destroy one, and so forth. Thus, the COM specs explain all the details of the implementation so that all you have to do is create all the interfaces and the code that goes with them.

Finally, because COM objects are dynamically linkable, you must use something like a .DLL to contain them. You don't have to, but that method is the easiest way. Also, because COM objects need to work with any language, they have an exact binary specification, which means that you must make sure that your compiler creates the exact binary footprint that a standard Windows C++ compiler does when it creates virtual classes. I know that you're probably saying, "what the #$@#$!" But these concepts become clearer as you actually use COM objects.

Another version of COM, called *DCOM* (Distributed COM), is even more advanced than COM and enables the use not only of components on your machine but components on other machines over a network. Is that wild or what?

The components of DirectX

The various components of DirectX delve into each aspect of video game design — graphics, sound, input, 3D, and networking. This book doesn't cover all the DirectX components, just the basic ones — DirectDraw (see Chapter 8), DirectSound (see Chapter 13), and DirectInput (see Chapter 14) — along with some quasi-DirectX components, such as DirectSetup (see Chapter 16) and AutoPlay (see Chapter 16). However, I want you to at least be familiar with all the components so that you can impress your friends at parties.

Take a look at Figure 7-6, which illustrates all the DirectX components and their relationship to Win32, GDI, and the hardware. Notice that GDI and DirectX are on different sides of the border: Each has access to the other and to the hardware. The blocks of DirectX called the HAL (Hardware Abstraction Layer) and HEL (Hardware Emulation Layer) are also very important, as I discuss next.

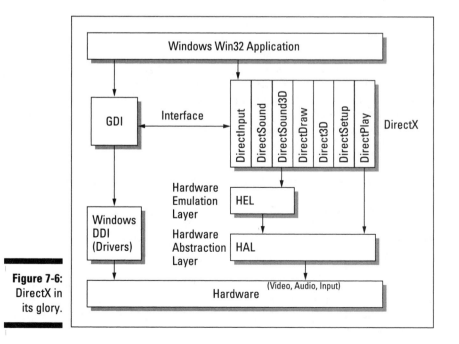

Figure 7-6: DirectX in its glory.

HAL: The Hardware Abstraction Layer

The Hardware Abstraction Layer (HAL) is the lowest level of software in DirectX, consisting of the hardware drivers provided by the manufacturer to control the hardware directly. This layer of software gives you the utmost performance because it talks directly to the hardware. Of course, you don't actually make calls to the HAL yourself; DirectX does that for you.

HEL: The Hardware Emulation Layer

The Hardware Emulation Layer (HEL) is built on top of the HAL. In general, DirectX is designed to take advantage of hardware if the hardware is there, but DirectX still works if hardware isn't available. For example, suppose that you write some graphics code, assuming that the hardware you're running on supports bitmap rotation and scaling. You therefore make calls to DirectX to scale and rotate bitmaps. On hardware that supports scaling and rotation, your code runs at full speed and uses the hardware, but if you run on hardware that doesn't support scaling and rotation, what then?

That's when the HEL kicks in. The HEL emulates the functionality of the HAL with software algorithms so that you don't know the difference. Of course, the code runs more slowly because it's being emulated, but it does run. That's the reason for the HEL. Some programmers query the hardware, see exactly what its capabilities are, and maybe use their own routines instead of the ones provided in the DirectX HEL, but you can just take advantage of the HEL instead.

DirectDraw

DirectDraw is probably the single most important component of DirectX. It enables you to access the video card, along with various hardware acceleration capabilities. In addition, DirectDraw knows how to set up every single video mode you may want, even high-resolution and True Color modes, so you don't have to worry about that stuff. And DirectDraw has support for palettes, clipping, and animation.

Direct3D

This component of DirectX is the only link between you and the 3D hardware. Direct3D enables you to use a standard API to communicate with and use any 3D hardware that you may have plugged into your computer, in a uniform manner. The API is based on a graphics engine created by a company called Rendermorphics (Microsoft bought the engine), so the API isn't really new.

And the battle between Direct3D and OpenGL isn't over, so you may want to think twice about using Direct3D for games, as it may get slowly phased out, like WinG. Remember WinG? Microsoft swears that they never heard of it . . . sounds like an X-File!

DirectSound

DirectSound is one of the greatest things on Earth. Writing sound drivers for the PC is nearly impossible; you just can't keep up with all the sound cards out there, so writing sound software is a full-time job. In the past, most game programmers (pretty much all of them) licensed their sound engines from a third party, such as John Miles Sound System or Diamondware Sound Toolkit. And these sound engines weren't cheap! But with DirectSound, this situation is no more.

DirectSound works with every sound card. It supports pure digital mixing of multiple channels in real-time. In addition, the newer versions of DirectSound support MIDI music. But MIDI has been dying off slowly, now that pure digital is CD quality and memory has become so cheap. On the other hand, new wave-table and wave-guide synthesizers are making a MIDI comeback, so supporting MIDI is nice insurance of compatibility.

DirectSound3D

DirectSound3D is based on DirectSound and is an implementation of 3D sound. The theory behind 3D sound is that you can simulate how a real object would sound at any position in space as long as you can control the input into each ear. You control the input by shifting the frequency of the sound and its amplitude, harmonics, and timing, based on mathematical models of how sound interacts with the geometry of your head along with how it travels through space.

DirectSound does all the math for you and enables you to place sounds in virtual 3D space. So you can place a monster behind the player, who will actually hear the monster as it would sound if it were actually behind him or her. A transfer function here, a Fourier transform there; cook with a convolution kernel. . . . Presto: 3D sound!

DirectInput

DirectInput was a long-awaited addition to DirectX. In the early releases of DirectX, input was accomplished by using Windows and the Win32 API. But now, as of Version 3.0, DirectX supports DirectInput, which allows a program to acquire data from the keyboard, mouse, and joystick in a uniform manner. And in DirectX Version 5.0, DirectInput supports Force Feedback devices — joysticks that vibrate.

The cool thing about DirectInput is the joystick support. Back in the '80s, just one kind of joystick was available, but today you have hundreds of joysticks — some digital, some analog, and all with weird button configurations. To use each joystick, you'd normally have to get the specs from the manufacturer and write a driver, but with DirectInput, the manufacturer writes a DirectInput driver for you!

DirectPlay

DirectPlay is probably the most underutilized of all the DirectX components because it's much harder to understand than the others. DirectPlay is networking support for games. It's a rather robust set of functions and systems that enable you to write network code for direct connections, local area networks, and Internet gaming without all the headache of using Winsock or your own code.

Unfortunately, DirectPlay takes about as long to learn as all the other DirectX components combined, but it is well worth the time investment if you want to write networked games. You simply would not want to write all this code yourself — believe me!

DirectSetup and AutoPlay

These two components aren't really DirectX objects. DirectSetup is a simple API that you use to install and set up DirectX and your game on client machines. AutoPlay is the standard Windows support for CDs to automatically load when they're placed in the machine. Microsoft probably wanted to call AutoPlay DirectPlay, but that was already used for networking. Maybe they should have called AutoPlay DirectLoad? (Hey, I think I'll patent that!)

Interfacing with Interfaces

DirectX is implemented as a number of components, each with a number of interfaces. To use DirectX, you need to understand a little about what's going on with COM and the interfaces — this understanding makes using DirectX much easier in cases where you have to create wrappers around all the DirectX COM stuff yourself.

A component consists of one or more interfaces. Each interface is like a communications port that you must use to call the functions within the interface. In this section, I show you a really rudimentary implementation of a COM object — it doesn't work, but it gives you a better idea of what's what.

First, you need to define your interface classes. Each interface contains a list of methods that you implement later but that nonetheless are the methods supported by the interface.

However, all interfaces are derived from the root interface IUnknown. For this example and the ones that follow, I use many keywords and definitions that you may not have seen before in your programming travels, so read the comments carefully.

GUIDs (pronounced "goo-ids") and IIDs (pronounced "eye-eye-deez") are special numbers that are very long (128 bits) and guaranteed to be unique from each other. Every COM object in existence must have its own GUID or IID. In addition, no two IIDs can be the same. So once you publish (distribute it to the world) a COM object with a number of interfaces, every interface must have its own IID. These numbers are generated with a Microsoft-supplied (with most compilers) program called GUIDGEN.EXE, which mathematically guarantees that it will never reproduce two identical GUIDS. Basically, using GUIDs is a way to name COM objects and interfaces uniquely.

```
// notice that all methods are pure virtual
// and they use the __stdcall or Pascal stack calling
// convention instead of the standard _cdecl;
// the interface IUnknown is defined by Windows like this

struct IUnknown
{
// this method is used to access the interface
virtual HRESULT __stdcall QueryInterface(const IId& iid,
(void **)ip)=0;

// this method increases the interfaces reference count
virtual ULONG __stdcall Addref() = 0;

// this method decreases the interfaces reference count
virtual ULONG __stdcall Release()=0;
};
```

IUnknown is the base class that all interfaces must derive from; hence, all interfaces must implement at least QueryInterface(), Addref(), and Release():

- QueryInterface(): Used to request a pointer to the interface of interest. You must pass an interface IID along with a pointer to hold the interface returned from the function. The only way to get access to an interface is through this method. You need to use it just once in a blue moon, when DirectX doesn't have a wrapper function or macro to do it for you.

- Addref(): Increases the internal reference count of the COM object. All COM objects allocate and deallocate themselves (so you don't have to) through *reference counting*. When an object is created, its internal reference count is incremented; when a reference to an object is no longer needed, its reference count is decremented. Thus, by tracking the reference count of an object, you can detect how many other objects are using it. When the reference count is zero, the object is no longer in use and can be deleted. You never need to use Addref() — it's called internally by all COM objects.

✔ Release(): Decrements the reference count of a COM object — a very important method that you use all the time after you're done using an interface or component.

Here's how to use IUnknown to create a couple of interfaces:

```
// a graphics interface
struct IGraphics : IUnknown
{
virtual int InitGraphics(int mode)=0;
virtual int SetPixel(int x, int y, int c)=0;
// more methods...
};

// a sound interface
struct ISound : IUnknown
{
virtual int InitSound(int driver)=0;
virtual int PlaySound(int note, int vol)=0;
// more methods...
};
```

C++ programmers please note that structs are just like classes except with default visibility of Public; that's why I'm using struct instead of class.

Now you have two interfaces, but still not a COM object. To make a COM object, you must contain the interfaces in a container class and actually implement the code for each independent interface, like this:

```
// create a new class based on the two interface classes
class CDumbX: public IGraphics, public ISound
{
public:
// implement IUnknown here
virtual HRESULT __stdcall QueryInterface(const IId& iid,
(void **)ip)
{ /* implementation */ }

// this method increases the interfaces reference count
virtual ULONG __stdcall Addref()
{ /* implementation */}

// this method decreases the interfaces reference count
virtual ULONG __stdcall Release()
{ /* implementation */}
```

```
// implement each interface
virtual int InitGraphics(int mode)
                     { /*implementation */}
virtual int SetPixel(int x, int y, int c)
                     {/*implementation */}
virtual int InitSound(int driver)
                     { /*implementation */}
virtual int PlaySound(int note, int vol)
                     { /*implementation */}
private:
// locals..
};
```

Of course, implementation involves a billion more details, but at least you have an idea of what a COM object looks like. To complete the COM objects, you need to add the code for all the functions and then implement the IUnknown interface, which means computing unique IIDs (by using the Microsoft program GUIDGEN.EXE) for the two interfaces and then making QueryInterface() obtain a pointer to the requested interface. And lastly, you need a way to create the COM object itself — CDumbX. Whether you use a .DLL or something else depends on the final implementation of the COM object; in most cases, the function that creates the initial COM object from which all interfaces are queried is called CreateInstance(), but you should never have to use this function with DirectX. DirectX puts wrappers around all the COM stuff to make it easier for you.

Using COM with DirectX and C/C++

Chapter 8 gets into all the details of using COM with DirectX, but for now, I just want to give you an idea of how to create and use a DirectX COM object, without getting hung up on COM stuff and pointers.

As you can imagine from the preceding COM discussion, lots of virtual things are going on, and you're going to be using function pointers a bit to access the functions of the COM interfaces. A function pointer is just like any other pointer, except that it points to a function instead of a variable or record. The cool thing about a function pointer is that you can point it to different functions and call it without changing one line of code. Take a look at Figure 7-7 to see how function pointers work.

For example, suppose that you have a function that plots a pixel on a display device SetPixelX(int x, int y, int color). The function takes *x, y,* and the color of the pixel. But now imagine that you have 3 or

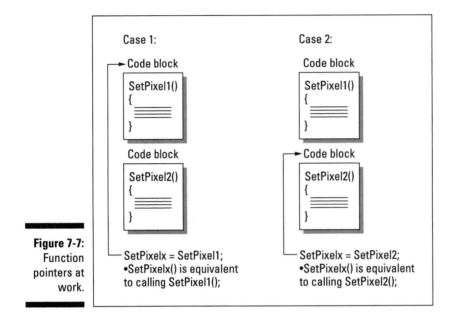

Figure 7-7:
Function
pointers at
work.

maybe 300 different display devices. What a pain to write your application, go through the code to find every single example of the call to the graphics function, and adjust for whatever display device is being used. But if you write a SetPixelX() for each display device, you can use a function pointer to make the call instead of making an explicit call. Then by changing the function pointer to the appropriate function in the initialization section of your program, you don't have to make a hundred changes in your code. Here's an example:

```
int SetPixel1(int x, int y, int color)
{ /* sets a pixel on a raster screen /*}

int SetPixel2(int x, int y, int color)
{ /* sets a pixel on a plotter */ }

// this is a function pointer; notice the position of *
int (* SetPixelX)(int x, int y, int color);
```

Now with the real functions and the pointer in hand, you can point the function pointer to either function, like this:

```
SetPixelX = SetPixel1;
```

or

```
SetPixelX = SetPixel2;
```

Then in your code, you make calls to the display function like this:

```
SetPixelX(x,y,c);
```

But the function can be pointing to either `SetPixel1()` or `SetPixel2()`, and that's the cool part. Now you see how powerful function pointers are and why COM uses virtual functions. COM creates a list of function pointers in what is called the *VTABLE*. You can then use this VTABLE to access any functions that have been plugged into it. I'm belaboring this point for the sole reason that C has no way to access VTABLEs implicitly because C doesn't know what a class is — but in C++, access is automatic.

Here's how you use COM to create a COM DirectDraw object:

```
LPDIRECTDRAW lpdd; // a pointer to the DirectDraw interface

// create the component and obtain a pointer to interface
DirectDrawCreate(NULL,&lpdd,NULL);
```

Now, what's really happening under the hood is that a function something like `CreateInstance()` is being called to create the COM object, and a `.DLL` is loaded, but this process is hidden by macros and wrappers. After the call, `lpdd` points to the DirectDraw interface and can be used to access the methods or functions that DirectDraw supports. One such function is to change the video resolution `SetDisplayMode()`. Here's how you use the interface pointer to make the call:

```
// now set the display mode
lpdd->SetDisplayMode(320,240,8);
```

In general, most DirectX calls look like

```
interface_ptr->function_name(parms...);
```

And that's it. Just one teeny-weeny pointer! And of course, DirectDraw has a number of interfaces itself, but you can get to them all from the initial `lpdd` interface pointer. That's one of the rules of COM: After you have an interface, you can get to any other interface within the component from that interface.

Finally, after you're done with an interface, you must call `Release()` on it, like this:

```
lpdd->Release();
```

The future of DirectX

As is the case with all Microsoft products, DirectX is out of version control. By the time I finish this sentence, a new version will probably be out. However, after Version 3.0, the foundation of DirectX was fairly solid, and by Version 5.0, everything really works well. So as a programmer, you probably won't be using much more than what was available in Version 3.0, let alone all the stuff in 6.0.

However, with the release of Version 5.0, Microsoft decided to take DirectX to the next level and created a whole slew of DirectX-based products and technologies. Here are a few:

✔ **DirectAnimation:** Performs graphics animation on the desktop and in Web browsers; basically competes with ShockWave

✔ **DirectShow:** Allows playback of numerous video and audio media such as .AVI; replaces ActiveMovie

✔ **DirectModel:** Helps in the construction, control, and use of 3D computer meshes for games and multimedia

✔ **DirectScript:** Helps networking and Web-page creators with scripting and interfacing to BackOffice

And then on top of these technologies, Microsoft is creating yet others, so the best thing to do is go to the Microsoft World Wide Web site (at www.microsoft.com) to keep up-to-date.

As far as the future for games and graphics, you'll see more Direct3D (yuck!). And hopefully a version of OpenGL (Graphics Language) for DirectX called DirectGL. Also, DirectX-capable games will soon contain more support for HMDs (Head Mounted Displays) and virtual-reality applications, which are going to start coming back now that we really do have the technology.

Writing DirectX/Win32 Applications: Yes, It Can Be Done!

DirectX, Win32, Windows, and COM all work together very well. You just write a skeleton Windows application (such as WINX.CPP back in Chapter 6) and then create your real application by using the functionality of DirectX instead of GDI. But if you need to use GDI or Win32, you can without any problems.

DirectX isn't built into every user's computer. It's an add-on .DLL library that must be loaded on the client machine by you, the game programmer, or previously by the user or another game. So you must make sure that the players of your game can get DirectX if they don't have it. However, this issue is becoming less important now that Windows 98 and Windows NT 5.0 both have DirectX built in, so at least most of, if not all, the new computers sold after the release of these operating systems have DirectX loaded.

Chapter 8

Getting to Know DirectDraw

• •

In This Chapter

▶ Cooperating with Windows

▶ Changing video modes

• •

DirectDraw is the drawing component of DirectX and is the most important of the components. Not only does it let you create 32-bit high-resolution games, but with it, you can almost circumvent Windows and — better yet — get rid of GDI. And if you're the type who has "DOS Forever" tattooed on your arm, you'll be happy to know that when you use DirectDraw, you're creating a DirectX application that's based on a shell such as `WINX.CPP`, which is almost like a DOS application. (For more about `WINX.CPP`, see Chapter 6.)

As one of the largest parts of DirectX (second only to Direct3D), DirectDraw can do a great deal. But you don't need to know everything about it to work effectively with it. This chapter covers the major aspects of DirectDraw. For more-advanced stuff, such as animation, see Chapter 9. If you're interested in anything beyond that, these chapters give you the tools to figure it out.

Introducing DirectDraw

DirectDraw is implemented in run-time as a `.DLL` or a set of `.DLL`s. But as long as DirectX has been installed on the computer, you don't need to worry about the physical implementation of the DirectX COM objects; all you need to worry about are the interfaces. (If you're a little shaky on the terminology in this section, take a look at Chapter 7 for a discussion of DirectX and the COM.) Figure 8-1 illustrates the interconnections between the run-time modules, the game executable, and the compiler.

To write a DirectX application that uses DirectDraw, you need only two files in your project:

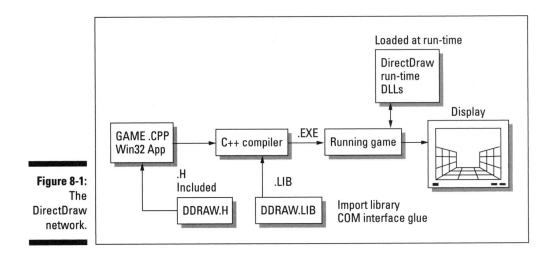

Figure 8-1:
The
DirectDraw
network.

> ✔ DDRAW.H: The header file for DirectDraw
>
> ✔ DDRAW.LIB: The library file that contains all the code, imports, and
> COM object .DLL loaders

You can find both files in the \SDK subfolder of your DirectX installation
under \INC and \LIB. Depending on your compiler, you need to either copy
the files into your local working directory or point your compiler's include
and library directories to them (I usually choose the latter method). In
either case, you must include DDRAW.H with all your program projects, and
you *must* use the C++ compiler, *not* the C compiler. In addition, you need to
add DDRAW.LIB to your project unless you tell your compiler to link it in
with the default library list.

Interfacing to DirectDraw

Every COM component has a number of interfaces, and DirectDraw is no
different. You must communicate with the component through these interfaces, period. Figure 8-2 diagrams all the DirectDraw interfaces.

The interfaces of DirectDraw are a bit arbitrary in their names and functionality from a software-design perspective. I think that the designers could
have selected the interfaces differently, but all my crank calls late at night to
the designers didn't seem to have an effect; so this is what we're stuck with.
Each interface is supposed to *model,* or represent, a different part of the
video system:

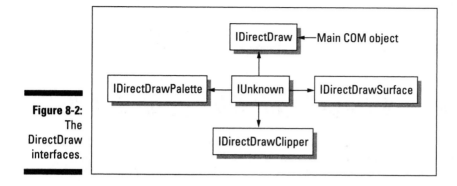

- ✔ IUnknown: The interface class that all interfaces must be derived from.

- ✔ IDirectDraw: Represents the video card. Use this interface to select video modes and set the overall system-cooperation level. It's the main interface (the core) of the COM object that you create; from it, you request other interfaces. You may have more than one DirectDraw object; therefore, you can drive more than one video card and display with the same computer — *MMS* (Multiple Monitor Support).

- ✔ IDirectDrawSurface: Represents the video memory or the drawing surface(s) that you draw on. However, DirectDraw surfaces can also be created in system memory so that you can transfer graphics from system memory to video memory by using hardware.

- ✔ IDirectDrawPalette: Represents the color palette associated with the drawing surface. This interface is most important in 256-color modes and Windows modes that have palettes. In Hi-Color or True Color modes, this interface isn't as important.

- ✔ IDirectDrawClipper: Represents a DirectDraw *clipper,* which is a set of rectangles that DirectDraw can draw into. This interface manages clipping rectangles and acts like a rendering filter. It's most important when running in windowed modes.

Of course, you need to know all the functions within each interface. I show you all the important functions (or *methods,* for C++ fanatics); if you want to know more, refer to the amazingly thorough DirectX SDK Help.

Here's a quick overview of how you use each interface:

1. **Create a DirectDraw object and obtain access to the main interface** IDirectDraw.

2. **Set a video mode and cooperation level; from there, create one or more DirectDraw surfaces (**IDirectDrawSurface**) to draw on.**

3. **Depending on the color depth, you may create a palette (IDirectDrawPalette).**

4. **Create a clipper (IDirectDrawClipper), if desired.**

Creating a DirectDraw Object with C/C++

Because DirectX and Windows are so well integrated, all you need to do to get DirectDraw working is create a DirectDraw object by creating a minimal Windows application and a single window for DirectDraw (and DirectX) to anchor itself to.

The window is more of a formality than anything else, but it is the conduit that all the DirectX components communicate through. So assume that you have created a window and have a working Windows application that does nothing — something like WINX.CPP, which you find on the CD that comes with this book. Then just add the header file DDRAW.H and the library DDRAW.LIB to your application, and you're ready to code. Of course, all the demos I supply on the CD include any necessary headers, which you should place in your current working directory if you want to compile. Before you create a DirectDraw object, be aware of the following about data structures:

- ✔ DirectX and, hence, DirectDraw have a veritable plethora of data structures, and these data structures are nested, with lots of fields in them — an inefficient design at times, but all part of designing with future developments in mind. I show you what you need to know as I go.

- ✔ The most important rule about DirectX data structures is that just about every one of them has a dwSize field, which indicates the size of the data structure and is used to compute the actual length of variant-length data structures that DirectX uses. *You must fill in this field yourself* — don't assume that Windows will do it for you. Leaving out this single assignment is the cause of most DirectX problems.

To create a DirectDraw COM object, use the function DirectDrawCreate(), which has the following prototype:

```
HRESULT DirectDrawCreate(GUID FAR *lpGUID,
                         LPDIRECTDRAW FAR *lplpDD,
                         IUnknown FAR *pUnkOuter);
```

- ✔ lpGuid: A GUID (Globally Unique Identifier) that selects the type of video driver you want to use. NULL selects the default driver — meaning the current driver.

✔ **lplpDD:** Where the function places the address of the COM interface, if successful.

✔ **PUnkOuter:** An advanced feature; always set it to NULL.

Notice that the return type is HRESULT, which is a standard return type for many DirectX calls. You must test the return value against predefined constants rather than test it for TRUE, FALSE, or NULL. In general, if a function worked, it returns DD_OK; otherwise, it returns something else. Thus, always test for DD_OK to see whether a function was successful.

Here's the code for creating a DirectDraw object:

```
LPDIRECTDRAW lpdd; // pointer to interface object

// create object and test for error
if (DirectDrawCreate(NULL,&lpdd,NULL)!=DD_OK)
    { /* error */ }
```

If the call was successful, lpdd points to a valid DirectDraw object interface, and you're free to use *lpdd* to call functions. But remember that all functions (methods) are in a virtual function table, or VTABLE; therefore, you must use the pointer dereferencing syntax:

```
lpdd->function(parms...);
```

Also, after you're done using the DirectDraw interface, you must release it when your application terminates, like this:

```
lpdd->Release();
```

PROG8_1.CPP on the CD is an example of creating and destroying a DirectDraw object. This program is based on the WinX game-console shell (see Chapter 6), so the object is created in Game_Init(), like this:

```
int Game_Init(void *parms)
{
// initialize game here

// create object and test for error
if (DirectDrawCreate(NULL,&lpdd,NULL)!=DD_OK)
    return(0);

// return success
return(1);
} // end Game_Init
```

And the DirectDraw object is released in `Game_Shutdown()`, like this:

```
int Game_Shutdown(void *parms)
{
// shutdown and release are resources here

// release the DirectDraw object
if (lpdd!=NULL)
   lpdd->Release();

// return success
return(1);
} // end Game_Shutdown
```

Notice the test to see whether `lpdd` is non-`NULL` — good defensive programming. Releasing a `NULL` object probably wouldn't hurt, but it may, so this test is insurance. In a hundred years, releasing a `NULL` COM object could result in a wormhole or something, so better safe than in the Delta quadrant!

Playing Nice with Windows: Cooperation

After creating a DirectDraw object, you need to set the *cooperation level*. Windows is a cooperative, shared environment, so DirectDraw (as all of DirectX) must cooperate with Windows — it can't just take over the entire video system, at least not without giving Windows a memo first!

You control the following kinds of things with the cooperation-level setting:

- Whether you're creating a windowed or a full-screen application
- Whether you want to use Mode X video modes (320 x 200, 320 x 240)
- Whether the user can Ctrl+Alt+Delete out of the game

The function used to set the cooperation level is `SetCooperativeLevel()` — now that's a good name! Here's the prototype:

```
HRESULT SetCooperativeLevel(HWND hWnd, // handle to window
            DWORD dwFlags); // cooperation level flags
```

Table 8-1 lists the various flag settings.

Table 8-1	DirectDraw Cooperation-Level Flags
Value	*Meaning*
DDSCL_ALLOWMODEX	Allows the use of Mode X display modes. This flag must be used with the DDSCL_EXCLUSIVE and DDSCL_FULLSCREEN flags.
DDSCL_ALLOWREBOOT	Allows Ctrl+Alt+Delete to function while in exclusive (full-screen) mode.
DDSCL_EXCLUSIVE	Requests exclusive access. This flag must be used with the DDSCL_FULLSCREEN flag.
DDSCL_FULLSCREEN	Indicates that DirectDraw will update the entire video display and Windows GDI won't write to the display. This flag must be used with the DDSCL_EXCLUSIVE flag.
DDSCL_NORMAL	Indicates that the application will function as a regular Windows application. This flag can't be used with the DDSCL_ALLOWMODEX, DDSCL_EXCLUSIVE, or DDSCL_FULLSCREEN flag.
DDSCL_NOWINDOWCHANGES	Indicates that DirectDraw can't minimize or restore the application window on activation.

The flags may sound a bit confusing, but here are some general rules:

✔ To create a windowed DirectX application, use DDSCL_NORMAL and set the cooperation level like this, where lpdd is the DirectDraw interface and hwnd is the handle to the target window (usually the only window in your application):

```
lpdd->SetCooperativeLevel(hwnd, DDSCL_NORMAL);
```

✔ To create a full-screen application, use DDSCL_ALLOWMODEX | DDSCL_FULLSCREEN | DDSCL_EXCLUSIVE | DDSCL_ALLOWREBOOT. Even though your application may not use Mode X, adding the flag doesn't hurt. Here's how to set the cooperation level:

```
lpdd->SetCooperativeLevel(hwnd,DDSCL_ALLOWMODEX |
    DDSCL_FULLSCREEN | DDSCL_EXCLUSIVE | DDSCL_ALLOWREBOOT);
```

With this flag setting, your application can go into Mode X as well as normal video modes. In addition, the user can kill the application with Ctrl+Alt+Delete, which is a nice feature because most games created from the beginning of time to the present allow the user to exit via Ctrl+Alt+Delete.

Here's a final example of creating a DirectDraw object and setting the cooperation level:

```
LPDIRECTDRAW lpdd; // a DirectDraw object pointer

// create window and get handle in hwnd..

// create directdraw object
if (DirectDrawCreate(NULL,&lpdd,NULL)!=DD_OK)
  { /* error*/ }

// set cooperation level to windowed mode normal
lpdd->SetCooperativeLevel(hwnd,DDSCL_NORMAL);
```

Simple as 3.1415926! Now, to see `SetCooperativeLevel()` in action, take a look at `PROG8_2.CPP` on the CD. This program implements the new cooperation level setting. The code is placed in the `Game_Init()` and `Game_Shutdown()` functions of the WinX console. The program doesn't do a whole lot, though; it just kind of sits there.

If you take a gander at the DirectX SDK for `SetCooperativeLevel()`, you see something like `IDirectDraw2::SetCooperativeLevel(...)`, which may look a little alien to C programmers. If you're a C++ programmer, it should look familiar, but what is `IDirectDraw2`? It's the second version of the original interface `IDirectDraw`. As each version of DirectX comes out, Microsoft changes the code. Changing an interface is illegal, so Microsoft must come up with another interface that takes the place of the last; that's where `IDirectDraw2` comes from. You don't need to worry about it — just use the `SetCooperativeLevel()` function, and COM takes care of the rest.

Selecting Video Modes

Changing the video mode is one of the most important features of DirectDraw. In the Win32 API, changing the video mode is possible, but it's like mixing matter with antimatter — you just don't do it! With DirectDraw, this task is almost trivial.

The function to change video modes is `SetDisplayMode()`, and you use it to select the horizontal and vertical resolution along with the color depth in bits per pixel. As long as your video card can support the mode and you have enough memory for it, DirectDraw computes the proper parameterizations to send to the video driver for the mode that you request. And abracadabra — the screen changes modes. Here's the prototype of `SetDisplayMode()`:

```
HRESULT SetDisplayMode(
    DWORD dwWidth,        // width of mode in pixels
    DWORD dwHeight,       // height of mode in pixels
    DWORD dwBPP,          // bits per pixel
    DWORD dwRefreshRate,  // refresh rate, set to 0
    DWORD dwFlags);       // flags, set to 0
```

At the end of the function signature are a couple of extra parameters:
dwRefreshRate and dwFlags, which are advanced features that you don't
need to worry about. Set them to 0 or leave them out — they default to 0.

Bringing DirectX Online

Here's a complete example of how you create a DirectDraw object, set the
cooperation level, and request a video mode of 640 x 480 with 8-bit color:

```
LPDIRECTDRAW lpdd; // a DirectDraw object pointer

// create window and get handle in hwnd..

// create directdraw object
if (DirectDrawCreate(NULL,&lpdd,NULL)!=DD_OK)
   { /* error*/ }

// set cooperation level to windowed mode normal
lpdd->SetCooperativeLevel(hwnd,DDSCL_ALLOWMODEX |
  DDSCL_FULLSCREEN | DDSCL_EXCLUSIVE | DDSCL_ALLOWREBOOT);

// set the display mode
if ((lpdd->SetDisplayMode(640,480,8))!=DD_OK)
   { /* error */ }
```

This code tests the result of the function call for an error. Of course, it only
tests for an error; if you want more information, you can compare the
HRESULT to a number of error constants that SetDisplayMode() may
return (refer to your DirectX SDK for more information on error codes).

Furthermore, you don't need the DDSCL_ALLOWMODEX flag unless you want
Mode X modes available, but it doesn't hurt even if you don't. Here's how
you request the 320-x-240, 256-color Mode X mode:

```
if ((lpdd->SetDisplayMode(320,240,8))!=DD_OK)
   { /* error */ }
```

And here's how you request an 800 x 600, 16-bit Hi-Color mode:

```
if ((lpdd->SetDisplayMode(800,600,16))!=DD_OK)
   { /* error */ }
```

This mode requires a minimum of 800 x 600 x 2 bytes (960,000) of video memory to be satisfied. So you need at least a 1MB video card.

`SetDisplayMode()` is one of the easiest functions to use in DirectDraw. Now, you may be wondering whether you can change the video mode multiple times during the life of your program. The answer is yes; each video change incurs a rather ugly monitor hiccup in most cases, but other than that, you can switch video modes as much as you like.

One of the tricks to performing smooth video-mode switches is this: When you create your main window, create it as `WS_POPUP` instead of `WS_OVERLAPPEDWINDOW`. Doing so creates a window, with no borders or controls, that looks like a full-screen mode. When you create the window, be sure to make it as big as the current video mode. Remember that you can request the current size of the screen by using `GetSystemMetrics()`. Here's an example:

```
// create a full-screen pop-up window
if (!(hwnd = CreateWindow(WINDOW_CLASS_NAME, // class
         "WinX Game Console",    // title
         WS_POPUP | WS_VISIBLE, // flags
         0,0,                   // x,y position
         GetSystemMetrics(SM_CXSCREEN), // max width
         GetSystemMetrics(SM_CYSCREEN), // max height
         NULL,    // handle to parent
         NULL,    // handle to menu
         hinstance,// instance
         NULL)))   // creation parms
return(0);
```

For a working example of all this stuff, look at `PROG8_3.CPP` on the CD. This program creates a DirectDraw object, sets the cooperation level, and sets the video mode to 640 x 480 with 8-bit color. For fun, you can try rewriting the program to change the video modes with a key press or even a menu.

Chapter 9
Using the DirectDraw Crayons

*I*n this chapter, I show you how to put DirectDraw to work and actually draw something on the screen. You see how to plot pixels, change colors, work with surfaces, and more. But be careful, the chapter offers a lot of vocabulary to absorb, and the information is important, so take your time.

Painting on the Canvas: DirectDraw Surfaces

DirectDraw refers to the displayable memory as *surfaces,* which is where you draw your imagery, whether it's 2D or 3D. Figure 9-1 illustrates the concept of surfaces. In most cases, you have at least one surface — the *primary* surface, which represents the visible video screen itself and in reality is mapped directly to the video memory on the video card (VRAM).

Although a surface is nothing more than memory, a number of concepts go along with it:

✔ **A surface can be any size.** The primary surface must be the same size as the current screen resolution, but other surfaces can be any size you want, as Figure 9-2 shows.

✔ **You can create surfaces in video memory (as long as you have room) or in system memory.** Of course, many operations are faster with video memory, but if you run out of video memory, you can create surfaces in system memory just as well.

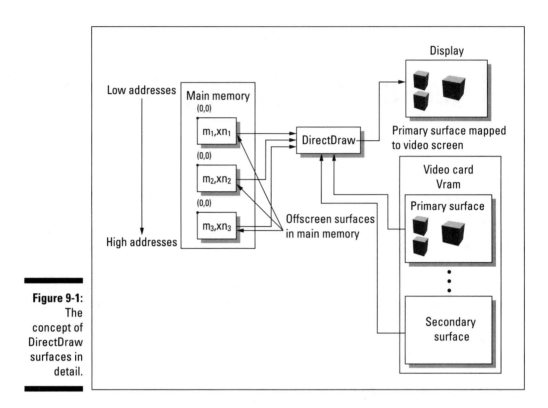

Display

Primary surface mapped to video screen

Low addresses

Main memory
(0,0)

m_1, xn_1

(0,0)

m_2, xn_2

(0,0)

m_3, xn_3

High addresses

DirectDraw

Offscreen surfaces in main memory

Video card Vram

Primary surface

Secondary surface

Figure 9-1: The concept of DirectDraw surfaces in detail.

Memory operations that are performed from video memory to video memory are faster in many cases because the memory can be moved on-board without using the slow system bus. Moreover, many video cards have multiported VRAM (video RAM), so you can access the memory at the same time that it's being rasterized into video.

✔ **All surfaces have the same properties, as far as bit depth and color space.** When you create a surface, it's compatible with the primary surface (as long as you created it from the same DirectDraw object), and you're able to copy data back and forth. This compatibility is necessary because the data in each surface must be in the same format — DirectDraw would be confused if you told it to copy an image from a surface that had 8 bits of color to a surface that had 24.

A typical Windows game has the following:

✔ **Primary display surface:** As I mention in the introduction to this section, the primary surface represents the visible video screen itself and is mapped directly to the video memory on the video card (VRAM).

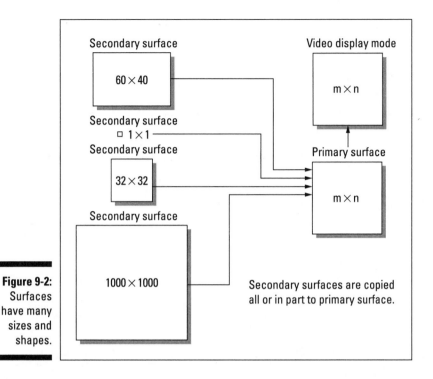

Secondary surface

60 × 40

Secondary surface
□ 1 × 1

Secondary surface

32 × 32

Secondary surface

1000 × 1000

Video display mode

m × n

Primary surface

m × n

Secondary surfaces are copied
all or in part to primary surface.

Figure 9-2:
Surfaces
have many
sizes and
shapes.

✔ **Secondary display surface for animation:** Also called the *backbuffer,* this surface has the same structure as the primary one, but is invisible and is used as a workspace to render the next frame of animation.

✔ **Offscreen surfaces:** These plain surfaces are used to hold bitmaps or *sprites,* or screen items (characters or spaceships, for example) that you want to quickly display by using hardware acceleration.

Working with primary surfaces

Creating a primary surface is the absolute minimum you need to do to draw anything. To create any surface, you need to fill out a DDSURFACEDESC data structure with the proper values and call CreateSurface() to actually create the surface.

Take a look at the CreateSurface() function first, and then I show you the details of the data structures:

```
HRESULT CreateSurface(
        LPDDSURFACEDESC lpDDSurfaceDesc,
        LPDIRECTDRAWSURFACE FAR *lplpDDSurface,
        IUnknown FAR *pUnkOuter);
```

✔ lpDDSurfaceDesc: Pointer to a DirectDraw surface description structure. Within this pointer, you set various fields that describe the surface you want to request.

✔ lplpDDSurface: Pointer to a DirectDraw surface interface to be returned from the function if successful.

✔ pUnkOuter: An advanced feature, used for COM aggregation; always make it NULL.

As always, the function returns DD_OK if successful or various other constants otherwise.

The DirectDraw surface descriptor structure

Now take a look at the DDSURFACEDESC structure, the key to creating a surface:

```
typedef struct _DDSURFACEDESC {
  DWORD dwSize;  // the size of this structure in bytes
                 // this field must be set by you
  DWORD dwFlags; // flags field indicating which fields
                 // of this structure are valid with data
  DWORD dwHeight;// height of surface
  DWORD dwWidth; // width of surface
  union
   {
   LONG  lPitch;           // number of bytes per line
   DWORD dwLinearSize;     // unused
   };
  DWORD dwBackBufferCount;  // number of backbuffers
  union
   {
   DWORD dwMipMapCount;      // number of mip levels
   DWORD dwZBufferBitDepth;  // size of z buffer
   DWORD dwRefreshRate;      // refresh rate
   };
  DWORD         dwAlphaBitDepth; // number of bits for alpha
  DWORD         dwReserved;
  LPVOID        lpSurface;       // pointer to surface memory
  DDCOLORKEY ddckCKDestOverlay;  // destination overlay
  DDCOLORKEY ddckCKDestBlt;      // destination
  DDCOLORKEY ddckCKSrcOverlay;   // source overlay
  DDCOLORKEY ddckCKSrcBlt;       // source blit
  DDPIXELFORMAT ddpfPixelFormat; // pixel format of surface
  DDSCAPS    ddsCaps;            // capabilities structure (important)
} DDSURFACEDESC;
```

Table 9-1 lists the various flags settings needed to define which members of the DDSURFACEDESC are valid.

Table 9-1   Flags Settings for DDSURFACEDESC dwFlags

Value	Meaning If Set
DDSD_ALL	All input members are valid.
DDSD_ALPHABITDEPTH	dwAlphaBitDepth member is valid.
DDSD_BACKBUFFERCOUNT	dwBackBufferCount member is valid.
DDSD_CAPS	ddsCaps member is valid.
DDSD_CKDESTBLT	ddckCKDestBlt member is valid.
DDSD_CKDESTOVERLAY	ddckCKDestOverlay member is valid.
DDSD_CKSRCBLT	ddckCKSrcBlt member is valid.
DDSD_CKSRCOVERLAY	ddckCKSrcOverlay member is valid.
DDSD_HEIGHT	dwHeight member is valid.
DDSD_LINEARSIZE	Unused.
DDSD_LPSURFACE	lpSurface member is valid.
DDSD_MIPMAPCOUNT	dwMipMapCount member is valid.
DDSD_PITCH	lPitch member is valid.
DDSD_PIXELFORMAT	ddpfPixelFormat member is valid.
DDSD_REFRESHRATE	dwRefreshRate member is valid.
DDSD_WIDTH	dwWidth member is valid.
DDSD_ZBUFFERBITDEPTH	dwZBufferBitDepth member is valid.

DDSURFACEDESC is rather complex, as you can see. It's used as a communications channel to surfaces. You can set fields within it to create or change a surface, or you can request fields to be filled in from a specific surface. I don't go over *all* the fields, just the ones you need right now. I cover the other fields if and when you need them. The important fields are

✔ dwSize: Must be set by you to the size of a DDSURFACEDESC structure.

✔ dwFlags: Contains the valid field information flags. In other words, you must set the flags field to the logical OR of all the fields that you want to modify or read. Table 9-2 lists the valid flags.

✔ dwHeight: Contains the height of the surface, in pixels.

✔ dwWidth: Contains the width of the surface, in pixels.

✔ lpSurface: Contains a pointer to the VRAM of the surface when the surface is locked. *Locking* is a procedure to instruct DirectDraw that you're going to mess with a portion of surface memory.

✔ dwBackBufferCount: Indicates the number of offscreen buffers or pages. DirectDraw allows you to create multiple surfaces, so you can create smooth animation by drawing on one while displaying another.

✔ lPitch: Contains the *memory pitch* of the surface — that is, the number of bytes per lines.

✔ ddsCaps: Contains further capabilities of the surface. It's actually just a DWORD flags register, as shown:

```
typedef struct _DDSCAPS
{
DWORD dwCaps; // contains the surface's capabilities
} DDSCAPS,FAR* LPDDSCAPS;
```

✔ dwCaps: Holds the capabilities that you want a surface to have. Most of them are advanced; Table 9-2 contains only a partial list, but it should be enough to get you started.

Table 9-2   DirectDraw DDSCAPS Surface Capabilities Flags

Value	Meaning
DDSCAPS_BACKBUFFER	The surface will be a backbuffer in a flipping chain.
DDSCAPS_COMPLEX	The surface is part of a complex surface, having more than a primary surface.
DDSCAPS_FLIP	The surface is flippable.
DDSCAPS_FRONTBUFFER	This surface is the first, or *frontbuffer,* in a flipping structure.
DDSCAPS_MODEX	The surface is a 320 x 200 or 320 x 240 Mode X surface.
DDSCAPS_OFFSCREENPLAIN	The surface is any offscreen surface that is not an overlay, texture, z-buffer, frontbuffer, backbuffer, or alpha surface. Normally, you use this flag for sprites and bitmaps.
DDSCAPS_OWNDC	The surface will have a Windows device context association for a long period.
DDSCAPS_PRIMARYSURFACE	The surface is the primary surface — that is, visible and being rendered.

Value	Meaning
DDSCAPS_STANDARDVGAMODE	The surface is a standard VGA mode surface, not a Mode X surface.
DDSCAPS_SYSTEMMEMORY	The surface memory should be allocated in system memory.

After reviewing all the data structures and flags, you should be thoroughly "frazzled." If you're not, go back and read them until you are. Microsoft may have been a little overzealous in this area, but you actually need to know very little of this stuff to get something working.

Creating a primary surface

In review, to create a primary surface, you must set up a DDSURFACEDESC description structure with the appropriate setting and flags within the DDSCAPS substructure, then make a call to CreateSurface(). Here's the general flow of the sequence to create a surface without error checking:

```
// pointer to DirectDraw object
LPDIRECTDRAW lpdd;

// used to hold the DirectDraw surface description
DDSURFACEDESC ddsd;

// where the interface pointer will be placed
// when the surface is created
LPDIRECTDRAWSURFACE lpddsprimary;

// create DirectDraw object
DirectDrawCreate(NULL,&lpdd,NULL)

// set cooperation level
lpdd->SetCooperativeLevel(hwnd, DDSCL_ALLOWREBOOT |
          DDSCL_ALLOWMODEX | DDSCL_FULLSCREEN |
          DDSCL_EXCLUSIVE );

// now set the display mode; assume constants defined
lpdd->SetDisplayMode(SCREEN_WIDTH,SCREEN_HEIGHT,
                  SCREEN_BPP);

// create the primary surface
// manually set the size; very important
ddsd.dwSize  = sizeof(ddsd);
```

(continued)

(continued)

```
// the only field you modify, so you
// must indicate in the flags that you want a primary
// drawing surface; in this case, you don't have to define
// anything else, because DirectDraw already knows the
// resolution and color of the video mode
ddsd.dwFlags = DDSD_CAPS;

// set the capabilities to what you want, a primary surf
ddsd.ddsCaps.dwCaps = DDSCAPS_PRIMARYSURFACE;

// create the surface and check for an error
if (lpdd->CreateSurface(&ddsd,&lpddsprimary,NULL)!=DD_OK)
    { /* error */ }
```

The error codes for `CreateSurface()` are in the DirectX SDK as usual, but testing for `DD_OK` is usually all you'll need to do unless you really need to know exactly what went wrong.

As a good game programmer, you must always remember to `Release()` each COM interface. In this case, because the surface derives from the DirectDraw object, you must first `Release()` the surface interface and then the DirectDraw object itself, like a stack. Here's how:

```
// first release the surface, but check for NULL
if (lpddsprimary)
    lpddsprimary->Release();

// now release the DirectDraw object itself
if (lpdd)
    lpdd->Release();
```

This code creates a DirectX application in any resolution, with a primary drawing surface attached and referenced by `lpddprimary`. For an example, check out `PROG9_1.CPP` on the CD, which implements this code and places the video card in 640 x 480 x 8. If your card can't support the mode, the program notifies you. Of course, all you see is a blank screen because you don't know how to draw on the primary surface yet. Guess what's next?

In general, I use two different conventions to write resolution: (Width x Height x Total_Colors) and (Width x Height x Bits_Per_Pixel). Therefore, 320 x 240 x 256 is the same as 320 x 240 x 8; likewise, 640 x 480 x 65,536 is the same as 640 x 480 x 16. Sometimes one form is more convenient than the other, depending on the context.

Linear versus nonlinear memory

A surface is a chunk of memory that exists on the video card or in system memory, but it is not necessarily linear (as the preceding section assumes). Figure 9-3 shows a surface that is 640 x 480 with a single byte per pixel. So you may think that this surface has 640 bytes per line and 480 lines. Those numbers are correct for linear-memory video modes but not for *nonlinear*.

If your video card can support the mode you're requesting in linear-memory mode, the *horizontal pixel pitch* is equal to the *horizontal memory pitch*. So if you have a resolution that's 640 pixels wide in 8-bit color, then there are 640 bytes of memory per video line. However, this number may not be the case in nonlinear modes.

A number of video cards (usually older ones) can't address high-resolution video modes linearly. So even though you may think that a 640 x 480 x 256-color mode has a memory pitch of 640 bytes per line, it may not! To get to the next video line, you may have to add something like 1,024 instead of 640. Here's an example:

```
UCHAR *video_buffer;
// point video buffer to primary surface...
// (check out the section "The details of rendering to the primary surface" for
            this code)

// write a single pixel; color is a palette index
video_buffer[x + 1024*y] = color;
```

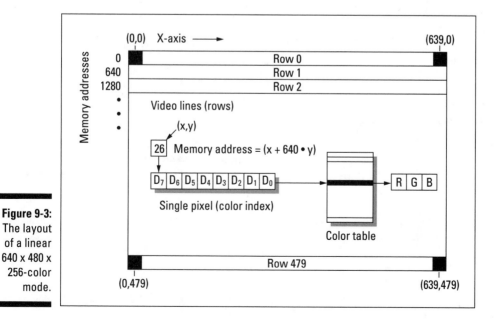

Figure 9-3:
The layout of a linear 640 x 480 x 256-color mode.

Alas, to make things worse, on a card that doesn't support linear memory, not all surfaces are nonlinear. In other words, you may have heterogeneous memory surfaces. For example, a system memory surface that you create is always linear, and when you create more than one surface on the video card itself, the surface may be linear as long as it's not the primary surface.

As you can see, using surfaces comes with plenty of caveats. But luckily, DirectDraw has variables (lpitch for one) that you can consult during run-time to make sure about the linearity of the video mode so that you can write to the surface correctly — and not do something dumb. (Check out Chapter 10 for more information on these variables.)

Basic drawing on the primary surface

To draw on the primary surface, you access it like a contiguous region of memory, where each video line or row increases in memory from left to right and from top to bottom, as Figure 9-4 shows. Therefore, to draw on the screen, you need a pointer to the video memory (surface); *then* you can write into it.

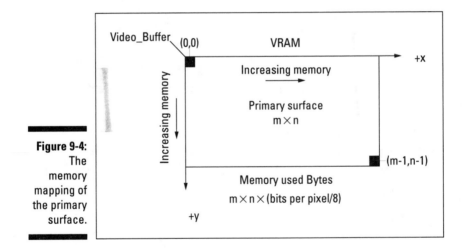

Figure 9-4:
The memory mapping of the primary surface.

For example, assume that you're in a linear 640 x 480 x 8 mode — 1 byte per pixel and 640 bytes per line. To access any pixel (x,y) on the screen, use the following code:

```
// used to access data
UCHAR *video_buffer;


// point video_buffer to primary surface...
// (check out the section "The details of rendering to the primary surface" for
            this code
```

```
// write a single pixel; color is a palette index
video_buffer[x + 640*y] = color;
```

And if you have to set up a 640 x 480 x 16-bit color mode, each pixel value actually contains the RGB values (5 bits each) for the color, and each line has 1,280 bytes because you're working with 2 bytes per pixel (640 x 2). Remember that 8-bit video modes support 256 colors using a palette (see Chapter 5), but 16-bit and higher actually encode the color in the bit pattern. To write a pixel in this mode, do this:

```
// this time, use a 16-bit short
USHORT *video_buffer;

// point video buffer to primary surface...

// write a single pixel; color is a palette index
video_buffer[x + 640*y] = color;
```

This code works because `video_buffer` is now a `USHORT` 16-bit pointer rather than a `UCHAR` 8-bit pointer. Any pointer arithmetic performed on `video_buffer` is scaled by 2 (2 bytes for a `USHORT`), so the code works properly.

The details of rendering to the primary surface

Drawing in DirectDraw is a little different from GDI. GDI has hundreds of functions to draw images, change colors, and so on. DirectDraw has very little rendering support — by design. Most game programmers write their own graphics engines and libraries, so all DirectDraw does is give the game programmer basic color support, access to the video buffer, and high-speed filling and blitting via hardware acceleration (if present). That's more than enough functionality to create any graphics functions that you may need.

The most basic graphics primitive is plotting a single pixel. If you can draw a pixel, you can draw anything. The primary surface is memory mapped to the video screen with (0,0) at the upper-left corner and *x* increasing to the right and *y* increasing down (refer to Figure 9-4). Therefore, to draw a pixel anywhere, all you need are the (x,y) position, the memory pitch per line, and the pixel format. Remember that the pixel format is either a single byte in palletized modes or a 16-, 24-, or 32-bit word in RGB modes.

Drawing in palletized modes

In palettized modes, each pixel on the display surface is represented by a single byte. Each byte is an index into a Color Look Up Table (CLUT) that has the actual RGB values for each color. Hence, palettized modes can be thought of as painting by colors. Each byte on the screen display is a number, and the number is used to look up the color in a color table.

I cover how to control the palette a little later in "Getting Down with Palettes," but for now, just assume that the color palette has some reasonable default values in it — maybe 26 is a blue, 190 a green, and so on. The specifics don't really matter at this point.

To draw on the primary surface, whether palettized or RGB, the first thing you need to do is get a pointer to it, with the Lock() function. Then with the pointer in hand, you can access the display memory and write to it or read from it. After you're done accessing memory, you Unlock() it so that DirectDraw can access it again. Here are the prototypes for Lock() and Unlock() — they're both part of the IDirectDrawSurface interface:

```
HRESULT Lock(
LPRECT lpDestRect,          // rectangle to lock; use NULL to lock
                            // the entire surface
LPDDSURFACEDESC lpDDSD,     // returns the properties of the
                            // surface being locked
DWORD dwFlags,              // control flags
HANDLE hEvent);             // unused; set to NULL
```

The function returns DD_OK if successful. Basically, you pass Lock() the rectangular region that you want locked (NULL locks the whole surface), along with the address of the DDSURFACEDESC structure that on return will receive information of the locked surface and finally the locking flags. These flags, which Table 9-3 shows, control how the surface is to be locked.

Table 9-3	Flags for Lock()
Value	*Meaning*
DDLOCK_READONLY	The surface locked will be readable only.
DDLOCK_SURFACEMEMORYPTR	The surface locked will return a memory pointer to the surface memory in lpSurface. This default action takes place if you don't send any flags.
DDLOCK_WAIT	If the surface can't be locked, wait for it until it can be.
DDLOCK_WRITEONLY	The surface being locked will be written to only.

After you have locked the surface and are done with it, you must unlock it:

```
HRESULT Unlock(LPVOID lpSurfaceData); // pointer to surface
```

In this prototype, lpSurfaceData is the pointer to the memory returned from Lock() in the lpSurface field of LPDDSURFACEDESC.

Or you can pass NULL to Unlock() if you originally locked the entire surface, which would be the case if you passed NULL for the LPRECT field.

You must be careful when computing addresses in display memory. Although most new video cards support linear display memory, some don't, so you need to acquire the correct memory line pitch for the mode you're in.

Here are the steps to plot a single pixel:

1. **Lock the surface.**

2. **Get a pointer to the display surface.**

3. **Compute the pixel address.**

4. **Write the pixel.**

5. **Unlock the surface.**

Here's an example complete with the standard DirectDraw setup calls to plot a pixel at (x,y) with color col:

```
// pointer to DirectDraw object
LPDIRECTDRAW lpdd;

// you use this function to access the surface memory
UCHAR video_buffer = NULL;

// used to hold the DirectDraw surface description
DDSURFACEDESC ddsd;

// primary surface
LPDIRECTDRAWSURFACE lpddsprimary;

// create DirectDraw object
DirectDrawCreate(NULL,&lpdd,NULL)

// set cooperation level
lpdd->SetCooperativeLevel(hwnd, DDSCL_ALLOWREBOOT |
        DDSCL_ALLOWMODEX | DDSCL_FULLSCREEN |
        DDSCL_EXCLUSIVE );

// now set the display mode to 320 x 200 x 256
lpdd->SetDisplayMode(320,200,8);
```

(continued)

(continued)

```
// set up data structure to create the primary surface
ddsd.dwSize  = sizeof(ddsd);
ddsd.dwFlags = DDSD_CAPS;
ddsd.ddsCaps.dwCaps = DDSCAPS_PRIMARYSURFACE;

// create the primary surface
lpdd->CreateSurface(&ddsd,&lpddsprimary,NULL);

// set up the surface description to lock the surface
// zero out the data structure and set its size
memset(&ddsd,0,sizeof(ddsd));
ddsd.dwSize = sizeof(ddsd);

// lock the primary surface
lpddsprimary->Lock(NULL,&ddsd,
            DDLOCK_SURFACEMEMORYPTR | DDLOCK_WAIT,NULL);

// get video pointer
video_buffer = (UCHAR *)ddsd.lpSurface;

//.. use video pointer to write to memory
// notice the use of lPitch (linear pitch)
video_buffer[x + y*ddsd.lPitch] = col;

// unlock the surface
lpddsprimary->Unlock(ddsd.lpSurface);
```

The following code would also work to unlock the surface:

```
// lpddsprimary->Unlock(video_buffer);
```

Even this code would work, because you lock the entire surface:

```
// lpddsprimary->Unlock(NULL);
```

The code is straightforward enough. The key elements are the locking and unlocking sequences. Also, notice the use of lPitch in the address calculation, to ensure that the memory is accessed correctly.

To see the code in action, check out PROG9_2.CPP on the CD, which draws to the primary buffer as in this example.

Drawing in RGB modes

The only difference between drawing in RGB modes and palettized modes is the setting of each pixel. Instead of the data being an index into a color table, the color is an actual RGB data word in 16-, 24-, or 32-bit format. You can use almost the identical code as in the preceding section, with a few small changes. However, you need one macro, to build up the RGB data. Here's a macro to build up a 16-bit RGB word, 5 bits per channel (that's what the MOD 32 is for):

```
#define _RGB16BIT(r,g,b) ((b%32)+((g%32)<<5)+((r%32)<<10))
```

Remember that in 16-bit modes, only 15 of the 16 bits are used (in most cases), so this macro fills them in with the proper shifting. To draw on a primary surface that has 16-bit color or higher, you must create the surface, of course, lock it, and finally write to the surface as before. The only changes are the writing of the pixel and the memory address calculation.

Writing to the primary surface

This section shows you how to write to the primary surface. (For code to create the DirectDraw object and the surface, see Chapter 8.) Here's an example of writing to location (x,y) with a color (r,g,b) in a 640 x 480 x 16 mode:

```
// assume you've created a 640 x 480 x 16-bit color surface

// set up the surface description to lock the surface
memset(&ddsd,0,sizeof(ddsd));
ddsd.dwSize = sizeof(ddsd);

// lock the primary surface
lpddsprimary->Lock(NULL,&ddsd,
              DDLOCK_SURFACEMEMORYPTR | DDLOCK_WAIT,NULL);

// get video pointer
video_buffer = (USHORT *)ddsd.lpSurface;

// use video pointer to write to memory..
// notice the use of lPitch (linear pitch)
// and the division by 2 (>>1); this is needed to keep
// the addressing correct because you're using USHORT
// pointers and lPitch is always in bytes
video_buffer[x + (y*ddsd.lPitch >> 1)]=
                    (USHORT)_RGB16BIT(r,g,b);

// unlock the surface
lpddsprimary->Unlock(ddsd.lpSurface);
```

You can use this code on any 16-bit surface.

Pay close attention to the way that the final array index is calculated. Instead of simply multiplying the *y* coordinate by `lPitch`, I had to divide it by 2. That's because all pointer arithmetic is done on 16-bit boundaries when using `USHORT`s, but `lPitch` is always in terms of bytes. So a `lPitch` of 1,280 (which is correct for a linear 640-word-per-line 16-bit mode) would get converted into 2*1,280 or 2,560 bytes per line when indexing a `USHORT` array! So, depending on how you do your pointer arithmetic, this bug can crop up.

Another, more straightforward way is to use a `UCHAR` pointer, like this:

```
UCHAR video_buffer = (UCHAR *)ddsd.lpSurface;
video_buffer[x*2 + ddsd.lPitch*y] = color;
```

Now you don't need to divide anymore, because you're using 8-bit data. But *x* is off by a factor of 2, so you must multiply that. Although that seems like a problem, it's not. At the top of your rendering loop, you figure out the correct memory addressing values and then just use the constants. To write to a 24- or 32-bit surface, you need a new macro to build the color `WORD` up. For example, a 24-bit color macro looks like this:

```
#define _RGB24BIT(r,g,b) ((b&255)+((g&255)<<8)+((r&255)<<16))
```

Remember that the code for this macro needs to be on the same line!

Many video cards use 32 bits even for 24-bit modes, so the upper 8 bits are always 0.

That's all there is to writing to surfaces. As long as you pay attention to the memory addressing and lock and unlock the surface, you won't have a problem.

As another example, `PROG9_3.CPP` on the CD creates a 640 x 480 x 16-bit display and writes to it. See whether you can successfully change it to 24-bit (assuming that your video card supports that color depth in that resolution).

I left out a lot of error checking in all the code thus far. Please check the `HRESULT`s as much as possible — making further calls with invalid results will cause crashes or lockup. Also, many of the functions return elaborate error codes, so take a look at each function's error codes to see whether they can help you write smarter code.

Creating secondary surfaces

Now I want to show you how to create a secondary (or backbuffer) surface attached to the primary surface for animation.

You use *secondary surfaces* (backbuffers) to perform smooth animation, among other things, by doing the following general steps:

1. **Create a primary surface and a single secondary surface off of the primary surface.**

2. **Draw on the secondary surface while the primary surface is being displayed.**

3. **Instantly switch or flip the surfaces, so that the secondary becomes the primary, and vice-versa, creating smooth animation.**

Figure 9-5 shows this procedure.

Creating a secondary surface off the primary requires only one new call: GetAttachedSurface(). Basically, you create a *complex* primary surface, meaning that it has more than one surface — that is, at least one secondary surface, or backbuffer. Then after creating the primary surface, you query it for the attached surface. The procedure sounds a lot more complex than it really is. Just look at the code (I have boldfaced areas that deal with the setup of the secondary surface, also called the *backbuffer*):

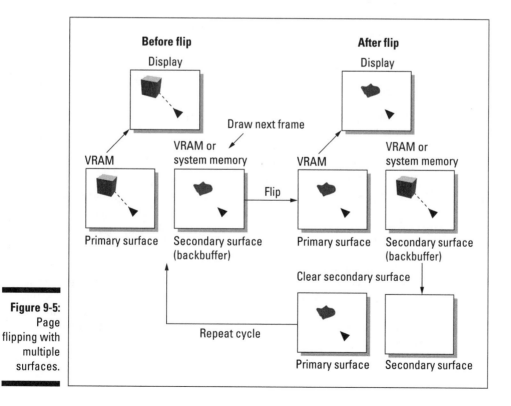

Figure 9-5:
Page flipping with multiple surfaces.

```
// DirectDraw surface description
DDSURFACEDESC ddsd;

// device capabilities structure, used to query for
// secondary backbuffer, among other things
DDSCAPS ddscaps;

LPDIRECTDRAWSURFACE lpddsprimary, // primary surface
        lpddssecondary; // secondary backbuffer surface

// prepare to create primary surface with one backbuffer
memset(ddsd,0,sizeof(ddsd));
ddsd.dwSize = sizeof(ddsd); // DDSURFACEDESC would work, too

// set the flags to validate both the capabilities
// field and the backbuffer count field
ddsd.dwFlags = DDSD_CAPS | DDSD_BACKBUFFERCOUNT;

// you need to let dd know that you want a complex
// flippable surface structure; set flags for that
ddsd.ddsCaps.dwCaps =
  DDSCAPS_PRIMARYSURFACE | DDSCAPS_FLIP | DDSCAPS_COMPLEX;

// set the backbuffer count to 1
ddsd.dwBackBufferCount = 1;

// create the primary surface
lpdd->CreateSurface(&ddsd,&lpddsprimary,NULL);

// query for the backbuffer or secondary surface
// notice the use of ddscaps to indicate what
// you're requesting
ddscaps.dwCaps = DDSCAPS_BACKBUFFER;

// get the surface
lpddsprimary->GetAttachedSurface(&ddscaps,&lpddsback);
```

If you're a little flabbergasted by this code fragment, don't stress — I just want you to go through the motions even though you haven't seen all the data structures yet. After this code executes, you have a surface structure like what Figure 9-6 shows. The primary surface has a single backbuffer, or secondary surface, that you can render to, and then you can swap the surfaces.

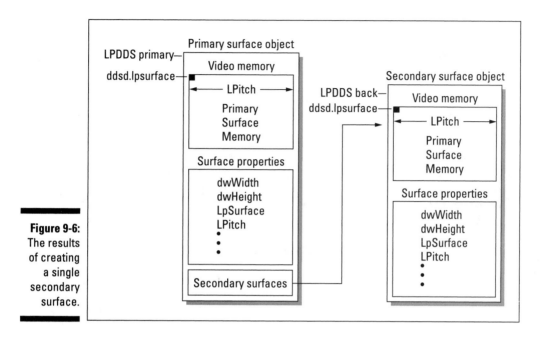

Figure 9-6:
The results of creating a single secondary surface.

To render to the secondary surface lpddsback, you must Lock() and Unlock() it, just as you do with the primary surface, like this:

```
// used to access secondary video buffer
UCHAR *video_buffer;

// lock the secondary surface
lpddsback->Lock(NULL,&ddsd,
            DDLOCK_SURFACEMEMORYPTR | DDLOCK_WAIT,NULL);

// draw on the surface: ddsd.lpSurface and
// ddsd.lPitch are valid as before
video_buffer = ddsd.lpSurface;

// unlock the surface
lpddsback->Unlock(ddsd.lpSurface);
```

After drawing the frame on the secondary "invisible" surface, you flip the primary surface with the secondary surface via the call Flip(), as shown here:

```
HRESULT Flip(
LPDIRECTDRAWSURFACE3 lpDDSurfaceOverride,  // always NULL
DWORD dwFlags); // always DDFLIP_WAIT
```

You always call Flip() from the primary surface interface, not the secondary. Also, the function call may fail if the surfaces can't be flipped at the time you request it, so you usually employ a while loop, like this:

```
// flip the primary and secondary surfaces
while(lpddsprimary->Flip(NULL, DDFLIP_WAIT)!=DD_OK);
```

The function may not succeed on the first call, but this while loop retries until the function does succeed.

After the primary and secondary surfaces have been flipped, only their memory is swapped — that's important to understand. The primary is still the visible, and the secondary is still invisible, as Figure 9-7 shows.

Creating offscreen surfaces

In a typical game you're going to have a primary surface, secondary surface for animation, and a number of bitmap images or "sprites" for the game objects. DirectDraw supports what are called *offscreen plain surfaces,* which are nothing more than bitmaps that have the same color depth and properties as the main primary surface but that exist either in system memory or in VRAM.

A *sprite* simply means a small object that moves around on a video game screen. It's nothing more than a bitmap, in most cases. Originally, the term was coined by the developer of an Apple II game, a long, long, time ago.

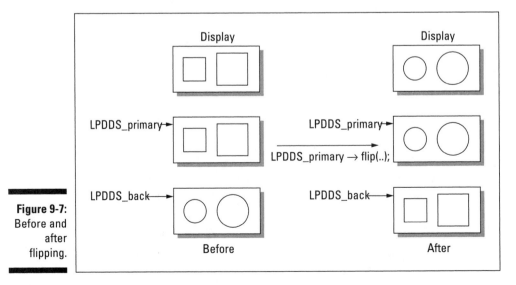

Figure 9-7: Before and after flipping.

The cool thing about offscreen plain surfaces is that they're DirectDraw objects; hence, DirectDraw knows how to draw them for you. In addition, if you have hardware acceleration, DirectDraw can draw them very quickly, using the hardware *blitter* (*bl*ock *i*mage *transfer*). I don't want to get into all kinds of detail right now; I just want to show you how to create an offscreen surface that's compatible with the current primary surface.

Assume that you've already created a DirectDraw object, and a primary surface. Here's how you create an offscreen plain surface in VRAM of size (width times height):

```
// .. assume DirectDraw has been set up and so on

DDSURFACEDESC ddsd;          // a DirectDraw surface descriptor
LPDIRECTDRAWSURFACE lpwork;  // the working surface

// set the size parameter as always
memset(&ddsd,0,sizeof(ddsd));
ddsd.dwSize    = sizeof(ddsd);

// set the flags; very important
// remember that you must set the flags of the fields
// that will be valid
ddsd.dwFlags   = DDSD_CAPS | DDSD_WIDTH | DDSD_HEIGHT;

// set dimensions of the new surface
ddsd.dwWidth   = width;
ddsd.dwHeight  = height;

// what kind of offscreen surface, system memory, or VRAM
// default is VRAM
ddsd.ddsCaps.dwCaps = DDSCAPS_OFFSCREENPLAIN;

// now create the surface and check for error
if (lpdd->CreateSurface(&ddsd,&lpwork,NULL)!=DD_OK)
   { /* error */ }
```

Simple! Now, you need to pay a little more attention to the error codes on this function call than you have before. If the call to `CreateSurface()` fails, the failure is probably a result of not enough VRAM being left to create surfaces. Remember that you have only 1MB or 2MB, so it's not like system RAM. Hence, you may need to create the surface in system memory, like this:

```
// set flags for an offscreen plain system memory surface
ddsd.ddsCaps.dwCaps =
              DDSCAPS_OFFSCREENPLAIN | DDSCAPS_SYSTEMMEMORY;

// now create the surface and check for error
if (lpdd->CreateSurface(&ddsd,&lpwork,NULL)!=DD_OK)
  { /* error */ }
```

You can create as many plain surfaces as you want. Then you can copy them to the primary (or secondary) surface very quickly, using hardware acceleration (that's the whole point of DirectDraw) — I get to that later.

If you're still scratching your head over all this stuff, you may want to try a new shampoo, or you may want to see the next chapter, which covers surfaces in more detail.

Getting Down with Palettes

The whole DirectDraw palette thing can leave anybody in the dark, and you may not even understand it now, but I'm just a doctor, Jim! Palettes in DirectDraw can be a very complex subject. Luckily, in most cases, you create full-screen applications, which makes palette management much simpler because you don't have to share colors with Windows. (See Chapter 5 for the scoop on why sharing colors with Windows is such a problem.)

In any 256-color mode, one palette contains the RGB values for each of the colors. When you write into video memory, each byte represents a color index, as Figure 9-8 shows. Basic drawing on the primary surface shows you how to write into video memory; now I show you how to actually create a DirectDraw palette and attach it to the primary surface.

Creating palettes

DirectDraw palettes are handled through the IDirectDrawPalette interface, so you must create a IDirectDrawPalette object when working with palettes. To create a DirectDraw palette, the first thing you need to do is create the palette data structure that contains the RGB values for each palette entry. Luckily, DirectX uses the standard PALETTEENTRY structure to hold each color:

```
typedef struct tagPALETTEENTRY { // pe
    BYTE peRed;   // the red component 8-bits
    BYTE peGreen; // the green component 8-bits
    BYTE peBlue;  // the blue component 8-bits
    BYTE peFlags; // the control flags
} PALETTEENTRY;
```

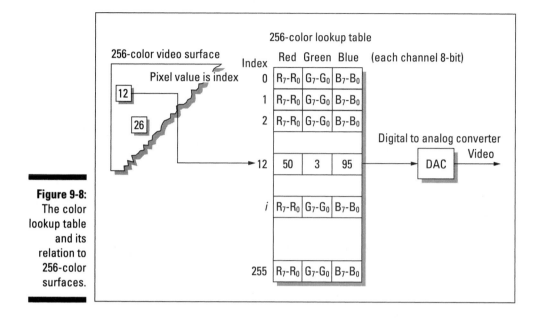

Figure 9-8:
The color lookup table and its relation to 256-color surfaces.

First create an array of 256 PALETTEENTRYs to hold the entire palette, like this:

```
PALETTEENTRY palette[256];
```

Then you can fill in the elements with any RGB values you want. However, you must set the peFlags field to PC_NOCOLLAPSE, to inform DirectDraw to leave the entries alone and interpret them as they are without any compression or optimization. So to create a palette with 64 shades of red, green, blue, and gray, do something like this:

```
// first clear out all the entries; defensive programming
memset(palette,0,256*sizeof(PALETTEENTRY));

// create a R,G,B,GR gradient palette
for (int index=0; index<256; index++)
    {
    if (index < 64) // shades of red
        palette[index].peRed = index*64;
    else            // shades of green
    if (index >=64 && index <128)
        palette[index].peGreen = (index-64)*4;
    else            // shades of blue
```

(continued)

(continued)

```
    if (index >=128 && index <192)
        palette[index].peBlue = (index-128)*4;
    else           // shades of gray
    if (index >=192 && index <256)
        palette[index].peRed = palette[index].peGreen =
        palette[index].peBlue = (index-192)*4;

    // set flags
    palette[index].peFlags = PC_NOCOLLAPSE;
    } // end for index
```

After generating the data for the palette, you have two more steps to get the palette working:

1. **Create a DirectDraw palette object with the palette data.**

2. **Attach the palette to the primary surface.**

The function to create a DirectDraw palette is `CreatePalette()`:

```
HRESULT CreatePalette(
DWORD dwFlags,                      // creation flags
LPPALETTEENTRY lpColorTable,        // pointer to palette data
LPDIRECTDRAWPALETTE FAR *lplpDDPal, // pointer to palette
                                    // interface object
IUnknown FAR *pUnkOuter);           // always NULL
```

`dwFlags` defines what kind of palette you want. In this case, you always use `DDPCAPS_8BIT | DDPCAPS_INITIALIZE | DDPCAPS_ALLOW256`, which informs DirectDraw that you want an 8-bit palette with 256 colors and that you're sending the values to initialize it with. Finally, the function returns an interface pointer object in `lplpDDPal`; that's what you use to communicate to the palette with. As usual, the function returns `DD_OK` if successful or something else if not. You may create as many palettes as you want, but only one can be attached to any one surface at a time. Here's how you create the palette object. Note that it's created from the main DirectDraw object.

```
LPDIRECTDRAWPALETTE lpddpal; // the palette object

// create the palette
if ((lpdd->CreatePalette(
    DDPCAPS_8BIT | DDPCAPS_INITIALIZE | DDPCAPS_ALLOW256,
    palette,&lpddpal,NULL))!=DD_OK)
    { /* error */ }
```

Finally, to attach the palette to a surface, use the `SetPalette()` function, which is part of the `IDirectDrawSurface` interface. The function works like this:

```
lpddsprimary->SetPalette(lpddpal);
```

When you make the call to `SetPalette()`, the palette is instantly utilized on the next frame, so you usually want to set up the palette in the initialization section of your program.

Changing palette entries on-the-fly

Creating palettes is no big deal, but what if you want to change one or more palette entries during program execution to simulate animation, or a glowing light, or something? You have yet another function, called `SetEntries()`:

```
HRESULT SetEntries(
    DWORD dwFlags,              // control flags, always 0
    DWORD dwStartingEntry,      // starting index to change
    DWORD dwCount,              // number of colors to change
    LPPALETTEENTRY lpEntries);  // pointer to data
```

You can use this function to change one or more palette entries in the palette. Here's how you change a single entry anywhere in the palette:

```
// create a single color, notice the flag
static PALETTEENTRY color = {10,0,20,PC_NOCOLLAPSE};

// change the palette entry at location 'index'
lpddpal->SetEntries(0,index,1,&color);
```

Notice that the function call is made from the palette interface object, not the DirectDraw object, nor the surface. If you want to change the entire palette, you can do something like this:

```
// define and initialize the new palette...
PALETTEENTRY new_palette[256];

// change the entire palette
lpddpal->SetEntries(0,0,256,new_palette);
```

If you're getting the itch to create functional wrappers around all these DirectDraw functions, feel free to do so. In fact, I already have, in some of the programs. Chapter 12 shows you how to encapsulate all these functions into one very large game-programming library — GPDUMB.LIB.

Querying palette entries

To find out what value a palette entry has in it, you use a function called GetEntries(). It works exactly like SetEntries(), except that it fills the array you send with data instead of changing the palette with the data you send. Here's its prototype:

```
HRESULT GetEntries(
    DWORD dwFlags,              // control flags, always 0
    DWORD dwStartingEntry,      // starting index to get
    DWORD dwCount,              // number of colors to retrieve
    LPPALETTEENTRY lpEntries);  // pointer to data storage
```

GetEntries() can retrieve one or more entries from the palette and fill in the destination data structure with the data. Here's an example of how you save the current palette for later use and then restore it:

```
// data storage for palette here
PALETTEENTRY save_palette[256];

// save the palette
GetEntries(0,0,256,save_palette);

//..manipulate the current palette

// restore the old palette
SetEntries(0,0,256,save_palette);
```

That's all there is to palettes. Of course, I'm lying, but the truth is always so boring! Again, if you have questions, peruse the DirectX SDK for more information. To complete the coverage on palettes, I wrote two programs for the CD: PROG9_4.CPP and PROG9_5.CPP. The first one creates a gradient palette and then draws some colored bars. The second one does the same, but then animates the palette colors, using the SetEntries() and GetEntries() functions.

Chapter 10

Digging into DirectDraw: Animation and Bitmaps

● ●

In This Chapter

▶ Using DirectDraw to access hardware acceleration

▶ Animating

▶ Loading bitmaps

▶ Using the blitter

● ●

*A*fter the SVGA video card, 2D and 3D hardware have become common-place. The whole point of DirectDraw is to allow you to access hardware acceleration in a drama-free manner. However, if all you do is lock the primary buffer and draw pixels into the buffer one by one, you're using only a portion of the capabilities of DirectDraw.

Because DirectDraw is primarily a 2D graphics system, you don't have a whole lot of things to accelerate, but you may as well accelerate as much as possible so that the main CPU works as little as possible on graphics and has more time to spend on artificial intelligence, game logic, physics, and so on.

This chapter covers some of the more advanced features of DirectDraw, related to acceleration hardware: animation and bitmapped graphics.

Smooooth Animation Techniques

The illusion that a video game creates is that of a film or video, meaning frame after frame of continuous animation in which you can't see the imagery being drawn or erased. You have two methods to choose from in accomplishing this illusion:

✔ **Page flipping:** As Chapter 9 discusses, you create two surfaces — a primary and a secondary — and then page-flip between them. Historically, page flipping has meant that the video hardware memory contains two or more video pages: The graphics are drawn to one of those video pages, the pages are flipped, then the graphics are drawn to the other, and so forth. However, if a video card doesn't have enough memory to provide two entire pages in the desired resolution and color within the VRAM, then the technique used is *double buffering*.

✔ **Double buffering:** This technique is very similar to page flipping, but the video card contains just a single primary buffer, and system memory has just a single double buffer, as Figure 10-1 shows. With double buffering, *you* do the page flipping manually with system memory instead of having the hardware do it.

With DirectX, you don't have to worry about using double buffering, because if you don't have enough video memory, DirectX goes ahead and simulates page flipping for you. And you won't know (or see) the difference. Basically, when you tell DirectDraw to flip the pages, DirectDraw copies the system-memory page into the primary buffer instead of using hardware to change which page is being displayed. But seeing how double buffering works in the next section can help you better understand page flipping, which you may need if you're abducted by aliens that want you to make a DOS game.

Another problem with this procedure is that a simple fill doesn't suffice for a nonlinear video card, but DirectDraw handles that for you, too, by using the blitter to do simple fills and clears.

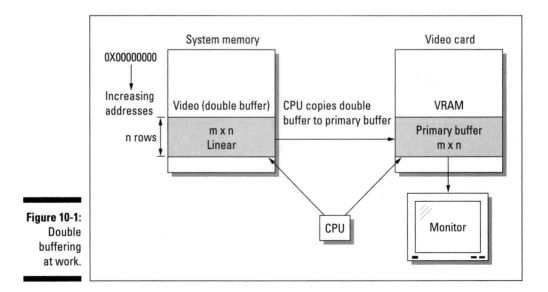

Figure 10-1:
Double
buffering
at work.

Double buffering

To achieve double buffering, draw your frame of animation in the double buffer (existing in system memory), which is off-screen, and then copy that frame to the primary buffer, usually with a memcpy( ) or another memory-move function. In this way, the entire frame is quickly copied into view, and the animation from frame to frame is smooth. Players never see the frame being built up; they see only the entire frame being instantly copied to the primary buffer.

For example, suppose that you've set up a single primary surface that's 640 x 480 with 256 colors referenced by lpddsprimary, and you want to use double buffering to draw into a double buffer and then copy the double buffer into the primary buffer each new frame. (If the "surface" stuff throws you for a loop, check out Chapter 9 for more info.) Here's a list of steps you must do:

1. **Allocate memory for the double buffer so that the double buffer has the same size width and height in pixels as the primary buffer does.**

2. **In the main loop, erase the image in the double buffer.**

3. **Perform game logic.**

4. **Render the next frame into the double buffer.**

5. **Copy the double buffer into the primary buffer.**

6. **Synchronize the display to a specific frame rate.**

7. **Go to Step 2 until CPU degrades into quarks, and pi mesons.**

The following is an example that sets up DirectDraw and a double buffer and enters into a rendering loop. I highlighted the key double-buffer code (in bold). Note that I left out the code declarations of the DirectDraw data structures. Also, you may want to split up the functionality of the following code into the appropriate sections: Game_Init( ), Game_Main( ), and Game_Shutdown( ).

```
// the double buffer
UCHAR *double_buffer = NULL,
      *primary_buffer = NULL;

// create DirectDraw object and test for error
if (DirectDrawCreate(NULL,&lpdd,NULL)!=DD_OK)
    return(0);
```

(continued)

(continued)

```
// set cooperation level to windowed mode normal
if (lpdd->SetCooperativeLevel(main_window_handle,
            DDSCL_ALLOWMODEX | DDSCL_FULLSCREEN |
            DDSCL_EXCLUSIVE | DDSCL_ALLOWREBOOT)!=DD_OK)
    return(0);

// set the display mode to 640 x 480 x 8
if (lpdd->SetDisplayMode(640,480,8)!=DD_OK)
    return(0);

// create the primary surface
memset(&ddsd,0,sizeof(ddsd));
ddsd.dwSize               = sizeof(ddsd);
ddsd.dwFlags              = DDSD_CAPS;
ddsd.ddsCaps.dwCaps = DDSCAPS_PRIMARYSURFACE;

if (lpdd->CreateSurface(&ddsd,&lpddsprimary,NULL)!=DD_OK)
    return(0);

// now create the 640 x 480 double buffer
double_buffer = (UCHAR *)malloc(640*480);

// enter main event loop
while(1)
    {
    if (PeekMessage(&msg,NULL,0,0,PM_REMOVE))
        {
        // test whether this is a quit
        if (msg.message == WM_QUIT)
            break;

        // translate any accelerator keys
        TranslateMessage(&msg);

        // send the message to the window proc
        DispatchMessage(&msg);
        } // end if

        // main game processing goes here
        // erase double buffer
        memset(double_buffer,0, 640*480);
```

```
// perform game logic...

// draw the next frame into the double buffer
// plot 1000 random pixels
for (int index=0; index<1000; index++)
    {
    int x = rand()%640;
    int y = rand()%480;
    UCHAR col = rand()%256;
    double_buffer[x+y*640] = col;
    } // end for index

// copy the double buffer into the primary buffer
memset(&ddsd,0,sizeof(ddsd));
ddsd.dwSize = sizeof(ddsd);

// lock the primary surface
lpddsprimary->Lock(NULL,&ddsd,
        DDLOCK_SURFACEMEMORYPTR | DDLOCK_WAIT,NULL);

// get video pointer to primary surface
primary_buffer = (UCHAR *)ddsd.lpSurface;

// copy memory from double buffer to primary
memcpy(primary_buffer, double_buffer, 640*480);

// unlock primary buffer
lpddsprimary->Unlock(primary_buffer);

// synchronize video to some constant rate
Sleep(30);

} // end while

// release double buffer
free(double_buffer);
```

To see this code in action, check out PROG10_1.CPP on the CD. The program implements this logic and creates a display that looks like a plasma fire — or a bunch of random dots, depending on how much you've had to drink.

The code has a potential problem. If the video card does not support linear memory, the video address from line to line isn't the same as the horizontal pitch — so you'll obviously have a problem when performing a memory-to-memory fill. True, you have the same number of bytes per line; however, the starting address of each line in video memory is found not by adding the width of the mode but by adding the value in the `ddsd.lPitch` field. If you want to write bulletproof code that uses a double buffer, you must check for the case in which the memory pitch is not the same as the video width, and take the appropriate action — such as filling line by line and updating the line addresses appropriately.

Page flipping with surfaces

Here's a brief summary of how to create a secondary surface (see Chapter 9 for more details):

First, you need to create a primary surface with the extra capabilities `DDSCAPS_PRIMARYSURFACE | DDSCAPS_FLIP | DDSCAPS_COMPLEX` and a backbuffer count of 1, like this:

```
// DirectDraw surface description
DDSURFACEDESC ddsd;

// device capabilities structure, used to query for
// secondary backbuffer, among other things
DDSCAPS ddscaps;

LPDIRECTDRAWSURFACE lpddsprimary, // primary surface
        lpddssecondary;          // secondary backbuffer surface

// prepare to create primary surface with 1 backbuffer
memset(ddsd,0,sizeof(ddsd));
ddsd.dwSize = sizeof(ddsd);

// set the flags to validate both the capabilities
// field and the backbuffer count field
ddsd.dwFlags = DDSD_CAPS | DDSD_BACKBUFFERCOUNT;

// you need to let dd know that you want a complex
// flippable surface structure; set flags for that
ddsd.ddsCaps.dwCaps =
  DDSCAPS_PRIMARYSURFACE | DDSCAPS_FLIP | DDSCAPS_COMPLEX;
```

```
// set the backbuffer count to 1
ddsd.dwBackBufferCount = 1;

// create the primary surface
lpdd->CreateSurface(&ddsd,&lpddsprimary,NULL);
```

Then you're ready to query for the single attached surface, which will become your secondary surface. Here's that bit:

```
// query for the backbuffer or secondary surface
// notice the use of ddscaps to indicate what
// you're requesting
ddscaps.dwCaps = DDSCAPS_BACKBUFFER;

// get the surface
lpddsprimary->GetAttachedSurface(&ddscaps,&lpddsback);
```

At this point, you have a primary surface and a secondary surface accessed via the interface pointers lpddsprimary and lpddsback, respectively. The primary surface is always visible, and the secondary surface is always invisible, or off-screen. To flip between the two surfaces, use the function Flip() from the interface pointer of the primary surface like this:

```
// flip the primary and secondary surfaces
while(lpddsprimary->Flip(NULL, DDFLIP_WAIT)!=DD_OK);
```

The following example takes the double-buffer code from the previous section and replaces the double buffer algorithm with page flipping and a secondary surface shown in bold (I left out the creation of the primary and secondary surfaces, which you can see in the preceding discussion):

```
// a general video buffer
UCHAR *video_buffer;

// set up DirectDraw and create surfaces...

// enter main event loop
while(1)
    {
    if (PeekMessage(&msg,NULL,0,0,PM_REMOVE))
        {
        // test whether this is a quit
        if (msg.message == WM_QUIT)
            break;
```

(continued)

(continued)

```
      // translate any accelerator keys
      TranslateMessage(&msg);

      // send the message to the window proc
      DispatchMessage(&msg);
      } // end if

   // main game processing goes here
   // erase secondary surface

   // lock secondary surface
   lpddsback->Lock(NULL,&ddsd,
        DDLOCK_SURFACEMEMORYPTR | DDLOCK_WAIT,NULL);

   // get video pointer to secondary surface
   video_buffer = (UCHAR *)ddsd.lpSurface;

   // clear the memory
   memset(video_buffer, 0, 640*480);

   // perform game logic...

   // draw the next frame into the double buffer
   // plot 1000 random pixels
   for (int index=0; index<1000; index++)
       {
       int x = rand()%640;
       int y = rand()%480;
       UCHAR col = rand()%356;
       video_buffer[x+y*640] = col;
       } // end for index

   // unlock the secondary surface
   lpddsback->Unlock(video_buffer);

   // flip the primary and secondary surfaces
   while(lpddsprimary->Flip(NULL, DDFLIP_WAIT)!=DD_OK);

   // synchronize video to some constant rate
   Sleep(30);

   } // end while
```

Much simpler than using a double buffer, huh? The only ugly part is the memory fill to clear out the secondary surface. This code still suffers from the potential problem of a nonlinear video card (as noted in the "Double buffering" subsection, earlier in this chapter), so a simple fill doesn't suffice. Here's the solution: DirectDraw has the capability to fill a surface itself with the *blitter* hardware (or the hardware emulation layer, if hardware is not available). The next section shows you how to use the blitter to do simple fills and clears.

Check out `PROG10_2.CPP` on the CD for an example of page flipping. It simply flips two pages of random pixels back and forth.

I want to hold off on the general discussion of bit blitting until the next section, but take a look at how to do simple fills and clears using the blitter.

The next subsection on "Using the blitter to fill" should be read before you read the section on "Bitmaps," because the discussion of using the blitter builds from this subsection to the next. If you're using this book as a reference, please be aware that the discussion of filling with the blitter and the bitmap discussion go together.

Using the blitter to fill

Normally, you use the bit blitter hardware to copy bitmap images from some source to a destination (usually the primary surface). In addition, you may request for the bitmaps to be scaled, rotated, or processed using various other effects. However, foregoing all the cool things the blitter can do, it also can simply clear out or fill a chunk of memory with a value.

To access the bit blitter, use one of the following functions:

  ✔ `Blt()` when you aren't concerned with clipping to the edges of the screen

  ✔ `BltFast()` when you are concerned with clipping to the edges of the screen

Here's the prototype for the `Blt()` function:

```
HRESULT Blt(
    LPRECT lpDestRect,      // the destination rectangle
    LPDIRECTDRAWSURFACE3 lpDDSrcSurf,  // the source surface
    LPRECT lpSrcRect,       // the source rectangle
    DWORD dwFlags,          // control flags
    LPDDBLTFX lpDDBltFx);   // the special fx structure
```

The function returns DD_OK if successful or various error codes if not. The parameters are a bit tricky:

- ✔ lpDestRect: Pointer to a RECT structure that contains the destination rectangle to blit to, as Figure 10-2 shows. If this pointer is NULL, the entire destination surface is used. Also, the destination rectangle can be a different size than the source, in which case the data is scaled to fit when blittered. However, if no hardware acceleration is available to support the scaling operation, software emulation is used — which isn't the fastest thing in the world!

- ✔ lpDDSrcSurf: Interface pointer to the source surface.

- ✔ lpSrcRect: Pointer to a RECT structure that contains the source rectangle to blit to, as Figure 10-2 shows. If this pointer is NULL, the entire source surface is used.

- ✔ dwFlags: The main control flag word, which instructs the blitter on what to do. Table 10-1 contains a partial list of the most important settings. Note that you can logically OR these settings together.

- ✔ lpDDBltFx: Pointer to a DDBLTFX structure; the lpDDBltFx field contains further information that the Blt() function needs for some operations, such as filling and rotating.

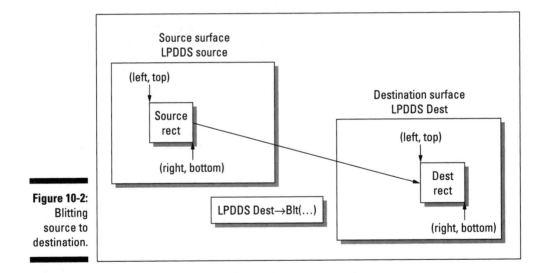

Figure 10-2: Blitting source to destination.

Table 10-1	Partial List of Control Flags for Blt()
Value	*Meaning*
DDBLT_COLORFILL	Uses the dwFillColor member of the DDBLTFX structure as the RGB color that fills the destination rectangle on the destination surface
DDBLT_DDFX	Uses the dwDDFX member of the DDBLTFX structure to specify the effects to use for this blit
DDBLT_DDROPS	Uses the dwDDROPS member of the DDBLTFX structure to specify the raster operations (ROPs) that are not part of the Win32 API
DDBLT_KEYDEST	Uses the color key associated with the destination surface
DDBLT_KEYSRC	Uses the color key associated with the source surface
DDBLT_ROP	Uses the dwROP member of the DDBLTFX structure for the ROP for this blit; these ROPs are the same as those defined in the Win32 API
DDBLT_ROTATIONANGLE	Uses the dwRotationAngle member of the DDBLTFX structure as the rotation angle (specified in $1/100$ of a degree) for the surface
DDBLT_WAIT	Instructs the blitter to keep trying the blit operation until the blit operation is successful; this way, you don't get errors back if the blitter is busy

The DDBLTFX structure contains a number of fields that are used to further qualify more complex blitter functionality. The structure is gnarly, but fortunately you don't have to worry about 90 percent of the fields, which are used for such advanced features as z-buffer (used for 3D) and alpha channeling (used for transparency). Nevertheless, this structure is important and is tied directly to the blitter, so you need to know it:

```
typedef struct _DDBLTFX{
DWORD dwSize;  // the size of this structure in bytes
DWORD dwDDFX;  // type of blitter fx
DWORD dwROP;   // Win32 raster ops that are supported
DWORD dwDDROP; // DirectDraw raster ops that are supported
DWORD dwRotationAngle; // angle for rotations
DWORD dwZBufferOpCode;    // z-buffer fieldsused for 3D

DWORD dwZBufferLow;    // advanced parameter
DWORD dwZBufferHigh;   // advanced parameter
```

(continued)

(continued)

```
DWORD dwZBufferBaseDest;    // advanced
DWORD dwZDestConstBitDepth; // advanced
union
{
DWORD              dwZDestConst;      // advanced...
LPDIRECTDRAWSURFACE lpDDSZBufferDest; // advanced...
};
DWORD dwZSrcConstBitDepth;            // advanced...
union
{
DWORD              dwZSrcConst;       // advanced...
LPDIRECTDRAWSURFACE lpDDSZBufferSrc;  // advanced...
};
DWORD dwAlphaEdgeBlendBitDepth;  // alpha stuff (advanced)
DWORD dwAlphaEdgeBlend;          // advanced...
DWORD dwReserved;                // advanced...
DWORD dwAlphaDestConstBitDepth;  // advanced...
union
{
DWORD              dwAlphaDestConst;  // advanced...
LPDIRECTDRAWSURFACE lpDDSAlphaDest;   // advanced...
};
DWORD dwAlphaSrcConstBitDepth;        // advanced...
union
{
DWORD              dwAlphaSrcConst;   // advanced...
LPDIRECTDRAWSURFACE lpDDSAlphaSrc;    // advanced...
};
union // the following are very important
{
DWORD dwFillColor; // color word used for fill
DWORD dwFillDepth; // z filling (advanced)
DWORD dwFillPixel; // color fill word for RGB(alpha) fills
LPDIRECTDRAWSURFACE lpDDSPattern;
};
// the following are very important
DDCOLORKEY ddckDestColorkey; // destination color key
DDCOLORKEY ddckSrcColorkey;  // source color key
} DDBLTFX,FAR* LPDDBLTFX;
```

Make sure that you take a look at the DirectX SDK Help for a more in-depth discussion and definition of the preceding structures. They are extremely complex and context sensitive.

Because filling is a destination-only operation — with no source, just a fill color — the parameters sent to Blt() are much simplified compared to a full bitmap blit operation. The only work is to set up the Blt() function correctly to perform a memory fill. You need to use the DDBLT_COLORFILL flag (refer to Table 10-1), in addition to DDBLT_WAIT, which is a general precaution that instructs the blitter to keep trying if the blitter can't satisfy the request right now. To use the DDBLT_COLORFILL flag correctly, you must provide a DDBLTFX structure with the dwFillColor set to the color index (or the RGB value, if in 16-, 24-, or 32-bit mode) of the fill. Here's an example of how to perform a color fill with the Blt() function:

```
DDBLTFX ddbltfx; // this contains the DDBLTFX structure
RECT fill_area;  // this contains the destination rectangle

// clear out the structure and set the size field
memset(&ddbltfx,0,sizeof(DDBLTFX));
ddbltfx.dwSize = sizeof(DDBLTFX);

// set the dwfillcolor field to the desired color
ddbltfx.dwFillColor = color; // <- your data 8,16,24 bit

// fill in the destination-rectangle data (your data)
fill_area.top    = top;
fill_area.left   = left;
fill_area.bottom = bottom;
fill_area.right  = right;

// ready to blit to surface; in this case, blit to primary
lpddsprimary->Blt(&fill_area, // pointer to dest rectangle
        NULL,                 // pointer to source surface, NA
        NULL,                 // pointer to source rectangle, NA
        DDBLT_COLORFILL | DDBLT_WAIT,   // fill and wait
        &ddbltfx);            // pointer to DDBLTFX structure
```

Note that the call to Blt() is relative to the destination surface, which in this case is lpddsprimary. This detail is very important; you must always call Blt() from the destination-surface pointer.

Here's how this code works:

1. **Clear out the DDBLTFX structure to make sure that it doesn't contain any garbage that could instruct the blitter to do something you're not requesting.**

2. **Set the** dwSize **field to the size of the** DDBLTFX **structure and set the** dwFillColor **field to the color descriptor.**

The setting of the color is very important and is context sensitive. If you're in a 256-color mode, the value placed in dwFillColor is interpreted as a color index. However, if you're in an RGB mode — say, 16-bit — the data in dwFillColor is interpreted as an RGB value. In either case, the data is used as the fill word.

3. **Fill in the** fill_area RECT **structure, which is simply the bounding box of the area to fill. If you want to fill the entire screen, make this field** NULL.

4. **Call the** Blt() **function, with all the parameters and the proper flags.**

You can use this code to fill any surface with any color, and hardware acceleration will be used (if available) — which is very cool. Not only does the hardware do the fill, but now the CPU doesn't have to fill 64K, 128K, 256K, or however many chunks of memory, and the fill operation can take place in parallel with the main CPU after fill is initiated.

As an example of using the blitter to perform simple fills, PROG10_3.CPP on the CD creates a 640 x 480 16-bit mode and fills the primary surface with randomly sized, colored rectangles, using the blitter.

Bitmaps

In the late '70s and early '80s, many games, such as *Tail Gunner* (one of my favorites; see Figure 10-3), still used vector graphics displays — displays made up of lines. After a while, raster displays that draw bitmaps replaced all the vector graphics games. The mainstay of any 2D and some 3D computer games is the *bitmap,* which is a 2D matrix of colored pixels that represents a single image, as Figure 10-4 shows.

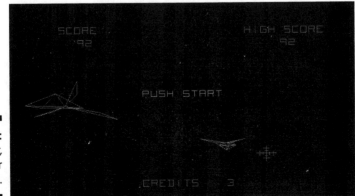

Figure 10-3:
Tail Gunner,
with vector
graphics.

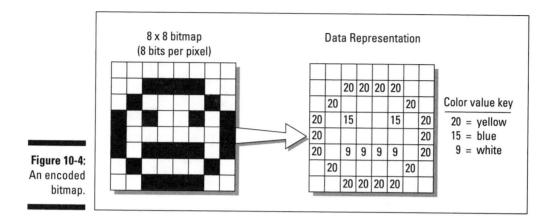

8 x 8 bitmap
(8 bits per pixel)

Data Representation

		20	20	20	20		
	20					20	
20		15			15		20
20							20
20		9	9	9	9		20
	20					20	
		20	20	20	20		

Color value key
20 = yellow
15 = blue
9 = white

Figure 10-4:
An encoded
bitmap.

Animation is achieved by drawing one or more bitmaps of some object and then rapidly flipping through them to create the illusion of motion or change, which is exactly how a movie is made. For example, Figure 10-5 depicts a number of 56 x 72 bitmaps of a skeleton-creature animation. If I write a program that draws each one of these bitmaps in rapid succession and then moves the bitmaps each frame, the skeleton will look as if it's walking. *That's* animation.

Figure 10-5:
A bitmap
animation
of a
skeleton
creature.

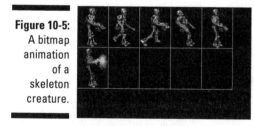

You want to be able to load and display bitmaps anywhere on the secondary or primary surface. Then you need to write software to animate the bitmaps, move them, check for collision, and generally control them as if they were game objects. You use the blitter to copy bitmaps from one surface to another, as the "Bit Blasting with the Blitter" section of this chapter discusses. But what about creating and loading the bitmaps?

Creating bitmaps

Creating bitmaps is more of an artistic thing than anything else, but the main idea is to use a paint program — JASC Paint Shop Pro, Corel PHOTO-PAINT, and so on — to draw your bitmaps. In addition, draw your bitmaps with some set of conventions so that the bitmaps can be easily loaded and manipulated. Most game programmers like to draw their bitmaps in templates.

Figure 10-6 illustrates a standard 8-x-8-pixel bitmap template. I created a number of 2 x 2 rectangles (cells), each containing an 8-x-8-pixel bitmap. The rectangles are like placeholders, so I know that if I draw each of my bitmaps in the rectangles and then load each of the bitmaps from the rectangles, I have a set of bitmaps all the same size with the desired imagery within. Moreover, I know that I can access each cell or bitmap with a pair of coordinates (cx,cy), which is the upper-left corner of any cell.

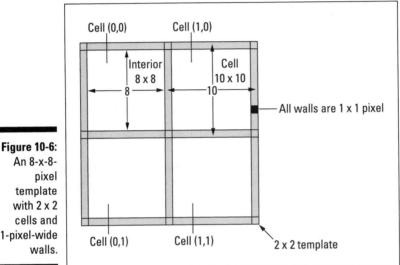

Figure 10-6:
An 8-x-8-pixel template with 2 x 2 cells and 1-pixel-wide walls.

Here are some things to be careful of when creating bitmaps:

✔ **Color:** You need to decide how many colors your bitmaps will have, and then draw them all in the same color space. For example, if you want to use an 8-bit 256-color mode, you must draw all your bitmaps with the same 256 colors — you can't use one palette for the good guys and one for the bad guys. Similarly, if you decide to use 16 bits per pixel to draw your bitmaps, all your bitmaps must be in 16 bits per pixel. One creature can't use 24 bits per pixel. Remember, the game will only run in a single video mode and all the graphics and bitmaps must be displayed in the same way.

✔ **Size:** Draw all your bitmaps in sizes that are powers of 2 — 2 x 2, 4 x 4, 8 x 8, 16 x 16, 32 x 32, and so on. Following this guideline helps with the blitter and with various optimizations that you perform in your games.

Also, when you create a page of bitmaps, use the same size for all the bitmaps; don't mix up different sizes on different pages. For example, suppose that you make a large, 600 x 600 bitmap image in your paint program. You're going to put all your 32-x-32-pixel bitmaps on this single image in a nice template that has, say, 16 x 16 cells, as Figure 10-7 shows. You then realize that you have some room left over on the image — you can fit a group of 4-x-4-pixel images. *Not* a good idea! Just make another large bitmap to hold the smaller bitmaps, and for any other sizes that you may have. Don't mix your bitmap sizes on a single image page.

If you're a detail-oriented person (or you're on your fifth Mountain Dew), you should realize that if the bitmaps are 32 x 32, for example, the cells enclosing them must be 34 x 34 each and have a common wall (1-pixel thick). That's a key point when building templates.

On the CD, you can find a number of templates, labeled BMPNxN.BMP, for various-sized bitmaps. They're all in 256-color mode, so if you want to use higher color modes, convert these templates to 16-, 24-, or 32-bit.

So you create one or more large bitmap files that contain your imagery for your game. You may have one file that has all the ships, another that has the explosions, another that has the terrain, and so on. Then you load all the bitmaps into memory (as the next section discusses) and, with program code, display the bitmaps when and where they're supposed to appear. Obviously, I'm glossing over details, but you can see how to display bitmaps in "Bit Blasting with the Blitter," later in this chapter.

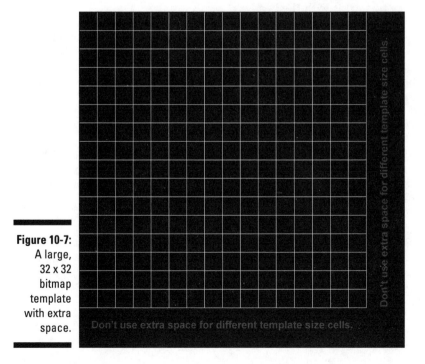

Figure 10-7:
A large, 32 x 32 bitmap template with extra space.

Loading bitmaps

Unfortunately, loading bitmaps isn't simple. Bitmaps come in hundreds of file formats — .TGA, .GIF, .JPG, .TIFF, and many others — all having various properties. However, the most common Windows bitmap file format is .BMP. If you prefer a different file format for memory reasons or if your favorite paint program doesn't support .BMP, you can just convert all your bitmap-image files to .BMP before trying to load them with the software that this section shows you how to write. (By the way, Paint Shop Pro by JASC is great at converting — not only file formats but color space also.)

The .BMP file format supports a great deal of functionality, such as large bitmaps, compression, and various color depths. But the .BMP file reader that this section shows you how to create uses the bare minimum of the file format — it can read .BMP files that are in 8-bit indexed color or 16- or 24-bit RGB color, and that's it. If the image is a 24-bit RGB image, the code converts the image into a 16-bit RGB image. Also, .BMP files must *not* be compressed for our loader. But the loader can load a file of any size (within reason).

Explaining exactly how to read in .BMP files would take a whole chapter all by itself, so I give you the 25-cent tour of the main points and then supply you with a function to load a bitmap into a region of memory. After the bitmap is in memory, you can manipulate the bitmap further yourself. The best place to start is with the headers.

Windows provides a function you can use to load bitmaps. You can add a bitmap resource to your project just as you do a menu, and then load it in with LoadBitmap(). The only problem with this method is that the .EXE must be updated with the new bitmap data and, hence, recompiled if you want to add new bitmaps, because the bitmaps are part of the .EXE. However, most game programmers prefer to have a little more flexibility and load the .BMP files manually. However, you can use LoadBitmap().

Every file format on Earth (and the planet I'm from) typically starts with a header section, which describes the file so that the file reader can load the file. .BMP files have two header sections followed by the binary data, as Figure 10-8 shows. The definitions of the header sections are BITMAPFILEHEADER and BITMAPINFO.

BITMAPFILEHEADER describes the bitmap type, total size, and the offset in bytes to get to the BITMAPINFO section. Here's the structure's definition:

```
typedef struct tagBITMAPFILEHEADER { // bmfh
  WORD  bfType;      // type of bitmap; 0x4D42 means .BMP
  DWORD bfSize;      // the total size of the file, in bytes
  WORD  bfReserved1; // always 0
  WORD  bfReserved2; // always 0
  DWORD bfOffBits;   // number of bytes from this
```

```
                              // structure to access the BITMAPINFO;
                              // basically an offset
} BITMAPFILEHEADER;
```

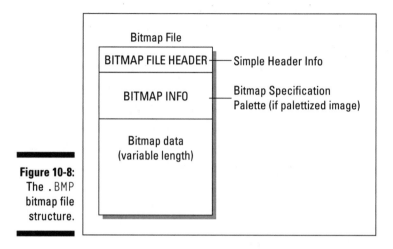

Figure 10-8:
The .BMP
bitmap file
structure.

BITMAPINFO is where all the information is. It describes every detail of the
.BMP file — dimensions, bits per pixel, palette (if 256-color mode), and
anything else. Actually, this structure is really composed of two more nested
data structures, as Figure 10-9 shows: BITMAPINFOHEADER and the color
palette. If a color palette exists, it's in the form of 256 RGB color descriptors,
very similar to the standard DirectDraw palettes but with one difference:
The palette data is composed of RGBQUADs, which are slightly different from
PALETTEENTRYs, as I discuss in a moment.

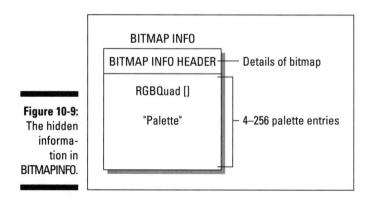

Figure 10-9:
The hidden
informa-
tion in
BITMAPINFO.

The BITMAPINFO structure is more of a container structure than anything
else. However, it can have variable size. If a palette is present in the file, the
bmiColors[] array contains the palette; otherwise, the bmiColors[] array
is empty. Here's the definition of the BITMAPINFO structure:

```
typedef struct tagBITMAPINFO
{
  BITMAPINFOHEADER bmiHeader;         // contains all the data
                                      // field definitions of the
                                      // .BMP file
  RGBQUAD          bmiColors[1]; // the color palette
} BITMAPINFO;
```

In the preceding code, RGBQUAD contains a single RGB- flags entry, but the
order of data is BGRF (Blue, Green, Red, Flags) instead of RGBF (Red, Green,
Blue, Flags). The following code shows the RGBF order:

```
typedef struct tagRGBQUAD { // RGBQ struct
BYTE rgbBlue;           // the blue component
    BYTE rgbGreen;      // the green component
    BYTE rgbRed;        // the red component
    BYTE rgbReserved;   // flags; must be zero
} RGBQUAD;
```

An RGBQUAD is similar to a PALETTEENTRY (see Chapter 5) but in reverse
order. You must preprocess the palette (if one exists) and be sure to extract
the RGB values correctly.

And finally, here's the actual BITMAPINFOHEADER structure:

```
typedef struct tagBITMAPINFOHEADER{
    DWORD   biSize;         // number of bytes in this structure
    LONG    biWidth;        // width of bitmap
    LONG    biHeight;       // height of bitmap
    WORD    biPlanes;       // number of color planes (always 1)
    WORD    biBitCount      // bits per pixel (1,4,8,16,24, or 32)
    DWORD   biCompression;  // type of compression;
                            // it will always be BI_RGB for
                            // noncompressed bitmaps
    DWORD   biSizeImage;    // size of image in bytes
    LONG    biXPelsPerMeter; // x res of target display
    LONG    biYPelsPerMeter; // y res of target display
    DWORD   biClrUsed;      // how many colors are used
    DWORD   biClrImportant; // number of important colors
                            // only important for Windows apps
} BITMAPINFOHEADER;
```

Reading in bitmaps

These data structures are the only ones you need to know. To read in a `.BMP` file, you can use whatever file I/O techniques you like, but basically, the goal is to load the first section of the file — the section containing the header information — into these data-structure templates and then load the bitmap data itself (which is straight byte data) into a chunk of memory determined by the color depth and dimensions that you extract from the header section.

`PROG10_4.CPP` on the CD contains the (rather long) code for this procedure.

The easiest approach is to create a single container structure to hold all the relevant data structures, as follows:

```
typedef struct BITMAP_FILE_TAG
   {
   BITMAPFILEHEADER bitmapfileheader;
   BITMAPINFOHEADER bitmapinfoheader;
   PALETTEENTRY palette[256]; // the 256-color palette
   UCHAR        *buffer;      // pointer to data
   } BITMAP_FILE, *BITMAP_FILE_PTR;
```

To load bitmaps, I created two functions:

- ✔ `Load_Bitmap_File()`: Loads the bitmap and fills in the `BITMAP_FILE` structure
- ✔ `Unload_Bitmap_File()`: Unloads the bitmap and frees the memory allocated to the bitmap

Here are the prototypes:

```
int Load_Bitmap_File(BITMAP_FILE_PTR bitmap,
                     char *filename)

int Unload_Bitmap_File(BITMAP_FILE_PTR bitmap)
```

Standard Windows `.BMP` images are inverted vertically, as Figure 10-10 shows. Originally, this inversion had a reason, but now it's just a problem. Alas, after you load any `.BMP` file, you must vertically invert the image data with software. Of course, you could draw your images upside down, but the blood would rush to your head. `Load_Bitmap_File()` includes a call to another function, `Flip_Bitmap()`, which will invert the `.BMP` files for you.

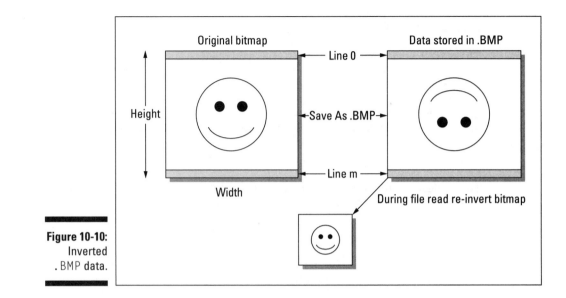

Figure 10-10:
Inverted
.BMP data.

Both functions return TRUE if successful or FALSE otherwise. The functions are used to load a bitmap into memory and delete the bitmap when finished. The bitmap file can be in 8-, 16-, or 24-bit format, but the function converts it to 16-bit RGB if it's a 24-bit image. Here's an example of loading a .BMP file:

```
BITMAP_FILE bitmap1; // the bitmap file

If (!Load_Bitmap_File(&bitmap1, "ANDRE.BMP"))
   { /* error */ }

// manipulate bitmap...

// unload the bitmap and release all memory
Unload_Bitmap_File(&bitmap1);
```

This fragment loads a file named ANDRE.BMP into the bitmap file bitmap1 and then deletes the bitmap data after the program's done with it. As the creator of the bitmap, you already know the width, height, and color depth of the image, so you could cheat and use these values directly in your code and leave it at that. However, that's not good programming practice. You should look up the properties of any bitmap you load from the header and use those values to be safe. For example, here's how you access the width, height, and bits per pixel of bitmap1:

```
bitmap1.bitmapinfoheader.biWidth
bitmap1.bitmapinfoheader.biHeight
bitmap1.bitmapinfoheader.biBitCount
```

In addition, if the .BMP file is a 256-color palletized image, you can access the palette entries via the array bitmap1.palette[index]. Here's an example of reading the components of the entry indexed by index:

```
red   = bitmap1.palette[index].peRed;
blue  = bitmap1.palette[index].peGreen;
green = bitmap1.palette[index].peBlue;
```

Loading 16-bit hi-color bitmaps

Although this stage of building a game is still a long way from using the bit blitter to draw animated bitmaps, you do have enough information to create a bitmap dump program, as long as the bitmaps are a certain size and color depth (so they can fit on the video mode). You just need to load a bitmap and then copy the bits to the primary buffer. Here's an example for a screen mode of 640 x 480 in 16-bit color:

```
// assume DirectDraw is set up and lppdsprimary is
// the primary surface

// used to access the 16-bit video memory
UCHAR *primary_buffer = NULL;

// the bitmap file you're going to load the image into
BITMAP_FILE bitmap16bit;

// load the bitmap
Load_Bitmap_File(&bitmap16bit, "ANDRE16.BMP");

// lock the primary surface
// set up the surface description to lock the surface
memset(&ddsd,0,sizeof(ddsd));
ddsd.dwSize = sizeof(ddsd);

lpddsprimary->Lock(NULL,&ddsd,
          DDLOCK_SURFACEMEMORYPTR | DDLOCK_WAIT,NULL);

// get video pointer
primary_buffer = (UCHAR *)ddsd.lpSurface;

// copy each bitmap line into primary buffer,
// taking into consideration nonlinear video
// modes and the memory pitch lPitch
for (int y=0; y<480; y++)
   {
   // copy the line
   memcpy(&primary_buffer[y*ddsd.lPitch], // destin address
```

(continued)

(continued)

```
        &bitmap16bit.buffer[y * 640*2], // source address
        640*2);                          // bytes to copy
  } // end for y

// unlock the surface
lpddsprimary->Unlock(primary_buffer);

// delete the bitmap
Unload_Bitmap_File(&bitmap16bit);
```

Notice that this code takes into consideration the `lPitch` of the video mode, which is important only if the video card does *not* support linear memory modes. Otherwise, you can simply use the width of the video mode multiplied by the bytes per pixel to move from video line to line.

If you want to see the code in action, look at `PROG10_5.CPP` on the CD.

Loading 8-bit 256-color bitmaps

The next example loads a 256-color image with a palette. The loader loads the bitmap and the palette (and fixes the backward BGR entries to RGB), but you must load the palette data manually into a DirectDraw palette from the bitmap file palette. This process is a bit more complex, but not too bad. Here's an example of how to load a 640 x 480 256-color image and display it (the palette load is shown in bold):

```
// assume DirectDraw is set up and lppdsprimary is
// the primary surface

// used to access the 8-bit video memory
UCHAR *primary_buffer = NULL;

// the bitmap file you're going to load the image into
BITMAP_FILE bitmap8bit;

// load the bitmap
Load_Bitmap_File(&bitmap8bit, "ANDRE8.BMP");

// now load the palette into DirectDraw;
// assume a palette has been created and attached to
// the primary surface
lpddpal->SetEntries(0,0,256,bitmap8bit.palette);

// lock the primary surface
// set up the surface description to lock the surface
memset(&ddsd,0,sizeof(ddsd));
```

```
ddsd.dwSize = sizeof(ddsd);

// lock the primary surface
lpddsprimary->Lock(NULL,&ddsd,
            DDLOCK_SURFACEMEMORYPTR | DDLOCK_WAIT,NULL);

// get video pointer
primary_buffer = (UCHAR *)ddsd.lpSurface;

// copy each bitmap line into primary buffer,
// taking into consideration nonlinear video
// modes and the memory pitch lPitch
for (int y=0; y<480; y++)
   {
   // copy the line
   memcpy(&primary_buffer[y*ddsd.lPitch], // dest address
         &bitmap16bit.buffer[y * 640],    // src address
         640);                            // bytes to copy
   } // end for y

// unlock the surface
lpddsprimary->Unlock(primary_buffer);

// delete the bitmap
Unload_Bitmap_File(&bitmap8bit);
```

The only differences between this fragment and the 16-bit version is in the access of the primary buffer and the call to SetEntries() to update the palette with the palette of the bitmap.

Check out PROG10_6.CPP on the CD to see the 8-bit version of the bitmap loader in action.

Of the two blitting functions — Blt() and BltFast() — BltFast() is a bit faster when you don't have hardware acceleration, because it doesn't perform clipping. Other than that, the two functions are identical. See Chapter 12 for more about bitmap clipping.

Bit Blasting with the Blitter

The _blitter_ is a piece of hardware (or software emulation) that copies bitmaps from some source to some destination. In addition, the blitter can fill memory with a particular word (color), and many blitters support features such as rotating, scaling, and other special effects.

About the backbuffer

You'll note that I often refer to the secondary surface as the backbuffer, or the secondary backbuffer. You can call the surface a backbuffer, but sometimes it is secondary — so it's a secondary backbuffer. But it's also a secondary surface, but it's a secondary surface that I have abstracted to think of as a backbuffer. Basically, this whole issue is just DirectX-speak. A secondary surface is a backbuffer; sometimes I just want to emphasize that it's secondary. Don't be confused by that usage.

What you want to do is create small bitmap surfaces, each representing a single image, and then blit them in video memory at will. To do this, you need to load a bitmap into memory (as the preceding section describes), copy the contents of the bitmap to a secondary backbuffer surface, and then use the blitter to copy any section of the bitmap to the primary buffer.

Here are the steps:

1. **Create a DirectDraw application — say, 640 x 480 with 8-bit color.**

2. **Create a primary surface and a single secondary surface of the same size.**

3. **Load the bitmap into the secondary surface memory (which is off-screen).**

4. **Load the palette information into the palette attached to the primary surface.**

5. **Scan out arbitrary rectangular regions in the secondary surface and blit them to the primary surface at random locations.**

Normally, you would only use the secondary backbuffer for page flipping, but for illustrative purposes, I use it here as a source for the blitter to feed from because I don't really have another surface lying around.

The following program performs a secondary surface to primary surface bit blit. The call to Blt() is later in the program because so much setup is necessary.

```
// assume all variables have been defined...

// create object and test for error
if (DirectDrawCreate(NULL,&lpdd,NULL)!=DD_OK)
    return(0);

// set cooperation level to windowed mode normal
if (lpdd->SetCooperativeLevel(main_window_handle,
```

```
                DDSCL_ALLOWMODEX | DDSCL_FULLSCREEN |
                DDSCL_EXCLUSIVE | DDSCL_ALLOWREBOOT)!=DD_OK)
    return(0);

// set the display mode
if (lpdd->SetDisplayMode(640,480,8)!=DD_OK)
    return(0);
```

Next, create the primary and secondary surfaces:

```
// create the primary surface
memset(&ddsd,0,sizeof(ddsd));
ddsd.dwSize  = sizeof(ddsd);
ddsd.dwFlags = DDSD_CAPS | DDSD_BACKBUFFERCOUNT;

// you need to tell DirectDraw that you want a complex
// flippable surface structure; set flags for that
ddsd.ddsCaps.dwCaps =
  DDSCAPS_PRIMARYSURFACE | DDSCAPS_FLIP | DDSCAPS_COMPLEX;

// set the backbuffer count to 1
ddsd.dwBackBufferCount = 1;

// create the primary surface
lpdd->CreateSurface(&ddsd,&lpddsprimary,NULL);

// query for the backbuffer; that is, the secondary surface
ddscaps.dwCaps = DDSCAPS_BACKBUFFER;
lpddsprimary->GetAttachedSurface(&ddscaps,&lpddsback);
```

Now create a black (all values 0,0,0) color palette and attach it to the primary surface:

```
// create palette
memset(palette,0,256*sizeof(PALETTEENTRY));

// set flags
for (int index=0; index<256; index++)
    palette[index].peFlags = PC_NOCOLLAPSE;

// now create the palette object
if (lpdd->CreatePalette(DDPCAPS_8BIT | DDPCAPS_INITIALIZE | DDPCAPS_ALLOW256,
            palette,&lpddpal,NULL)!=DD_OK)
    return(0);

// attach the palette to the primary surface
if (lpddsprimary->SetPalette(lpddpal)!=DD_OK)
    return(0);
```

The next step is to load the 8-bit 256-color bitmap, set the palette, and copy the data into the secondary surface:

```
// load the bitmap
Load_Bitmap_File(&bitmap8bit, "HOLLY8.BMP");

// now load the palette into DirectDraw
lpddpal->SetEntries(0,0,256,bitmap8bit.palette);

// lock the secondary surface
memset(&ddsd,0,sizeof(ddsd));
ddsd.dwSize = sizeof(ddsd);
lpddsback->Lock(NULL,&ddsd,
            DDLOCK_SURFACEMEMORYPTR | DDLOCK_WAIT,NULL);

// get video pointer
secondary_buffer = (UCHAR *)ddsd.lpSurface;

// copy the bitmap data into secondary surface;
// this time, assume linear memory
memcpy(secondary_buffer, bitmap8bit.buffer, 640*480);

// unlock the secondary backbuffer
lpddsback->Unlock(secondary_buffer);
```

Now you're ready to rock 'n' roll! Figure 10-11 shows the state of the system at this point. The source data is in the secondary surface, while the primary surface is the current display. So all you need to do is write a small loop that blits random rectangles from the source to the destination.

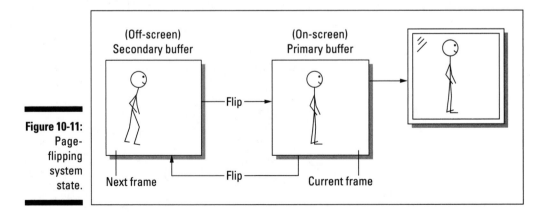

Figure 10-11: Page-flipping system state.

The following code shows that loop. The bold text in this code deals with Color Keys, which Chapter 11 explains in detail. Basically, Color Keys define what colors should or shouldn't be blitted from the source to the destination, so you can have holes and transparent objects.

```
// select source position to grab bitmap from
int source_x = rand()%640;
int source_y = rand()%480;

// select destination position to blit to
int dest_x = rand()%640;
int dest_y = rand()%480;

// select width and height of rectangle
int width = rand()%640;
int height = rand()%480;

// set up rectangles
RECT source_rect, dest_rect;

source_rect.left   = source_x;
source_rect.top    = source_y;
source_rect.right  = source_x + width;
source_rect.bottom = source_y + height;

dest_rect.left   = dest_x;
dest_rect.top    = dest_y;
dest_rect.right  = dest_x + width;
dest_rect.bottom = dest_y + height;

// set up the color key so that color 0 is transparent
DDCOLORKEY col_key;
col_key.dwColorSpaceLowValue  = 0;
col_key.dwColorSpaceHighValue = 0;

// set the key
lpddsback->SetColorKey(DDCKEY_SRCBLT, &col_key);

// perform the blit
lpddsprimary->Blt(&dest_rect, lpddsback, &source_rect, DDBLT_KEYSRC |
                DDBLT_WAIT, NULL);
```

Not bad for government work. Using the blitter to copy bitmaps is extremely easy (and very fast). Basically, I base this book's entire game engine (which is built in Chapters 12 and 16) on the blitter and little more.

To see this code in action, check out PROG10_7.CPP on the CD. Also, try rewriting the programs in this chapter to take command-line parameters for the input files. Better yet, before going into full-screen DirectDraw mode, put up a File Selection dialog and let the user select the .BMP file to load.

Chapter 11

Digging Deeper into DirectDraw: Advanced Features

*T*his chapter covers the advanced stage of bitmapped graphics and gives you the final details you need in order to create a full-bitmapped sprite engine. After that, I round off the chapter with advanced DirectDraw features such as using GDI on DirectDraw surfaces, and creating windowed DirectDraw applications. The latter is important if you want to keep the Windows "look" in your games, but with the performance of DirectDraw. With these concepts under your belt, you can follow the building of the GPDUMB library in Chapter 12.

Color Keying and Transparency

Writing a bitmapped graphics engine is simple. More or less, all you are doing is copying chunks of memory from one place to another. About the only problem people have when writing bitmap engines is properly taking transparent pixels into consideration. Hence, after you understand *transparency* and *color keying,* writing a bitmap engine is a snap.

Why manually set transparency?

If you read the sections on color keying and transparency in this chapter, you may wonder why you'd ever need to know how to manually set bitmap transparency. After all, apparently DirectDraw gives you the perfect tools in its color-keying functions so that you'd never need to write code for making a background transparent.

However, you still need the information presented in the section "Transparency." In some instances, you need to write bitmap functions and other image-processing algorithms. So be aware that the subsections "Color keying" and "Transparency" complement each other; one method of making a bitmap background transparent is not more useful than the other.

Transparency

Transparency always seems to confuse people. Suppose that you create a bitmap image of a character. The character bitmap is contained within a 64-x-64-pixel bitmap, but the character is an irregular shape: It has a head, arms, legs, and so on, so it doesn't take up the entire 64-x-64-pixel bitmap. The area devoid of color should be transparent — that is, only the parts of the character image that have color should be drawn.

Figure 11-1 (on the left) shows an example of blitting a character down without transparency on a background. (If the word *blitting* makes no sense to you, check out Chapter 10 for a comprehensive discussion.) See what happens? The black background is drawn along with the character itself, and the result is a big rectangle — definitely not what you want. The solution is to draw the bitmap with transparency, as shown on the right of Figure 11-1. In this case, only the character is drawn, not the background around the character; hence, the image looks correct.

Figure 11-1:
Blitting
without
transparency
(left) and
blitting with
transparency
(right).

Implementing transparency is very simple. All you need to do is decide on a color or color index that will be transparent. Most people select RGB black (0,0,0) in RGB modes or color index 0 in 256 modes. Therefore, if you want to write a blitting function with transparency, you have to test for the transparent index or RGB value in each pixel of the bitmap that you draw. This testing is basically unavoidable (without preprocessing or tricks).

Suppose that you load a bitmap; extract the pixels for a single, 32-x-32-pixel game character; and store the pixels in a linear byte array image[]. You want to draw the image pixel by pixel, row by row, but with transparency. Assume that you're in 8-bit color mode and that everything is already set up so that primary_buffer is pointing to the video memory. Here's a fragment that copies the bitmap image to the primary buffer at location (x,y) with color 0 as the transparent color:

```
// these two loops blit a 32 x 32 bitmap
for (int index_y=0; index_y<32; index_y++)
{
// copy next row of pixels
for (int index_x=0; index_x<32; index_x++)
    {
    // get the next pixel
    UCHAR pixel = image[index_x+index_y*32];
    // test if pixel is transparent
if (pixel!=0)
        primary_buffer[x+index_x+(y+index_y)*ddsd.lPitch] =
                                            pixel;
// else do nothing
    } // end for index_x
} // end for index_y
```

The selection of the transparent color is up to you, but most programmers use color 0 or RGB (0,0,0).

The preceding code is much slower than what you would actually use in practice — you definitely don't want to perform multiplication on each pixel in the inner loop, as this code does.

In graphics code, avoid multiplication as much as possible and divide only if no other mathematical trick can do the same thing. I made the code in these examples as easy to understand as possible, without optimization; however, the code that I provide in the GPDUMB library *is* optimized. Here's how to write that code in an optimized fashion, without the multiplication:

```
// alias a pointer to the source bitmap image
UCHAR *src_ptr = image;
// find the starting address of the bitmap destination
UCHAR *dest_ptr =
        primary_buffer + x + y * ddsd.lPitch;
// these two loops blit a 32 x 32 bitmap
for (int index_y=0; index_y<32; index_y++)
    {
    // copy next row of pixels
    for (int index_x=0; index_x<32; index_x++)
        {
        // get next pixel
        UCHAR pixel = *src_ptr;

        // test if pixel is transparent
if (pixel!=0)
            dest_ptr =  pixel;
        // advance pointers
        src_ptr++;
        dest_ptr++;
        } // end for index_x

    // move destination pointer to start of next line
    dest_ptr+=(ddsd.lPitch - 32);
    } // end for index_y
```

This code may look a bit more complex than the previous one, but it's about 80 to 100 times faster. You can also eradicate the initial single multiplication before the loop if you use *shifting* to multiply.

In general, shifting a binary number to the left is equivalent to multiplying by 2, while shifting to the right is equivalent to dividing by 2, as Figure 11-2 shows. Moreover, multiple shifts are accumulative. Therefore, to multiply player_x*64, you can use player_x << 6 because 2^6 is 64. Multiplying player_x by 100 can be done in two parts: (player_x << 6) + (player_x<<5); that works because player_x*100 = player_x*64 + player_x*32 = (player_x << 6) + (player_x<<5) — 2^6 = 64 and 2^5 = 32.

You can do lots of things with transparency. You can select any color for the transparent color, or a number of colors, or a range of colors, and so on. You can turn the tables and think in terms of the destination instead of the source — that is, instead of writing software that keeps the transparent color(s) from being blitted, you may write it so that you blit any color from the source as long as the current destination pixels are of a certain color. For example, using a destination key, you might say that anything that's blue in the destination image can't be blitted on. This way, the blue objects always seem to be in the foreground. These techniques are used to accomplish overlays and simulated 3D layering or parallax scrolling.

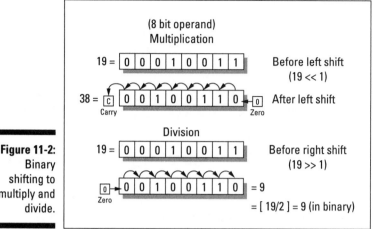

Figure 11-2:
Binary
shifting to
multiply and
divide.

Color keying

DirectDraw has a much more complex set of options for transparency than you could ever want; this technology is referred to as color keying. You can control which colors are transparent, which aren't, the z-ordering of bitmaps, and a lot more with color keying, but I don't go into all that stuff. You just need to know about *source* and *destination* color keys to get the job done.

Source keys

The beauty of using the blitter is that you don't have to write the software to perform the blitting or the transparency effects. DirectDraw handles these actions for you; but of course, you have to set it up. *Source color keying* is identical to the standard concept of defining transparent colors, as shown in the preceding section's code example. You set the range of colors that should be transparent and then instruct the blitter not to copy this range during the blit operation.

To perform a source color key blit, all you need to do is set the color key with the function SetColorKey():

```
HRESULT SetColorKey(DWORD dwFlags, // what kind of key
        LPDDCOLORKEY lpDDColorKey); // range of key
```

The function returns DD_OK if all went well or something else if not.

To set the color key system to use source blit color keying, you must set the dwFlags to DDCKEY_SRCBLT and set the color key range in a DDCOLORKEY structure:

```
typedef struct _DDCOLORKEY {
  DWORD dwColorSpaceLowValue; // starting color (inclusive)
  DWORD dwColorSpaceHighValue;// ending color (inclusive)
} DDCOLORKEY,FAR* LPDDCOLORKEY;
```

The reason for having both a low and a high value is in case you want a range of colors to be transparent. With that in mind, look at the following example of performing a standard source color key blit with color 0 as the transparent color:

```
DDCOLORKEY key; // color key
// set transparent color range to 0
key.dwColorSpaceLowValue  = 0;
key.dwColorSpaceHighValue = 0;
// set color key now on the source surface, which
// is usually the backbuffer
lpddsback->SetColorKey(DDCKEY_SRCBLT, &key);
// perform the blit from backbuffer to primary buffer
lppddsprimary->Blt(...);
```

If you want to set as transparent a range of colors such as colors 0 to 3, set `key.dwColorSpaceLowValue = 0` and `key.dwColorSpaceHighValue = 3`.

Review `PROG10_7.CPP` on the CD to see this technique in its entirety.

Destination keys

This book doesn't use destination keys as much as source keys, because destination keys are for more advanced bitmapping, such as layers and 3D simulations. Destination keys give you a range of colors on the destination surface that can be written to. So you can think of destination keys as more of an indicator describing what colors on the destination image are writable.

The flag to set up a destination key is `DDCKEY_DESTBLT`. You must set up a `DDCOLORKEY` structure with the destination range, similar to the previous example. The only difference is that the destination key is in relation to the destination surface, so you must set the color key of that surface interface rather than the source surface interface. As an example, here's how you set up a destination color key that allows the first 250 color values, but not colors 250 to 255, to be overwritten:

```
DDCOLORKEY key; // color key
// set writable values from 0 to 249
key.dwColorSpaceLowValue = 0;
key.dwColorSpaceHighValue = 249;
// set color key now on the destination surface
lpddsprimary->SetColorKey(DDCKEY_DESTCBLT, &key);
```

```
// perform the blit from backbuffer to primary buffer
// or whatever is the source surface...
lppddsprimary->Blt(...);
```

That's all there is to color keying. You can use a number of additional key types for advanced features; you probably won't need them, but if you're curious, check out the DirectX SDK Help for more information about support for 3D sprite overlays and sprite Z-buffering.

Building Little Bitmapped Objects

The section, "Transparency," earlier in this chapter, shows you how to load in a bitmap and manually display it with a software loop; and the section, "Color keying," shows another method of blitting the bitmap from the secondary surface to the primary surface using DirectDraw to handle transparency. However, these methods are a bit crude; you need something a little more . . . Lexus.

Your goal is to create a complex bitmap graphics engine that supports both hardware acceleration and software rendering. This section doesn't create a full-blown sprite engine yet, but it does take a couple more steps in the right direction. It shows you how to take 8-, 16-, or 24-bit images that you load into memory and extract each of the bitmap images out of the large bitmap template, as Figure 11-3 shows. Basically, you need a function that takes the large image bitmap along with the dimensions of each container cell and the coordinates of a cell to scan. The function scans the bits out of the image and places them into a smaller bitmap that contains only the image.

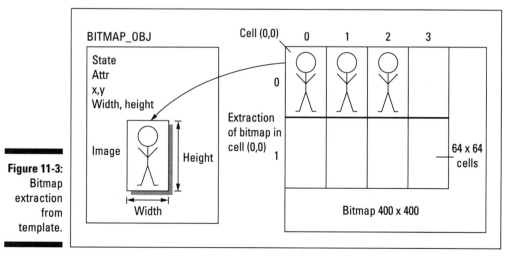

Figure 11-3: Bitmap extraction from template.

Furthermore, you want all the smaller bitmaps to be DirectDraw surfaces so that you can use DirectDraw to blit them instead of blitting them yourself with software. So you need a function to do the scanning, a bitmap data structure to hold the bitmapped objects, and a couple more functions to create the objects and draw them.

That's a lot of software. I show you just the bare bones of the functions and data structures. Take a look at the complete source code with PROG11_1.CPP on the CD.

This version of the blitter object engine supports only 256-color bitmaps. When I create the game library for the next chapter, I create much better BOBs that support multiple frames, motion, collision, and more, but the following BOBs are sufficient for this chapter's discussion. All the functions return TRUE if successful or FALSE if not.

Here are the steps involved for a simple example of loading and displaying a little bitmapped object bitmap (which I call *BOB* — I think I got that term from my Amiga 500 days, when *BOB* stood for *blitter object*):

1. **Set up DirectDraw.**

2. **Load a 256-color bitmap image with the objects in it as in Chapter 10.**

3. **Create a BOB with** Create_BOB().

4. **Load an image into the BOB with** Load_BOB().

5. **Draw the BOB with** Draw_BOB().

6. **After you are done, delete the BOB with** Destroy_BOB().

Setting things up for BOB

Begin with the data structure to hold BOB. Start off with something simple that contains at least the surface containing the bitmap, the bitmap's (x,y) position, and its width and height. Finally, the structure should have a state and flags field, to be well rounded. Here it is:

```
typedef struct BITMAP_OBJ_TYP
{
int state; // the state of the object (general)
int attr; // attributes pertaining to the object (general)
int x,y;   // position bitmap will be displayed at
int xv,yv; // velocity of object
int width, height; // the width and height of the bitmap
LPDIRECTDRAWSURFACE image; // the bitmap surface itself
} BITMAP_OBJ, *BITMAP_OBJ_PTR;
```

And here are a few #defines to define the state of each BOB:

```
// defines for BOBs
#define BOB_STATE_DEAD    0  // this is a dead BOB
#define BOB_STATE_ALIVE   1  // this is a live BOB
#define BOB_STATE_LOADED  2  // the BOB has been loaded
```

You may wonder what a "dead BOB" or a "live BOB" is. *Live* means being processed by game logic; *dead* means not being processed by game logic. The visual of being dead or alive has absolutely nothing to do with those terms. For example, in my game *Rex Blade,* hundreds of "dead" animated figures were lying around as the player progressed through the game, and these animations were all still "live objects," meaning that the AI, logic, and rendering still had to process them.

Creating BOB

Here's the prototype of the function to create the BOBs:

```
int Create_BOB(BITMAP_OBJ_PTR bob,     // the BOB to create
               int width, int height,  // size of BOB
               int attr,               // attrs
               int flags = 0)          // memory flag
{
// create the BOB object; note that all BOBs
// are created as off-screen surfaces in VRAM as the
// default; if you want to use system memory,
// set flags equal to DDSCAPS_SYSTEMMEMORY
DDSURFACEDESC ddsd; // used to create surface
// set state and attributes of BOB
bob->state = BOB_STATE_ALIVE;
bob->attr  = attr;
bob->image = NULL;

// set position and velocity to 0
bob->x = bob->y = bob->xv = bob->yv = 0;
// set to access caps, width, and height
memset(&ddsd,0,sizeof(ddsd));
ddsd.dwSize  = sizeof(ddsd);
ddsd.dwFlags = DDSD_CAPS | DDSD_WIDTH | DDSD_HEIGHT;
// set dimensions of the new bitmap surface
ddsd.dwWidth  = bob->width = width;
ddsd.dwHeight = bob->height = height;
```

(continued)

(continued)

```
// set surface to off-screen plain
ddsd.ddsCaps.dwCaps = DDSCAPS_OFF-SCREENPLAIN | flags;
// create the surface
if (lpdd->CreateSurface(&ddsd,&(bob->image),NULL)!=DD_OK)
   return(0);
// set color key to color 0
DDCOLORKEY color_key; // used to set color key
color_key.dwColorSpaceLowValue  = 0;
color_key.dwColorSpaceHighValue = 0;
// now set the color key for source blitting
(bob->image)->SetColorKey(DDCKEY_SRCBLT, &color_key);
// return success
return(1);


} // end Create_BOB
```

To use `Create_BOB()`, you simply send the blank BOB along with the parameters of the BOB. `Create_BOB()` then creates a DirectDraw off-screen surface big enough to hold your BOB and sets all the internal variables of the structure. Creating an off-screen surface is much simpler than creating a secondary backbuffer because off-screen surfaces don't have to be queried from the primary surface and have nothing to do with page flipping. Basically, the `Create_BOB()` function sets the width and height of the requested surface along with flags instructing DirectDraw to create the surface in system memory (`DDSCAPS_SYSTEMMEMORY`) or in the video RAM (default).

Loading BOB with bitmap data

`Load_BOB()` is probably the most complex of these functions — if you can call any of them complex. Its goal is straightforward enough; getting it to work is the problem. Here's how you load a BOB with bitmap data:

```
int Load_BOB(BITMAP_OBJ_PTR bob, // BOB to load with data
BITMAP_FILE_PTR bitmap, // bitmap to scan image data from
 int cx,int cy, // cell or absolute pos to scan image from
 int mode)      // if 0, then cx,cy is cell position; else
                // cx,cy are absolute coordinates
{
// this function extracts a bitmap out of a bitmap file
UCHAR *source_ptr,  // working pointers
      *dest_ptr;
DDSURFACEDESC ddsd; //  DirectDraw surface description
// test the mode of extraction, cell-based or absolute
if (mode==0)
   {
```

```
     // re-compute x,y
     cx = cx*(bob->width+1) + 1;
     cy = cy*(bob->height+1) + 1;
     } // end if

// extract bitmap data
source_ptr = bitmap->buffer +
        cy*bitmap->bitmapinfoheader.biWidth+cx;
// get the addr to destination surface memory
// set size of the structure
ddsd.dwSize = sizeof(ddsd);

// lock the display surface
(bob->image)->Lock(NULL,
                   &ddsd,
                   DDLOCK_WAIT | DDLOCK_SURFACEMEMORYPTR,
                   NULL);
// assign a pointer to the memory surface for manipulation
dest_ptr = (UCHAR *)ddsd.lpSurface;
// iterate through each scanline and copy bitmap
for (int index_y=0; index_y<bob->height; index_y++)
    {
    // copy next line of data to destination
    memcpy(dest_ptr, source_ptr,bob->width);
    // advance pointers
    dest_ptr   += bob->width;
    source_ptr += bitmap->bitmapinfoheader.biWidth;
    } // end for index_y

// unlock the surface
(bob->image)->Unlock(ddsd.lpSurface);
// set state to loaded
bob->state |= BOB_STATE_LOADED;

// return success
return(1);

} // end Load_BOB
```

The function takes as parameters the destination BOB and the source bitmap file to scan from. Then the position of the scan is determined by (cx,cy) and `mode`. If `mode` equals 0, (cx,cy) are interpreted as cell coordinates, but if `mode` equals 1, (cx,cy) are interpreted as absolute coordinates in the source bitmap. In either case, the size of the bitmap scanned out fits exactly into the BOB, which is defined to be `bob->width` and `bob->height`. Take a look at Figure 11-4 to illuminate this otherwise complex situation.

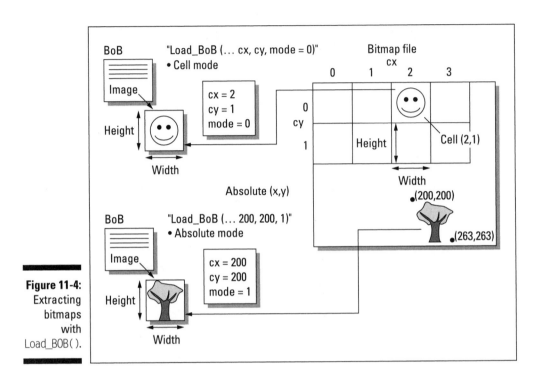

Figure 11-4:
Extracting
bitmaps
with
Load_BOB( ).

Drawing BOB

The next function you need is a way to draw a BOB:

```
int Draw_BOB(BITMAP_OBJ_PTR bob, // BOB to draw
  LPDIRECTDRAWSURFACE dest) // surface to draw the BOB on
{
// draw a BOB at the x,y defined in the BOB
// on the destination surface defined in dest
RECT dest_rect,   // the destination rectangle
    source_rect; // the source rectangle
// fill in the destination rect
dest_rect.left   = bob->x;
dest_rect.top    = bob->y;
dest_rect.right  = bob->x+bob->width-1;
dest_rect.bottom = bob->y+bob->height-1;
// fill in the source rect
source_rect.left   = 0;
source_rect.top    = 0;
source_rect.right  = bob->width-1;
source_rect.bottom = bob->height-1;
// blt to destination surface
```

```
dest->Blt(&dest_rect, bob->image,
          &source_rect,(DDBLT_WAIT | DDBLT_KEYSRC),
          NULL);
// return success
return(1);
} // end Draw_BOB
```

Because the position of the BOB is internal to the structure, you don't need to send coordinates to draw the BOB at. The only thing the function needs to know is the BOB to draw and the destination surface to draw it on (usually a backbuffer or the primary surface).

Destroying BOB

To destroy a BOB after you're done with it, just call `Destroy_BOB()`:

```
int Destroy_BOB(BITMAP_OBJ_PTR bob)
{
// destroy the BOB; simply release the surface
if (bob->image)
   (bob->image)->Release();
else
   return(0);
// return success
return(1);

} // end Destroy_BOB
```

Using the function to make BOB dance

Here's the whole sequence of BOB functions calls to create, load, display, and destroy those little suckers:

```
BITMAP_FILE bitmap; // working bitmap file
BITMAP_OBJ car;     // the bitmapped object
// load the bitmap
Load_Bitmap_File(&bitmap,"cars8.bmp");
// create a 32 x 32 VRAM BOB
Create_BOB(&car,32,32,0,0);

// load the BOB with first cell of bitmap template image
Load_BOB(&car,0,0,0);
// unload the bitmap; you're done with it
```

(continued)

(continued)

```
Unload_Bitmap_File(&bitmap);
// set position of BOB
car.x = 100;
car.y = 200;

// draw BOB on primary surface
Draw_BOB(&bob, lppdsprimary);

// your game code goes here...
// delete the BOB
Delete_BOB(&car);
```

If you want to see a demonstration of this crude first attempt at sprite objects, check out `PROG11_1.CPP` on the CD — it's an asteroid field made of BOBs.

Tricks with Color

In the old days (about five years ago), 2D acceleration was very expensive, and 3D acceleration was still taking baby steps. Game programmers had to use tricks to make the graphics system look as if it had more colors than it really did, as well as special lighting effects that looked impossible to do with the available hardware. Even though the technology is now available to accomplish these feats without tricks, some of these techniques are still great for adding a lot of visual excitement for a little price. I discuss two color tricks of the game-programming trade in the following sections: palette animation, and color rotation.

Palette animation

Palette animation is a technique that's only applicable to 8-bit color modes. The idea of palette animation is to continually update one or more palette entries with new data in real-time. This way, any on-screen pixel that's drawn with these colors animates or changes instantly. Use this technique to simulate blinking lights, pulsing energy sources, explosions, and so on.

The only downside to palette animation is that you must set aside one or more palette colors for animation. For example, say that you want to have three colors that blink on and off in red, green, and blue. You have to decide on three palette values — maybe 253, 254, and 255 — that you're going to animate. Then you continually update these palette entries with the new values, and any pixel in your images that has these colors changes instantly.

Remember, in palletized modes, such as the 8-bit 256-color modes, if you change the palette entry, you change every pixel drawn with that entry.

For example, suppose you write a program that loads in a bitmap background — an image of some machinery. To make the image look more realistic, you want blinking red, green, and blue lights. So you take the bitmap image into your painting program and draw the lights, using color indices 253, 254, and 255 (the actual working colors that you use in your paint program are irrelevant because they're going to be changed by the software anyway, they're just placeholders). Then you load the image in and animate the color entries (253 to 255) with a simple algorithm to make them look like they're blinking. Here's such an algorithm, assuming that all the DirectDraw stuff is set up as usual:

```
void Blink_Em(int r_rate, // rate of red blink in cycles
      int g_rate,  // rate of green blink in cycles
      int b_rate,  // rate of blue blink in cycles
      int r_i, int g_i, int b_i) // indices of colors
{
// this is a self-contained autonomous function
// define colors
static PALETTEENTRY black={0,0,0,PC_NOCOLLAPSE},
                    red   = {255,0,0,PC_NOCOLLAPSE},
                    green = {0,255,0,PC_NOCOLLAPSE},
                    blue  = {0,0,255,PC_NOCOLLAPSE};
// state variables
static int red_count   = 0,
           green_count = 0,
           blue_count  = 0,
           red_state   = -1,
           blue_state  = -1,
           green_state = -1;


// run algorithm
// red
if (++red_count>=r_rate)
   {
   // toggle state of red light
   red_state=-red_state;
red_count = 0;
   // change color entry
   if (red_state==1)
      lpddpal->SetEntries(0,r_i,1,&red);
   else
      lpddpal->SetEntries(0,r_i,1,&black);
   } // end if
// green
if (++green_count>=g_rate)
   {
```

(continued)

(continued)

```
    // toggle state of green light
    green_state=-green_state;
    green_count = 0;
    // change color entry
    if (green_state==1)
        lpddpal->SetEntries(0,g_i,1,&green);
    else
        lpddpal->SetEntries(0,g_i,1,&black);
    } // end if
// blue
if (++blue_count>=b_rate)
    {
    // toggle state of blue light
    blue_state=-blue_state;
    blue_count = 0;
    // change color entry
    if (blue_state==1)
        lpddpal->SetEntries(0,b_i,1,&blue);
    else
        lpddpal->SetEntries(0,b_i,1,&black);
    } // end if
} // end Blink_Em
```

To use the function, send it the rate of blinkage for the red, green, and blue lights, along with their color indices. For example, if you want to blink each light at a rate of 2, 4, and 8 cycles and you want the colors animated to be 253, 254, and 255, make the following call each cycle of your game in Game_Main() or a similar position:

```
// blink the lights
Blink_Em(2,4,8, 253,254,255);
```

To see this code in action, check out the CD's PROG11_2.CPP, which animates a piece of digital hardware.

Color rotation

Color rotation is a very powerful method of simulating motion. For example, have you ever seen a game with a waterfall, running stream, or conveyor belt? Chances are that the effect was achieved with color rotation. You can also see this trick in Chapter 9, in the program PROG9_5.CPP that creates an RGB gradient screen and then scrolls the colors to make them look like they're moving. That program uses color animation with the following code:

```
// get the color palette
lpddpal->GetEntries(0,0,256,work_colors);
// shift and store at 1 to 255
lpddpal->SetEntries(0,1,255,work_colors);
// now store color 255 at 0
lpddpal->SetEntries(0,0,1,&work_colors[255]);
```

Pretty simple stuff! Color rotation is basically the shifting of colors, as Figure 11-5 shows. The technique is a great way to make a bunch of pixels look like they're moving when in fact they aren't.

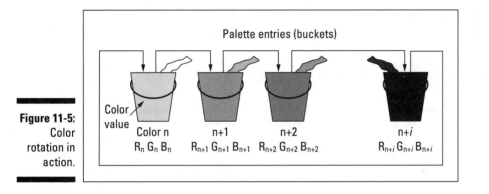

Figure 11-5: Color rotation in action.

Of course, color rotation works only in 256-color modes because the entire basis of the algorithm is color indirection (see Chapter 9). That is, changing some entries in a table changes every pixel on-screen. You can't do color rotation in a standard 16- or 24-bit color mode, because these modes don't support indirection. Here's a general code function that rotates a section of colors one step:

```
void Rotate_Colors(LPDIRECTDRAWPALETTE pal,
                   int start_index, // starting color
                   int colors) // number of colors
{
// this function rotates the color between start and end
PALETTEENTRY work_pal[256]; // working palette
// get the color palette
pal->GetEntries(0,start_index,colors,work_pal);
// shift the colors
pal->SetEntries(0,start_index+1,colors-1,work_pal);
// fix up the last color
pal->SetEntries(0,start_index,1,&work_pal[colors - 1]);
} // end Rotate_Colors
```

The function shifts the colors to the right, in a positive direction, so you have to rewrite it to shift in the other direction. To use the function, simply call it with the DirectDraw palette that you want to rotate and the starting index, along with the number of colors.

If you want to rotate the blinking lights from the previous example, do this:

```
Rotate_Colors(lpddpal, 253, 3);
```

Then the lights would blink and shift! Now that is coooool.

For the CD, I created the quintessential example of color rotation: the trench in the Death Star from *Star Wars*. Check out PROG11_3.CPP to see it!

Getting Clipped on the 50-Yard Line

Clipping means not drawing parts of an image that aren't visible. For example, if you have a large bitmap ship that's moving from right to left on-screen, as in Figure 11-6, you don't want to draw the nose of the ship after that part has moved past the left edge of the screen. Another example of clipping is a control panel, in the middle of your screen, that you want nothing drawn on; you want any images drawn into the control panel area to be clipped. Without clipping, games would look pretty bad.

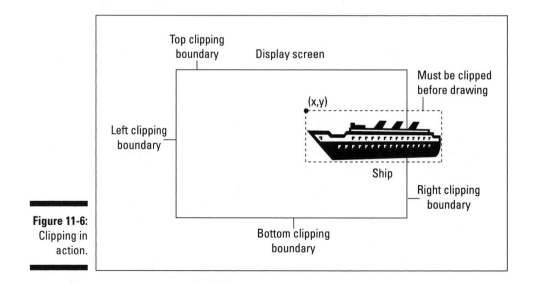

Figure 11-6:
Clipping in action.

Clipping comes in two flavors:

✔ **Image-space clipping:** Clipping an image as it's drawn pixel by pixel. This task is time-consuming and usually works well with hardware acceleration only. But the idea is that as you're drawing each pixel of the object, you make sure that it isn't being drawn in a clipped area. Of course, you can use many optimizations. For example, you can draw a scan line, and when a pixel is needed to be clipped in either the right or left direction, you don't need to continue testing the remaining pixels.

✔ **Object-space clipping:** Analyzing the geometry of the object being drawn and computing how much of it to draw instead of letting the drawing algorithm continually compare each pixel to the clipping region. This technique is a little more mathematical than image-space clipping. Figure 11-7 depicts cases of rectangles being drawn on-screen. Assuming that the screen is the clipping region means that you don't need to draw the portions of the rectangle that extend beyond the screen; so the end points of the rectangle are recomputed to make sure that they stay on-screen, and then the preclipped rectangle is resubmitted to the drawing software and can be drawn without clipping.

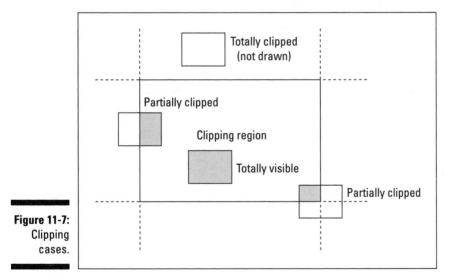

Figure 11-7:
Clipping
cases.

For an example of object space clipping, say that a rectangle is defined by (x1,y1) at the top-left corner and (x2,y2) at the bottom-right corner, and you want to clip this rectangle to a screen clipping region that's defined by MIN_X, MIN_Y, MAX_X, and MAX_Y, as in Figure 11-8. Use this code:

```
// trivial rejections test first
// is the rectangle totally off the screen?
if (x1 > MAX_X || x2 < MIN_X || y1 > MAX_Y || y2 < MIN_Y)
   { /* totally clipped, do nothing */ }

// check x coords
if (x1 < MIN_X) x1 = MIN_X;
else if (x2 > MAX_X) x2 = MAX_X;

// now y coords
if (y1 < MIN_Y) y1 = MIN_Y;
else if (y2 > MAX_Y) y2 = MAX_Y;

// at this point, (x1,y1) through (x2,y2) contain the
// clipped rectangle...
```

In short, clipping means that you don't draw what's not on the screen!

Introducing the DirectDrawClipper

DirectDraw supports the DirectDrawClipper, which can be attached to any surface that you want to blit into (clipping works for the blitter only). In addition, the clipper can have multiple clipping regions.

But the system has a little quirk. Normally, graphics programmers like to think of clipping regions as where not to draw, but DirectDraw thinks of them as where you *can* draw. So the clipping regions you supply to DirectDraw are the valid drawing regions, and everything else is clipped. Not a big deal, but it takes a little getting used to. Figure 11-8 clears this up.

Here are the steps for creating a DirectDrawClipper:

1. Create the DirectDrawClipper object itself.

2. Create a list of clipping rectangles and assign it to the clipper.

3. Attach the clipper to a surface.

Steps 1 and 3 are simple; Step 2 gives you the headache. As usual, DirectDraw tries to use data structures that are already available to Win32, which makes things harder than they really need to be because most of these data structures are old and weren't designed with speed or DirectX in mind.

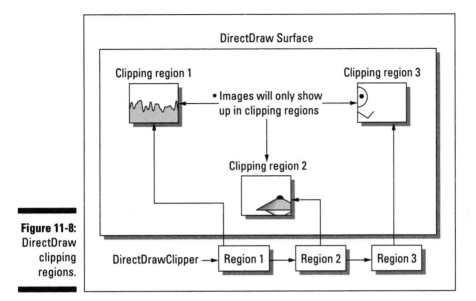

Figure 11-8:
DirectDraw
clipping
regions.

Creating the DirectDrawClipper

Here's the prototype for DirectDrawClipper:

```
HRESULT CreateClipper(DWORD dwFlags, // unused; make 0
LPDIRECTDRAWCLIPPER FAR *lplpDDClipper, // ptr to result
IUnknown FAR *pUnkOuter); // always NULL
```

To create a clipper, simply do this:

```
LPDIRECTDRAWCLIPPER lpddclipper; // the clipper
if ((lpdd->CreateClipper(0,&lpddclipper,NULL))!=DD_OK)
   return(NULL);
```

It won't do much, but at this point, lpddclipper is a valid clipper object.

Filling the clipping list

After you create the DirectDrawClipper, you need to fill in the clipping list with data — that's the hard part. The clipping list is contained in a special data structure called RGNDATA, as shown here:

```
typedef struct _RGNDATA { // rgnd
  RGNDATAHEADER rdh; // the header
  char Buffer[1]; // a list of RECTs defining clipping
} RGNDATA;
```

So `rdh` has some kind of header, which I know you can't wait to see, and `Buffer[]` contains a list of `RECT`s that are the clipping regions. Now take a look at the `rdh` field, which is a `RGNDATAHEADER` structure:

```
typedef struct _RGNDATAHEADER { // rgndh
  DWORD dwSize;    // size of this header
  DWORD iType;     // must be RDH_RECTANGLES
  DWORD nCount;    // number of rectangles in buffer
  DWORD nRgnSize;  // size of the buffer
  RECT  rcBound;   // a bounding box around all the rects
} RGNDATAHEADER;
```

You have to provide a list of `RECT`s that you want as the clipping region, then fill out the `RGNDATA` and `RGNDATAHEADER` structures, and send all this stuff to DirectDraw, with `SetClipList()`:

```
HRESULT SetClipList(
   LPRGNDATA lpClipList,  // ptr to RGNDATA
   DWORD dwFlags);        // unused; must be 0
```

Assuming that you've created the clipping list and set up the `RGNDATA` structure properly, here's how you set the clipping list:

```
RGNDATA region_data; // holds the RECTs and data header
// fill in region_data...
// set clipping list
if ((lpddclipper->SetClipList(region_data, 0))!=DD_OK)
   { /* error */ }
```

Attaching the clipper to a surface

After you create the DirectDrawClipper object itself, create a list of clipping rectangles, and assign the list to the clipper, tell DirectDraw what surface to use the clipping list on. This association is done with `SetClipper()`:

```
HRESULT SetClipper(LPDIRECTDRAWCLIPPER lpDDClipper);
```

But where's the surface? `SetClipper()` is actually a method from the surface interface `IDIRECTDRAWSURFACE`, so call `SetClipper()` like this, where `lpdds` is a pointer to a surface (primary, secondary, off-screen, and so on):

```
if ((lpdds->SetClipper(lpddclipper))!=DD_OK)
{ /* error */ }
```

I've danced around the setup of the clipping list and `RGNDATA` a little, but that's one of those things where you have to see the code for yourself — in the next section.

Creating one function to do it all

Here's a function that uses the surface you want the clipper attached to, along with the clipping list of rectangles, to create a DirectDrawClipper and attach it:

```
LPDIRECTDRAWCLIPPER
DD_Attach_Clipper(LPDIRECTDRAWSURFACE lpdds,
                  int num_rects,
                  LPRECT clip_list)
{
// this function creates a clipper from the sent clip list
// and attaches it to the sent surface
int index;                          // looping var
LPDIRECTDRAWCLIPPER lpddclipper;    // pointer to the newly
                                    // created dd clipper
LPRGNDATA region_data;   // pointer to the region
                         // data that contains
                         // the header and clip list

// first create the DirectDraw clipper
if ((lpdd->CreateClipper(0,&lpddclipper,NULL))!=DD_OK)
   return(NULL);
// now create the clip list from the sent data
// first allocate memory for region data
region_data = (LPRGNDATA)malloc(sizeof(RGNDATAHEADER) +
              num_rects*sizeof(RECT));
// now copy the rects into region data
memcpy(region_data->Buffer, clip_list,
      sizeof(RECT)*num_rects);
// set up fields of header
region_data->rdh.dwSize    = sizeof(RGNDATAHEADER);
region_data->rdh.iType     = RDH_RECTANGLES;
region_data->rdh.nCount    = num_rects;
region_data->rdh.nRgnSize  = num_rects*sizeof(RECT);

region_data->rdh.rcBound.left   =  64000;
region_data->rdh.rcBound.top    =  64000;
region_data->rdh.rcBound.right  = -64000;
region_data->rdh.rcBound.bottom = -64000;
// find bounds of all clipping regions
for (index=0; index<num_rects; index++)
    {
    // test whether the next rectangle unioned with the
    // current bound is larger
```

(continued)

(continued)

```
    if (clip_list[index].left <
            region_data->rdh.rcBound.left)
        region_data->rdh.rcBound.left =
                            clip_list[index].left;
    if (clip_list[index].right >
            region_data->rdh.rcBound.right)
        region_data->rdh.rcBound.right =
                            clip_list[index].right;
    if (clip_list[index].top <
            region_data->rdh.rcBound.top)
        region_data->rdh.rcBound.top = clip_list[index].top;
    if (clip_list[index].bottom >
            region_data->rdh.rcBound.bottom)
        region_data->rdh.rcBound.bottom =
                            clip_list[index].bottom;
    } // end for index
// you've computed the bounding rectangle region and
// set up the data; now set the clipping list
if ((lpddclipper->SetClipList(region_data, 0))!=DD_OK)
    {
    // release memory and return error
    free(region_data);
    return(NULL);
    } // end if

// now attach the clipper to the surface
if ((lpdds->SetClipper(lpddclipper))!=DD_OK)
    {
    // release memory and return error
    free(region_data);
    return(NULL);
    } // end if

// all is well, so release memory and send back the pointer
// to the new clipper
free(region_data);
return(lpddclipper);

} // end DD_Attach_Clipper
```

The function returns a DirectDrawClipper, which you can use later to access the clipping information or make changes. Here's how you actually set up a clipping list on the primary surface:

```
// create clip list (4) rectangles
RECT cliplist[4] = { {0,0,100,100}, {200,200,300,300},
                     {400,100,500,200}, {500,400,550,450}};
// attach clipper and save in lpddclipper
lpddclipper = DD_Attach_Clipper(lpddsprimary,4,cliplist);
```

You can start to appreciate subroutines! To see the clipper function in action, look at the CD's PROG11_4.CPP, which creates clipping regions and then blits at random positions on the screen — but you only see imagery within the clipping regions themselves because everything else is clipped.

Using GDI with DirectDraw

As Chapter 5 explains, GDI isn't the fastest thing in the world. But it's very good at many things that DirectX isn't as good at, such as drawing text, creating charts or tactical displays, drawing menus, displaying dialog boxes, and so on. This section covers high-level (using message boxes, menus, and so on) and low-level (drawing objects and text) mixing of Windows and DirectDraw, as well as windowed modes.

Note one detail about mixing GDI and DirectDraw: You must make the calls yourself. Windows will *not* be able to draw on your application surfaces. In other words, if another application needs to draw a window or control, you'll never see the application's image. That's because most of the time, you set the cooperation level to DDSCL_FULLSCREEN | DDSCL_EXCLUSIVE, thus indicating to Windows that the video system is off-limits — which is a good thing because it gives you total control of all things graphical.

With that in mind, you can see that GDI can draw almost anything on your application's surfaces. If you want to use the graphics primitives used by GDI, you can draw on any video surface; however, the controls, dialog boxes, and objects that are more high-level always display on the primary buffer.

You have three choices in which to use GDI within DirectDraw:

- **Via high-level controls:** The simplest way to use GDI is to avoid *GDCs* — Graphics Device Contexts (note that a GDC is simply a special case of an HDC, or Handle to Device Context) — and use high-level controls such as message boxes, dialog boxes, menus, and so on, instead.

- **Via the GDC:** You can use a GDC, which in reality is nothing more than a description of the video mode, memory, resolution, color space, and so on, to draw on any surface. You request a GDC from DirectDraw by using a function from IDIRECTDRAWSURFACE.

✔ **Via windowed modes:** You can choose to use DirectDraw with GDI by using the standard windowed modes. Most of the graphics-using code in this book involves taking over the entire video surface and switching the graphics mode. Sometimes, however, you may not want to do that, so you draw with DirectDraw in a standard window on the desktop.

Hooking it up

To use high-level GDI controls (message box, dialog box. and so forth) in DirectDraw, all you need is the window handle for the destination GDI operations, and DirectDraw and Windows work out the rest.

For example, if you want to display a message box on top of a bitmap image that's sitting in the primary buffer, you do something like this:

```
// this will pop up a message box on top of the image
if (KEY_DOWN('M'))
   {
   // show the mouse cursor
   ShowCursor(TRUE);

   // display the GDI message box
   MessageBox(main_window_handle,"What's Up Baby!",
            "Message Box Test",MB_OK);
   // hide the mouse cursor
   ShowCursor(FALSE);
   } // end if
```

This code waits for the user to press M; then it displays a message box. Notice the use of the global variable main_window_handle, which is how the communication between DirectDraw and Windows is accomplished. In addition, the mouse cursor is temporarily enabled during the display of the message box so that the user can navigate with the mouse (throughout the code in this book, you turn off the mouse in the initialization section of the code, right after window creation).

Program PROG11_5.CPP on the CD illustrates this code. Figure 11-9 shows the program running. Press M to display the message box, and press ESC to exit.

Figure 11-9:
A message box spawned from a DirectDraw application.

Drawing stuff

To draw on any surface, all you need is a Graphics Device Context (GDC). And a GDC is nothing more than a description of the video mode, memory, resolution, color space, and so on. You can request a GDC from DirectDraw by using the following function from IDIRECTDRAWSURFACE:

```
HRESULT GetDC(HDC FAR *lphDC); // ptr to graphics context
```

And after you're done with the GDC, you release it with

```
HRESULT ReleaseDC(HDC hDC); // the GDC to release
```

You can get a GDC from any surface you want — primary, secondary, or even small off-screen surfaces. After you have the GDC, you're free to draw whatever you want on the surface, using the standard GDI calls. For example, this code draws a bunch of random lines on the secondary backbuffer:

```
HDC xdc; // a DirectX GDC handle
HPEN old_pen, hpen; pens used to draw
// get the DirectDraw GDC handle from the surface
lpddsback->GetDC(&xdc);
// draw some lines
for (int index=0; index<100; index++)
    {
    // create a random colored pen
    hpen = CreatePen(PS_SOLID,1,
                RGB(rand()%256,rand()%256,rand()%256));
    // select the pen into context
    old_hpen = SelectObject(xdc,hpen);
    // move to a random position
    MoveToEx(xdc, rand()%WINDOW_WIDTH,
            rand()%WINDOW_HEIGHT, NULL);
    // draw a line
    LineTo(hdc,rand()%WINDOW_WIDTH, rand()%WINDOW_HEIGHT);
    // now delete the pen
    SelectObject(xdc,old_hpen);
    DeleteObject(hpen);

} // end for index
// release the DirectDraw-compatible GDC
lpddsback->ReleaseDC(xdc);
```

You can use any GDI functions that you like and do stuff more complex than this code. PROG11_6.CPP on the CD mixes GDI graphics and DirectDraw. This program moves a BOB creature from left to right on-screen and uses GDI to draw a string of text above the BOB creature.

Using windowed modes

The final way in which you can use DirectDraw with GDI is in standard windowed modes. Up to this point in the book, the code has been fairly aggressive about taking over the entire video surface and switching the graphics mode. However, you may not always want to do that. So how do you draw with DirectDraw in a standard window on the desktop? As easily as drawing with DirectDraw in full-screen modes. The only difference is that you create only a primary surface (most of the time), and you must draw only in the client area of your own window (unless you don't want to).

Here's the code from earlier in the book (see Chapter 8) to set up a more civilized cooperative DirectDraw windowed application (no error checking):

```
// create DirectDraw object
DirectDrawCreate(NULL,&lpdd,NULL);
// set cooperation level to windowed mode normal
lpdd->SetCooperativeLevel(main_window_handle,DDSCL_NORMAL);
// create the primary surface
memset(&ddsd,0,sizeof(ddsd));
ddsd.dwSize = sizeof(ddsd);
ddsd.dwFlags = DDSD_CAPS;
ddsd.ddsCaps.dwCaps =   DDSCAPS_PRIMARYSURFACE ;
lpdd->CreateSurface(&ddsd,&lpddsprimary,NULL);
```

If you Lock() the primary surface and draw into it, you draw right on top of all the windows on the desktop. That's good if you're writing a virus, but bad if you only want to draw in your window. You have two ways to approach the problem: You can set up a DirectDrawClipper to clip all output to your client window area, or you can do the clipping yourself.

In either case, you need to figure out where your window is on the desktop — that is, its client coordinates — which you can do with one of two functions: GetClientRect() if you want the interior dimensions of your window or GetWindowRect() if you want the actual screen coordinates of the window relative to the screen itself. Figure 11-10 shows the difference.

Using the functions is very simple. All you do is call either of them with your DirectDraw window handle and a RECT to save the data in. Here are the prototypes of the functions:

```
BOOL GetClientRect(HWND hWnd,  // handle of window
      LPRECT lpRect); // ptr to RECT for coordinates
BOOL GetWindowRect(HWND hWnd,  // handle of window
    LPRECT lpRect); // ptr to RECT for coordinates
```

The functions return TRUE if successful or FALSE otherwise.

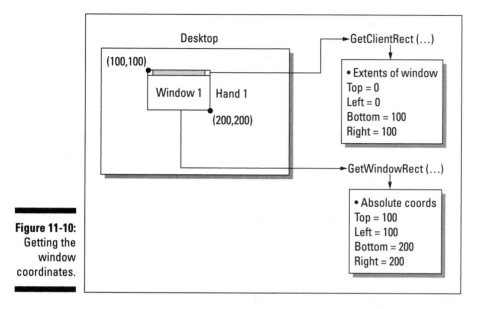

Figure 11-10:
Getting the
window
coordinates.

For a quick example, suppose that you have a DirectDraw application that's
running in windowed mode, and the resolution is 800 x 600 in 256 colors.
You want to draw only in your window's client area. Here's what you do:

```
RECT ddclient; // holds the client area of the window
// get the client rectangle of the DirectDraw window
GetWindowRect(main_window_handle, &ddclient);
// lock the primary buffer into primary_buffer....
// the starting address of the client area at
// pixel (0,0) is
primary_buffer[ddclient.left+
            (ddclient.top*ddsd.lPitch)] = color;
// and the bottom-right corner is
primary_buffer[ddclient.right+
            (ddclient.bottom*ddsd.lPitch)] = color;
// unlock primary surface ....
```

The better approach is probably knowing where the client area is; blindly
setting up a clipping area to it ends up drawing off the surface of your
window a great deal. In addition, your window may be moved around a lot,
so it may not stay in the same place — and neither will the clipping area.

For example, check out the CD's PROG11_7.CPP, which draws random pixels
in a DirectDraw window in windowed mode.

Making DirectDraw Talk Back

Getting information back from DirectDraw and DirectX in general is yet another skill that you need to master. As you may imagine, DirectX has a veritable plethora of informational functions that you can call to find things out. If the information is there, you can find it with DirectDraw's `Get_` class of functions. I cover just `GetCaps()` here, but once you've used one of these functions, you've used them all.

`GetCaps()` stands for (drum roll) Get Capabilities. And just about every DirectX interface and object has a `GetCaps()` for it. Here is a short list of the DirectDraw interfaces that have the method: DirectDraw, DirectDrawSurface, and DirectDrawPalette. You can make a call to `GetCaps()` from any of these interfaces. Of course, the information will be relative to the interface, but you get the idea. All the `GetCaps()` functions return `DD_OK` if successful or something else otherwise.

GetCaps() from the main DirectDraw object

The DirectDraw capabilities from `GetCaps()` are mainly concerned with the capabilities of the HAL (Hardware Abstraction Layer) and HEL (Hardware Emulation Layer); see Chapter 7. Here's the prototype:

```
HRESULT GetCaps(
  LPDDCAPS lpDDDriverCaps, // hardware capabilities
  LPDDCAPS lpDDHELCaps);  // software-emulation capabilities
```

The `GetCaps()` function takes pointers to two `DDCAPS` structures: one for the hardware capabilities and one for the software HEL capabilities. If you're not interested in either, send a `NULL` pointer. Here's how you make the call to get all the information:

```
// these variables will store all the capabilities
DDCAPS HELddcaps, HALddcaps;
// get the capabilities
lpdd->GetCaps(&HALddcaps, &HELddcaps);
```

After the call, you can query through the `DDCAPS` structures and check things out. For example, if you want to know how much VRAM the video card has, look at these variables in the `HALddcaps`:

```
HALddcaps.dwVidMemTotal // total video memory
HALddcaps.dwVidMemFree  // video memory free
```

GetCaps () from a DirectDraw surface object

The GetCaps() for a DirectDraw surface works as you may think it would: It returns a DDSCAPS structure with the capabilities of the surface in question. Here's the prototype, where lpDDSCaps is a pointer to the data storage for DirectDraw to place the results in:

```
HRESULT GetCaps(LPDDSCAPS lpDDSCaps);
```

See Chapter 8 for the DDSCAPS structure. Basically, this structure contains a description of the surface. Is the surface complex? Is there alpha channeling? And so on. Making the call is simple, as usual. Here's how you get the primary surface's capabilities:

```
DDSCAPS primaryddscaps; // used to hold the capabilities
// get the data
lpddsprimary->GetCaps(&primaryddscaps);
```

GetCaps () from a DirectDraw palette object

This GetCaps() is probably the easiest of all. About all it sends back are the various palettes that are supported. Here's the prototype:

```
HRESULT GetCaps(LPDWORD lpdwCaps);
```

On return, lpdwCaps contains the bit-encoded flags, as Table 11-1 lists.

Table 11-1	Bit Encoding for Palette Capabilities
Value	*Meaning*
DDPCAPS_1BIT	Supports 1-bit color palettes.
DDPCAPS_2BIT	Supports 2-bit color palettes.
DDPCAPS_4BIT	Supports 4-bit color palettes.
DDPCAPS_8BIT	Supports 8-bit color palettes.
DDPCAPS_8BITENTRIES	Supports 8-bit color palettes.
DDPCAPS_ALLOW256	All 256 colors can be defined.
DDPCAPS_PRIMARYSURFACE	Primary surface can have a palette.
DDPCAPS_VSYNC	Supports palette switches during vertical blank period.

Here's how to see whether the palette hardware supports 256-color palettes:

```
DWORD pal_flags;
// make the call
lpddpal->GetCaps(&pal_flags);

// test the flags for 8-bit
if (pal_flags && DDPCAPS_8BIT)
   { /* do the dew */ }
```

Chapter 12

The GPDUMB Game Engine, Part I

. . . .

In This Chapter

▶ Designing the GPDUMB I engine

▶ Creating a simple DirectDraw interface

▶ Including primitive graphics

▶ Manipulating color

▶ Getting Windows GDI support

▶ Using bitmap graphics

▶ Exploring the advanced BOB engine

▶ Tracking your game's time

. . . .

*E*arlier chapters of this book discuss Windows programming, DirectDraw, multimedia, and a lot more. For this chapter, I've applied all that information and created a game engine library — GPDUMB.

By using the GPDUMB library, you could probably write a whole game. In Chapter 16, you finish the library and add functionality for DirectInput, DirectSound, and DirectSetup, but for now I cover the design of Part I of the library and all the functions in it.

The Design of the GPDUMB I Engine

I had two goals in mind when I designed the GPDUMB engine: I wanted to simplify the use of DirectDraw and Windows, while at the same time writing a library that you may actually use! So what I did was make a list of everything that I cover in earlier book chapters and then sort those tasks into groups. Then I thought of a set of functions (as orthogonal as possible) to help you accomplish these tasks. The resulting library consists of about 60 or so functions that handle these jobs.

But I wanted to create more than a bunch of functions; I had a design goal for the GPDUMB engine: to create 256-color video games on the PC. Hence, the engine is built around an animation system that supports a primary video buffer and a secondary backbuffer, as shown in Figure 12-1. All graphics are rendered into these buffers. Moreover, the majority of graphics will be represented by BOBs and/or simple drawing primitives. (For more information about what I call a BOB, see Chapter 11.) I wanted to give you the ability to set up DirectDraw and create animation and graphics very quickly. Therefore, I took the BOB engine that I discuss in the last chapter and improved it with further animation capabilities. Now, the BOB engine is a fairly complete object-based animation package.

I didn't want you to have to write boring utility functions to manipulate the palette, perform timing, use the GDI, and so on. So, in addition to the main BOB animation system, I wrote a number of functions to do just about everything you need to do in a complete game. But you aren't locked into using all these functions. If you just want to start up DirectDraw and draw into the primary or backbuffer yourself, you can. You can take what you want and leave the other stuff behind. To tell you the truth, I don't expect you to use any of these functions as is. I hope that you optimize them and tailor them for your games. These functions are more of a way to get you started and show you the kinds of functionality that a game engine needs to have.

The game engine consists of a single `.CPP` file (called `GPDUMB1.CPP`) and a header (`GPDUMB1.H`). That's all there is to the engine. Include the header in your program and make sure to include `GPDUMB1.CPP` in your project, and the game engine will work. Of course, your application must create a window, and you need to supply the code for `Game_Init()`, `Game_Main()`, and `Game_Shutdown()`, but that's it.

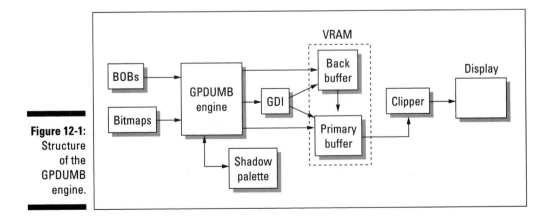

Figure 12-1:
Structure
of the
GPDUMB
engine.

For an example of a skeleton application that you can use as a template, take a look at GPTEMP.CPP on the CD. All you need to do is fill in the game console functions and this application does the rest. Basically, it's the WinX Game console file (see Chapter 6) with a few changes to incorporate the GPDUMB library functions. Figure 12-2 illustrates the relationship between the WinX file and the GPDUMB library, so you can see it in black and white.

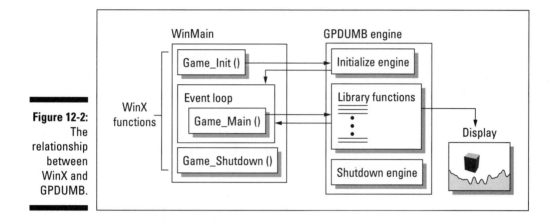

Figure 12-2:
The relationship between WinX and GPDUMB.

The GPDUMB engine consists of a number of #defines, macros, types, data structures, globals, and functions, so I may as well start with the #defines.

The #defines

The #defines for the GPDUMB engine cover everything from screen size to BOB attributes. Some of them are for future use; some are just to make the code look cleaner. Here they are:

```
// default screen size
#define SCREEN_WIDTH    640    // size of screen
#define SCREEN_HEIGHT   480
#define SCREEN_BPP      8      // bits per pixel
// bitmap defines
#define BITMAP_ID   0x4D42         // universal id for a bitmap
#define BITMAP_STATE_DEAD    0 // states of bitmaps
#define BITMAP_STATE_ALIVE   1
#define BITMAP_STATE_DYING   2
#define BITMAP_ATTR_LOADED   128
```

(continued)

(continued)

```
#define BITMAP_EXTRACT_MODE_CELL  0
#define BITMAP_EXTRACT_MODE_ABS   1
// defines for BOBs
#define BOB_STATE_DEAD            0  // this is a dead bob
#define BOB_STATE_ALIVE           1  // this is a live bob
#define BOB_STATE_DYING           2  // this BOB is dying
#define BOB_STATE_ANIM_DONE       1  // done animation state
#define MAX_BOB_FRAMES           64  // max BOB frames
#define MAX_BOB_ANIMATIONS       16  // max anim sequences
#define BOB_ATTR_SINGLE_FRAME     1  // BOB has single frame
#define BOB_ATTR_MULTI_FRAME      2  // multiple frames
#define BOB_ATTR_MULTI_ANIM       4  // multiple animations
#define BOB_ATTR_ANIM_ONE_SHOT    8  // perform animation once
#define BOB_ATTR_VISIBLE         16  // BOB is visible
#define BOB_ATTR_BOUNCE          32  // BOB bounces off edges
#define BOB_ATTR_WRAPAROUND      64  // BOB wraps around edges
#define BOB_ATTR_LOADED         128  // the BOB has been loaded
```

In the preceding code block, the purpose and usage of the screen and bitmap #defines are either explained in a comment or are easy to determine by the #define name. However, some of the #defines for the BOBs aren't quite so self-explanatory, so I cover those next.

The engine includes a lot of bitmap and BOB stuff, so these #defines help describe the capabilities of these objects for you. The general design of the GPDUMB engine is for each object to have a *state* and *attributes*.

- The state is a real-time indicator of the object. For example, is the BOB dead? alive? dying? These concepts are completely up to you. Usually, alive means running around, dying means in the process of dying and soon to be dead. And dead of course, means no longer alive.

- The attributes define the capabilities that the object can have after it's created.

Bitmap images aren't that smart, meaning that they have no state information, but the new BOBs have a lot of functionality to support animation. You can create a number of different BOB types:

- **Single Frame:** The BOB has one single frame; maybe the BOB is just a rock.

- **Multiple Frame:** The BOB has multiple frames, but always animates the frames in a linear sequence. Take a look at Figure 12-3.

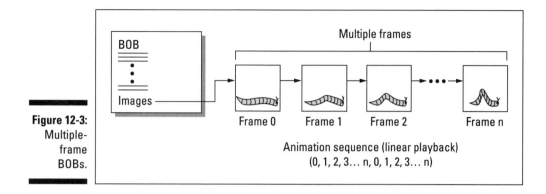

✔ **Multiple Animations:** The BOB has multiple frames of animation, but there is another level of control called an animation sequence. For example, the BOB may have 3 frames of a walking animation (frame 0 is left leg forward, 1 is neutral, 2 is right leg forward). If you were to play that animation over and over, the BOB would look like it was missing a step — no second occurrence of the neutral leg position. But if you were to create another list with the animation steps 0,1,2,1,0, the BOB would look like it was walking without missing a step. In addition, by using multiple animation BOBs, you can load in 50 (up to 64) frames, and create animations that use subsets of the animation cells. One animation may be a figure walking, another an explosion, and so on. (This concept will become clearer when you see the functions in the upcoming section, "BOB: The Next Generation.")

The macros

In the example programs of earlier chapters, I use macros here and there to make tasks easier. I rounded up all the good ones and wrote a couple more for inclusion in this section.

The following macros read the keyboard asynchronously (later I explain how to do this with DirectInput in Chapter 14):

```
#define KEY_DOWN(vk_code) ((GetAsyncKeyState(vk_code) & 0x8000) ? 1 : 0)
#define KEY_UP(vk_code)   ((GetAsyncKeyState(vk_code) & 0x8000) ? 0 : 1)
```

Here's an example of checking whether the A key is pressed:

```
if (KEY_DOWN('A')) {/* do it */ }
```

The following macro builds up a 16-bit color value. Although the BOB and bitmap image software of the GPDUMB engine are for 8-bit graphics, you can still set the system to 16-bit and do the process manually.

```
#define RGB16BIT(r,g,b) ((b%32)+((g%32)<<5)+((r%32)<<10))
```

Here's how to create a bright green:

```
USHORT green = _RGB16BIT(0,31,0);
```

Notice that the maximum value for any 16-bit RGB component is 31.

The following are a couple of useful macros that take a data word and set or reset a bit or bits in the word based on the parameters:

```
#define SET_BIT(word,bit_flag) ((word)=((word) | (bit_flag)))
#define RESET_BIT(word,bit_flag) (word)=((word) & (~bit_flag)))
```

For example, to set the 8-bit in a data value named `counter`:

```
SET_BIT(counter, 0x0008);
```

And to reset the value to 0:

```
RESET_BIT(counter, 0x0008);
```

Finally, I got tired of clearing out all the DirectDraw structures and setting their size, so I wrote this macro to do the job:

```
#define DD_INIT_STRUCT(ddstruct) { memset(&ddstruct,0,sizeof(ddstruct));
        ddstruct.dwSize=sizeof(ddstruct); }
```

Use the macro like this:

```
DDSURFACEDESC ddsd; // any DirectDraw data structure
// call macro
DD_INIT_STRUCT(ddsd);
```

Due to the width of code listings, some of the previous macros are shown on multiple lines. Please note that this isn't the case; the lines that appear indented very far actually reside on single lines. To see this single-line display, look at the source on the CD.

Types and data structures

I have created a few data structures for the game engine. These structures aren't particularly efficient or space saving, but they do the job. The function of each data field becomes more obvious when you see the functions, but the comments clarify their workings. First, here are the simple types:

```
// basic unsigned types
typedef unsigned short USHORT;
typedef unsigned short WORD;
typedef unsigned char  UCHAR;
typedef unsigned char  BYTE;
```

Now for the bitmap file structure:

```
// container structure for bitmaps .BMP file
typedef struct BITMAP_FILE_TAG
  {
  BITMAPFILEHEADER bitmapfileheader; // bitmapfile header
  BITMAPINFOHEADER bitmapinfoheader; // all info defining bitmap
  PALETTEENTRY     palette[256];     // copy of palette is stored here
  UCHAR            *buffer;          // pointer to data
  } BITMAP_FILE, *BITMAP_FILE_PTR;
```

After I created the BOBs, I realized that you need a simpler code for elements such as backgrounds. Moreover, I wanted a graphic object that was made of simple system memory and had nothing to do with DirectDraw, so I came up with BITMAP_IMAGEs. These objects are like very simple single-frame BOBs, but without all the bells and whistles. Here is the data structure:

```
// the simple bitmap image
typedef struct BITMAP_IMAGE_TYP
       {
       int state;         // state of bitmap
       int attr;          // attributes of bitmap
       int x,y;           // position of bitmap
       int width, height; // size of bitmap
       int num_bytes;     // total bytes of bitmap
       UCHAR *buffer;     // pixels of bitmap
       } BITMAP_IMAGE, *BITMAP_IMAGE_PTR;
```

A BITMAP_IMAGE has a state (alive, dead, or dying), a set of attributes (not well defined in the code just yet), a size, and a position. That's it. These objects are great for backgrounds and elements that don't need to be animated.

Now for the big dog of the data structures — BOB:

```
// the blitter object structure BOB
typedef struct BOB_TYP
   {
   int state;       // the state of the object (general)
   int anim_state;  // an animation state variable (up to you)
   int attr;        // attributes of BOB object (general)
   int x,y;         // position at which BOB is displayed
   int xv,yv;       // velocity of BOB
   int width, height; // size of the BOB
   int width_fill;  // used to force 8*x wide surfaces
   int counter_1;   // general counters
   int counter_2;
   int max_count_1; // general threshold values;
   int max_count_2;
   int varsI[16];   // stack of 16 integers
   float varsF[16]; // stack of 16 floats
   int curr_frame;  // current animation frame
   int num_frames;  // total number of animation frames
   int curr_animation; // index of current animation
   int anim_counter;   // used to time animation transitions
   int anim_index;     // animation element index
   int anim_count_max; // number of cycles before animation
   int *animations[MAX_BOB_ANIMATIONS]; // animation sequences
   LPDIRECTDRAWSURFACE images[MAX_BOB_FRAMES]; // the bitmap images DD surfaces
   } BOB, *BOB_PTR;
```

Great scott! The good thing is: You don't have to worry about all those data fields, the BOB engine takes care of them for you. That's the beauty of the juice weasel. But if you must know; new fields have been added for animation state control, internal timing and counting (so you don't have to use outside variables), animation timing, and motion. Finally, notice that the images[] array is an array and not a single image as in the previous BOB version in Chapter 11. The array exists so that the BOB can hold multiple frames.

In the prior code block, the number of frames a BOB can hold is limited to MAX_BOB_FRAMES (which was set at 64 in the code found in the section "The #defines," earlier in this section). If you want more frames for your BOBs, increase this constant in the file GPDUMB1.H, which is on the CD.

I tried to think of all the object data items you may want to track, and then I put them in the BOB. I included these items so that you don't have to create a container structure to add more functionality to the BOB.

Global, globals, where are my globals?

Global variables, often called simply *globals,* have been persecuted for eternity — at least, an eternity for programmers. I think that globals have a bad rap! These variables are good, and game programmers use them a lot. They are fast, they are always there, and they are . . . well . . . global!

To track all the action of the game engine, the engine needs a number of globals. Some of them you will read, some of them you will write, but most of them are used internally, so you won't have to worry about them. However, if you mess with global variables (and you will know when you are), the result will probably be a little message box that reads, `"GPFAULT at 0x349fdc34"` or something similar. Here are the global variables as they exist in `GPDUMB1.CPP` (I have highlighted globals of interest in boldface, and note that *dd* stands for DirectDraw):

```
LPDIRECTDRAW        lpdd        = NULL; // dd object
LPDIRECTDRAWSURFACE lpddsprimary = NULL; // primary surface
LPDIRECTDRAWSURFACE lpddsback   = NULL; // back surface
LPDIRECTDRAWPALETTE lpddpal     = NULL; // dd palette
LPDIRECTDRAWCLIPPER lpddclipper = NULL; // dd clipper
PALETTEENTRY        palette[256];       // color palette
PALETTEENTRY        save_palette[256]; // copy of palette
DDSURFACEDESC       ddsd;      // a dd surface desc. struct
DDBLTFX             ddbltfx;   // used for filling
DDSCAPS             ddscaps;   // dd surface caps struct
HRESULT             ddrval;    // result from dd calls
UCHAR    *primary_buffer = NULL; // primary video buffer
UCHAR    *back_buffer    = NULL; // secondary backbuffer
int       primary_lpitch = 0;    // memory line pitch
int       back_lpitch    = 0;    // memory line pitch
BITMAP_FILE bitmap16bit;     // a 16-bit bitmap file
BITMAP_FILE bitmap8bit;      // an 8-bit bitmap file
DWORD       start_clock_count = 0; // used for timing
// these defined the general clipping rectangle
int min_clip_x = 0, // clipping rectangle
    max_clip_x = SCREEN_WIDTH-1,
    min_clip_y = 0,
    max_clip_y = SCREEN_HEIGHT-1;
// these are overwritten globally by DD_Init()
int screen_width  = SCREEN_WIDTH,  // width of screen
    screen_height = SCREEN_HEIGHT, // height of screen
    screen_bpp    = SCREEN_BPP;    // bits per pixel
FILE *fp_error    = NULL;          // general error file
```

All the global variables in the code here are important, but you will work with the highlighted ones most often. After you set up DirectDraw, all the DirectDraw-related interface pointers will be valid. `lpddsprimary` and `lpddsback` are the interface pointers to the primary and secondary surfaces, so they are important. Also, when locking video memory, `primary_buffer` and `back_buffer` point to the linear VRAM of the primary or secondary buffer, respectively. In addition, `primary_lpitch` and `back_lpitch` contain the memory pitch of the surfaces, so you can access the surfaces properly.

The next important global is `palette[]`, which contains a copy of the color palette that is currently active. Normally, you don't have to access this global directly because functions are available to do this task, but the global is there if you need it. Finally, `bitmap8bit`, and `bitmap16bit` are for you to use when loading bitmap files, just as a convenience more than anything else.

The remaining globals should be obvious by their names; most of them are working globals to get information, and so on. The only values that are somewhat interesting define the clipping rectangle (`min_clip_x`, `min_clip_y . . .`), which controls the clipping for the line-drawing primitive.

That's about it for the preliminaries of the GPDUMB game engine. The next section looks at each subsystem of the engine in detail.

Mission Impossible: A Simple DirectDraw Interface

The task of creating a DirectDraw interface isn't as easy as you may think. The problem is deciding what the interface should support and what it should automate within the budget of time and space. In the end, I tried to keep the interface as simple as possible and give it enough capability to get things up and running very quickly. Here's a list of the functional classes, in no particular order:

- ✔ Initializing DirectDraw
- ✔ Shutting down DirectDraw
- ✔ Creating off-screen plain surfaces
- ✔ Page flipping the surfaces for animation
- ✔ Filling a DirectDraw surface with a color

- ✔ Attaching DirectDrawClippers to surfaces
- ✔ Waiting for the vertical blanking period
- ✔ Locking the primary buffer and backbuffer

In the following sections, I cover each function prototype, explain its purpose, and provide a short example of usage (if appropriate).

Unless otherwise stated, all functions return TRUE if successful and FALSE if a problem occurs.

DD_Init

Function prototype:

```
int DD_Init(int width, // width of fullscreen videomode
    int height, // height of fullscreen videomode
    int bpp);   // bits per pixel of mode
```

Purpose: DD_Init() initializes the entire DirectDraw system. It creates the DirectDraw object lpdd, sets the cooperation level, sets the video mode, creates a palette accessed via lpddpal, and creates primary and secondary surfaces accessed via lpddsprimary, and lpddsback. This function is the only one you need to start a DirectDraw application. Here's an example of setting up an 800 x 600 256-color mode:

```
if (!DD_Init(800,600,8)) { /* error */ }
```

DD_Shutdown

Function prototype:

```
int DD_Shutdown(void);
```

Purpose: DD_Shutdown() shuts down and releases all the DirectDraw interfaces that were created with DD_Init(). Call DD_Shutdown() when your game application is complete. In most cases, you will place this function call in Game_Shutdown(). Here's an example of a complete DirectDraw application start-up and shutdown sequence:

```
DD_Init(640,480,8); // start up DirectDraw
// .. do whatever
DD_Shutdown(); // shut down directdraw
```

DD_Create_Surface

Function prototype:

```
LPDIRECTDRAWSURFACE DD_Create_Surface(
                    int width, // width of surface
                    int height, // height of surface
                    int mem_flags); // memory flags
```

Return value: This function returns an interface pointer to the newly created surface if successful, and NULL otherwise.

Purpose: DD_Create_Surface() creates an off-screen plain surface for your own internal programming usage. Simply send to the function the width and height (in pixels) of the surface you want along with the memory flags. The memory flags default to DDSCAPS_OFFSCREENPLAIN, which will create a surface in VRAM. You are free to add more flags, such as DDSCAPS_SYSTEMMEMORY, to request that the surface be constructed in system memory. This example creates a 64 x 64 surface in VRAM:

```
LPDIRECTDRAWSURFACE lpddsplayer; // surface holding player
// create surface
if (!(lpddsplayer = DD_Create_Surface(64,64,0)))
   { /* error */ }
```

Of course, the surface needs to be compatible with the primary surface and use the same palette. Also, color index 0 should be transparent for blit operations (see Chapter 10 for more on transparency).

All surfaces you create with this code must have a width that is divisible by 8. This is a DirectDraw quirk.

DD_Flip

Function prototype:

```
int DD_Flip(void);
```

Purpose: DD_Flip() is used to page flip the primary and secondary surfaces lpdds_primary and lpdds_back. Call this function after rendering the next frame on the secondary backbuffer lpddsback. Here's an example of making the call:

```
// draw the next frame in lpdds_back....
// flip the surfaces
if (!DD_Flip()) { /* error - serious problem!!! */ }
```

DD_Fill_Surface

Function prototype:

```
int DD_Fill_Surface(
        LPDIRECTDRAWSURFACE lpdds, // surface to fill
        int color);  // color to fill surface with
```

Purpose: DD_Fill_Surface() takes a surface pointer along with a color and fills the entire surface. This function simply saves you the time of using the blitter to fill the surface — or worse yet, locking the surface and performing a memory fill that way. Here's an example of filling the primary surface with color 25:

```
if (!DD_Fill_Surface(lpddsprimary,25)) { /* error */ }
```

And here's how to clear the surface like the one you created a minute ago named lpddsplayer with color 0:

```
if (!DD_Fill_Surface(lpddsplayer,0)) { /* error */ }
```

DD_Attach_Clipper

Function prototype:

```
LPDIRECTDRAWCLIPPER DD_Attach_Clipper(
  LPDIRECTDRAWSURFACE lpdds, // surface to attach clipper to
  int num_rects,      // number of rectangles in clipping list
  LPRECT clip_list); // a list of RECTs making up the clipping list
```

Return value: The function returns a pointer to the DirectDrawClipper after creating and attaching it to the surface. In most cases, you'll have only one clipper in your application, so you can assign the return value to the global clipper object lpddclipper to keep track of it. (Check out Chapter 8 for more about the DirectDrawClipper.)

Purpose: DD_Attach_Clipper() is used to create a clipper object, attach the clipper to a surface (which I cover in Chapter 11), and set the clipping regions, all in one fell swoop. In most cases, you will attach the clipper to the backbuffer (secondary surface) because that's where you will be doing most of your blitting. Although you can send multiple clipping rectangles to the function, most of the time you will send only one: the screen boundary. Here's an example of attaching a clipper to a secondary surface that is the same size as the screen:

```
// define screen rectangle for 640x480 video mode
RECT screen_rect = {0,0,640,480};
```

```
// create and attach the clipper to the secondary back surface
if (!(lpddclipper = DD_Attach_Clipper(lpddsback,1,&screen_rect)))
   { /* error */ }
// all blitter operations to the secondary surface lpddsback will be clipped
```

DD_Wait_For_Vsync

Function prototype:

```
int DD_Wait_For_Vsync(void);
```

Purpose: DD_Wait_For_Vsync() is used to wait for the vertical blank to start. Take a look at Figure 12-4. The image on your computer screen is drawn line by line, left to right and top to bottom, by an electron gun. After the image is drawn, the electron gun moves back to the top left-hand corner and starts again. This process is called the *vertical retrace.* The point in time in which the gun is moving back to the top-left corner is the best time to update the screen because the image isn't being drawn. DD_Wait_For_Vsync helps you with this task.

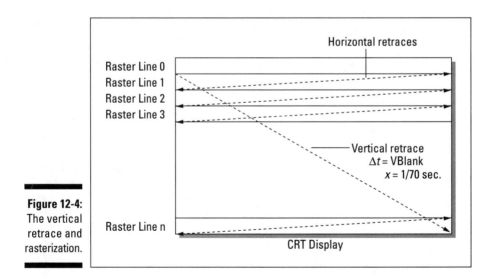

Figure 12-4:
The vertical retrace and rasterization.

At the end of your graphics loop right before you call DD_Flip(), **first** call DD_Wait_For_Vsync() to make sure that the vertical retrace has started, and then call DD_Flip(). This method insures a rock-steady display without shearing or flicker. Here's an example:

```
DD_Wait_For_Vsync(); // wait for vsync
DD_Flip(); // flip pages
```

Locking and unlocking functions

Now I want to cover the locking and unlocking functions. In essence, there are two video buffers: the primary and the backbuffer (secondary). The locking functions enable you to lock the memory and obtain a pointer to each of the video buffers along with the memory pitch.

DD_Lock_Primary_Surface
Function prototype:

```
UCHAR *DD_Lock_Primary_Surface(void);
```

Return value: This function, if successful, returns a pointer to the video memory of the primary surface, or NULL if the function fails. In addition, the function aliases the value primary_buffer to the memory and sets primary_lpitch equal to the memory pitch of the primary buffer.

Purpose: DD_Lock_Primary_Surface() locks the primary surface, so you can write to or read from the memory. After the function call, you can access the surface memory via the pointer primary_buffer and its memory pitch is stored in primary_lpitch. Before locking, both of these values are invalid, so don't use them unless you have locked the surface at a point in the code prior to the point in which you want to use the values. Here's an example of locking the primary surface and writing a pixel at (x,y) in color col.

```
if (!DD_Lock_Primary_Surface()) // lock the primary surface buffer
   { /* error */}
primary_buffer[ x + y*primary_lpitch] = col; // write the pixel
```

DD_Unlock_Primary_Surface
Function prototype:

```
int DD_Unlock_Primary_Surface(void);
```

Return value: The function returns TRUE if successful and FALSE if it fails or if the surface wasn't locked to begin with.

Purpose: DD_Unlock_Primary_Surface() unlocks the previously locked primary surface. This process is necessary if you want to flip pages, or use DirectDraw to blit or draw on the surface.

While you have the surface locked, you are the only one that can mess with it! So after you're finished using the primary buffer (as in the preceding example), you make the unlock call like this:

```
if (!DD_Unlock_Primary_Surface()) {/ *error */}
```

DD_Lock_Back_Surface

Function prototype:

```
UCHAR *DD_Lock_Back_Surface(void);
```

Return value: This function, if successful, returns a pointer to the video memory of the backbuffer or NULL if the function fails. In addition, the function aliases the pointer back_buffer to the memory and sets back_lpitch equal to the memory pitch of the primary buffer.

Purpose: DD_Lock_Back_Surface() locks the secondary backbuffer surface, so you can write or read from the memory. After the function call, you can access the surface memory via the pointer back_buffer, and its memory pitch is stored in back_lpitch. Before locking, both of these values are invalid, so don't use them until after you have locked the surface. Here's an example of locking the backbuffer surface and writing a pixel at (x,y) in color col.

```
if (!DD_Lock_Back_Surface()) // lock the secondary backbuffer surface
   { /* error */}
back_buffer[ x + y*back_lpitch] = col; // write the pixel
```

DD_Unlock_Back_Surface

Function prototype:

```
int DD_Unlock_Back_Surface(void);
```

Return value: The function returns TRUE if successful and FALSE if it fails or the surface wasn't locked to begin with.

While you have the surface locked, your program is the only one that can access it!

Purpose: DD_Unlock_Back_Surface() simply unlocks the previously locked backbuffer surface. This task is necessary if you want to flip pages, or use DirectDraw to blit or draw on the surface. So after you're done with the backbuffer (as in the preceding example), make the call like this:

```
if (!DD_Back_Primary_Surface()) {/ *error */}
```

DD_Lock_Surface

Function prototype:

```
UCHAR *DD_Lock_Surface(
          LPDIRECTDRAWSURFACE lpdds,  // surface to lock
          int *lpitch); // pitch of locked surface
```

Return value: This function returns a pointer to the memory of the locked surface.

Purpose: DD_Lock_Surface() locks a general surface, maybe one you created. The function takes the surface to lock along with a pointer to a variable to store the memory pitch of the surface after locking. After you have locked the surface, you are free to read or write it. For example, suppose that you want to read the pixel (1,1) out of the lpddsplayer surface that you created earlier in your code:

```
UCHAR *surface_buffer = NULL; // will hold the memory
int memory_pitch; // will hold the memory pitch
// lock the surface
if (!(surface_buffer = DD_Lock_Surface(lpddsplayer, &memory_pitch)))
{ /* error */ }
UCHAR pixel = surface_buffer[1+1*memory_pitch]; // read the pixel
```

DD_Unlock_Surface
Function prototype:

```
int DD_Unlock_Surface(LPDIRECTDRAWSURFACE
        lpdds,                  // pointer to surface
        UCHAR *surface_buffer); // pointer to surface memory
```

Purpose: DD_Unlock_Surface() unlocks a surface previously locked with DD_Lock_Surface(). You need to send the function a pointer to the memory surface along with the surface itself. Here's an example of unlocking the surface that was locked in the DD_Lock_Surface example:

```
DD_Unlock_Surface(lpddsplayer, surface_buffer); // unlock lpddsplayer
```

Primitive Graphics: Someone Has to Do It!

Most 2D games use bitmapped graphics alone, but being able to draw lines, rectangles, and plot pixels is nice. In this section, I provide some functions to do those tasks for you.

This book doesn't contain a discussion of line-drawing algorithms, so I want to quickly brief you on how they work. Take a look at Figure 12-5. It depicts a simple line from (x1,y1) to (x2,y2). Up until now, you have used Windows GDI to draw lines, but I can assure you that drawing a simple line is not as simple as it seems. A number of algorithms can do it, but one of the most popular is *Bresenham's algorithm*.

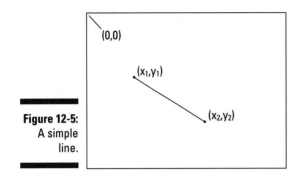

Figure 12-5:
A simple
line.

When you want to draw a line from point to point, you must draw it with single pixels. Start from the starting point (x1,y1) and draw the proper points in-between to arrive at (x2,y2) and be as mathematically correct as possible.

The problem is: The computer screen is composed of an integer matrix of pixels, and you can't plot fractional coordinates such as (23.5,34.6). Any good line algorithm must take this limitation into consideration. Bresenham's algorithm functions by using an *error term:* The algorithm takes this fractional error and tracks it, and then plots pixels that are the best approximation to the real line.

Sounds confusing, huh? Good thing I've written a version of Bresenham's algorithm for you! If you are interested in finding out more about line drawing, take a close look at the line-drawing function's code. It's short, and if you look at it long enough and make some sketches, you should get the idea.

The following sections take a look at the pixel-plotting, rectangle, and line-drawing functions.

All functions return TRUE if successful or FALSE otherwise.

Draw_Pixel

Function prototype:

```
int Draw_Pixel(int x, int y,      // position of pixel
               int color,          // color of pixel
               UCHAR *video_buffer, // pointer to memory buffer
               int lpitch);        // horizontal memory pitch
```

Purpose: This function draws a single pixel in the destination memory buffer at the sent position and color. Also, note that you must send the memory pitch of the destination surface. You may use this function on pure system memory or on DirectDraw surfaces. The function doesn't know the difference. Here's an example of drawing a pixel at (100,100) with color index 20 on the primary surface:

```
DD_Lock_Primary_Surface(); // lock primary surface
Draw_Pixel(100,100,20, primary_buffer, primary_lpitch); // draw the pixel
DD_Unlock_Primary_Surface(); // unlock the primary surface
```

Draw_Clip_Line and Draw_Line

Function prototype(s):

```
int Draw_Clip_Line(int x0,int y0, // starting point
            int x1, int y1,     // ending point
            UCHAR color,        // color of line
            UCHAR *dest_buffer, // destination memory
            int lpitch);        // memory pitch of destination memory

int Draw_Line(int x0, int y0,   // starting point
            int x1,int y1,      // ending point
            UCHAR color,        // color of line
            UCHAR *vb_start,    // destination memory
            int lpitch);        // memory pitch of dest memory
```

Purpose: Both functions Draw_Line() and Draw_Clip_Line() draw a line from (x0,y0) to (x1,x2) on the destination memory surface. The only difference is that Draw_Clip_Line() clips the line to a clipping rectangle defined by min_clip_x, min_clip_y, max_clip_x, max_clip_y (see Figure 12-6).

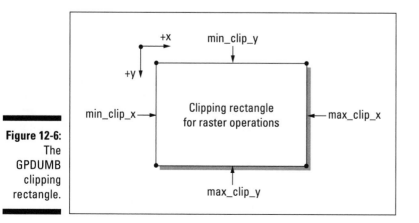

Figure 12-6:
The
GPDUMB
clipping
rectangle.

The Draw_Line() version doesn't clip and is a bit faster. However, if you send it coordinates that are out of range, trouble will result! Here's an example of drawing on the secondary backbuffer (I'm assuming a video mode of 640 x 480):

```
DD_Lock_Back_Surface(); // lock the backbuffer
for (int index = 0; index<100; index++) // draw 100 lines
Draw_Line(rand()%640, rand()%480, rand()%640,rand()%480,
                back_buffer, back_lpitch);
DD_Unlock_Back_Surface(); // unlock the backbuffer surface
```

And here's the same example, but using the clipping version with a clipping rectangle in the middle of the screen:

```
min_clip_x = 200; // set clipping rectangle globals
min_clip_y = 200;
max_clip_x = 500;
max_clip_y = 300;
DD_Lock_Back_Surface(); // lock the backbuffer
for (int index=0; index<100; index++) // draw 100 lines
    Draw_Clip_Line(rand()%640, rand()%480,
                rand()%640,rand()%480,
                back_buffer, back_lpitch);
DD_Unlock_Back_Surface(); // unlock the backbuffer surface
```

Draw_Rectangle

Function prototype:

```
int Draw_Rectangle(
    int x1, int y1, // upper-left corner of rectangle
    int x2, int y2, // lower-right corner of rectangle
    int color,      // color of rectangle
    LPDIRECTDRAWSURFACE lpdds); //destination surface
```

Purpose: Draw_Rectangle() draws a filled rectangle on a DirectDraw surface rather than working with arbitrary memory regions (which is what the previous line and pixel functions do). The reason for this difference is that I wanted to put the blitter to use. (Go to Chapter 10 to find out more about the blitter.) The function takes the upper-left and lower-right corners of the rectangle along with the rectangle's color and fills them in on the destination surface. If a clipper is attached to the surface, the rectangle will be clipped.

This function only draws filled rectangles. If you want a hollow rectangle, you need to make a function from the line drawing functions.

Here's an example of drawing a square centered at (320,200) on the primary surface:

```
Draw_Rectangle(320-50,200-50,320+50,200+50,10,lpddsprimary);
```

Painting the Town with Color

Along with an animation system, I created some kind of color interface so that you could manipulate the color palette. To this end, I came up with a *shadow buffer* system, meaning that the color palette is shadowed in memory in an array made of PALEETENTRYs called *palette[]*. However, don't access this array directly; use the functions that I provide. Technically, you can always read from the array, but if you write to it, GPDUMB won't know that you have written data to the color array and you will desynchronize the color management system.

The color system includes functions to read and write single palette entries or the entire palette. In addition, you can read and write palettes to and from the disk, which is cool if you want to load in multiple palettes from a disk and do some kind of animation with them. Here are the globals that the color system tracks:

- lpddpal: The DirectDraw palette

- palette[]: The color palette shadow of the DirectDraw palette

- save_palette[]: A convenient global variable for you to save the palette in if you want to destroy or modify the palette temporarily

The following is the function listing. As usual, all functions return TRUE if successful, and FALSE otherwise.

Set_Palette_Entry

Function prototype:

```
int Set_Palette_Entry(
   int color_index,         // color index to change
   LPPALETTEENTRY color); // pointer to RGB color
```

Purpose: `Set_Palette_Entry()` changes a single color palette entry in the palette. Send it the index of the color to change along with a standard `PALETTEENTRY`, and the function does the rest. Here's an example of changing color 50 to pure blue:

```
// define a pure blue, note the PC_NOCOLLAPSE flag
PALETTEENTRY blue = {0,0,255,PC_NOCOLLAPSE};
Set_Palette_Entry(50, &blue); // set the palette entry
```

Get_Palette_Entry

Function prototype:

```
int Get_Palette_Entry(
  int color_index,          // color index to retrieve
  LPPALETTEENTRY color);    // pointer to color-entry storage
```

Purpose: `Get_Palette_Entry()` retrieves the RGB components of a palette entry in the currently active palette. You must provide the function with the color index you wish to retrieve along with storage for the results. The following code, which includes error checking, shows how to read color palette entry 100:

```
PALETTEENTRY color; // store result here
if (!Get_Palette_Entry(100,&color)) // get a single palette entry
  { /* error */ }
```

Save_Palette

Function prototype:

```
int Save_Palette(
  LPPALETTEENTRY sav_palette); // array to save palette in
```

Purpose: `Save_Palette()` saves the entire color palette in one call. You may want to do this step before performing any kind of color animation.

The array you send to `Save_Palette()` must have enough space to hold 256 `PALETTEENTRY`s. If it doesn't, you will probably crash the computer!

Here is an example of saving the entire palette:

```
PALETTEENTRY old_palette[256]; // storage
Save_Palette(old_palette); // save the palette
```

Set_Palette

Function prototype:

```
int Set_Palette(LPPALETTEENTRY set_palette); // 256-color palette to set
```

Purpose: Set_Palette() sets or restores the entire palette with a previously saved palette or one that you have algorithmically generated. Simply call the function with a pointer to the 256 PALETTENTRYs and the new palette loads. This method is great to use with Save_Palette() in stack-based push/pop analogy. Here's an example of saving and restoring the palette:

```
PALETTEENTRY old_palette[256]; // storage
Save_Palette(old_palette); // save the palette
// code to mangle the palette goes here
Set_Palette(old_palette); // restore the palette
```

Load_Palette_From_File

Function prototype:

```
int Load_Palette_From_File(
        char *filename,           // filename to read palette from
        LPPALETTEENTRY palette); // pointer to destination palette storage area
```

Purpose: Load_Palette_From_File() loads a previously saved palette from a disk file. The format of the data file is 256 lines, each line containing one color entry of Red, Green, Blue, Flags (without the commas). Here's an example of the file format:

```
R0 G0 B0 F0
R1 G1 B1 F1
R2 G2 B2 F2
.
.
.
R255 G255 B255 F255
```

To use the function, pass it the name of the file containing the palette information along with a storage array. Here's an example of reading a palette from the file GPPAL.PAL:

```
PALETTEENTRY colors[256]; // storage palette
// load the palette, must test for error; file may not be there!
if (!Load_Palette_From_File("GPPAL.PAL",colors))
   { /* file not found or more serious problem */ }
```

Save_Palette_To_File

Function prototype:

```
int Save_Palette_To_File(
   char *filename,         // filename to save palette
   LPPALETTEENTRY palette); // array of 256 colors to save
```

Purpose: `Save_Palette_To_File()` saves a palette to disk in the previously mentioned format. Call the function with a filename and the palette to save, and `Save_Palette_To_File` does the rest. Here's an example of saving the main DirectDraw palette to disk:

```
if (!Save Palette To File("GPPAL.PAL",palette)) // save to disk. errors less
                          probable
   { /* some kind of error */ }
```

Rotate_Colors

Function prototype:

```
int Rotate_Colors(
     int start_index,   // starting index of colors to rotate
     int colors);       // number of colors to rotate
```

Purpose: `Rotate_Colors()` is a simple color rotation function that rotates the requested colors one slot in clockwise fashion, that is, (0⇨1, 1⇨2, . . . n⇨n+1). This function is almost identical to the one in the preceding color rotation demo of the *Star Wars* trench (`PROG11_3.CPP` in Chapter 11), but modified to integrate with the GPDUMB system. Here's an example of rotating the entire palette one click:

```
Rotate_Color(0,256);
```

Just a Bit of GDI

The Windows GDI isn't my first choice for doing anything more than printing text and maybe drawing tactical displays that don't need real-time speed. To access GDI, all you need to do is get a compatible graphics device context from the surface you want to draw in. Here's an example:

```
HDC xdc;
// get the device context that is compatible with windows from DirectDraw
xdc = lpdds->GetDC(&xdc);
// use xdc here ....
lpdds->ReleaseDC(xdc); // release the device context back to Windows
```

As long as you hold the device context, an internal lock is on the surface and neither DirectDraw nor you can draw on the surface; only GDI can, so watch out.

In general, when you lock surfaces, you should lock the surface, do the work, and unlock it. Doing so makes all the library functions work smoothly. Although you can hold a lock on a surface as long as you wish, doing so isn't a good idea.

Originally, I was going to create a number of wrapper functions around all the more important GDI functions, but I decided that the effort was not really useful because calling these functions is almost as easy. Alas, I decided to supply you with two versions of a single function, Draw_Text_GDI, to draw text, which is about the only task that you'll want to do with GDI. However, these functions must get a device context from the surface you send; if you are drawing on the primary or secondary surface, you must make sure that they aren't locked! The versions of this function return TRUE if successful, and FALSE otherwise.

Function prototype(s):

```
int Draw_Text_GDI(char *text, // text to draw
        int x,int y,    // position of text
        COLORREF color, // RGB color of text
        LPDIRECTDRAWSURFACE lpdds); // surface to draw on

int Draw_Text_GDI(char *text, // text to draw
        int x,int y,    // position of text
        int color,      // RGB color of text
        LPDIRECTDRAWSURFACE lpdds); // surface to draw on
```

Purpose: Draw_Text_GDI() uses GDI to draw text on a DirectDraw surface in any color and position that you desire. The function has two versions with the same name, but each version requires a different kind of color parameter, so to C++ they are different. This duplication is called *function overloading*. To get the proper version of the function, just call the function either with a color index or an RGB COLORREF, and C++ picks the right version for you.

Here's an example of drawing *Hello Dumb World* on the primary surface with color index 6:

```
if (!Draw_Text_GDI("Hello Dumb World",10,20,6,lpddsprimary))
  { /* error */ }
```

And here's an example of using the other overloaded version that uses a COLORREF to draw the text in green:

```
if (!Draw_Text_GDI("Hello Dumb World", 10, 20, RGB(0,255,0),lpddsprimary))
  { /* error */ }
```

It's possible for the above fragment to work, but not print in green. When you request an RGB color from GDI, it scans the color palette in 256 modes and finds the closest match. If it can't find green, it will find the closest match to it (which, according to the palette, may be red or blue!). So remember to always have at least one red, green, blue, yellow, white, black, and brown value in all your palettes. That way, problems like this won't happen! A good way to do this is to use the Include windows colors option when you make palettes. Most paint programs have this option when you convert from RGB color to 256 colors.

Support Your Local BMP

I won't go into detail in this section about what bitmap file loading and unloading routines do; if you need more information, check out Chapter 10. However, here are the basics:

- ✔ A .BMP file is a file format that contains a digital image.
- ✔ The format consists of a header section and a data section.
- ✔ The bitmap images can be any size, but my bitmap loader only supports 8-, 16-, and 24-bit images. However, if the image is 24-bit, it will be converted to 16-bit.

I cleaned up the functions a bit internally and added them to the GPDUMB library (see the following sections).

Load_Bitmap_File

Function prototype:

```
int Load_Bitmap_File(
  BITMAP_FILE_PTR bitmap, // bitmap file obj to store data
  char *filename);        // filename of .BMP file to load
```

Purpose: Load_Bitmap_File() loads a .BMP compliant file into memory and fills in the sent BITMAP_FILE record with the headers, data, and palette. Here is an example of loading an 8-bit color file called LASER.BMP:

```
if (!Load_Bitmap_File(&bitmap8bit, "LASER.BMP")) { /* error */ }
```

If you want to load the palette attached in the bitmap file, do this:

```
Set_Palette(bitmap8bit.palette);
```

You must check for errors to see whether the file was loaded, because the filename may be incorrect. If so, you don't want your program to use the data. Also, notice the use of the variable bitmap8bit. This variable and bitmap16bit are globals I have created for your convenience. Use them if you wish.

Unload_Bitmap_File

Function prototype:

```
int Unload_Bitmap_File(BITMAP_FILE_PTR bitmap); // bitmap object to unload
```

Purpose: Unload_Bitmap_File() unloads and frees the memory allocated by a bitmap file loaded via Load_Bitmap_File(). Call it with the previously loaded bitmap file object, like this:

```
Unload_Bitmap_File(&bitmap8bit); // unload bitmap8bit
```

Basic Bitmap Graphics

The bitmap file loader loads a bitmap and its palette (if one exists) into memory, but no other support functions were available to do anything useful with the data, so I decided to create a bitmap engine that can do a few cool things. The bitmap engine enables you to create `BITMAP_IMAGE` objects and then load images into an object one at a time. After the images are loaded, you can draw them on any surface or destination buffer. The bitmap system doesn't do much, but with it you can make an asteroid field or a moving background. Only five functions are supported, and they all return `TRUE` if successful and `FALSE` otherwise.

Create_Bitmap

Function prototype:

```
int Create_Bitmap(
    BITMAP_IMAGE_PTR image,     // pointer to object to create
    int x, int y,               // initial position of bitmap object
    int width, int height);     // size of object
```

Purpose: The `Create_Bitmap()` function creates a `BITMAP_IMAGE` object in memory and fills in the internal fields with the sent data. Use this function to create and initialize a `BITMAP_IMAGE` object. Here's an example of creating a monster that is 32 x 32 pixels at location (100,100):

```
BITMAP_IMAGE monster; // the monster
if (!Create_Bitmap(&monster, 100,100, 32,32)) // create the object
   { /* error */ }
```

After the call, zeros appear in the bitmap data, so the data still has to be loaded by you via `monster.buffer` or the load function (`Load_Image_Bitmap`).

Destroy_Bitmap

Function prototype:

```
int Destroy_Bitmap(BITMAP_IMAGE_PTR image); // bitmap image to destroy
```

Purpose: `Destory_Bitmap()` destroys a previously created `BITMAP_IMAGE` object. Just call the function with a pointer to the `BITMAP_IMAGE` that you want to eliminate. Here's an example of destroying the object created in the example for `Create_Bitmap()`:

```
if (!Destroy_Bitmap(&monster)) { /* error, object wasn't valid */ }
```

Load_Image_Bitmap

Function prototype:

```
int Load_Image_Bitmap(
  BITMAP_IMAGE_PTR image, // bitmap image object to load
  BITMAP_FILE_PTR bitmap, // bitmap file to load data from
  int cx,int cy,// cell or absolute coords to load image data from
  int mode);    // loading mode (cell or absolute)
                // if equal to BITMAP_EXTRACT_MODE_CELL
                // then cx,cy are cell coords
                // if equal to BITMAP_EXTRACT_MODE_ABS
                // then cx,cy are absolute coords
```

Purpose: Load_Image_Bitmap() loads an image from a previously loaded bitmap file out of the bitmap buffer itself. The parameters are straightforward except maybe for cx,cy and mode. Take a look at Figure 12-7. I cover the cell-based template system in Chapter 10, and you are seeing it again here. If mode is equal to BITMAP_EXTRACT_MODE_CELL, then cx,cy are interpreted as cell coordinates. Otherwise, cx,cy are interpreted as absolute coordinates in the source bitmap file and the bitmap is scanned from that point. In either case, the size of the scanned bitmap is equal to the original width and height of the BITMAP_IMAGE object.

As a more complete example, the following shows how to create a BITMAP_IMAGE object (in this case, a graphic of a monster) that is 32 x 32 and then scan its image data from the absolute coordinates (0,0) of the TREK.BMP file:

```
BITMAP_IMAGE monster; // image of a monster
if (!Load_Bitmap_File(&bitmap8bit, "TREK.BMP")) { /* error */ }
// create the object
if (!Create_Bitmap(&monster, 0,0, 32,32)) { /* error */ }
// load the image
if (!Load_Image_Bitmap(&monster, &bitmap8bit,0,0,BITMAP_EXTRACT_MODE_CELL ))
  { /* error */ }
// unload bitmap8bit now that we are done with it
Unload_Bitmap_File(&bitmap8bit);
// .. do whatever with the object
if (!Destroy_Bitmap(&monster)) { /* error */ }
```

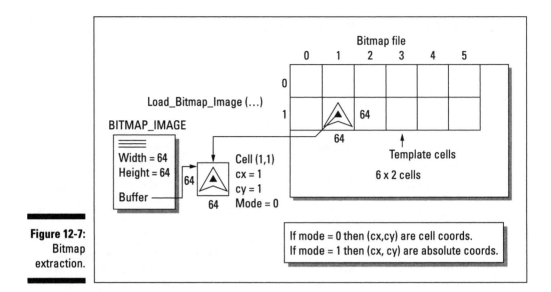

Figure 12-7:
Bitmap
extraction.

Draw_Bitmap

Function prototype:

```
int Draw_Bitmap( BITMAP_IMAGE_PTR source_bitmap, // pointer to bitmap object
   UCHAR *dest_buffer,  // destination buffer to draw to
   int lpitch, // horizontal memory pitch
   int trans); // if 1 then draw with color 0 transparent; else draw opaque
```

Purpose: Draw_Bitmap() draws the bitmap image on a memory surface having horizontal memory pitch lpitch. If the destination is system memory, then the lpitch is equal to the width of the memory — that is, the virtual width that you decided it has. But if the destination is a DirectDraw surface that was locked, then the memory pitch may be unequal to the width. I discuss the memory pitch problem in Chapter 8. Take a look at Figure 12-8 to see this memory line length problem graphically.

The last parameter to the function is used to enable or disable transparency. Because the function uses software to draw the bitmap, I decided to send a flag to instruct the function to draw with color 0 transparent or opaque. So if you want color 0 to be transparent, then make trans equal to 1. Also, the transparent version of the software blitter is slower than the opaque version,

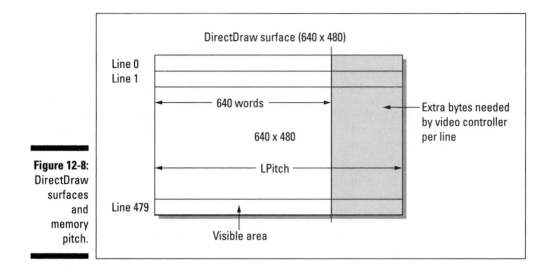

Figure 12-8:
DirectDraw
surfaces
and
memory
pitch.

so don't use it unless the object is in the foreground. Assuming that the bitmap image object has already been created (as in the previous examples), here's how to draw the BITMAP_IMAGE on the backbuffer screen at any (x,y):

```
monster.x = x; // set position
monster.y = y;
Draw_Bitmap(&monster,back_buffer, back_lpitch,1); // draw bitmap
```

That's all there is to BITMAP_IMAGEs. If you haven't had enough of graphics, check out the new and improved BOBs in the next section; they're sure to satisfy all your animation needs.

BOB: The Next Generation

The last chapter shows you how to create a BOB engine that does the job, but is fairly limited. In fact, the new BITMAP_IMAGE system has about the same capabilities as the old BOB engine. The new BOB engine is state-of-the-art — and monkeys can fly! In reality, a state-of-the-art animation system takes a couple of months to write, so I am exaggerating a bit; but, nevertheless, the new BOB engine offers quite a bit of utility.

✔ The most important improvement is that the BOB engine I describe in this chapter supports multiple frames of animation; thus you can load up to 64 frames and then animate them! (Take a look at Figure 12-9.)

✔ The BOB engine in this chapter supports animation sequences, so you can load in a set of frames and an animation sequence and the sequence plays while feeding from the frames. This feature is very cool. In addition to the new multiple-frames feature, the new BOB engine has an object-oriented feel to it, in that I have created functions to access the data member so you don't have to.

✔ The new BOB supports motion. In other words, the BOB engine offers built-in functionality for creating a simple motion, such as an object bouncing around the screen or flying in a single direction and wrapping around when it hits a boundary.

✔ I included in the engine functions to animate and move the BOBs for you, so you don't have to. The functions take into consideration how the BOB was created and the environment it's in (the screen) and do the right thing.

Obviously, the new BOB engine has a lot of features, and I can't describe them all here; heck, the code is 20 pages or more! But I give you a function listing (as I have done thus far) that shows a sample use of each function. I tried to place the functions in the best possible order. But if I show you something that doesn't make sense, bear with me because the concept may become clearer as you continue through the functions.

A demo program called Star Ferret (filename STARFERR.CPP) on the CD incorporates BOBs and a lot of the other stuff into an embryonic game, so make sure that you check it out. And if you want to compile the demo yourself, remember to include the GPDEM01.CPP library and, of course, the DirectDraw library (DDRAW.LIB).

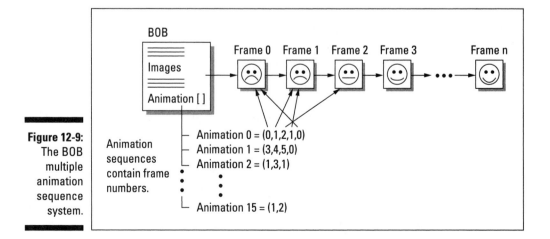

Figure 12-9:
The BOB
multiple
animation
sequence
system.

Before starting, make sure to place your thumb on the first couple pages of this chapter so that you can refer back to the data structure for a BOB from time to time. Also, all functions return TRUE if successful and FALSE otherwise.

Create_BOB

Function prototype:

```
int Create_BOB(BOB_PTR bob, // pointer to BOB to create
    int x, int y,           // initial position of BOB
    int width, int height,  // size of BOB
    int num_frames, // total number of frames for BOB
    int attr,       // attributes of BOB
    int mem_flags); // surface memory flags, 0 is VRAM
```

Purpose: Create_BOB() creates a single BOB object and sets it up. The function sets up all the internal variables in addition to creating a separate DirectDraw surface for each frame. Most of the parameters are self-explanatory; the only value that needs a little explanation is the attribute variable attr. Take a look at Table 12-1 to see a better description of each of the attributes that you can logically OR together and send in this field.

Table 12-1	Attributes for a BOB
Value	*Meaning*
BOB_ATTR_SINGLE_FRAME	Create BOB with a single frame.
BOB_ATTR_MULTI_FRAME	Create BOB with multiple frames, but the animation of the BOB will be a linear sequence through the frames 0..n.
BOB_ATTR_MULTI_ANIM	Create a multiple-frame BOB that supports animation sequences.
BOB_ATTR_ANIM_ONE_SHOT	Set an animation sequence to play only once and then stop. At this point, the internal variable anim_state is set. To play the animation again, reset this variable.
BOB_ATTR_BOUNCE	Make the BOB bounce off the screen boundaries like a ball. This value only works if you use Move_BOB().
BOB_ATTR_WRAPAROUND	Make the BOB wrap around to the other side of the screen as it moves. This value only works if you use Move_BOB().

Here are some examples that create BOBs. First, a single frame BOB at (50,100) with a size of 96 x 64:

```
BOB car; // a car BOB
// create the BOB
if (!Create_BOB(&car, 50,100,96,64,1,BOB_ATTR_SINGLE_FRAME,0))
    { /* error */ }
```

And here's a multiple-frame BOB with 8 frames and a size of 32 x 32:

```
BOB ship; // a spaceship BOB
// create the BOB
if (!Create_BOB(&ship, 0,0,32,32,8,BOB_ATTR_MULTI_FRAME,0))
    { /* error */ }
```

Finally, a multiple-frame BOB that supports animation sequences:

```
BOB greeny; // a little green man BOB
// create the BOB
if (!Create_BOB(&greeny, 0,0,32,32,32,BOB_ATTR_MULTI_ANIM,0))
        { /* error */ }
```

Destroy_BOB

Function prototype:

```
int Destroy_BOB(BOB_PTR bob); // pointer to BOB to destroy
```

Purpose: Destroy_BOB() destroys a previously created BOB. For example, to destroy the green man BOB created in the prior example, do this:

```
Destroy_BOB(&greeny);
```

Draw_BOB

Function prototype:

```
int Draw_BOB(BOB_PTR bob,  // pointer of BOB to draw
    LPDIRECTDRAWSURFACE dest); // dest surface to draw on
```

Purpose: Draw_BOB() is a very powerful function. It draws the sent BOB on the DirectDraw surface that you send it. The BOB is drawn in its current position and current frame (as defined by its animation parameters).

For this function to work, the destination surface must *not* be locked.

Here's an example of how to position a multiframe BOB at (50,50) and draw the first frame of it on the backbuffer surface:

```
BOB ship; // a spaceship BOB
// create the bob
if (!Create_BOB(&ship, 0,0,32,32,8,BOB_ATTR_MULTI_FRAME,0))
// load the BOB images in (see Load_Frame_BOB())
ship.x = 50; // set the position and frame of BOB
ship.y = 50;
ship.curr_frame = 0; // this contains the frame to draw
Draw_BOB(&ship, lpddsback); // draw BOB
```

Draw_Scaled_BOB

Function prototype:

```
int Draw_Scaled_BOB(BOB_PTR bob, // pointer of BOB to draw
    int swidth, int sheight,      // new width and height of BOB
    LPDIRECTDRAWSURFACE dest);    // dest surface to draw on
```

Purpose: Draw_Scaled_BOB() works exactly like Draw_BOB(), except that you can send a new width and height to draw the BOB with. If you have acceleration, this method is a great way to scale a BOB to make it look 3D! Here's an example of drawing the ship 128 x 128 even though it was created as only 32 x 32 pixels:

```
Draw_Scaled_BOB(&ship, 128,128,lpddsback);
```

Load_Frame_BOB

Function prototype:

```
int Load_Frame_BOB(
  BOB_PTR bob, // pointer of BOB to load frame into
  BITMAP_FILE_PTR bitmap,// pointer of file to scan data
  int frame,    // frame number to place image into (0,1,...)
  int cx,int cy, // cell position or absolute position to scan from
  int mode);    // scan mode, same as Load_Frame_Bitmap()
```

Purpose: The Load_Frame_BOB() function works identically to the Load_Frame_Bitmap() function, so refer to it in this chapter for details. The only addition is the control of the frame to load via frame. If you create a BOB that has four frames, you will load the frames in one-by-one. Here's an example of loading four frames into a BOB from a bitmap file in cell mode:

```
BOB ship; // the BOB
// loads frames 0,1,2,3 from cell position (0,0), (1,0),
// (2,0), (3,0)
// from bitmap8bit bitmap file; assume it has been loaded
for (int index=0; index<4; index++)
    Load_Frame_BOB(&ship,&bitmap8bit, index, index,0,
                BITMAP_EXTRACT_MODE_CELL );
```

Load_Animation_BOB

Function prototype:

```
int Load_Animation_BOB(
    BOB_PTR bob,     // BOB to load animation into
    int anim_index,  // which animation to load (0 to 15)
    int num_frames,  // number of frames of animation
    int *sequence);  // pointer to array holding sequence
```

Purpose: Load_Animation() takes a little explaining. The function is used to load one of 16 arrays internal to the BOB that contain animation sequences. Each sequence contains an array of indices or frame numbers to display in sequence. For example, you may have a BOB that has 8 frames (0,1, . . . 7), but you may have four animations that look like this:

```
int anim_walk[]  = {0,1,2,1,0};
int anim_fire[]  = {5,6,0};
int anim_die[]   = {3,4};
int anim_sleep[] = {0,0,7,0,0};
```

Then to load the animations into the BOB, do this:

```
// create a multi-animation BOB
if (!Create_BOB(&alien, 0,0,32,32,8,BOB_ATTR_MULTI_ANIM,0))
    { /* error */ }
// load in the BOB frames here...
// load walk into animation 0
Load_Animation_BOB(&alien, 0,5,anim_walk);
// load fire into animation 1
Load_Animation_BOB(&alien, 1,3,anim_fire);
// load die into animation 2
Load_Animation_BOB(&alien, 2,2,anim_die);
// load sleep into animation 3
Load_Animation_BOB(&alien, 3,5,anim_sleep);
```

After loading the animations, you can set the active animation and play them with the animation functions, which are declared later in this chapter.

Set_Pos_BOB

Function prototype:

```
int Set_Pos_BOB(BOB_PTR bob, // pointer to BOB to set position
               int x, int y);  // new position of BOB
```

Purpose: Set_Pos_BOB() is a simple way to set the position of the BOB. This function does nothing more than assign the internal (x,y) variables, which is nice. Here's how to set the position of an "alien" BOB:

```
Set_Pos_BOB(&alien, player_x, player_y);
```

Set_Vel_BOB

Function prototype:

```
int Set_Vel_BOB(BOB_PTR BOB, // pointer to BOB to set velocity
        int xv, int yv);    // new x,y velocity
```

Purpose: Each BOB has an internal velocity contained in (xv,yv). Set_Vel_BOB() simply assigns the new values sent in the function to these values. The velocity values in the BOB won't do anything unless you use the function Move_BOB() to move your BOBs. However, even if you don't, you can use (xv,yv) to track the velocity of the BOB yourself. Here's an example to make the BOB move in a straight horizontal line:

```
Set_Vel_BOB(&alien, 10,0);
```

Set_Anim_Speed_BOB

Function prototype:

```
int Set_Anim_Speed_BOB(BOB_PTR bob, // pointer to BOB
                int speed); // speed of animation
```

Purpose: Set_Anim_Speed() sets the internal animation rate for a BOB anim_count_max. The higher this number is, the slower the animation; the lower the number (0 is the lowest), the faster the animation. However, this function only matters if you use the internal BOB animation function `Animate_BOB()`. And you must have created a BOB that has multiple frames. Here's an example of setting the rate to change frames every 30 frames:

```
Set_Anim_Speed_BOB(&alien, 30);
```

Set_Animation_BOB

Function prototype:

```
int Set_Animation_BOB(
        BOB_PTR bob,      // pointer of BOB to set animation
        int anim_index); // index of animation to set
```

Purpose: `Set_Animation_BOB()` sets the current animation that will be played by the BOB. In the earlier example of `Load_Animation_BOB()`, you created four animations. To make number two active, do this:

```
Set_Animation_BOB(&alien, 2);
```

This step also resets the BOB animation to the first frame in the sequence.

Animate_BOB

Function prototype:

```
int Animate_BOB(BOB_PTR bob); // pointer to BOB to animate
```

Purpose: `Animate_BOB()` animates a BOB. Normally, you call this function once every frame to update the animation of the BOB. Here's an example:

```
// erase everything here...
// move everything here...
Animate_BOB(&alien); // animate everything
```

Move_BOB

Function prototype:

```
int Move_BOB(BOB_PTR bob); // pointer of BOB to move
```

Purpose: Move_BOB() moves the BOB a delta (or change from original position) of (xv,yv), and then, depending on the attributes, either bounces the BOB off the walls, wraps it around, or does nothing. Similarly to the Animate_BOB() function, place the following call once in the main loop right after (or before) Animate_BOB():

```
Animate_BOB(&alien); // animate BOB
Move_BOB(&alien);    // move it
```

Hide_BOB

Function prototype:

```
int Hide_BOB(BOB_PTR bob); // pointer to BOB to hide
```

Purpose: Hide_BOB() sets the invisible flag on the BOB and hence Draw_BOB() won't display it. Here's an example:

```
Hide_BOB(&alien);
```

Show_BOB

Function prototype:

```
int Show_BOB(BOB_PTR bob); // pointer to BOB to show
```

Purpose: Show_BOB() sets the visible flag on a BOB so that it is drawn (undoes a Hide_BOB() call). Here's an example of hiding and showing a BOB because you are displaying a GDI object or some other element and don't want the BOB to occlude it:

```
Hide_BOB(&alien);
// make calls to Draw_BOB and GDI etc.
Show_BOB(&alien);
```

Collision_BOBS

Function prototype:

```
int Collision_BOBS(BOB_PTR bob1,  // pointer to first BOB
                   BOB_PTR bob2); // pointer to second BOB
```

Return value: The function returns TRUE if a collision occurred, FALSE otherwise.

Purpose: `Collision_BOBS()` detects if the bounding rectangles of two BOBs overlap. Use this function for collision detection in a game to see if a player BOB hits a missile BOB. Here's an example of checking whether a missile BOB hit a player BOB:

```
if (Collision_BOBS(&missile, &player)) { /* make explosion sound */ }
```

What Time Is It?

Time is like a predator that stalks you. . . . I heard that somewhere, and it couldn't be more true. No matter what you do, time is always an issue, and games are no different. Back in Chapter 5 on Windows programming, I show you a few ways to deal with time by using timers, retrieving the current clock count, and so on. Now I want to give you a few simple functions to make tracking time on a millisecond level a little easier.

If you study all the demo programs, you may notice that I usually include something like

```
Sleep(10);
```

at the end of each main loop. This inclusion is to slow the `Game_Main()` down and lock it to a specific frame rate. However, sleeping isn't the best way for a video game to count time — mainly because sleeping is a waste of time and processing. A more accurate way to track time is to record the time at the top of the loop; then at the end of the loop, compare that time to the current time until a certain amount has elapsed. The amount — 1 millisecond or 10 — doesn't matter, but this technique is better than sleeping.

Here's the reason. Suppose that you want your main loop to run at 30 frames per second (fps), which means that each frame should take $1/30$ second or roughly 33 milliseconds to complete. If you `Sleep()` at the end of the loop for 33 milliseconds, this method will work fine on a super fast Pentium II 266, but terrible on a Pentium 75. The lack in performance is because, on a Pentium 75, the loop itself may take 20 to 30 milliseconds and waiting another 33 milliseconds means a total of 53 to 63 milliseconds!

A better solution is to record the time at the top of the loop; then at the bottom of the loop, monitor the current time and wait until the 33 milliseconds have elapsed. If 33 milliseconds have already elapsed, then bail out of the loop; otherwise continue to wait. This way your timing is more precise, and slower machines will not wait any longer than necessary.

To accomplish this functionality, I encapsulated the `GetTickCount()` Win32 API function in a wrapper function, added a global variable to track time, and wrote the following functions to start the counter, to wait for a specific amount of time, and to just read the counter.

Start_Clock

Function prototype:

```
DWORD Start_Clock(void);
```

Return value: This function returns the current counter value in milliseconds. Note that the absolute value is relative to some arbitrary event such as starting the computer, or the number of milliseconds that have elapsed since 1970, or something. So the bottom line is this: You must use this value relative to another reading in the future and compute the difference.

Purpose: Start_Clock() records the current time in the global timer-state variable. This function is used at the top of a timing loop that you want to ensure takes a specific amount of time. So, at the top of your loop, simply make a call to it like this:

```
Start_Clock();
```

You don't need to worry about the return value unless you want to because it is cached internally in a global.

Wait_Clock

Function prototype:

```
DWORD Wait_Clock(DWORD count);
```

Return value: This function returns the current value of the clock timer, the same as the preceding.

Purpose: Wait_Clock() waits for a specific amount of time to elapse. When the function is called, it will look at the time that Start_Time() was called and wait count milliseconds from then. For example, here is how to make a loop run at 100 milliseconds (or 10 frames per second) a cycle:

```
while(1)
    {
    // start the clock here; the current clock count is recorded
    Start_Clock()
    // do whatever..game logic etc.
    Wait_Clock(100); // force it to wait 100
    }// end while
```

Get_Clock

Function prototype:

```
DWORD Get_Clock(void);
```

Return value: This function returns the current clock count, the same as the preceding function.

Purpose: Use Get_Clock() if you just want the current clock count. The result is identical to calling GetTickCount(). Here's an example:

```
DWORD count = Get_Clock();
```

That's All Folks!

Well, if you read this entire chapter, you understand that GPDUMB is a complete graphics engine that offers some decent capabilities. It won't hold a candle to the final engine in this book, but for now it's pretty high-tech! Make sure to check out the demo on the CD named STARFERR.CPP and the accompanying executable for a good example use of the engine (see Figure 12-10).

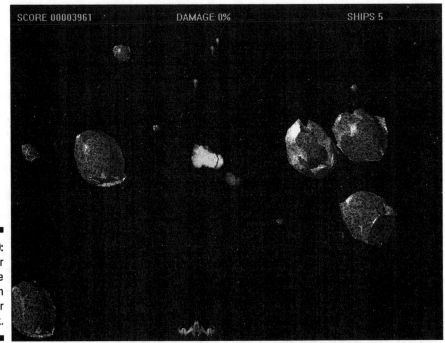

SCORE 00003961   DAMAGE 0%   SHIPS 5

Figure 12-10:
Star
Ferret — the
culmination
of your
work.

Part III

The Rest of the Puzzle: Sound, Input, and Setup

The 5th Wave   By Rich Tennant

"...and you say a giant has your mother and father locked in a dungeon? And your sister's being held hostage in a tower? You just sit tight, Davey – a SWAT team is on its way."

In this part . . .

Y
ou need to know a great deal about DirectX to create a well-rounded Windows game, and this part provides the missing pieces of the DirectX puzzle. Read on to find out about DirectSound, DirectInput, and DirectSetup. You can finish up by adding the final touches to the game engine GPDUMB.

This part is my favorite in the book, because you can use the software-programming knowledge gained in earlier parts to do something interesting. Here you really see the awesome power of DirectX in action.

I end this part by revamping *Star Ferret* into a complete playable game with sound, solid input controls, and the works. Check out *Star Ferret Deluxe* on the CD-ROM!

Chapter 13

Making Noise with DirectSound

In This Chapter

▶ The fundamentals of sound

▶ Digital sound versus synthesized sound

▶ Sound hardware

▶ DirectSound API

▶ Sound file formats

*P*rogramming sound is one of those tasks that's just a pain! Writing a sound system is difficult because not only do you have to understand sound and music, but you must make sure that the sound system works on every single sound card – and therein lies the problem. In the past, most game programmers used a third-party sound library, such as Miles Sound System or Diamondware Sound Toolkit. Each system has its pros and cons, but the biggest problem is price; a sound library that works for DOS and Windows can cost thousands of dollars.

Luckily, you don't have to worry about DOS anymore, but you do have to worry about Windows. It's true that Windows offers sound and multimedia support, but it was never designed to provide the ultra high performance needed by a real-time video game. Thankfully, DirectSound solves all these problems and more. DirectSound is free, is extremely high-performance, has support for a million sound cards, and now has 3D sound capabilities — so clap your hands because life just got easier. In this chapter, I cover the physics of sound and then the basics to get you up and running with DirectSound in less than a quarter beat!

Music 0101: The Fundamentals of Sound

If you were to go out on the streets and ask people what sound is, most of them would probably offer a circular definition like: "Hmmm, stuff you hear with your ears, like sounds and noises." Go ahead; try it. . . . However, that definition won't help you understand the actual physics of sound, and that concept is important if you are going to record, manipulate, and play sound.

Sound is a mechanical pressure wave emitted from a source, as shown in Figure 13-1. Sound can only exist in a viscous environment — such as our atmosphere — that is filled with gases such as nitrogen, oxygen, helium, and so on. Sound can also travel in liquid or solids, but at much higher velocities.

A sound wave is really the motion of molecules. When a speaker vibrates in and out to the rhythm of music, it moves the air in and out. This motion is transmitted to the surrounding air mechanically — that is, by contact of the molecules — and, at some point, the sound wave reaches you.

However, because a sound travels by a wave propagating through the air via mechanical collisions, it takes time to get to you. That's why sound travels so slowly (relatively speaking). You can see something happen and not hear it for a second or two, if the sound is far enough away. This delay is because a mechanical wave, or sound wave, can only travel at about 600 to 700 miles per hour depending on the density and temperature of the air.

Sound is a wave that travels through air at a constant velocity — the speed of sound. A traveling sound wave can have the following two parameters:

✔ **Amplitude:** How much air volume is moved. A large speaker (or someone with a big mouth) moves a lot of air, thus the sounds are stronger or more intense.

✔ **Frequency:** How many complete waves or cycles per second are emanating from the source (measured in hertz and abbreviated Hz). Most humans can hear in the range of 20 to 20,000 Hz. The average male has a voice that ranges from 20 to 2,000 Hz, and a female voice ranges from 70 to 3,000 Hz.

A *waveform* can be thought of as the shape of the sound's amplitude changes. In other words, some sounds smoothly go up and down, and others rise up and then sharply fall off. Even if two sounds have the same amplitude and frequency, their shapes make them sound different.

Sounds have shape, meaning they travel in different waveforms, such as sine waves, square waves, sawtooth waves, and so on. Figure 13-2 shows a graphical representation of the amplitude and frequency of some standard waveforms.

A single pure tone will always have the shape of a sine wave, but can have any frequency and amplitude. Single tones sound like electronic toys. My point: Most sounds, such as voices or music, are composed of hundreds or even thousands of pure tones all mixed together. Hence, sounds have a spectrum.

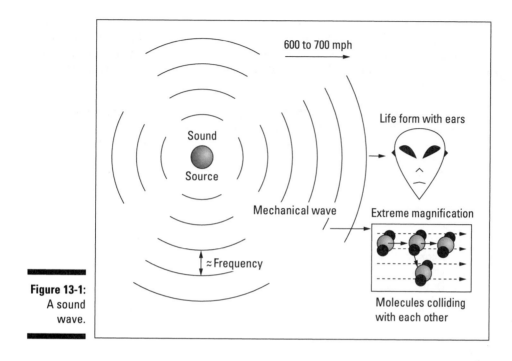

Figure 13-1:
A sound
wave.

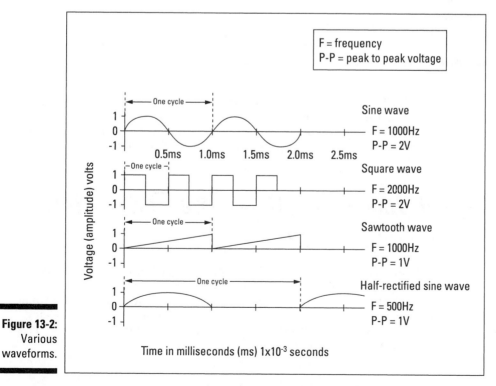

Figure 13-2:
Various
waveforms.

The most basic waveform in the universe is the sine wave — mathematically symbolized by SIN(t). All other waveforms can be created by one or more sine waves. This fact can be mathematically proven with the *Fourier Transform,* which is a method of breaking a waveform down into its sinusoidal components.

The spectrum of a sound is its *frequency distribution.* Figure 13-3 shows the frequency distribution for my voice. As you can see, my voice contains many different frequencies, but most of them are low. To make truly realistic sounds, you must understand that sounds are composed of many simple pure tones, all at different frequencies and amplitudes.

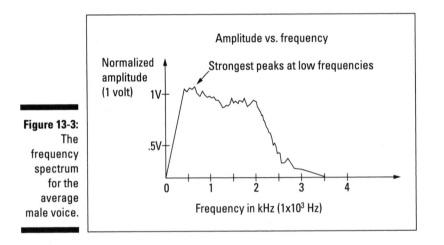

Figure 13-3: The frequency spectrum for the average male voice.

That's all great, but your goal is to make the computer make sounds. No problem; the computer can control a speaker with electrical signals to force it to move in and out at any rate with any force (within reason). So you can make sounds with the computer. Read on to find out how.

Digital versus MIDI — The Federation versus The Empire

A computer can make two kinds of sounds: *digital* and *synthesized.* Digital sounds are recordings of sound, and synthesized sounds are programmed reproductions of sounds based on algorithms and hardware. Digital sounds are usually used for sound effects such as explosions and people talking, and synthesized sounds are used for music. And in most cases these days, synthesized sound is *only* used for music.

Digital sound

Digital sound comes from the word *digitize,* which means to encode data in the digital form of ones and zeros. Just as an electrical signal can make a speaker move. If you talk into a speaker, the opposite happens. That is, the speaker generates an electrical signal based on the vibrations of your voice. This signal has the sound information encoded in it as an analog or linear voltage (as shown in Figure 13-4).

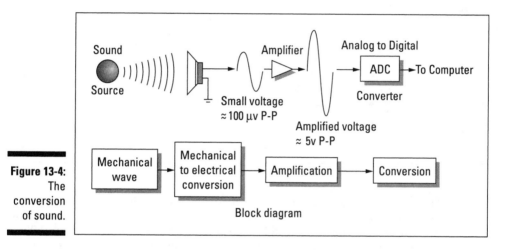

Figure 13-4:
The
conversion
of sound.

By using the proper hardware, this linear voltage (which has the sound information encoded in it) can be sampled and digitized. This process is exactly how your CD player works. The information on each CD is in the digital form of ones and zeros, whereas information on cassette tapes and so forth is stored in analog form. Digital information is much easier to process and is the only information that digital computers *can* process. So for a computer to process sound, the sound must be converted into a digital data stream with an analog-to-digital converter, as shown in Figure 13-5.

After a sound is recorded into the memory of the computer, the sound can be processed or played back with a digital-to-analog converter (see Figure 13-5). The sound information must be in digital format before processing, and you need to get it in that format before working with it.

But recording digital sound is a bit tricky. Sound has a lot of information in it. If you want to sample a sound realistically, you must consider two factors: frequency and amplitude.

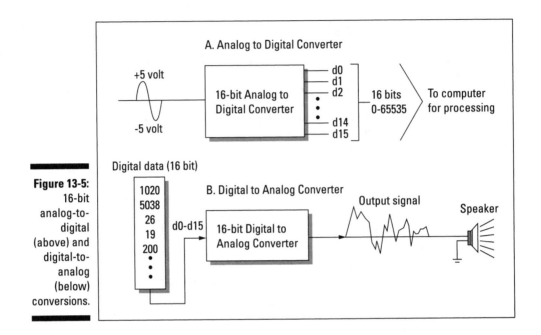

Figure 13-5:
16-bit
analog-to-
digital
(above) and
digital-to-
analog
(below)
conversions.

The number of samples per second of an input sound is called the *sample rate*. This sample must be two times the frequency of the original sound. For example, if you are sampling a human voice that has a range of 20 to 2,000 Hz, you must sample the sound at 4,000 Hz. (The mathematical reason for this requirement — Shannon's Theorem — is based on being able to reconstruct the original waveform from samples, so just trust me.)

The second sampling parameter is the *amplitude resolution* — meaning the number of different values for the amplitude. If you have only 8 bits per sample, the result is only 256 different amplitudes. This number is enough for games. But for reproduction of professional sounds and music, you need 16-bits (providing 65,536 different values).

Synthesized sound and MIDI

Although digital sound is currently the highest quality sound, synthesized sound has been around a long time and is getting better and better. Synthesized sound isn't digitally recorded; it's more of a mathematical reproduction of a sound from a description. Synthesizers use hardware and algorithms to generate sounds based on a description of the desired sound. For example, suppose that you want to hear a 440 Hz, pure concert A. You could design a piece of hardware that could generate a pure analog sine wave of any frequency from 0 to 20,000 Hz and then instruct it to create a 440 Hz tone. This process is the basis of synthesis.

The only problem is that most people want to hear more than a single tone (unless they're listening to a musical birthday card), so you must create hardware that supports approximately 16 to 32 different tones at the same time (as shown in Figure 13-6).

To meet the challenge, *FM synthesis* was invented. Remember the old Ad-Lib sound card? It was the precursor to the Sound Blaster and the first PC card to support multiple-channel FM synthesis. The FM stands for *frequency modulation.* An FM synthesizer can not only alter the amplitude of the sound, but the frequency of the sound. FM synthesis operates on the mathematical basis of feedback. FM synthesizers feedback the output of the signals back into themselves, thereby modulating the signal and creating harmonics and phase-shifted tones. The bottom line is that the result sounds very real.

MIDI enters, stage left

At about the same time all this FM synthesis stuff came out, a file format for music synthesis — called *MIDI (Musical Instrument Digital Interface)* — was catching on. MIDI is a language that describes musical compositions as a function of time. Instead of digitizing sound, a MIDI piece describes it. For example, a MIDI file may look like this:

```
Turn on Channel 1 with an A.
Turn on Channel 2 with a C sharp.
Turn off Channel 1.




Turn all channels off.
```

Of course, the information is encoded in binary serial stream, but you get the picture. Moreover, each channel in the MIDI specification is connected to a different instrument or sound. So you may have 16 channels, each representing a different instrument, such as a piano, drums, guitar, base, flute, trumpet, and so on. MIDI is an indirect method of encoding. It leaves the synthesis up to the hardware and only records the actual musical notes to play and when to play them. Hence, a MIDI file for an hour of music may only be a few hundred kilobytes of memory instead of megabytes for the same digital piece!

The only problem with MIDI and FM synthesis is that they are more or less good only for music. Sure, you can design FM synthesizers to create white noise for explosions or laser blasts, but the sounds will always be simple in nature and not have the variety or organic feel of a digitized sound. More advanced methods of synthesis have been created, such as wave table and wave guide technology.

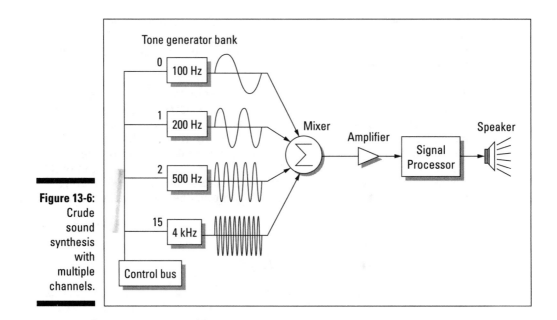

Figure 13-6:
Crude
sound
synthesis
with
multiple
channels.

Sound Hardware

Are any sound cards left besides Creative Labs Sound Blasters these days? If there are other cards around, I don't think they'll last much longer. Sound Blasters are the most prevalent sound cards — at least for 2D sound. And Creative Labs produces both wave table and wave guide models, which I discuss in the next sections.

Wave table synthesis

Wave table synthesis is a mix between synthesis and digital recording. It works like this: The wave table has a number of real-sampled digital sounds within it. The data is then processed by a DSP (Digital Signal Processor) that takes the real sample and plays it back in any frequency and amplitude that you need. Hence, you can sample a real piano and then play any note on that piano by using wave table synthesis. The result sounds almost as good as digital, but you still have to have the original sources sampled — and that process takes memory.

Wave guide synthesis

Wave guide synthesis is the ultimate synthesis technology. By using DSP chips and very special hardware, the sound synthesizer can actually generate a mathematical model of a virtual instrument and then play it! This concept may seem like science fiction, but it's a fact. With this technology, you *cannot* perceive the difference between a sampled instrument, the real one, and the wave guide simulated instrument. Thus, you can create MIDI files that control a wave table or wave guide synthesizer and get great results.

Finally, DirectSound only supports digital sound, so MIDI becomes irrelevant anyway.

Digital Recording: Tools and Techniques

Before I finish off the sound and music preceptor program, I want to give you some hints on recording sound and music for your games. You can choose among three ways to create digital samples:

- ✔ Sample them from the real world with a microphone or outside input.
- ✔ Buy sampled sounds in digital or analog format and download or record them for use.
- ✔ Synthesize digital sounds with a waveform synthesizer, such as Sound Forge.

The third method may seem a little backward, but it's useful if you want to create a pure tone(s) with digital hardware and you don't have a convenient source for the sound. But methods one and two are the most important for the purpose of this book's examples.

If your game will have lots of speech in it, you may need to sample your own voice (or the voice of a friend), tweak it with a piece of software, and then use it in your game. For games that use standard explosions, doors, or growls, you can probably get away with generic sound clips; just about everybody in the game business has a copy of the Sound Ideas General 6000 sound library. It includes about 40 CDs full of thousands of sound effects. This library is used for movies, so it offers any sound you may need.

However, because I'm a nice guy, I supply you with a complete set of cool sounds from one of my games. You can find them on the CD within the folder called SOUNDS. These sounds are all in .VOC format, but you can load them into Sound Forge or any other sound program and convert them to whatever file format you wish.

Recording sounds

If you record your own sounds, I suggest the following settings. Create your originals with 16-bits per sample in 22 kHz, mono. Remember, *no* stereo. DirectSound works best with mono sound, so recording in stereo won't help. Also, because most sounds you can make or record are mono anyway, recording in stereo is a waste of memory.

If you want to record from a microphone plugged into your sound card, buy a good one (a good microphone feels heavy). Also, do your recording in an enclosed room without background noise or any interruptions. If you are recording direct from a device (such as a CD or radio), make sure that the connections are good and that you use high-quality audio connectors.

Finally, give your sound files reasonable names; don't be cryptic. You will never remember what's what unless you're organized!

Processing your sounds

After you sample your sounds with Sound Forge or a similar piece of software, you may want to post process the sounds. Sound Forge or a similar package can do all the processing. During processing, crop all the dead air, normalize the volumes, remove noise, add echoes, and so on.

I suggest that you make backups of your sounds before you perform these steps; don't mess with the originals. Use an approach such as renaming the processed sounds with numbers appended at the end. Once the original file is gone, it's gone!

While you process sound, try to experiment with frequency shifting, echoes, distortion, and various other effects. When you find a cool effect, make sure that you write down the formula on paper so that you can reproduce the effect. I can't tell you how many times I've had the perfect female computer voice (synthesized from my own voice), and I lost the formula.

Finally, after you're done with all your sounds, save the data files all out in the same format (such as 22 or 11 kHz, mono with 8-bit). This method tremendously helps DirectSound when it processes your sounds. If you have sounds with different sample rates and bits per sample, then DirectSound will always have to convert to its native rate of 22 kHz, 8-bit.

Technically, DirectSound's native, format is 22 kHz, 8-bit stereo. However, most sounds are mono in nature and sending stereo data to DirectSound is a waste of data.

DirectSound Overture

DirectSound comprises a number of components or interfaces, just like DirectDraw. However, because this is a book on game programming, I don't cover them all — just the most important ones. Thus, I won't be discussing the 3D sound component (DirectSound3D), or the new sound-capturing interface (DirectSoundCapture). I'm going to focus on the primary interfaces of DirectSound and that's it. Believe me, that's enough to turn someone's brains to mush!

Figure 13-7 depicts the relationship of DirectSound to the rest of the Windows system. Notice that DirectSound is very similar to DirectDraw. However, DirectSound has a really cool feature that DirectDraw doesn't offer: If you don't have a DirectSound driver for your sound card, then DirectSound will still work, but it will use emulation and the Windows DDI (Device Driver Interface) instead. So as long as you ship your product with the DirectSound .DLLs — even if the user doesn't have DirectSound drivers — your code will still work. It won't be as fast, but it will work.

DirectSound basically has three components: a run-time .DLL that is loaded when you use DirectSound, a compile-time library named DSOUND.LIB, and a header named DSOUND.H. To create a DirectSound application, you just include these files in your application.

To use DirectSound, you must create a DirectSound Component Object Model (COM) object and then request the various interfaces from the main object. (For more about the COM, check out Chapter 7.) Figure 13-8 illustrates the main interfaces of DirectSound.

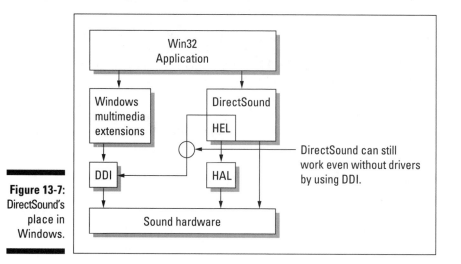

Figure 13-7: DirectSound's place in Windows.

Win32 Application

Windows multimedia extensions

DirectSound

HEL

DDI

HAL

Sound hardware

DirectSound can still work even without drivers by using DDI.

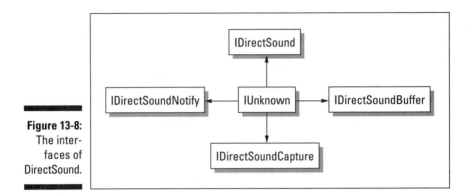

Figure 13-8:
The inter-
faces of
DirectSound.

The following are the DirectSound main interfaces:

- ✔ **IUnknown:** The base COM object of all COM objects.

- ✔ **IDirectSound:** The main COM object of DirectSound, representing the audio hardware itself. You may have one or more sound cards in your computer. If so, you need a DirectSound object for each of them.

- ✔ **IDirectSoundBuffer:** The mixing hardware and actual sounds. DirectSound has two kinds of buffers: *primary* and *secondary* (just like DirectDraw). The single primary buffer represents the sound that is currently playing and mixed either by hardware (hopefully) or software. Secondary buffers represent sounds that are stored for playback. They may exist in system memory or SRAM (Sound RAM) on the sound card. In either case, you can play as many secondary buffer sounds as you wish as long as you have the horsepower and memory to do so. Figure 13-9 represents the relationship between the primary sound buffer and secondary sound buffers.

- ✔ **IDirectSoundCapture:** You aren't going to use this interface in this book, but it's used to record and capture sounds. You can use it to allow the player to record his or her name, or if you're more of a techno-superfreak, it can be used to capture voice in real-time for voice recognition.

- ✔ **IDirectSoundNotify:** Sends messages back to DirectSound. In a game with a complex sound system, you may need this, but you can get along without it.

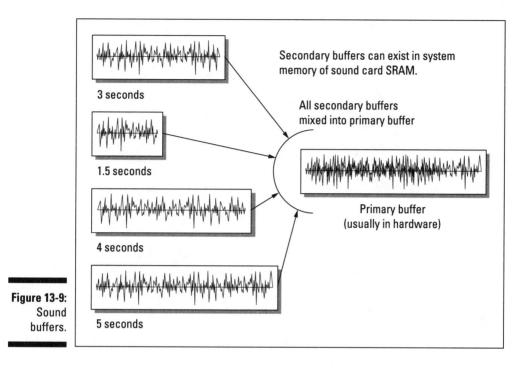

Figure 13-9:
Sound
buffers.

Using DirectSound

To use DirectSound, you first create a DirectSound object, a number of secondary sound buffers, load them with sounds, and then play any sound you want. DirectSound will take care of the rest. I cover each stage in the remaining sections of this chapter.

Summoning a DirectSound object

The main DirectSound object represents the sound card itself. If you have more than one sound card, then you will have to detect them and request their GUIDs (Globally Unique Identifiers). But if you just want to connect to the default sound device, then you don't have to mess with detection; you can simply create a DirectSound object that represents the main sound card.

Creating a DirectSound object

Here's the interface pointer that represents a DirectSound object:

```
LPDIRECTSOUND  lpds; // DirectSound interface pointer
```

To create a DirectSound object, you must make a call to `DirectSoundCreate()`, prototyped in the following:

```
HRESULT DirectSoundCreate(
    LPGUID lpGuid, // GUID of sound card
                   // NULL for default device
    LPDIRECTSOUND *lpDS,    // interface pointer to object
    IUnknown FAR *pUnkOuter) // always NULL
```

Look familiar? This DirectX stuff all looks alike. Once you have mastered one part of DirectX, you have mastered them all. The problem is that Microsoft keeps making new components as fast as you can learn them!

To create a DirectSound object, do the following:

```
LPDIRECTSOUND lpds; // pointer to DirectSound object

// create DirectSound object
if (DirectSoundCreate(NULL, &lpds, NULL)!=DS_OK )
   { /* error */ }
```

Notice that the success value is now DS_OK (DirectSound OK) rather than DD_OK (DirectDraw OK).

And, of course, after you're done with the DirectSound object, you must release it like this:

```
lpds->Release();
```

Setting the cooperation level

After creating the main DirectSound object, you need to set the cooperation level of DirectSound. DirectSound is a little more finicky than DirectDraw as far as cooperation level is concerned. You can't be as brutal when you take over the sound system as you can with graphics. (Well, you can if you want to, but Microsoft advises that you don't. They made the product, so I recommend that you take their advice.)

You can set DirectSound into a number of cooperation levels. They are divided into two groups: settings that enable your control over the primary sound buffer, and settings that don't.

The primary sound buffer represents the actual mixing hardware (or software) that is mixing sounds at all times and sending them out to the speaker. If you mess with the primary buffer, DirectSound wants you to make sure that you know what you're doing because you could not only crash or distort your application's sound, but the sound of other applications as well.

Here's a general briefing on each cooperation level:

- ✔ **Normal cooperation:** The most cooperative of all the settings. While your application has the focus, it will be able to play sounds, but so will other applications. Furthermore, you don't have to write permission to the primary buffer, and DirectSound will create a default primary buffer for you of 22 kHz, stereo, 8-bit. I suggest using this setting most of the time.

- ✔ **Priority cooperation:** With this setting, you have first access to all the hardware. You can change the setting of the primary mixer, and you can request the sound hardware to perform advanced memory operations (such as compaction). This setting is only necessary if you must change the data format of the primary buffer — rarely needed.

- ✔ **Exclusive cooperation:** The same as priority, but your application will be the only one audible when it's in the foreground.

- ✔ **Write_Primary cooperation:** The highest priority. You have total control and must control the primary buffer yourself to hear anything. Use this mode only if you are writing your own sound mixer or engine.

Bottom line — use the normal priority level until you get the hang of DirectSound. It's the easiest to make work and has the smoothest operation.

To set the cooperation level, use the SetCooperativeLevel() function from the interface of the main DirectSound object. Here's the prototype:

```
HRESULT SetCooperativeLevel(HWND hwnd, // window handle
    DWORD dwLevel); // cooperation level setting
```

The function returns DS_OK if successful and a number of other constants otherwise (you can find these and other error constants in the DirectX SDK Help). But make sure to check for errors, because it's more than possible that another application has taken control of the sound card. Table 13-1 lists the flags settings for the various cooperation levels.

Table 13-1   Settings for DirectSound SetCooperativeLevel()

Value	Meaning
DSSCL_NORMAL	Sets normal cooperation.
DSSCL_PRIORITY	Sets priority cooperation level allowing you to set the data format of the primary buffer.
DSSCL_EXCLUSIVE	Gives you priority cooperation in addition to exclusive control when your application is in the foreground.
DSSCL_WRITEPRIMARY	Gives you total control of the primary buffer.

Here's how to set the cooperation level to normal after creating the DirectSound object:

```
if (lpds->SetCooperativeLevel(main_window_handle,
              DSSCL_NORMAL)!=DS_OK)
  { /* error setting cooperation level */ }
```

Cool, huh? Take a look at PROG13_1.CPP on the CD. It creates a DirectSound object, sets the cooperation level, and then releases the object on exit. Of course, it doesn't make any sound; that's next!

Primary and secondary sound buffers

The DirectSound object that represents the sound card itself has a single primary buffer. The primary buffer represents the mixing hardware (or software) on the card and is working all the time. Primary buffer mixing is very advanced and, luckily, you don't have to do it. DirectSound takes care of the primary buffer as long as you don't set the cooperation level to the highest priority. In addition, you don't need to create a primary buffer; DirectSound creates one for you as long as you set the cooperation level to one of the lower levels, such as DSSCL_NORMAL.

The only drawback is that the primary buffer will be set for 22 kHz stereo in 8 bits. If you want 16-bit sound or a higher playback rate, you need to at least set the cooperation level to DSSCL_PRIORITY and then set a new data format for the primary buffer. But for now, just use the default because it makes life much easier.

Working with secondary buffers

Secondary buffers represent the actual sounds that you want to play. They can be any size that you want as long as you have the memory to hold them. However, the SRAM on the sound card can only hold so much sound data, so be careful when you request sounds to be stored on the sound card itself, because memory is at a premium. With that said, keep in mind that sounds stored on the sound card itself take much less processing power to play.

These are the two kinds of sound buffers:

- **Static sound buffers:** Sounds that you plan to keep around and play over and over. These are good candidates for SRAM.

- **Streaming sound buffers:** If you want to play an entire CD with DirectSound, you most likely won't have enough system RAM or SRAM to store all 650 megabytes of audio data in memory, so you need to read the data in chunks and stream it out — the purpose of streaming buffers. You continually feed them with new sound data as they are playing. Sound tricky? Take a look at Figure 13-10 to see the write pointers and their relationship to the data.

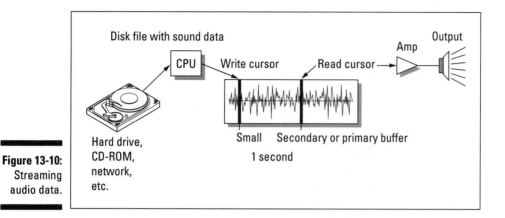

Figure 13-10:
Streaming
audio data.

In general, all secondary sound buffers can be written to static or streaming. However, it's possible that the sound may be playing as you're trying to write to it. But DirectSound has a scheme to take this problem into consideration: *circular buffering*. Circular buffering means that each sound is stored in a data array that is continually read from one point by the *play cursor* and written to at another (slightly behind) point called the *write cursor*. Of course, if you don't need to write to your sound buffers as they are playing, then you don't have to worry about this; when you are streaming audio however, you need to know about circular buffering.

To facilitate this complex buffered real-time writing capability, the data access functions for sound buffers may return a memory space that's broken into two pieces, because the data block you're trying to write may exist at the end of the buffer and overflow into the beginning of the buffer. You need to know this fact if you're going to stream audio. However, in most games, as long as you keep all the sound effects to a few seconds each and the musical tracks are loaded on demand, you can usually fit everything into a few megabytes of RAM (and this explanation is moot). Using 2MB to 4MB of storage for sound in a computer with 16MB to 32MB of RAM isn't much of a problem.

Creating a secondary sound buffer

To create a secondary sound buffer, you must make a call to CreateSoundBuffer() with the proper parameters. If successful, the function creates the sound buffer, initializes it, and returns an interface pointer of this type:

```
LPDIRECTSOUNDBUFFER lpdsbuffer; // a DirectSound buffer
```

Before you make the call to CreateSoundBuffer(), however, you must set up a DirectSoundBuffer description structure similar to a DirectDrawSurface description. The description structure is of the type DSBUFFERDESC, as follows:

```
typedef struct {
DWORD   dwSize;       // size of this structure
DWORD   dwFlags;      // control flags
DWORD   dwBufferBytes; // size of the sound buffer in bytes
DWORD   dwReserved;   // unused
LPWAVEFORMATEX  lpwfxFormat; // the wave format
} DSBUFFERDESC, *LPDSBUFFERDESC;
```

The dwSize field is the standard DirectX structure size, dwBufferBytes is how big you want the buffer, and dwReserved is unused. The only fields that should set off a yellow alert are dwFlags and lpwfxFormat. dwFlags contains the creation flags of the sound buffer. Take a look at Table 13-2, which contains a partial list of the more basic flag settings.

Table 13-2 DirectSound Secondary Buffer Creation Flags

Value	Meaning
DSBCAPS_CTRLALL	The buffer must have all control capabilities.
DSBCAPS_CTRLDEFAULT	The buffer should have default-control options. This value is the same as specifying the DSBCAPS_CTRLPAN, DSBCAPS_CTRLVOLUME, and DSBCAPS_CTRLFREQUENCY.
DSBCAPS_CTRLFREQUENCY	The buffer must have frequency-control capability.
DSBCAPS_CTRLPAN	The buffer must have pan-control capability.
DSBCAPS_CTRLVOLUME	The buffer must have volume-control capability.
DSBCAPS_STATIC	Indicates that the buffer will be used for static sound data. Most of the time, you create these buffers in hardware memory (if possible).
DSBCAPS_LOCHARDWARE	Use hardware mixing and memory for this sound buffer if memory is available.
DSBCAPS_LOCSOFTWARE	Forces the buffer to be stored in software memory and use software mixing, even if DSBCAPS_STATIC is specified and hardware resources are available.
DSBCAPS_PRIMARYBUFFER	Indicates that the buffer is a primary sound buffer. Set this value only if you want to create a primary buffer, and you are a sound god.

In most cases, you'll set the flags to DSBCAPS_CTRLDEFAULT |
DSBCAPS_STATIC | DSBCAPS_LOCSOFTWARE — for default controls, static
sound, and the use of system memory. If you want to use hardware memory,
use DSBCAPS_LOCHARDWARE instead of DSBCAPS_LOCSOFTWARE.

Now consider the WAVEFORMATEX structure. It contains a description of the
sound that you want the buffer to represent. Parameters such as playback
rate, number of channels (mono or stereo), bits per sample, and so on are
recorded in this structure. Here it is for your review:

```
typedef struct {
  WORD   wFormatTag; // always WAVE_FORMAT_PCM
  WORD   nChannels;  // number of audio channels (1 or 2)
  DWORD  nSamplesPerSec;  // samples per second
  DWORD  nAvgBytesPerSec; // average data rate
  WORD   nBlockAlign;     // nchannels * bytespersample
WORD  wBitsPerSample;     // bits per sample
  WORD   cbSize;          // advanced, set to 0
} WAVEFORMATEX;
```

Simple enough. Basically, this structure contains the description of the
sound.

Enough talk; now you can see some action. Here's the prototype of the
CreateSoundBuffer() function (ptr means *pointer*):

```
HRESULT CreateSoundBuffer(
  LPCDSBUFFERDESC lpcDSBuffDesc,   // ptr to DSBUFFERDESC
  LPLPDIRECTSOUNDBUFFER lplpDSBuff,// ptr to sound buffer
  IUnknown FAR *pUnkOuter);        // always NULL
```

And here's an example of creating a secondary DirectSound buffer at 11 kHz
mono, 8-bit with storage for two seconds:

```
// pointer to DirectSound
LPDIRECTSOUNDBUFFER lpdsbuffer; buffer

DSBUFFERDESC dsbd;   // DirectSound buffer description
WAVEFORMATEX  pcmwf; // holds the format description

// set up the format data structure
memset(&pcmwf, 0, sizeof(WAVEFORMATEX));
pcmwf.wFormatTag = WAVE_FORMAT_PCM; // always need this
pcmwf.nChannels  = 1; // MONO, so channels = 1
```

(continued)

(continued)

```
pcmwf.nSamplesPerSec = 11025; // sample rate 11khz
pcmwf.nBlockAlign    = 1; // set to the total data per
// block, which in our case 1 channel times 1 byte per
// sample, so 1 byte total; if it were stereo, then it
// would be 2, and if stereo and 16 bit then it would be 4

pcmwf.nAvgBytesPerSec =
                pcmwf.nSamplesPerSec * pcmwf.nBlockAlign;
pcmwf.wBitsPerSample = 8; // 8 bits per sample
pcmwf.cbSize         = 0; // always 0

// set up the DirectSound buffer description
memset(dsbd,0,sizeof(DSBUFFERDESC));
dsbd.dwSize = sizeof(DSBUFFERDESC);
dsbd.dwFlags= DSBCAPS_CTRLDEFAULT | DSBCAPS_STATIC |
              DSBCAPS_LOCSOFTWARE ;
dsbd.dwBufferBytes   = 22050; // enough for 2 seconds at
// a sample rate of 11025

dsbd.lpwfxFormat     = &pcmwf; // the WAVEFORMATEX struct

// create the buffer
if (lpds->CreateSoundBuffer(&dsbd,&lpdsbuffer,NULL)!=DS_OK)
   { /* error */ }
```

If the function call was successful, `lpdsbuffer` is ready to be played. The only problem is that nothing is in it! You must fill the sound buffer with data yourself. You can do this step by reading in a sound file, such as a `.VOC` or `.WAV`, and then parsing the data and filling up the buffer. Or you can just algorithmically write data (such as a sine wave) into the buffer yourself just for a test. In the next section, you can find out how to write the data into the buffer. In the section "Reading the jams from disk," later in this chapter, I show you how to read sound files from a disk.

Writing data to secondary buffers

Secondary sound buffers are circular in nature and are a little more complex to write to than a standard linear array of data. For example, with DirectDraw surfaces, you just lock the surface memory and write to it. DirectSound works in a similar fashion: You lock it, but instead of getting one pointer back, you get two! Therefore, you must write some of your data to the first pointer and the rest to the second. Take a look at the prototype for `Lock()` to see what I mean:

```
HRESULT Lock(
   DWORD dwWriteCursor,      // position of write cursor
   DWORD dwWriteBytes,       // size of buffer you want to lock
LPVOID lplpvAudioPtr1,       // return pointer to first chunk
   LPDWORD lpdwAudioBytes1,// number of bytes in first chunk
   LPVOID lplpvAudioPtr2,    // return pointer to second chunk
   LPDWORD lpdwAudioBytes2,// num of bytes in second chunk
   DWORD dwFlags);           // locking flags
```

If you set dwFlags to DSBLOCK_FROMWRITECURSOR, then the buffer is
locked from the current write cursor of the buffer. If you set dwFlags to
DSBLOCK_ENTIREBUFFER, the entire buffer is locked. This is the way to go.
Keep it simple.

For example, suppose that you create a sound buffer that's 1,000 bytes long.
When you lock the buffer for writing, you will get two pointers back — along
with the length of each memory segment to write to. The first chunk may be
900 bytes long and the second may be 100 bytes long. You have to write
your first 900 bytes to the first memory region and the second 100 bytes to
the second memory region. Take a look at Figure 13-11 to clarify this idea.

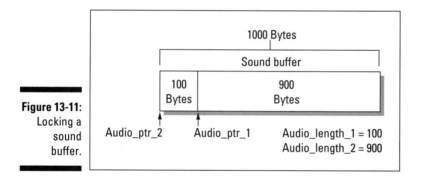

Figure 13-11:
Locking a
sound
buffer.

Here's an example of locking the 100-byte-long sound buffer:

```
UCHAR *audio_ptr1,  // used to retrieve buffer memory
      *audio_ptr_2;
int audio_length_1, // length of each buffer section
    audio_length_2;

// lock the buffer
if (lpdsbuffer->Lock(0,1000,
    (void **)&audio_ptr_1, &audio_length_1,
    (void **)&audio_ptr_2, &audio_length_2,
    DSBLOCK_ENTIREBUFFER )!=DS_OK)
    { /* error / }
```

After you lock the buffer, you are free to write into the memory. The data can be from a file or algorithmically generated. After you finish with the sound buffer, you must unlock it with `Unlock()`. `Unlock()` takes both pointers and both lengths like this:

```
if (lpdsbuffer->Unlock(audio_ptr_1, audio_length_1,
        audio_ptr_2, audio_length_2)!=DS_OK)
    { /* problem unlocking */}
```

And as usual, after you're done with the sound buffer, you must destroy it with `Release()`, like this:

```
lpdsbuffer->Release();
```

Manipulating, mangling, and mastering sounds

After you have created all your sound buffers and loaded them with sounds, you're ready to rock. DirectSound offers a number of control functions that enable you to play sounds and alter their parameters as they play. You can change volume, frequency, stereo panning, and so on.

Playing a sound

To play a sound from the buffer, use the `Play()` function as prototyped in the following:

```
HRESULT Play(
    DWORD dwReserved1, DWORD dwReserved2,    // both 0
    DWORD dwFlags); // control flags to play
```

The only flag that is defined is `DSBPLAY_LOOPING`. Setting this value causes the sound to loop. If you want the sound to play only once, set `dwFlags` to 0. Here's an example of playing a sound over and over:

```
if (!lpdsbuffer->Play(0,0,DSBPLAY_LOOPING))
    { /* error */ }
```

Use looping for music and other stuff that you want to repeat.

Stopping a sound

After you have started a sound, you may want to stop it before it's finished playing. Use the function `Stop()`. Here's its prototype:

```
HRESULT Stop(); // that's easy enough
```

Here's how to stop the sound you just started in the preceding example:

```
if (!lpdsbuffer->Stop())
   { /* error */ }
```

Now you have enough code for a complete demo of DirectSound. Check out PROG13_2.CPP on the CD. It creates a DirectSound object and a single secondary sound buffer. It then loads the buffer with a synthesized sine wave and plays it. Simple, but the code effectively shows you everything you need to know to play a sound.

Controlling the volume

DirectSound gives you the ability to manipulate the volume or amplitude of a sound. However, this ability isn't free of drains on your resources. If your hardware doesn't support volume changes, then DirectSound must remix the sound with the new amplitude. This task can take a little more processing power. In any case, here's the prototype:

```
HRESULT SetVolume(LONG lVolume); // attenuation in decibels
```

SetVolume() works a little strangely. Instead of instructing DirectSound to increase or decrease the amplitude, SetVolume() controls the attenuation (volume decrease). If you send a 0 (which is equal to DSBVOLUME_MAX), then the sound is played without attenuation. A value of –10,000 or DSBVOLUME_MIN sets the attenuation to maximum –100dB (decibels), and you won't hear a thing.

The best thing to do is create a wrapper function around SetVolume(), so you can send a value from 0 to 100 or something more natural. The following macro transformation will do the job:

```
#define DSVOLUME_TO_DB(volume)
                   ((DWORD)(-30*(100 - volume)))
```

In the preceding code snippet, volume is from 0 to 100 — 100 being full volume and 0 being totally silent. Here's an example that will make a sound play at 50 percent of full volume:

```
if (!lpdsbuffer->SetVolume(DSVOLUME_TO_DB(volume)))
   { /* error */ }
```

Are you wondering what a *decibel* is? It's a measure of sound or power. In electronics, many things are measured in tenths or some other scale — in other words, logarithmically. The decibel scale is one of those scales. 0 dB means no attenuation, –1 dB means that the sound is $^1/_{10}$ its original value, –2 dB means $^1/_{100}$, and so on. Therefore, a sound that's attenuated –100 dB couldn't be heard by an ant! Note that on some scales dB is also scaled by a factor of 10. So –10 dB is $^1/_{10}$ and –20 dB is $^1/_{100}$. This scale is one of those things that everybody has their own version of.

Changing the frequency

One of the coolest ways to alter a sound is to change its playback frequency. This change has the effect of changing the pitch (sort of), and you can make sounds slow and evil or fast and happy. This method is how you can make your own voice sound like that of a chipmunk or of Darth Vader in real-time. To change the frequency of playback, use the SetFrequency() function as shown in the following:

```
HRESULT SetFrequency(
    DWORD dwFrequency); // new frequency from 100-100,000 Hz
```

Here's how to make a sound play faster:

```
if (!lpdsbuffer->SetFrequency(22050))
    { / * error */ }
```

If the original sound was sampled at 11,025 Hz (11 kHz), then the sound would play twice as fast, have two times the pitch, and play for exactly half as long. Get it?

Panning in 3D

The final cool thing you can do with a sound is change the stereo pan or the amount of power coming from each speaker. For example, if you play a sound at the same volume in both speakers (or headphones), it seems like the sound source is right in front of you; but if you shift the volume to the right speaker, the sound seems like it's moving to the right. This technique is called *panning* and can help you create localized 3D sounds (in a crude manner).

The function to set the stereo panning is called SetPan(), and here's its prototype:

```
HRESULT SetPan(
        LONG lPan); // the pan value-10,000 to 10,000
```

The pan value is logarithmic again, so a value of 0 is dead center, and a value of –10,000 means that the right channel is attenuated by –100 decibels (dB), and 10,000 means that the left channel is attenuated by –100 dB. Stupid, huh? Here's how to attenuate the right channel by –5 dB:

```
if (!lpdsbuffer->SetPan(-500))
    { /* error */ }
```

Interrogating DirectSound

You may wonder whether you have any way to query information from DirectSound about the sound system and/or a sound that is playing. For example, can you find out whether the sound is finished playing? Of course! DirectSound has a number of functions for querying like that. Here's the general DirectSound capability function to determine the capabilities of your hardware:

```
HRESULT GetCaps(LPDSCAPS lpDSCaps);// ptr to DSCAPS structure
```

The function simply takes a pointer to a DSCAPS structure and fills it in. Check out the DSCAPS in the DirectX SDK for a complete description of each field; most of them are decipherable by their names.

Call the function like this:

```
DSCAPS dscaps; // hold the caps
if (!lpds->GetCaps(&dscaps))
    { /* error */ }
```

Then you can test any of the fields you want and determine what capabilities your sound hardware has.

There's also a similar function for a DirectSound buffer that returns a DSBCAPS structure:

```
HRESULT GetCaps(LPDSBCAPS lpDSBCaps); // ptr to DSBCAPS struct
```

The preceding code takes a DSBCAPS structure that looks like this:

```
typedef struct {
  DWORD dwSize;                 // size of structure (you must set this)
  DWORD dwFlags;                // flags buffer has
  DWORD dwBufferBytes;          // size of buffer
  DWORD dwUnlockTransferRate;   // sample rate
  DWORD dwPlayCpuOverhead;      // percentage of processor needed
                                // to mix this sound
} DSBCAPS, *LPDSBCAPS;
```

Here's how to check out the sound buffer `lpdsbuffer` in the examples:

```
DSBCAPS dsbcaps;                    // hold the results
// set up the struct
dsbcaps.dwSize = sizeof(DSBCAPS); // ultra important


// get the caps
if (!lpdsbuffer->GetCaps(&dsbcaps))
   { /* error */ }
```

That's all there is to it. Of course, functions are available to retrieve the volume, do pan setting, set the frequency, and so on, of any sound buffer, but you can look up those options.

The last "get info" function I want to show you determines the status of a playing sound buffer:

```
HRESULT GetStatus(LPDWORD lpdwStatus); // ptr to result
```

Just call the function from the interface pointer of the sound buffer you're interested in with a pointer to the DWORD you want the status stored in, like this:

```
DWORD status; // used to hold status
if (!lpdsbuffer->GetStatus(&status))
  { / * error */ }
```

The data in status will be one of the following:

- ✔ **DSBSTATUS_BUFFERLOST:** Something happened to the buffer — very bad.

- ✔ **DSBSTATUS_LOOPING:** The sound is playing in looped mode.

- ✔ **DSBSTATUS_PLAYING:** The sound is currently playing. If this bit isn't set, the sound isn't playing at all.

Reading the jams from disk

I held off on this subject until last in this section because it's one of those things that you wish you could just use a function call for. Unfortunately, DirectSound has no support to load sound files. I mean *no* support. No .VOC loader, no .WAV loader, no nothing! It's a darn shame. So programmers have to write their own loaders. The problem: Sound files are extremely complex and explaining the process of loading one would require half a chapter to do a good job, so I'm giving you a .VOC loader now along with a brief explanation on how it works, and then later I give you a .WAV loader when you create Part II of the GPDUMB library in Chapter 16.

Don't worry if you have never heard of the .VOC format. All good sound programs can read and write the format, so you can still work with .WAV files, but if you want to use my function, you need to convert your .WAVs to .VOCs before loading. Before I show you the guts to the .VOC loader, take a quick look at the .WAV format, so you have at least an idea of why reading it is so difficult.

Using the .WAV format

The .WAV format is a Windows sound format based on the .IFF format created originally by Electronic Arts. IFF stands for Interchange File Format and is a standard that allows many different file types to be encoded using a general header/data structure with nesting. The .WAV format uses this encoding and — although it's very clean and logical — it's a pain to read these files into a program. You must parse a lot of header information, which takes a lot of code, and then you finally have to extract the sound data.

The parsing is so difficult that Microsoft created a set of functions called the Multimedia I/O interface to help you, which are all prefixed with mmio*. So the moral of the story is: Writing a .WAV file reader isn't that easy, and it's tedious programming that has nothing to do with game programming. So I'm just going to give you a .WAV loader in Chapter 16, but now you know what you're up against if you want to write your own.

Reading .VOC files

The .VOC file format was created by Creative Labs and can hold sound files just as complex as .WAV files. But because .VOC files are only used to hold sound data, there isn't all the data abstraction as with .IFF wave files. A .VOC file can hold 8- or 16-bit samples in mono or stereo. Each sample is in a block. Take a look at Figure 13-12, which shows a few different data formats of blocks with various data sizes.

The beauty of .VOC files is that they are easy to read. A .VOC file has a header section followed by the data blocks. The data blocks also have a small header that describes the sound (see Figure 13-13). .VOC files can support mono or stereo files, but stereo uses the extended format that I don't want to deal with. So to keep things simple, use the basic mono, 8-bit format that includes one byte per sample. Simple, just the way I like it!

If you examine Figure 13-13, you can see that the header block can be of variable length (although it has remained about 26 bytes long for 10 years). This variable length was to keep things open for future expansion. The only way you can figure out the length of the header is to read its length from the header itself. This information is stored in byte index positions (20,21) of the header section. Confusing, huh? The header contains the following data in the first 25 bytes:

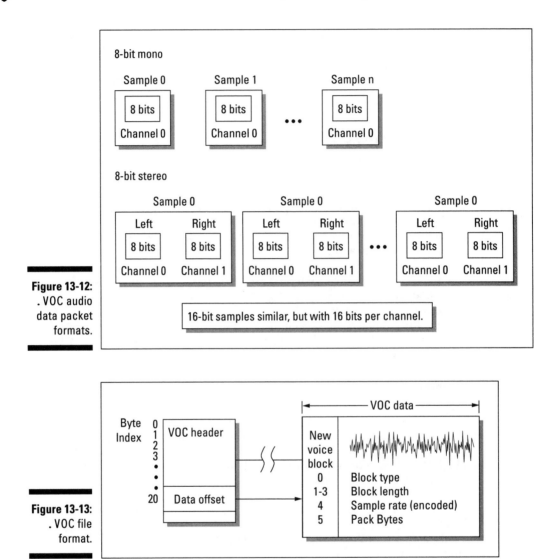

Figure 13-12:
. VOC audio
data packet
formats.

Figure 13-13:
. VOC file
format.

- ✔ **Bytes 0 to 19:** The Words "Creative Voice File." Read this section to make sure that you have a . VOC file.

- ✔ **Bytes 20 to 21:** The length of the header that I discuss earlier in this section. Rarely do you need the high byte in location 21.

- ✔ **Bytes 22 to 23:** Version number in major-minor byte encoded format.

- ✔ **Bytes 24 to 25:** More version number stuff, mostly unused.

Or if you were to create a data structure template to hold the data, use this:

```
typedef VOC_HEADER_TYP
   {
   char name[20];      // "Creative Voice File"
USHORT header_length; // length of this header
USHORT version1;      // version info
USHORT version2;      // version info
   } VOC_HEADER, *VOC_HEADER_PTR;
```

So that's it. To read a .VOC file, here are the steps:

1. **Open the .VOC.**

2. **Read the first 25 bytes of the file into a template (like** VOC_HEADER**).**

3. **Check whether the** name **field contains the words** *Creative Voice File.*

4. **Access the** header_length **field and use it as an offset from the beginning of the file to find the start of the .VOC data.**

After you reach the data section, you find another header called the *New Voice Block.* It's exactly 6 bytes long and has the following format:

```
typedef struct VOC_NVB_TYP
   {
UCHAR block_type; // type of block (1 is new voice block)
UCHAR block_length[3]; // 3-byte word indicating
                       // length of sound in bytes
UCHAR sample_rate; // sample rate of data in encoded form
UCHAR compression; // compression (0 means no compression)
UCHAR data[];      // here's where the data goes
} VOC_NVB, *VOC_NVB_PTR;
```

Just read the 6 bytes into the VOC_NVB, and you are ready to go. The block_type should always be 1, the block_length is unused, and compression should be equal to 0 (no compression). The only field that is encrypted is sample_rate. You'll notice that it's a single byte, so it can't describe sample rates greater than 255 right? Wrong! The actual sample rate is computed using this formula:

```
DWORD actual_sample_rate = -1000000/(sample_rate - 256);
```

Writing a .VOC reader is straightforward from this point on; just read the data and parse it based on the header and data structure. I don't have room to show you a complete listing of a .VOC file reader, but the CD contains one within the final demo program PROG13_3.CPP. The .VOC loader function is called Load_VOC(), which both loads a .VOC from disk and creates a sound buffer to hold it. Here's its prototype:

```
LPDIRECTSOUNDBUFFER int Load_VOC(
    char *voc_file, // name of .VOC file to load from disk
    VOC_FILE_PTR voc_data); // pointer to structure
                            // to hold data
```

In the preceding prototype, VOC_FILE is defined as:

```
typedef struct VOC_FILE_TYP
    {
    int sample_rate; // sample rate of sound
    int length;      // length of sound data
    LPDIRECTSOUNDBUFFER lpdsbuffer; // pointer to sound buffer
    } VOC_FILE, *VOC_FILE_PTR;
```

To use the function, send it a filename to load along with an empty VOC_FILE structure to the function. If the requested .VOC file is on the disk, then the Load_VOC() loads it in, allocates the memory necessary to hold it, loads the data, creates a DirectSound buffer to hold the sound data, loads the data into the buffer, and finally fills out the various fields of the VOC_FILE and returns with a TRUE. If the file isn't on the disk, then the function returns FALSE. Here's an example:

```
VOC_FILE voc_file; // used to hold .VOC data

// load explosion .VOC file
if (!Load_VOC("EXPLOS.VOC",&voc_file))
   { /* file not found */ }

// at this point voc_file will be filled in
// and voc_file.lpdsbuffer will be valid and ready
// for use...

// to play the sound, you would do this
voc_file.lpdsbuffer->Play(0,0,DSBPLAY_LOOPING);
```

Make sure that you check out PROG13_3.CPP on the disk. It's a complete demo of DirectSound and the Load_VOC() function. The program lets you manipulate the sound in real-time with scroll bars, so not only is it cool, but you can see how to add scroll bar controls to your applications!

In Chapter 16, which contains the second part of building the GPDUMB library, you can create an entire sound library that performs tasks such as releasing the sound buffer and managing multiple sounds.

Chapter 14

The Ins and Outs of DirectInput

· ·

In This Chapter

▶ Finding out about DirectInput

▶ Creating and using a keyboard device

▶ Playing with a mouse

▶ Setting up a joystick

· ·

*I*n this chapter, I cover DirectInput, which is the input component of DirectX. With DirectInput, you can access the keyboard, mouse, joystick, and all other forms of input devices in a uniform manner.

When Microsoft finally got DirectInput working in DirectX 3.0, I almost popped a blood vessel in my brain! Working with Windows messaging to get input from the keyboard, mouse, and joystick is definitely cruel and unusual. Lucky for us, the Dark Ages are over. DirectX 3.0 offers full support for every input device you can think of in a DirectX COM kind of way. The following list details some of the input devices DirectX supports:

✔ **Keyboards:** The standard QWERTY keyboard

✔ **Mice:** Two- and three-button mice

✔ **Joysticks and flight yokes:** Both analog and digital joystick/flight yoke support with six degrees of freedom and up to 32 buttons

✔ **Driving controls:** Both analog and digital driving simulation setups

✔ **Paddles:** Various rotational devices

✔ **Force feedback devices:** Joysticks or other devices that have mechanical actuators enabling the computer to make them vibrate and/or change shape

✔ **Virtual reality headgear tracking systems:** Position and orientation support for virtual reality headgear that sends back the state of the wearer's head

That about covers every kind of input device you could hook to your computer. And I would imagine that when full virtual reality suits come out, DirectInput will support them!

This chapter discusses using DirectInput in your game program. I start off with an explanation of what makes DirectInput tick, and the remaining sections show you how to make DirectInput work for you.

The Guts of DirectInput

DirectInput works by using the standard COM model with a single COM object representing DirectInput and a number of other objects, each representing an input device attached to the PC — as shown in Figure 14-1. (For more about COM models and such, check out Chapter 7.) In essence, the main DirectInput object manages all the input devices that are `IDirectInputDevice`s.

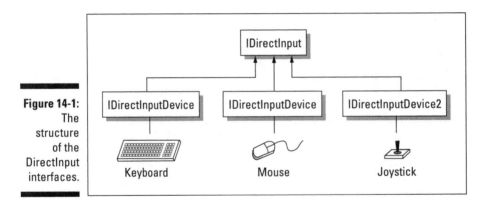

Figure 14-1:
The structure of the DirectInput interfaces.

Although DirectInput can be extremely complex if you use all its features, it can be quite manageable at the lowest level of functionality — which is how you use it with this book. In fact, you need only three interfaces:

- ✔ `IDIRECTINPUT`: The main DirectInput object, representing the entire input system that devices can be attached to

- ✔ `IDIRECTINPUTDEVICE`: Any simple input device

- ✔ `IDIRECTINPUTDEVICE2`: Same as `IDIRECTINPUTDEVICE`, but supports more advanced features, such as force feedback devices and virtual reality headgear

Too many input devices are available to have a different interface for each one, so instead DirectInput uses a single generic input device — `IDIRECTINPUTDEVICE` — that you must set up by sending a GUID along with the properties that you desire. This arrangement will make sense as you read this chapter.

If you're a little stumped by the two IDIRECTINPUTDEVICE interfaces, remember that each time a new release of DirectX comes out, Microsoft adds a little bit to each subsystem. When a subsystem undergoes major external changes, Microsoft creates a new interface with the same root name, but with a new, higher number appended to the end. Therefore, IDIRECTINPUTDEVICE2 is the second interface version of DirectInput, even though Microsoft is on Version 6.0 of DirectX. Makes perfect sense. (Not!)

Using DirectInput

DirectInput consists of run-time DLLs (that you don't worry about) and two compile-time files: DINPUT.LIB and DINPUT.H. They import the library and the header, respectively. Just make sure to include these in your project, and you won't have a problem.

Using DirectInput is fairly straightforward:

1. **Create a main DirectInput object with** DirectInputCreate().

2. **Create one or more input devices with** CreateDevice(); **you need a GUID for each one, so you may have to request that DirectInput enumerate all input devices.**

3. **Set the cooperation level for each device with** SetCooperativeLevel().

4. **Set the data format of each device with** SetDataFormat(), **and set any special properties with** SetProperty().

5. **Acquire each input device with** Acquire().

   This step attaches each input device to the main DirectInputDevice.

6. **Receive input with** GetDeviceState().

   Call Poll() if the device needs manual polling.

Read the input for each device as a record and then parse the record for the information that you want. Each different type of input device has slightly different record formats, but amazingly enough they are also very similar. That is, a lot of thought went into generalizing input data.

You can request input from DirectInput in two different ways:

 ✔ **Immediate input:** Represents the current state of the device.

 ✔ **Buffered input:** Keeps a database or list of events that have occurred since the last time you requested input.

For the examples in this book, I use immediate data format because it's easier to set up and a more intuitive way of reading input data.

With DirectInput, you don't have to worry about messages, stalls, slow response, and so on. DirectInput works directly with the hardware drivers. In fact, it works so well that it can completely cut Windows out of the loop!

DirectInput's capability to work without Windows can be a problem in windowed applications. If you set the priority level high enough in your DirectInput application, then Windows never gets any keyboard or mouse messages. If you don't want Windows to get these messages, then great. But if you want to use Windows controls or menus in your application, keep this limitation in mind when you set the DirectInput cooperation level.

Luckily, DirectInput is smart enough to allow you to set the cooperation level of each input device separately, so that's a good thing, but I would still be generous instead of greedy with cooperation.

The following sections explain each step in detail. Repeat the list three times, and click your heals before reading on.

Bringing DirectInput Online

The first step to using DirectInput is to create the main COM object that represents the DirectInput device manager (for lack of a better description). The main DirectInput COM object is referenced by the type:

```
LPDIRECTINPUT lpdi; // main DirectInput object
```

To create a DirectInput object, use this `DirectInputCreate()` function prototype:

```
HRESULT DirectInputCreate(
    HINSTANCE hinst,  // instance of application
    DWORD dwVersion,  // backward version compatibility
    LPDIRECTINPUT * lplpDirectInput,  // pointer to interface to
                                      // receive object
    LPUNKNOWN punkOuter); // COM stuff, always NULL
```

The function returns `DI_OK` (DirectInput Okay) if successful and another constant otherwise (take a look at the DirectX SDK for details).The parameters for `DirectInputCreate()` are a bit different from anything I cover in earlier chapters. In particular, `dwVersion` and `hinst.dwVersion` are used to request older versions of DirectInput if you want backward compatibility. But for now, always send `DIRECTINPUT_VERSION`, which means: Use the latest version.

On the other hand, hinst is a bit unusual. It's the *instance* of your application, and this is odd because rarely do you use an instance handle to create a DirectX COM object. In the case of hinst, make sure to save the application instance in the WinMain() function and send the instance handle to this function when you create a DirectInput object. Here's an example of creating a DirectInput object:

```
// make sure to include this and the library DINPUT.LIB
#include "DINPUT.H"

// more includes, defines, and so on....

LPDIRECTINPUT lpdi; // pointer to DirectInput object

// create DirectInput object
if (DirectInputCreate(hinstance,DIRECTINPUT_VERSION, &lpdi,NULL)!=DI_OK)
   { /* error */ }
```

That's it. And after you're done using the DirectInput object, release the object with a call to Release() like this:

```
lpdi->Release();
```

Just as DirectSound can operate independently of DirectDraw, so can DirectInput. In fact, every DirectX component can run by itself; all you need is a window to anchor it to. You don't have to start up DirectDraw to make DirectInput work. This flexibility is great when you are figuring out how to use DirectX components.

Keyboarding at the Speed of X

The keyboard is definitely the simplest of all DirectInput devices. I suffered only one or two headaches to get a keyboard to work with DirectX, and that's pretty good. (But don't worry; now that I've had my headaches, I can tell you how to avoid them!)

Because the keyboard is so straightforward, I go into detail on every step involved in setting it up for use in DirectInput. The sections of this chapter that discuss the mouse and joysticks don't go into detail about many procedural issues; I just cover the details specific to those devices. Use this section on keyboarding to get any other information.

1. **Create the keyboard device.**

2. **Set the cooperation level for the keyboard.**

3. **Set the data format for the keyboard device.**

4. **Acquire the keyboard device.**

Creating a keyboard device

The first step in using the keyboard is creating a keyboard device. This step is accomplished with the function `CreateDevice()`, which is used to create any and all DirectInput devices.

However, before I show it to you, I want to clarify a possible confusion with the DirectInput device/object metaphor. A device usually represents a single input device such as a keyboard, mouse, joystick, and so on — but not necessarily.

Some input devices, such as a steering wheel control for a race game, may have one device for the wheel, one for the pedals, and one for all the buttons (as shown in Figure 14-2). Moreover, DirectInput does not refer to an *object* as a complete input device, but as an individual input actuator. For example, a joystick is an input *device* that has a number of input *objects:* the joystick yoke and each button (as shown in Figure 14-3). I may warp in and out of these terms, and I don't want you to fall back in my trans-warp wake.

So with all that in mind, here's the function to create a device (note that *ptr* stands for *pointer*):

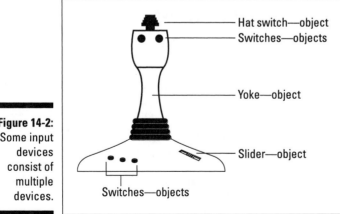

Figure 14-2: Some input devices consist of multiple devices.

Hat switch—object
Switches—objects

Yoke—object

Slider—object

Switches—objects

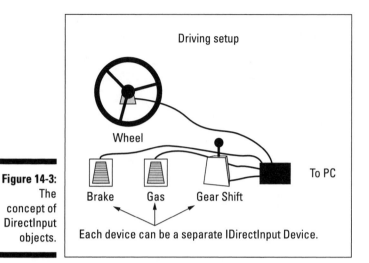

Figure 14-3:
The concept of DirectInput objects.

Driving setup

Wheel

Brake   Gas   Gear Shift   To PC

Each device can be a separate IDirectInput Device.

```
HRESULT CreateDevice(
  REFGUID rguid,     // GUID of device to create
  LPDIRECTINPUTDEVICE *lplpDIDev,// ptr to device interface
  LPUNKNOWN pUnkOuter); // always NULL
```

The first parameter to the function is the *GUID* (Globally Unique Identifier) that identifies the device you want to create. Normally, you must enumerate devices with `EnumDevices()` to get the GUIDs for any weird nonstandard devices such as joysticks, flight sticks, and so on. But DirectInput has a GUID predefined for the keyboard and mouse:

- ✔ `GUID_SysKeyboard`: The default system keyboard
- ✔ `GUID_SysMouse`: The default system mouse

However, to use these GUIDs, you must include them with #define `INITGUID` at the very top of your C/C++ file along with including the header file `OBJBASE.H` in your program. This method makes the compiler include all the COM stuff, including these predefined GUIDs.

The next parameter to `CreateDevice()` is the address of the interface pointer you want to receive the device. No differentiation exists between devices, so always use the same type, namely:

```
LPDIRECTINPUTDEVICE lpdikey; // keyboard device
```

Now use all this new knowledge to create a keyboard device. Remember to do the following at the top of your file:

```
#define INITGUID     // needed to get the GUIDS in here
#include <OBJBASE.H> // COM stuff
#include "DINPUT.H"  // you need this!
```

Then create a DirectInput object:

```
LPDIRECTINPUT lpdi; // main DirectInput object

// create DirectInput object
if (DirectInputCreate(hinstance,DIRECTINPUT_VERSION, &lpdi,NULL)!=DI_OK)
   { /* error */ }
```

And now create the keyboard device:

```
LPDIRECTINPUTDEVICE lpdikey; // the keyboard device

// create keyboard device
if (lpdi->CreateDevice(GUID_SysKeyboard, &lpdikey,NULL)!=DI_OK)
   { /* error */ }
```

Notice that `CreateDevice()` is an interface function of the main DirectInput object; that should be no surprise. After the preceding code fragment executes, `lpdikey` should point to the keyboard device and you are ready to set the cooperation level.

Setting the cooperation level

Each DirectInput device has its own cooperation level, although there aren't that many of them. To set the cooperation level of a device, use the `SetCooperativeLevel()` from the device interface as in the following prototype:

```
HRESULT SetCooperativeLevel(HWND hwnd,  // window handle
   DWORD dwFlags); // cooperation flags
```

The function returns `DI_OK` if successful.

The cooperation level really has only four settings: *background, foreground, exclusive,* and *nonexclusive.* The names are a bit misleading, so take a look at Table 14-1 for details.

Table 14-1 **General** `SetCooperativeLevel()` **Settings for All DirectInput Devices**

Value	Meaning
DISCL_BACKGROUND	Your application can use a DirectInput device when the application is idling in the background or active in the foreground.
DISCL_FOREGROUND	The application requires foreground access. If foreground access is granted, the device is automatically unacquired when the associated window moves to the background.
DISCL_EXCLUSIVE	After you acquire the device, no other application can request exclusive access to it; however, other applications can still request nonexclusive access.
DISCL_NONEXCLUSIVE	The application requires nonexclusive access. Access to the device will not interfere with other applications that are accessing the same device.

I'm not sure if even Microsoft knows what they mean, but as far as I can tell you should use `DISCL_BACKGROUND | DISCL_NONEXCLUSIVE` for the cooperation setting. This approach gives the best all-around performance. And because your games are going to run in full-screen mode most of the time, using the nonexclusive setting is no problem. Using exclusive access can really jack up Windows and take it completely out of the input loop, which you may not want to do.

Based on the previous cooperation level briefing, set the cooperation level of your new keyboard input device:

```
if (lpdikey->SetCooperativeLevel(main_window_handle,
    DISCL_BACKGROUND | DISCL_NONEXCLUSIVE)!=DI_OK)
  { /* error */ }
```

Setting the data format

The next step in getting the keyboard to talk to your program is setting the data format. The data format controls how you want the data from the device to be formatted and represented. This phase of initialization can be very complicated if you do it yourself. You have to make a call to `SetDataFormat()` as in the following prototype:

```
HRESULT SetDataFormat(LPCDIDATAFORMAT lpdf); // pointer to data format
```

The single parameter to `SetDataFormat()` uses a `DIDATAFORMAT` structure as shown in the following:

```
typedef struct {
  DWORD dwSize;       // size of this structure in bytes
  DWORD dwObjSize;    // size of DIOBJECTDATAFORMAT in bytes
  DWORD dwFlags;      // flags: either DIDF_ABSAXIS or
                      // DIDF_RELAXIS for absolute or
                      // relative reporting
  DWORD dwDataSize;   // size of data packets
  DWORD dwNumObjs;    // number of objects that are defined in
                      // the following array of object
  LPDIOBJECTDATAFORMAT rgodf; // pointer to array of objects
} DIDATAFORMAT, *LPDIDATAFORMAT;
```

As you can see, this data structure is a nightmare. Not only is this structure rather cryptic, but it's basically the header for an array of "object" (single inputs) records defining all the input controls for the device. Suffice it to say, the designers of DirectInput realized that making the user set up all these complex data structures was too much to ask, and henceforth, they created a number of predefined data formats. Hip hip hooray! They are shown in Table 14-2.

Table 14-2	Predefined Data Formats
Value	*Usage*
`c_dfDIKeyboard`	Predefined data format for the keyboard
`c_dfDIMouse`	Predefined data format for the mouse
`c_dfDIJoystick`	Predefined data format for a standard joystick

These predefined data formats are actually global variables, so use them as if they were variables you created. Here's how to set the data format:

```
// set format; notice the use of the address operator
if (lpdikey->SetDataFormat(&c_dfDIKeyboard )!=DI_OK)
  { /* error */ }
```

After the data format is set, the last step (at least for the keyboard) is to acquire the input device with `Acquire()`. This step attaches the device to the input stream and makes its data available. Here's the prototype for `Acquire()`:

```
HRESULT Acquire();
```

If successful, the return value can either be DI_OK or S_FALSE, so a little extra error-checking may be in order to be bulletproof.

Finally, here's how to acquire the keyboard device you create:

```
if (lpdikey->Acquire()!=DI_OK)
   { /* error */ }
```

That's it! Now you're finally ready to read the data from the keyboard.

Reading the data from the keyboard

Keep in mind that the DirectInput default keyboard data format is *state data*. In other words, when you read the data, you're reading the current state of the keyboard as if it were a set of momentary switches. However, it is possible to get a buffered input going, but most of the time you want simple on/off state data, so leave the data format as is.

To read the keyboard data — or any data, for that matter, from any device — you must use the GetDeviceState() function. This function reads the instantaneous data state of the device, or what the device did on the last input cycle. Here's the prototype:

```
HRESULT GetDeviceState(
    DWORD cbData,     // size of data record
    LPVOID lpvData);  // pointer to data storage area
```

As usual, the function returns DI_OK if successful and various other DirectInput error codes (see DirectX SDK Help for more details) if an error occurs.

The interesting thing about GetDeviceState() is that it's so general. This function is used whether you are reading the keyboard, mouse, joystick, or any other device. The only thing that changes is cbSize, which is the size of the receiving record in bytes, and lpvData, which is a pointer to the place where the data should be stored in memory.

For example, the keyboard state consists of an array of 256 BYTE elements. Each element represents a single key. This arrangement is identical to the way the Win32 GetAsyncKeyState() function works, so if you're familiar with Windows API programming, you should feel right at home. To use the GetDeviceState() function to retrieve the entire keyboard state, send that function the size of the data array (256 in this case) and a pointer to the array. Here's an example:

```
// storage for the keyboard data
UCHAR keystate[256];
// ...

// do this in your main loop
if (lpdikey->GetDeviceState(256, keystate)!=DI_OK)
  { /* something's amiss */ }

// test data entries...
```

Easy enough, but do you see how I slipped in that little "test data entries" comment? Well, DirectInput has a constant for each key, just as Win32 does for the GetAsyncKeyState(). The constants all begin with "DIK_" and are followed with the key. Table 14-3 is an extremely abridged version of all the key codes. For a complete reference, take a look at the DirectX SDK or just look in DINPUT.H within the DirectX SDK directory.

Table 14-3	DirectInput Keyboard Virtual Key Codes
Value	*Meaning*
DIK_ESCAPE	Escape key
DIK_0 – DIK_9	0–9 on the main keyboard
DIK_A – DIK_Z	A–Z
DIK_RETURN	Enter key on the main keyboard
DIK_LCONTROL	Left Ctrl key
DIK_RCONTROL	Right Ctrl key
DIK_SPACE	The spacebar
DIK_F1 – DIK_F12	Function keys F1–F12
DIK_UP	↑ (Up) arrow key
DIK_DOWN	↓ (Down) arrow key
DIK_LEFT	← (Left) arrow key
DIK_RIGHT	→ (Right) arrow key
DIK_PRIOR	Page Up
DIK_NEXT	Page Down

After getting the device state of the keyboard, you're free to query the data array. If a key is ON (pressed), the bit 0 x 80 is 1. If a key is OFF (released), the bit 0 x 80 is 0. For example, here's how you can test for arrow movements to move a ship:

```
int ship_x = 100, ship_y = 100; // initial ship position

// storage for the keyboard data
UCHAR keystate[256];
// ...

// in your main loop, you would do this
if (lpdikey->GetDeviceState(256, keystate)!=DI_OK)
    { /* something's amiss */ }

// test whether the player is "moving" the ship
if (keystate[DIK_RIGHT] & 0x80) ship_x++;
if (keystate[DIK_LEFT]  & 0x80) ship_x--;
if (keystate[DIK_DOWN]  & 0x80) ship_y++;
if (keystate[DIK_UP]    & 0x80) ship_y--;
```

Of course, you may want to put a macro around the call, so you don't have to explicitly do the AND bit test.

After you're done with your toys, you need to put them away. Thus, for each input device you create and acquire, you need to do the following:

```
// unacquire first
lpdikey->Unacquire();
// then release the object
lpdikey->Release();
```

The code above is basically the prototype to Unacquire(). There's nothing to it; just a call.

I hope you know how to use DirectInput to read the keyboard and, more generally, understand that the steps involved are pretty much the same for each input device. For example, check out PROG14_1.CPP on the CD; it's a demo of the keyboard under DirectInput. In the program, you're in control of a demon skeleton (as shown in Figure 14-4). You control the character with the arrow keys. Make sure to look at the other features of the demo and the use of the engine. Also, this demo uses the GPDUMB1 game engine, so if you want to recompile, make sure that you include GPDUMB1.CPP and the library files DDRAW.LIB and DINPUT.LIB.

If you want to compile the demo yourself, make sure that you include DINPUT.LIB from the DirectX SDK in your project.

WHERE IS EVERYBODY? I HAVE A BONE TO PICK!

USE ARROW KEYS TO MOVE ME.

Figure 14-4:
The
keyboard
demo.

Setting a Trap for the Mouse

Establishing communications with the mouse is almost identical to the
process for the keyboard. Reading the mouse position is really the only task
that's different.

I provide an explanation of all the functions and their prototypes earlier in
the keyboard discussion, "Keyboarding at the Speed of X." In this section, I
only show you the actual calls and software rather than all the setup details,
which I cover in the discussion of the keyboard.

Begin by creating the mouse input device.

1. **Create the mouse device.**

2. **Set the cooperation level.**

3. **Set the data format.**

4. **Acquire the mouse.**

Creating the mouse device

To create the mouse device, you must call `CreateDevice()` with the predefined GUID for the mouse, which is `GUID_SysMouse`. Here's how:

```
LPDIRECTINPUTDEVICE lpdimouse; // the mouse device

// create mouse device
if (lpdi->CreateDevice(GUID_SysMouse, &lpdimouse,NULL)!=DI_OK)
   { /* error */ }
```

Please cooperate with me!

Assuming that `CreateDevice()` was successful, the next step is to set the cooperation level of the device. Again, you want to be fair, so use the nonexclusive access with background processing, like this:

```
if (lpdimouse->SetCooperativeLevel(main_window_handle,
    DISCL_BACKGROUND | DISCL_NONEXCLUSIVE)!=DI_OK)
   { /* error */ }
```

Setting the data format

The next step is to set the data format. Similar to the keyboard process, you can use a predefined data format called `c_dfDIMouse` (as shown in Table 14-2). However, this predefined data type is in *relative mode,* which means that every time you request a mouse data record, the mouse position will be in delta (change from current position) format rather than absolute format. Figure 14-5 illustrates this arrangement. For example, you may get back something like: `dx=5, dy=-4`. This result means that the mouse moved 5 *mickeys* to the right and 4 *mickeys* upward.

What's a mickey?

A *mickey* is a virtual unit of movement that the mouse driver uses to represent the smallest amount of motion. Mickeys were invented to give Minnies something to do.

Just kidding! Seriously, mickeys are needed because some people have a large mouse pad, some have a small mouse pad, some have a big screen monitor, and some have a tiny 10-inch screen. Basically, no correlation exists between mouse motion on the mouse pad and the motion on the screen. Thus, mickeys were invented to artificially control the relationship.

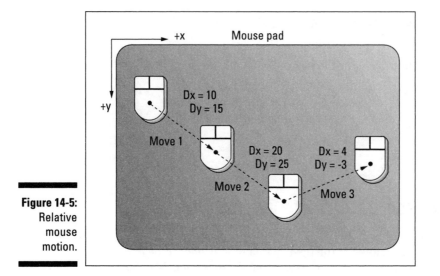

Figure 14-5:
Relative
mouse
motion.

DirectInput overrides the control panel settings for both the mouse and the keyboard, so don't be alarmed if you change a setting and it doesn't have any effect on your DirectInput application. On the other hand, the joystick settings and calibration *are* taken into consideration by DirectInput, so you can make changes there.

After you set the cooperation level, the next step is to set the data format. Fortunately, you can use a predefined data format. However, as I mention in the sidebar discussion "What's a mickey?" the data packets sent back will be relative deltas instead of absolute coordinates. This formatting may seem like a pain, but it's actually better. If you want absolute coordinates, you can surely keep a running (x,y) position of the mouse and simulate them, so it's really not a problem.

If you set the data format yourself, you can request an absolute position format, but it is relative to an arbitrary origin, so the position data isn't that useful.

To set the data format of the mouse, use the SetDataFormat() function as before, but with the predefined data format:

```
// set data format, notice the use of the address operator
if (lpdikey->SetDataFormat(&c_dfDIMouse)!=DI_OK)
   { /* error */ }
```

No problem! Moving on, the next step is to acquire the mouse.

Trapping the mouse

Acquiring the mouse means to attach it to the DirectInput main input handler and make its data available. This task is accomplished with a single call to Acquire() from the interface pointer of the mouse device IDIRECTINPUTDEVICE. Here's how:

```
// acquire the mouse
if (lpdimouse->Acquire()!=DI_OK)
    { /* error */ }
```

Isn't DirectInput cool? Well, that's about all there is to setting up the mouse. If you look back at all the code, you'll see only 10 to 20 lines (if that, but I'm too lazy to count).

Now you need to find out how to retrieve data from the mouse.

Making the mouse squeal!

Retrieving data from the mouse is accomplished with GetDeviceState(); however, the data record returned is, of course, different than that returned by the keyboard. Because I ask you to use the earlier discussion in "Keyboarding at the Speed of X" as a source for subjects not fully detailed in this discussion on using the mouse, I need to explain the data retrieved from the mouse.

The mouse sends back a DIMOUSESTATE structure that looks like this:

```
typedef struct {
    LONG lX; // x-axis of mouse
    LONG lY; // y-axis of mouse
    LONG lZ; // z-axis of mouse, typically a wheel or dial
    BYTE rgbButtons[4]; // buttons of the mouse
                        // high bit means pressed
} DIMOUSESTATE, *LPDIMOUSESTATE;
```

Now, that's a nice structure! The x, y, and wheel positions of the mouse are sent in lX, lY, lZ, and the buttons are sent as four bytes in rgbButtons[]. I still can't figure out why the buttons are in an array called rgbButtons[], but I have learned not to ask.

To retrieve the data state of the mouse, all you need is some storage for the data and to make a call to GetDeviceState(). Here's the code:

```
// this holds the mouse data
DIMOUSESTATE mouse_state;

// get mouse data
if (lpdimouse->GetDeviceState(sizeof(DIMOUSESTATE),
                (LPVOID)&mouse_state)!=DI_OK)
   { /* problem */ }
```

Then you can interrogate the data and see what's what. For example, to check whether the mouse buttons are down, do this:

```
// test left button
if (mouse_state.rgbButtons[0])
   { /* do whatever */ }
else // check right mouse button
if (mouse_state.rgbButtons[1])
   { /* do whatever */ }
```

Checking the position of the mouse can't really be done with your current data format. You can always write code to track an arbitrary (x,y) coordinate, but in many cases all you want to know is the mouse's (dx,dy) from its last position. Anyway, absolute coordinates are the native data format information returned.

For example, suppose that you want to know if the mouse was moved right, left, up, or down:

```
// is the mouse moving right
if (mouse_state.lX > 0 )
   { /* right */}
else // check for left motion
if (mouse_state.lX < 0)
   { /* left */ }

// is the mouse moving down
if (mouse_state.lY > 0 )
   { /* down */}
else // check for upward motion
if (mouse_state.lY < 0)
   { /* up */ }
```

That's all there is to reading the mouse.

When you have the mouse acquired, Windows will *not* receive any mouse messages, so keep that in mind. Finally, you must unacquire and release the mouse device when your application terminates, like this:

```
// unacquire first
lpdimouse->Unacquire();

// then release the object
lpdimouse->Release();
```

For an example of using the mouse, I include on the CD a very simple painting program named PROG14_2.CPP and, of course, the executable is PROG14_2.EXE. Figure 14-6 is a screen shot. The program is icon-based, so you shouldn't have any trouble figuring it out. Also, this demo uses the game engine, so if you want to recompile, make sure that you include GPDUMB1.CPP and the library files DDRAW.LIB and DINPUT.LIB.

Joysticks, Yokes, and Other Freudian Input Devices

A few years ago, a joystick was a joystick, and that's all there was to it. Today, a joystick has come to mean just about anything that's not a keyboard or mouse. Originally, only one kind of joystick existed for the PC, and it consisted of two perpendicular X-Y axes and two buttons (refer to Figure 14-2). The PC joystick was analog, meaning that as the yoke was moved, the position information returned was linear and had some finite range.

The problems with analog joysticks were their performance, calibration, and nonstandard construction. The basis of data acquisition for analog joysticks was a timing loop with a variable resistor or potentiometer used in a hardware timing loop. As the joystick yoke was moved around, it changed the values of two internal potentiometers that were, in turn, connected to timing circuits within the PC's joystick card.

To read a joystick position, a software program created a timing loop around the variable resistor in the joystick via I/O port control. Because the timing loop took more or less time to complete based on the resistance, this time variation could be used to convert the physical position of the joystick into a digital number and then could be passed to the CPU for processing.

That process is simplified at best, and 100 details can make joysticks send different readings — even joysticks made by the same manufacturers! This variation is due to different processor speeds, internal circuitry tolerances, and so on. So the moral of the story is that analog joysticks are not a very reliable input device and that's why you always have to calibrate them.

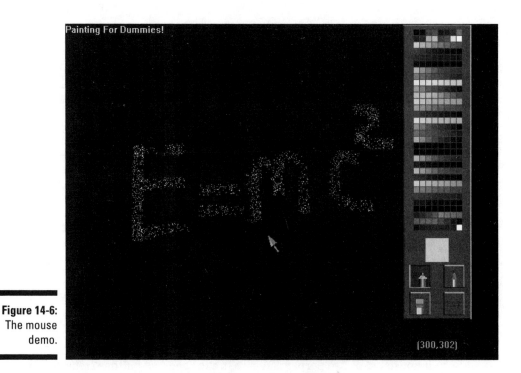

Figure 14-6:
The mouse
demo.

Joysticks under DirectInput

Today, analog joysticks still exist, but new digital joysticks have emerged, and these convert their analog motion into digital values. For example, the Microsoft Sidewinder is a purely digital joystick. The Sidewinder can still work with an older analog joystick card as an old-style analog stick, or its hardware can be taken advantage of with special software drivers. DirectInput takes care of handling digital and analog sticks for you. In addition, DirectInput understands any and all joystick-like devices, including joypads, flight sticks with multiple axes, or six-degrees-of-freedom space balls.

To facilitate this process, DirectInput came up with a generic virtual joystick that has the following data fields:

```
typedef struct DIJOYSTATE {
  LONG lX;   // x-axis of joystick
  LONG lY;   // y-axis of joystick
  LONG lZ;   // z-axis of joystick
  LONG lRx;  // x-rotation of joystick (context sensitive)
```

```
  LONG lRy;  // y-rotation of joystick (context sensitive)
  LONG lRz;  // y-rotation of joystick (context sensitive)
  LONG rglSlider[2];// slider-like controls (pedals, etc.)
  DWORD rgdwPOV[4]; // Point Of View hat controls (up to 4)
  BYTE  rgbButtons[32]; // 32 standard momentary buttons
} DIJOYSTATE, *LPDIJOYSTATE;
```

Now that's a joystick! As you can see, DIJOYSTATE has more than enough
fields to handle any kind of joystick-like device that may be plugged in. For
example, a steering wheel assembly may use the X-axis, one of the sliders,
and a couple of the buttons for the starter, lights, windshield wipers, and
so on.

But what if you have 12 degrees of freedom on your joystick device? No
problem; then you need two joystick devices to handle it — that's all. In
most cases, you only have to worry about the X-Y axis controls and a few
buttons.

Jacking into joysticks

Setting up a joystick is almost the same as in the keyboard and mouse
examples (check out "Keyboarding at the Speed of X" and "Setting a Trap for
the Mouse," earlier in this chapter), but you need to do a few more steps.
First, because so many different kinds of joysticks exist, a generic joystick
GUID isn't available as for the keyboard and mouse. You must query the
computer for the joystick(s) that are plugged in, get the GUIDs of these
devices, and use one of the IDs. Thus, you must write a device enumeration
function (bummer) to enumerate and scan all joystick-like devices plugged
into the system.

Assuming that you have successfully found the right GUID for the
Megablaster 3D joystick or whatever device is plugged into your computer,
then you have to do something ugly — query for a new interface. The
joystick interface that you need is IDIRECTINPUTDEVICE2 not
IDIRECTINPUTDEVICE. You need this new interface because it supports
some necessary functions — for example Poll(), which is necessary to
retrieve joystick device data (I get to this topic in "Pulling on the stick,"
later in this chapter). The bottom line: You must make some low-level
COM calls to query for the IDIRECTINPUTDEVICE2 interface from the
IDIRECTINPUTDEVICE interface. After you have the new interface, everything is smooth sailing. But don't worry; I take you through every step of
the way.

After all the dramatics of querying for the new interface, the remaining steps of setting up a joystick are the same as the mouse and keyboard — as is the actual retrieving of data, but with the single addition of a call to Poll().

To set you straight if you're a little bent on using joysticks, here's the game plan:

1. **Scan for all joysticks plugged into the system with** EnumDevices() **and record the GUIDs.**

2. **With a GUID from Step 1, create the joystick device with** CreateDevice().

3. **With the** IDIRECTDRAWDEVICE **interface created in Step 2, query for a** IDIRECTDRAWDEVICE2 **interface and release the original** IDIRECTDRAWDEVICE **interface.**

4. **Now set the cooperation level with** SetCoopertiveLevel().

5. **Set the data format with** SetDataFormat() **and properties with** SetProperty().

6. **Acquire the joystick with** Acquire().

7. **Read the data from the joystick in your main loop with the calling pair:** Poll() **and** GetDeviceState().

Spying for joysticks

I was hoping that I would never have to show you how to enumerate for anything. The technique DirectX uses is a little overkill in my opinion, but DirectX is modeled after older Microsoft software, and a lot of systems in Windows use "call back" functions, of which enumeration is one.

To request DirectInput to scan for any kind of input device and enumerate it, you must use the following EnumDevices() function (note that *func* stands for *function*):

```
HRESULT EnumDevices(
 DWORD dwDevType, // type of device to scan for
 LPDIENUMCALLBACK lpCallback, // pointer to callback function
 LPVOID pvRef, // 32-bit value passed back
 DWORD dwFlags); // type of search to do
```

You can begin by seeing what all the parameters do. First, dwDevType indicates what kind of devices you want to scan for. The possibilities are shown in Table 14-4:

Table 14-4	The Basic Device Types for DirectInput
Value	**Meaning**
DIDEVTYPE_MOUSE	A mouse or mouse-like device (such as a trackball)
DIDEVTYPE_KEYBOARD	A keyboard or keyboard-like device
DIDEVTYPE_JOYSTICK	A joystick or similar device, such as a steering wheel
DIDEVTYPE_DEVICE	A device that doesn't fall into one of the previous categories

If you want EnumDevices() to be more specific, then you can also give it a subtype that you connect via a logical OR with the preceding main type. Table 14-5 contains a short list of subtypes for mouse and joystick. Two or three dozen more types are available that I haven't listed.

Table 14-5	DirectInput Subtypes (Partial Listing)
Value	**Meaning**
DIDEVTYPEMOUSE_TOUCHPAD	Standard touchpad
DIDEVTYPEMOUSE_TRACKBALL	Standard trackball
DIDEVTYPEJOYSTICK_FLIGHTSTICK	General flightstick
DIDEVTYPEJOYSTICK_GAMEPAD	Nintendo-like gamepad
DIDEVTYPEJOYSTICK_RUDDER	Simple rudder control
DIDEVTYPEJOYSTICK_WHEEL	Steering wheel
DIDEVTYPEJOYSTICK_HEADTRACKER	Virtual reality head tracker

Be aware that DirectInput can be as general or specific in the search as you want it to be. However, in the example put forth in this section, you're just going to use good old DIDEVTYPE_JOYSTICK as the value for dwDevType.

The next parameter in EnumDevices() is a pointer to the callback function that DirectInput is going to call for each device it finds. Yes, this approach seems a bit odd. Instead of simply returning with a list of devices, the designers of DirectInput thought it would be better to have a function (that you supply) called each time it finds a device — I guess so that you can initialize each device as it's found or some dumb reason like that. Whatever the reasoning, you must supply your own callback function.

The next parameter `pvRef` is a 32-bit pointer that points to a value that will be passed to the callback function. Thus, you can modify the value in the callback if you want to or use it to pass data back explicitly instead of globally. Gee thanks, Microsoft!

Finally, `dwFlags` controls the way the enumeration function should scan. That is, should the function scan for all devices, only for devices that are plugged in, or just for force feedback devices? Here are the constants for enumeration:

- ✔ `DIEDFL_ALLDEVICES`: Scans for all devices that have been installed, even if they aren't currently connected
- ✔ `DIEDFL_ATTACHEDONLY`: Scans for devices that are installed *and* connected
- ✔ `DIEDFL_FORCEFEEDBACK`: Scans only for force feedback devices

Use the `DIEDFL_ATTACHEDONLY` value because it doesn't make sense to allow the player to use a device that he or she doesn't have plugged into the computer. (Of course, if you were writing a system analysis suite, then you *would* be interested in all devices even if they weren't plugged in.)

Callback function

Now I want to take a more complete look at the callback function. The way `EnumDevices()` works is that it sits in a loop, calling your callback over and over for each device it finds. Hence, it's possible that your callback could be called 10 to 20 times if a lot of devices are installed or attached to the PC. Thus, it's up to you and the callback function that you supply to record all these devices in a table or similar data structure, so you can later review them after the `EnumDevices()` returns.

Here's the generic prototype for the callback function to be compatible with DirectInput:

```
BOOL CALLBACK EnumDevsCallback(
  LPDIDEVICEINSTANCE lpddi, // a pointer from DirectInput
                            // containing info about the device it
                            // just found on this iteration
  LPVOID data);   // the pointer sent in
                  // pvRef to EnumDevices()
```

You just write a function with the preceding prototype (and fill in the stuff in the middle) and pass it as `lpCallback` to `EnumDevices()`, and you're all set. And, of course, the name can be anything you want. What you put inside the function is up to you, but you may want to record or catalog the names of all the devices and their GUIDs as they come in. Then with the list in hand, your program can select one or can let the user select one from a list.

Also, DirectInput allows you to continue the enumeration or stop it at your command. This process is controlled via the value you return from the callback function. At the end of the function, you can return one of two constants:

- ✔ DIENUM_CONTINUE: Continues enumeration
- ✔ DIENUM_STOP: Stops enumeration

If you simply return DIENUM_STOP as the return value of the function, then EnumDevsCallback() only enumerates one device even if more exist.

I don't have enough room in the chapter to show you a function that catalogs and records all the device GUIDs, so I'm going to give you the bargain version! This version simply enumerates the first device and stops.

Before I show that function to you, take a look at the DIDEVICEINSTANCE data structure that is sent to your callback function with each enumeration; it is chock-full of information:

```
typedef struct {
    DWORD dwSize;        // the size of the structure
    GUID guidInstance;   // instance GUID of the device
                         // this is the GUID we need
    GUID guidProduct;    // product GUID of device, general
    DWORD dwDevType;     // dev type as listed in Tables 14-4,5
    TCHAR tszInstanceName[MAX_PATH]; // generic instance name
                         // of joystick device, like "joystick 1"
    TCHAR tszProductName[MAX_PATH]; // product name of device
                         // like "Microsoft Sidewinder Pro"
    GUID guidFFDriver;   // GUID for force feedback driver
    WORD wUsagePage;     // advanced; don't worry about it
    WORD wUsage;         // advanced; don't worry about it
} DIDEVICEINSTANCE, *LPDIDEVICEINSTANCE;
```

In most cases, the only fields of interest are tszProductName and guidInstance.

With all that simmering in your noodle, here's an enumeration function that you can use to get the GUID of the first joystick device enumerated:

```
BOOL CALLBACK DI_Enum_Joysticks(
LPCDIDEVICEINSTANCE lpddi, LPVOID guid_ptr)
{
// this function enumerates the joysticks, but stops at the
// first one and returns the instance GUID
// so that we can create it
*(GUID*)guid_ptr = lpddi->guidInstance;

// copy product name into global variable
strcpy(joyname, (char *)lpddi->tszProductName);

// stop enumeration after one iteration
return(DIENUM_STOP);
} // end DI_Enum_Joysticks
```

To use the function to enumerate for the first joystick, do this:

```
char joyname[80]; // space for joystick name
GUID joystickGUID; // used to hold GUID for joystick

// enumerate attached joystick devices only with
// DI_Enum_Joysticks() as the callback function
if (lpdi->EnumDevices(
            DIDEVTYPE_JOYSTICK, // joysticks only
            DI_Enum_Joysticks, // enumeration function
            &joystickGUID, // send GUID back in this var
            DIEDFL_ATTACHEDONLY)!=DI_OK)
    { /* error */ }
```

Note that the EnumDevices() is called from the main DirectInput object.

At this point, joystickGUID should have the GUID of the joystick device and joyname should have the text string describing it.

Creating the device

After you get the callback function and enumeration squared away, you're ready to create the device, like this:

```
LPDIRECTINPUTDEVICE lpdijoy; // joystick device interface
// create the joystick with GUID
if (lpdi->CreateDevice(joystickGUID, &lpdijoy, NULL)!=DI_OK)
    { /* error */ }
```

Querying for IDIRECTINPUTDEVICE2

This query is the hard part in preparing your program for joystick use. The problem is that you have created an old DirectX 3.0 IDIRECTINPUTDEVICE interface, but you need the new IDIRECTINPUTDEVICE2 interface. Refer to the stuff on COM interfaces back in Chapter 7. To retrieve a different interface from any interface, use the Query_Interface() function with the GUID of the interface.

That's exactly what I do in this section. Here's how to request the new interface:

```
// version 2 interface pointer
LPDIRECTINPUTDEVICE2 lpdijoy2;

// query for the new interface from the old one
lpdijoy->QueryInterface(IID_IDirectInputDevice2,(void **) &lpdijoy2);
```

The syntax may seem a little confusing, but basically the first parameter is the IID (Interface ID) to the new interface, and the second is a spot to stuff it in — that's what the (void **) is for.

After the call, lpdijoy needs to be released because you don't need it anymore now that you have the much improved second version:

```
lpdijoy->Release();
```

Finally, you have the interface pointer; you can set the cooperation level and data format, and then acquire the joystick. Here's the cooperation level setting:

```
if (lpdijoy2->SetCooperativeLevel(hwnd,
        DISCL_NONEXCLUSIVE | DISCL_BACKGROUND)!=DI_OK)
{ /* error */ }
```

Next, set the data format. As usual, use a predefined format setting c_dfDIJoystick:

```
if (lpdijoy2->SetDataFormat(&c_dfDIJoystick)!=DI_OK)
    { /* error */ }
```

The next step would normally be to acquire the joystick, but you need to deal with a teeny-weeny problem first: the properties of the joystick.

Setting the properties right

Because the joystick is inherently an analog device, the motion of the yoke has some finite range. Because of this limitation, you must set the joystick to known values, so you can interpret it. In other words, when you query the joystick for its position and it returns 1X = 2000, 1Y=-3445, what does it mean? You can't interpret the data because you have no frame of reference.

You need to set the ranges of any analog axis that you wish to read. For example, you may decide to set both the X and Y axes to (–1,000 to 1,000) and (–2,000 to 2,000), respectively, or maybe (–128 to 128) for both, so you can fit them in a BYTE. Whatever you decide to do, *you* must implement it in the code; you won't have any way of interpreting the data when you retrieve it unless you set the range yourself.

Setting the ranges of the joystick is done with the SetProperty() function:

```
HRESULT SetProperty(
  REFGUID rguidProp,        // GUID of property to change
  LPCDIPROPHEADER pdiph);  // pointer to property header struct
  // containing detailed information relating to the change
```

SetProperty() sets a number of various properties such as relative or absolute data format, range of each axis, dead band (area that is neutral), and so on. Using the SetProperty() function is extremely complex due to the nature of all the constants and nested data structures. Suffice it to say, don't call SetProperty() unless you have to!

Because you only need to set the range of the X-Y axes to make things work, that's all I'm going to show you. If you are interested in finding out more, refer to the DirectX SDK on this subject. Nonetheless, the following code should shed light on how to set various other properties:

```
// this structure holds the data for the property changes
DIPROPRANGE joy_axis_range;

// first set x axis to -1024 to 1024
joy_axis_range.lMin = -1024;
joy_axis_range.lMax = 1024;

joy_axis_range.diph.dwSize      = sizeof(DIPROPRANGE);
joy_axis_range.diph.dwHeaderSize = sizeof(DIPROPHEADER);

// this holds the object you want to change
joy_axis_range.diph.dwObj  = DIJOFS_X;
```

```
// X can be any of the following:
//DIJOFS_BUTTON(n) - for buttons buttons
//DIJOFS_POV(n)  - for point-of-view indicators
//DIJOFS_RX - for x-axis rotation
//DIJOFS_RY - for y-axis rotation
//DIJOFS_RZ - for z-axis rotation (rudder)
//DIJOFS_X - for x-axis
//DIJOFS_Y - for y-axis
//DIJOFS_Z - for the z-axis
//DIJOFS_SLIDER(n) - for any of the sliders

// object access method; use this way always
joy_axis_range.diph.dwHow = DIPH_BYOFFSET;

// finally, set the property
lpdijoy2->SetProperty(DIPROP_RANGE,&joy_axis_range.diph);

// now y-axis
joy_axis_range.lMin = -1024;
joy_axis_range.lMax = 1024;
joy_axis_range.diph.dwSize       = sizeof(DIPROPRANGE);
joy_axis_range.diph.dwHeaderSize = sizeof(DIPROPHEADER);
joy_axis_range.diph.dwObj        = DIJOFS_Y;
joy_axis_range.diph.dwHow        = DIPH_BYOFFSET;
lpdijoy2->SetProperty(DIPROP_RANGE,&joy_axis_range.diph);
```

At this point, the joystick has both the X-Y axes set to a range of (–1,024 to 1,024). This range is arbitrary, but I like it.

The 1,834th rule of joystick acquisition

You can acquire the joystick now that its range has been set (technically, you could have set the range after acquisition). To acquire the joystick, use `Acquire()` from the device interface as usual:

```
if (lpdijoy2->Acquire()!=DI_OK)
   { /* error */ }
```

Then you're ready to get input from the joystick, which is a two-step process detailed in the next section.

Pulling on the stick

Reading a joystick device is done with a call to `GetDeviceState()` — the same as with the mouse and keyboard. But before you make the call, you must make a call to `Poll()` from the joystick's device interface, like this:

```
lpdijoy2->Poll();
```

All this step does is latch the data into the hardware and get the data ready for reading. If the data is already ready, then this function call is free, so don't worry about using it.

After polling the joystick, you can request a data record with `GetDeviceState()`. The record returned will be of the format `DIJOYSTATE`, which you can see in "Joysticks under DirectInput," earlier in this chapter. So to read the joystick, all you need to do is poll it and read the data like this:

```
DIJOYSTATE joy_state; // used to hold the data

lpdijoy2->Poll(); // this is needed for joysticks only
// read the data
lpdijoy2->GetDeviceState(sizeof(DIJOYSTATE), (LPVOID)&joy_state);
```

Then you can access the data fields and do whatever you want with them. But remember that all the axes are in relative mode, so you will get back positive and negative deltas. On the other hand, the buttons are simple ON/OFF switches and can be treated as booleans. For example, if you want to check whether the X-axis is in a position greater that 500 and whether button 0 is pressed, use the following code:

```
if (joy_state.lX > 500 && joy_state.rgbButtons[0])
    { /* fire photon torpedo! */ }
```

That's the basics of the joystick interface. I agree that it's a bit complicated, but if you really want to lose sleep, read up on force feedback!

Lastly, after you're done with the joystick, put it away by unacquiring it and releasing it like this:

```
lpdijoy2->Unacquire();
lpdijoy2->Release();
```

As a final example, I have created a little insect simulation that uses the joystick to control the bug blaster. It's called `PROG14_3.CPP`. Check it out. Make sure that you have a joystick plugged in before you try it. Also, notice that the name of your joystick prints out on the demo at the bottom left. If you want to compile the program yourself, you need `GPDUMB1.CPP` and the library files `DDRAW.LIB` and `DINPUT.LIB`.

Chapter 15

Press OK to Install: Using DirectSetup and Autoplay

In This Chapter

▶ Conquering the installation blues

▶ Using DirectSetup

▶ Understanding Autoplay

*Y*ou're finally finished with the most incredible game of all time and the only thing you have to do is write an installation program. Sounds easy enough? Not! Installation programs are one of the most time-consuming and tedious pieces of software that can be written. They aren't that complex or technical, but they absolutely *must* work very smoothly and be completely dummy-proof. Hence, the goal of this chapter is to show you how to use the built-in DirectSetup system to install DirectX and to give you some ideas on how to go about creating an installation program.

The Installation Blues

Figure 15-1 is a screen shot of a typical game installation program. Notice how nice and professional it looks. The basic role of a game installer is to load the game from the user's CD or floppy disk drive onto the main hard drive. This process can be complex due to the widely varying hardware platforms that users may have. In the past, writing installation programs was always one of those tasks that developers put off as long as possible.

Writing an installer is really a systems programming kind of task. In a nutshell, the installer must perform the following functions:

✔ Determine the system capabilities (optional).

✔ Allow the user to load the game onto the hard drive in whatever folder the user desires.

✔ Configure the game options and sound.

✔ Calibrate the input devices.

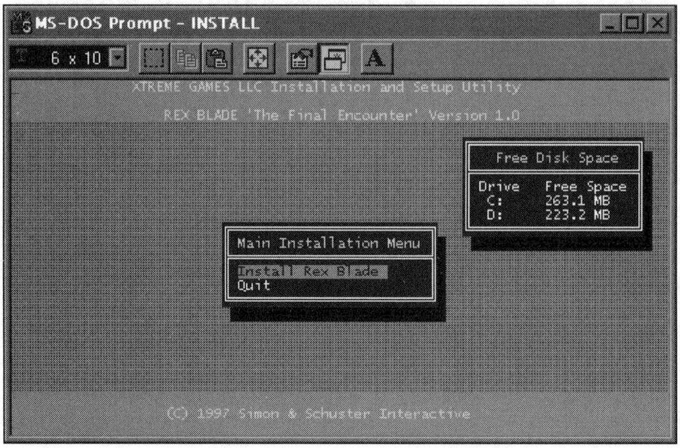

Figure 15-1:
A pro-
fessional
setup
program.

Although the task may seem trivial, it's not. The method for determining all the system capabilities is not at all intuitive, and creating a file navigation dialog box that's clean and functional is a pain. Finally, writing configuration dialog boxes and GUIs is a bummer, too.

The bottom line: Writing your own installation program takes a lot of work, and these days it's better to use an installation generator to create the framework for your installer. You can supply it with artwork, sounds, and small applets that are executed as the installation runs. By using the generator, you don't have to write all the mundane functions that navigate disk drives, draw dialogs, and so on.

A number of commercial programs allow you to write an "installation script" of sorts via pointing and clicking. The two main programs are

✔ **Wise Installer:** You can find information at the www.glbs.com Web site.

✔ **InstallShield:** Look for information at the www.installshield.com Web site.

Both programs are excellent, and just about every Windows program and/or game uses one of them. I can only briefly cover them here. The programs enable you to create a script of commands with a scripting language. This scripting language includes commands that enable you to load the game software anywhere on the hard drive, draw bitmap backgrounds, play music, launch other applications, ask questions of the user, and so forth.

After you're done writing the installation script, the installation generator uses all your files and the script you wrote to generate one or more compressed files and a single executable, usually named SETUP.EXE (as shown in Figure 15-2). You copy the file(s) on the CD or floppy disk and ship or upload to your Web site, depending on how you want to release your product. Whatever the release media is, a file or two contains the entire game including the installation engine (very small) that runs and lets the user load the game.

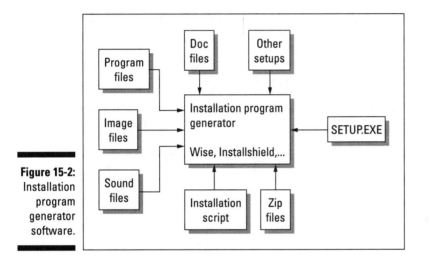

Figure 15-2:
Installation
program
generator
software.

You can use an installation program to generate the installer, or you can write one yourself. Or if you really want to be crude, you can simply archive (using an archiving program such as WinZip) the entire directory structure and just let the user unarchive the files onto their hard drives. This approach is fine for Internet launching. However, even after the files are decompressed and loaded onto the user's hard drive, a number of configuration and or other installations may need to be performed for sound, graphics, and DirectX.

But whatever you do, you must install DirectX (if you're doing a DirectX game) on the user's computer, and this task is nearly impossible unless you use DirectSetup.

As a quick checklist, here are the steps to getting your game ready for release:

1. **Write and test the game!**

2. **Write an installation program (or use a commercial installer).**

3. **Create all the README and legal files.**

4. **Put all the files together (including any 3rd-party files, such as DirectX) into a single compressed file for Internet distribution or in the most appopriate format for hard-media distribution.**

DirectSetup Basics

The complete DirectX run-time files are over 135MB as of version 5.0, and I imagine that they will grow. Of course, only a subset is installed on any one machine, but that's still a lot of hard-drive space! Ever since the release of DirectX Version 3.0, the program has included a very clean setup API. That API — `DirectXSetup()` — is available to install all of DirectX for you. All you do is call the API function, and DirectX is properly installed. Of course, a number of other support API functions also detect currently installed versions of DirectX as well as alter the default behavior of `DirectXSetup()`.

DirectSetup can't use any DirectX COM objects because they may not be installed on the user's machine. Thus, the DirectSetup installer directory must contain a number of special .DLLs to operate properly. To write a DirectSetup application, you need a minimal Windows application (actually you don't even need a window; you can just launch the setup calls from `WinMain()` without creating a window), and you must include `DSETUP.H` and `DSETUP.LIB`.

In addition to the `DSETUP.H` and `DSETUP.LIB` files, you need the actual DirectX files themselves on your distribution CD. (I say "your distribution *CD*" instead of *disk* because DirectX alone is more than 135MB.) Luckily, you don't have to round these files up; Microsoft has done it for you.

On the DirectX SDK disc (or directory), a folder called `REDIST\` usually exists in the root or within the `SDK\` folder. In either case, this folder contains all the files you need and the proper directory structure that DirectSetup expects. Here's a list of what you can find in the `REDIST\` folder: `DSETUP.DLL`; `DSETUP16.DLL`; `DSETUP32.DLL`; and the folder `DIRECTX\`.

You need to copy the `REDIST\` folder to your game's CD if you want to include DirectX. Then when your DirectX installation program calls `DirectXSetup()`, you tell it the exact path on the CD where it can find the `REDIST\` folder, and everything will work out and load correctly.

In addition, you must make sure that the preceding list of .DLL files is in the folder with your DirectSetup application. They are needed to run `DirectXSetup()` as well as link to `DSETUP.LIB`. The `DIRECTX\` folder can be anywhere, but you need a copy of the `DSETUP*.DLL` files in your setup's working directory. Take a look at Figure 15-3, which illustrates the relationship between all the files and the DirectX setup program.

Now that you have a general idea of what is going on, you can move to the master setup function `DirectXSetup()`.

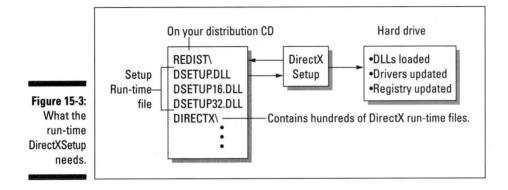

Figure 15-3:
What the
run-time
DirectXSetup
needs.

Making the call

The entire DirectX system can be installed with a single call to `DirectXSetup()`. Its prototype is shown here:

```
int WINAPI DirectXSetup(HWND hWnd, // parent's window
LPSTR lpszRootPath,            // path to REDIST files
    DWORD dwFlags);            // control flags
```

The function has a number of return values that indicate what happened during the installation. The list of return values is too long to include here, but you can take a look at it in the DirectX SDK Help file. However, in most cases, you only need to check for `DSETUPERR_SUCCESS`. Otherwise, the installation failed.

To review the parameters: `hWnd` is needed because `DirectXSetup()` generates dialog boxes and messages, and it needs a window handle to anchor to. `lpszRootPath` is the full path to the location that contains the contents of the DirectX run-time files `REDIST\`. For example, suppose that your game CD had `REDIST\` on the root; then `lpszRootPath` would be equal to

```
"CDROM:\\REDIST"
```

When you declare path names that use the "\" character, you must use a double slash or "\\", otherwise, the next character will be interpreted as an escape character. Also, you can use a single forward slash "/" to delineate path names. That's a secret!

As another example, suppose that you copied everything from REDIST\ into your game's main folder, called RAPTORX\; then RAPTORX\ would contain all your files plus

```
RAPTORX\
    DIRECTX\
    DSETUP.DLL
    DSETUP16.DLL
    DSETUP32.DLL
    (Your files)
```

In this case, the full path is: "CDROM:\\RAPTORX".

Notice that, in this case, I didn't need to use REDIST\ because I copied the contents of it into my games root directory, and lpszRootPath pointed to the place with the three necessary .DLLs and the DIRECTX\ folder. That's it.

Now move on to the dwFlags flags parameter. In most cases, you'll probably install all of DirectX by using the DSETUP_DIRECTX flag, but Table 15-1 contains all the valid values for this parameter.

Table 15-1	Valid DirectXSetup() Flags
Value	*Meaning*
DSETUP_DIRECTX	Installs DirectX run-time components as well as DirectX-compatible display and audio drivers.
DSETUP_DDRAWDRV	Installs display drivers provided by Microsoft.
DSETUP_DSOUNDDRV	Installs audio drivers provided by Microsoft.
DSETUP_DXCORE	Installs DirectX run-time components. Does not install DirectX-compatible display and audio drivers.
DSETUP_TESTINSTALL	Performs a test installation. Does not actually install new components.

Here's a complete example of loading DirectX:

```
if (DirectXSetup(main_window_handle,
                "CDROM:\\REDIST",
                DSETUP_DIRECTX)!=DSERR_SUCCESS)
    { /* error */}
```

For an example of using the DirectXSetup() function, take a look at PROG15_1.CPP and the executable PROG15_1.EXE on the CD. However, you must execute the program from the CD, because the path name is relative to the CD's location of the REDIST\ folder. If you want to recompile the program, remember to include DSETUP.LIB.

Make sure that you understand the difference between the SDK installer you run to install the DirectX SDK and this installer that just installs the run-time files. The SDK installs all the files needed to *write* DirectX games, whereas, the run-time installer installs only the files needed to *run* DirectX games.

Listening to DirectSetup talk back

Although the DirectX setup program runs fairly snag free, you may want a little more control. DirectSetup enables your control by specifying a *callback* function for `DirectXSetup()`. As DirectX is installed, a number of messages and events occur that you don't see. But if you have a callback function set up, your callback will be called and you can make better decisions or let the user make better decisions.

All the workings of the callback function are a bit advanced, so I just want to show you how to set one up and emulate what happens in the default case (without the callback). Later, you can add more code and break out the cases that you are more interested in using to query the user for more detail.

The function used to set the callback function is called `DirectXSetupSetCallback()` and takes a single parameter — the callback function. Here's the prototype:

```
INT WINAPI DirectXSetupSetCallback(
  DSETUP_CALLBACK Callback);  // pointer to
                              // callback function
```

And here's the generic callback function with the proper prototype:

```
DWORD DirectXSetupCallbackFunction(
  DWORD Reason,      // reason for the callback
  DWORD MsgType,     // same as MessageBox parameter
  char *szMessage,   // message string
  char *szName       // depends on Reason
  void *pInfo);      // upgrade information
```

Most of the fields are decipherable, but basically the return value you must return in your callback should emulate the action of a standard `MessageBox()` call, that is, return the Windows constant `IDOK` when things are okay, and so on. Here's a fully functional callback function:

```
DWORD WINAPI DSetupCallback(DWORD Reason,
                            DWORD MsgType,
                            char *szMessage,
                            char *szName,
                            void *pUpgradeInfo)
{
// this is the most generic callback function you can have;
// it simply returns IDOK for status calls, otherwise
// it pops up a messagebox and allows you to make the
// decision
if (MsgType==0)
    return(IDOK);

// call the messagebox function and return its value;
// remember, DirectSetup is designed to respond to the
// return values of MessageBox
return(MessageBox(main_window_handle, szMessage,
    "DirectX Setup Demo -- Running", MsgType));
} // end DSetupCallback
```

To install the callback, do this:

```
DirectXSetupSetCallback(DSetupCallback);
```

That's all there is to it. When you make the call to `DirectXSetup()`, `DSetupCallback()` is called whenever any messages or problems occur during the installation of DirectX.

For an example of using the callback function feature, take a look at `PROG15_2.CPP` and the executable `PROG15_2.EXE`. The program is basically a version of `PROG15_1.CPP` with the callback function pointer set. To compile and run it, you need to perform the same steps as with `PROG15_1.CPP`.

Getting info directly

The final part of DirectSetup I want to explain is the version acquisition function, `DirectXSetupGetVersion()`. It gets the version number and revision number of DirectX, each encoded as a 32-bit number. Here's its prototype:

```
INT WINAPI DirectXSetupGetVersion(
  DWORD *pdwVersion   // gets the version in 16.16 format
  DWORD *pdwRevision); // gets the revision in 16.16 format
```

Here's an example of printing out the version and revision number of DirectX:

```
DWORD version;    // used to hold version information
DWORD revision;   // used to hold revision information
char buffer[256]; // used to hold messages

// test whether DirectX is installed; if so, then print
// version and revision; otherwise print error message
if (DirectXSetupGetVersion(&version, &revision))
   {
   // build up message
   sprintf(buffer,"DirectX version is %d.%d.%d.%d\n",
               HIWORD(version), LOWORD(version),
               HIWORD(revision), LOWORD(revision));

   // display a message box with the info
   MessageBox(NULL,buffer,
               "DirectX Setup Version Demo",MB_OK);
   } // end if
else
   MessageBox(NULL,"Previous Versions of DirectX not Installed!",
               "DirectX Setup Version Demo",MB_OK);
```

To see the code in action, check out PROG15_3.CPP and the executable PROG15_3.EXE. It runs in any working directory and checks for the version and revision of DirectX. If you want to recompile it, you need to include DSETUP.LIB in your project, of course.

AutoPlay

AutoPlay a fairly old feature of Windows 95 (rather than DirectX) that enables you to create a CD-ROM that automatically starts up when it is placed in the CD-ROM drive like a console game machine such as a Playstation. AutoPlay functions by reading a special file — AUTORUN.INF — from the root directory of the CD. If the file exists, it is loaded and interpreted as an AutoPlay file.

An AUTORUN.INF file can contain a number of commands, but you need to know only two of them: open and icon. open is used to start up an executable, usually with your setup or installer, and icon is used to set the icon that represents the CD-ROM. Here are the steps to create an AutoPlay CD-ROM:

1. **Create a file called** AUTORUN.INF.

2. **Place these lines in the** AUTORUN.INF **file in order:**

```
[autorun]
open=yoursetup.exe
icon=youricon.ico
```

3. **Copy the** AUTORUN.INF **file to the root directory of your master CD-ROM.**

Then burn about 500,000 copies of your game and ship them out! (You are going to sell 500,000 copies, aren't you? Think big!)

CD-ROM writers used to cost over $1,000 for the bottom-of-line model, but today you can pick one up for less than $300, so burning your own CD-ROMs isn't that much of a stretch. Furthermore, if you do make a great game and a publisher publishes it for you, then you will probably want to make the CD an AutoPlay, so this AutoPlay stuff is good to know.

Chapter 16

GPDUMB Part II — The Final Conflict

*T*he last couple of chapters have been like a vacation, so the next couple are going to make up for it! However, before I dive into neural networks and frictional coefficients, I want to introduce the finishing touches on the GPDUMB game engine that was developed in Chapter 12, so you can use it to create more demos with cool graphics and sound. I add support for DirectInput, DirectSound, and take the BOB engine to the next level. With all these new features, you'll definitely be able to create your own games!

What's New in GPDUMB2?

Version II of the GPDUMB game engine — or more formally *GPDUMB2* — adds to the game engine full support for DirectSound (see Chapter 13) and DirectInput (see Chapter 14) in a very simple and concise API. Of course, whenever you simplify something and create a wrapper API, you lose a little control, but the functions I provide will get you up and running with these systems in a few lines of code, so the lack of control is worth it. Obviously, you don't have to use these new APIs, but I missed a lot of *Star Trek* to make them for you, so at least give them a try!

In addition to the sound and input stuff, I threw in a few extra functions for good measure, including some highly optimized line-drawing functions for horizontal and vertical lines, and a screen-transition system. I offer a couple more collision functions, and I provide a little more functionality to the BOB system (see Chapter 11) to handle multiple objects with the same visual bitmaps without wasting memory. All in all, the new stuff really rounds out the engine, and writing a game should be a snap. Take a look at Figure 16-1 to see how everything relates.

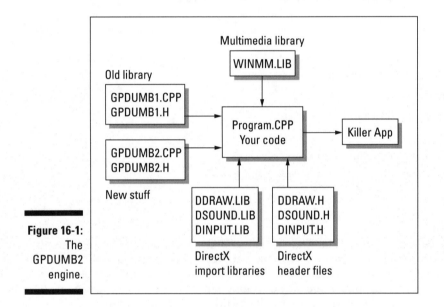

Figure 16-1:
The
GPDUMB2
engine.

You can begin with the following new files:

✔ GPDUMB2.H: The header file for the C/C++ module

✔ GPDUMB2.CPP: The main C/C++ file containing all the new library code

That's all the new files. Of course, the added features are built on top of the old library files GPDUMB1.CPP/H, so you must include them in your applications. (See Chapter 15 for an explanation of why this is so.) And you need to include all the primary DirectX libraries in your application: DirectDraw, DirectSound, and DirectInput. Therefore, you must include these headers in your source:

✔ DDRAW.H

✔ DSOUND.H

✔ DINPUT.H

And include these library files in your project to make everything compile better:

- DDRAW.LIB
- DSOUND.LIB
- DINPUT.LIB
- WINMM.LIB — the multimedia stuff

I include a template application as before called GPTEMP2.CPP that handles all the source includes for you, so use it as a starting point for your applications that use the GPDUMB libraries. The following section shows the main elements of the GPDUMB2.H header file.

The header

The header file GPDUMB2.H is a lot shorter than its older brother GPDUMB.H, and mostly the new file is made of function prototypes. However, a few new constants have been added to GPDUMB2.H (mostly for the screen-transition system) and a data structure for the sound system. Here's the header for your review (I have highlighted constants that you may want to muck with).

The following constants have to do with the new sound system in the revised game engine; they are fairly well explained by the comments:

```
#define MAX_SOUNDS      64 // max sounds in system at once
#define SOUND_NULL       0 // sound not loaded
#define SOUND_LOADED     1 // sound has been loaded
#define SOUND_PLAYING    2 // sound is currently playing
#define SOUND_STOPPED    3 // sound has been stopped
#define NVB_SIZE         6 // size of new voice block in bytes
```

The new engine has a screen-transition function, so you can do fades, swipes, dissolves, and so on. The following constants control that function:

```
#define SCREEN_DARKNESS   0  // fade to black
#define SCREEN_WHITENESS  1  // fade to white
#define SCREEN_SWIPE_X    2  // do a horizontal swipe
#define SCREEN_SWIPE_Y    3  // do a vertical swipe
#define SCREEN_DISSOLVE   4  // a pixel disolve
#define SCREEN_SCRUNCH    5  // a square compression
#define SCREEN_BLUENESS   6  // fade to blue
#define SCREEN_REDNESS    7  // fade to red
#define SCREEN_GREENNESS  8  // fade to green
```

A single BOB function *clones* a BOB, which is a duplication method that I cover later in this chapter in "The Six Million Dollar BOB." I decided to encode a clone in the attributes, so here's that:

```
#define BOB_ATTR_CLONE   256 // the bob is a clone
```

The new engine doesn't contain much in the way of new macros. I added a single function to help convert from 0–100 to the Microsoft decibels scale, which is what DirectSound uses. This way, you don't have to think in logarithms:

```
#define DSVOLUME_TO_DB(volume) ((DWORD)(-30*(100 - volume)))
```

And, finally, I offer a sound object record. This sound record is very similar to the one developed in Chapter 13.

```
typedef struct pcm_sound_typ
    {
    LPDIRECTSOUNDBUFFER dsbuffer;  // the DirectSound buffer
                                   // containing the sound
    int state;   // state of the sound
    int rate;    // playback rate
    int size;    // size of sound
    int id;      // id number of the sound
    } pcm_sound, *pcm_sound_ptr;
```

I told you that there wasn't much in the way of defines, data structures, or macros. Now take a look at the global variables.

Global awareness

The GPDUMB2 engine uses a number of global variables (or *globals,* as they are commonly referred to). However, most of them are related to the DirectSound and DirectInput systems.

Here are the globals for the sound system:

```
LPDIRECTSOUND   lpds;     // DirectSound interface pointer
DSBUFFERDESC    dsbd;     // DirectSound description
DSCAPS      dscaps;       // DirectSound caps
HRESULT     dsresult      // general DirectSound result
DSBCAPS     dsbcaps;      // DirectSound buffer caps

pcm_sound   sound_fx[MAX_SOUNDS]; // array of sound buffers
WAVEFORMATEX    pcmwf;    // generic waveformat structure
```

And here are the DirectInput globals. Notice the extra joystick variables:

```
LPDIRECTINPUT          lpdi;        // dinput object
LPDIRECTINPUTDEVICE  lpdikey;     // dinput keyboard
LPDIRECTINPUTDEVICE  lpdimouse;   // dinput mouse
LPDIRECTINPUTDEVICE  lpdijoy;     // dinput joystick
LPDIRECTINPUTDEVICE2 lpdijoy2;    // dinput joystick
GUID               joystickGUID; // GUID for main joystick
char               joyname[80];  // name of joystick

// these contain the target records
// for all DirectInput input packets
UCHAR keyboard_state[256];// contains keyboard state table
DIMOUSESTATE mouse_state; // contains state of mouse
DIJOYSTATE joy_state;     // contains state of joystick
int joystick_found;       // tracks if stick is plugged in
```

You shouldn't have to mess with any of these globals except to access the input device data after it has been read. This access is accomplished via `mouse_state`, `keyboard_state`, and `joy_state` for the mouse, keyboard, and joystick, respectively.

That's it for the preliminaries on the new code in the engine. Check out the next sections for more detailed information of the new capabilities of the GPDUMB2 game engine.

Sound Just Got a Whole Lot Easier

DirectSound can be complicated or simple depending on how you use it. If you want a "can do it all" API, then you're going to end up using most of the DirectSound functions themselves. But if you want a simpler API that enables you to initialize DirectSound and load and play sounds of a specific format, that task is a lot easier to wrap up in a few functions.

So I've formalized much of the work in the DirectSound chapter (see Chapter 13) into functions for you. In addition, I've created an abstraction around the sound system, so your program refers to a sound with an ID that is given to it during the loading process. Thus, you can use this ID to play the sound, check its status, or terminate it. This way, you don't need to mess with any ugly interface pointers.

The new API supports the following functionality (see Chapter 13 for more detailed information of why these attributes are so useful):

- Initializing and shutting down DirectSound with single calls
- Loading both .VOC and .WAV files that are in 11 kHz 8-bit mono format
- Playing a loaded sound file
- Stopping a sound
- Testing the play status of a sound
- Changing the volume, playback rate, or stereo panning of a sound
- Deleting sounds from memory

Take a look at each function one by one in the following sections.

Unless otherwise stated, all functions return TRUE (1) if successful and FALSE (0) if not.

DSound_Init

Function prototype:

```
int DSound_Init(void);
```

Purpose: DSound_Init() initializes the entire DirectSound system. It creates the DirectSound COM object, sets the priority level, and so on. Just call the function at the beginning of your application if you want to use sound. Here's an example:

```
if (!DSound_Init(void))
   { /* error */ }
```

DSound_Shutdown

Function prototype:

```
int DSound_Shutdown(void);
```

Purpose: DSound_Shutdown() shuts down and releases all the COM interfaces created during DSound_Init(). However, DSound_Shutdown() does not release all the memory allocated to all the sound. You must do this task yourself with another function. Here's how to shut down DirectSound:

```
if (!DSound_Shutdown())
   { /* error */ }
```

Load_VOC and Load_WAV

Function prototypes:

```
int Load_VOC(char *filename);
int Load_WAV(char *filename);
```

Purpose: Both Load_VOC() and Load_WAV() create a DirectSound buffer, load the sound data file into memory, and prepare the sound to be played. The functions take the complete path and filename of the sound file to be loaded (including extensions .VOC and .WAV) and load the file from disk. If successful, the functions return a non-negative ID number. You must save this number because it is used as a handle to reference the sound. If the function can't find the file or too many sounds are loaded, then it returns –1.

Here's an example of loading a .VOC file named BOOM.VOC:

```
int boom_id = Load_VOC("BOOM.VOC");

// test for error
if (boom_id==-1)
   { /* error */}
```

And here's how to load a .WAV file named FIRE.WAV:

```
int fire_id = Load_WAV("FIRE.WAV");

// test for error
if (fire_id==-1)
   { /* error */}
```

Of course, it's up to you to decide how you want to save the IDs. You may want to use an array or something else. You may even want to wrap the two functions into one function — called Load_Sound() — that tests for the .VOC or .WAV extension and then calls the proper function.

You may wonder where the sound data is and how to manipulate it. If you really must, you can access the data within the pcm_sound array sound_fx[] using as the index the ID you get back from either load function. For example, here's how to access the DirectSound buffer for the sound with ID sound_id.

```
sound_fx[sound_id].dsbuffer
```

Replicate_Sound

Function prototype:

```
int Replicate_Sound(int source_id); // id of sound to copy
```

Purpose: Replicate_Sound() copies a sound without copying the memory that holds the sound. For example, suppose that you have a gunshot sound, and you want to fire three gunshots one right after another. The only way to do this task with the original GPDUMB engine is to load three copies of the gunshot sound into three different DirectSound memory buffers, which would be a waste of memory.

Fortunately, I've prepared a solution with the Replicate_Sound function. You can create a duplicate (or *replicant,* if you're a *Blade Runner* fan) of the sound buffer, except for the actual sound data. Instead of copying it, just point a pointer to it and DirectSound is smart enough to use it as a source for multiple sounds using the same data.

Therefore, if you want to play a gunshot up to eight times, for example, load the gunshot once and then make seven copies of it and acquire a total of eight unique IDs. Replicated sounds work exactly the same as normal sounds; instead of using Load_WAV() or Load_VOC() to load and create them, copy them with Replicate_Sound(). Get it? Good! I'm starting to get dizzy!

Here's an example of creating eight gunshots:

```
int gunshot_ids[8]; // this holds all the ids

// load the master sound
gunshot_ids[0] = Load_WAV("GUNSHOT.WAV");

// now make copies
for (int index=1; index<8; index++)
    gunshot_ids[index] = Replicate_Sound(gunshot_ids[0]);

// use gunshot_ids[0..7],they all go bang!
```

Play_Sound

Function prototype:

```
int Play_Sound(int id,         // id of sound to play
               int flags=0,  // 0 or DSBPLAY_LOOPING
               int volume=0, // unused
```

```
          int rate=0,    // unused
          int pan=0);    // unused
```

Purpose: `Play_Sound()` plays a previously loaded sound. Send the ID of the sound along with the play flags — 0 for single, or `DSBPLAY_LOOPING` to loop — and the sound will start playing. If the sound is already playing, then it will restart at the beginning. Here's an example of loading and playing a sound:

```
int fire_id = Load_WAV("FIRE.WAV");
Play_Sound(fire_id,0);
```

Note that you can leave out the 0 for flags entirely, because that default parameter is 0, as shown in the following:

```
int fire_id = Load_WAV("FIRE.WAV");
Play_Sound(fire_id);
```

Either way, the `FIRE.WAV` sound plays once and then stops. To make it loop, send `DSBPLAY_LOOPING` for the flag's parameter.

Stop_Sound and Stop_All_Sounds

Function prototypes:

```
int Stop_Sound(int id);
int Stop_All_Sounds(void);
```

Purpose: `Stop_Sound()` stops a single sound from playing (if it is playing). Simply send the ID of the sound, and that's it. `Stop_All_Sounds()` stops all the sounds currently playing. Here's an example of stopping the `fire_id` sound:

```
Stop_Sound(fire_id);
```

At the end of your program, insert a code to stop all the sounds from playing before exiting. You can do this with separate calls to `Stop_Sound()` for each sound or a single call to `Stop_All_Sounds()`, like this:

```
//system shutdown code goes here
Stop_All_Sounds();
```

Delete_Sound and Delete_All_Sounds

Function prototypes:

```
int Delete_Sound(int id); // id of sound to delete
int Delete_All_Sounds(void);
```

Purpose: Delete_Sound() deletes a sound from memory and releases the DirectSound buffer associated with it. If the sound is playing, then the function stops it first. Delete_All_Sounds() deletes all previously loaded sounds. Here's an example of deleting the boom_id sound:

```
Delete_Sound(boom_id);
```

Status_Sound

Function prototype:

```
int Status_Sound(int id);
```

Purpose: Status_Sound() tests the status of a loaded sound based on its ID. All you do is pass to the function the ID number of the sound and the function returns one of these values:

- ✔ DSBSTATUS_LOOPING: The sound is currently playing and is in loop mode.
- ✔ DSBSTATUS_PLAYING: The sound is currently playing and is in single play mode.

If neither of these constants is the value returned from Status_Sound(), then the sound is not playing. Here's a complete example that waits until a sound has finished playing and then deletes it:

```
// initialize DirectSound
DSound_Init();

// load a sound
int fire_id = Load_WAV("FIRE.WAV");

// play the sound in single mode
Play_Sound(fire_id);
```

```
// wait until the sound is done (key following on one line)
while(Sound_Status(fire_id) &
            (DSBSTATUS_LOOPING | DSBSTATUS_PLAYING));

// delete the sound
Delete_Sound(fire_id);

// shut down DirectSound
DSound_Shutdown();
```

Pretty cool, huh? A lot better then the couple hundred or so lines of code to do the same action manually with DirectSound!

Set_Sound_Volume

Function prototype:

```
int Set_Sound_Volume(int id,    // id of sound
                     int vol); // volume from 0-100
```

Purpose: Set_Sound_Volume() changes the volume of a sound in real-time. Send the ID of the sound along with a value from 0–100 and the sound will change instantly. Here's an example of reducing the volume of a sound by 50 percent:

```
Set_Sound_Volume(fire_id, 50);
```

You can always change the volume back to 100 percent like this:

```
Set_Sound_Volume(fire_id, 100);
```

Set_Sound_Freq

Function prototype:

```
int Set_Sound_Freq(
    int id,    // sound id
    int freq); // new playback rate from 0-100000
```

Purpose: Set_Sound_Freq() changes the playback frequency of the sound. Because all sounds must be loaded at 11 kHz mono, here's how to double the perceived playback rate:

```
Set_Sound_Freq(fire_id, 22050);
```

And to make a sound file of your voice sound like Darth Vader, do this:

```
Set_Sound_Freq(fire_id, 6000);
```

Set_Sound_Pan

Function prototype:

```
int Set_Sound_Pan(
    int id,    // sound id
    int pan); // panning value from -10000 to 10000
```

Purpose: `Set_Sound_Pan()` sets the relative intensity of the sound on the right and left speakers. A value of –10,000 is hard left and 10,000 is hard right. If you want equal power in both speakers, set the pan to 0. Here's how to set the pan all the way to the right side:

```
Set_Sound_Pan(fire_id, 10000);
```

A Generalized DirectInput System

I can't wait until video games are played with mind control; then we won't have to worry about all these different input devices! Unfortunately, that innovation is a few years off (but not many). Nevertheless, DirectInput does a lot of the work of *normalizing* or abstracting the various input devices for you, so you can really put together a good input system on top of DirectInput with very little effort.

Originally, I was going to merge all the input from all the devices into one input event. However, after thinking about the situation for a while, I decided that creating one input event may not be such a good idea, because in some circumstances you may want more control.

Alas, the final input system is more of a housekeeper function than anything else. The system performs the following functions for you:

- ✔ Initializes the DirectInput system
- ✔ Sets up and acquires the keyboard, mouse, and joystick — or any subset
- ✔ Reads data from any of the input devices
- ✔ Shuts down and releases everything

In essence, I put wrapper functions around the few lines of code needed to set up and read each of the input devices. You still receive input in terms of a device state, and you have to process the various fields within each device state structure (keyboard, mouse, and joystick), as I detail in Chapter 14. However, the method in the updated GPDUMB engine gives you the most freedom.

Before reviewing the functions, take a look at Figure 16-2, which depicts the relationship between each device and the data flow.

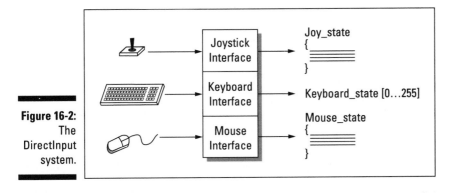

Figure 16-2:
The
DirectInput
system.

Input from the keyboard is placed in keyboard_state[], which is defined as an array of 256 values, each representing a particular key on the keyboard. The mouse data is stored in mouse_state and the joystick data is stored in joy_state by the input system. The structure of each of these records is the standard DirectInput device state structure. But in general, the mouse and joystick are roughly equivalent in terms of the (x,y) position; that is, you access them via the fields 1X, 1Y, and the buttons are Booleans in rgbButtons[].

DInput_Init

Function prototype:

```
int DInput_Init(void);
```

Purpose: DInput_Init() initializes the DirectInput input system. It creates the main COM object and returns TRUE if successful, FALSE otherwise. And, of course, the global lpdi (defined in GPDUMB2.CPP) will be valid. The function does not create any devices, though. Here's an example of initializing the input system:

```
if (!DInput_Init())
  { /* error */ }
```

DInput_Shutdown

Function prototype:

```
void DInput_Shutdown(void);
```

Purpose: `DInput_Shutdown()` releases all the COM objects and any resources allocated during the call to `DInput_Init()`. Normally, you would call `DInput_Shutdown()` at the very end of your application after you have released all the input devices themselves — which I get to after reviewing the initialization functions. Here's an example of shutting down the input system:

```
DInput_Shutdown();
```

DI_Init_Keyboard

Function prototype:

```
DI_Init_Keyboard(void);
```

Purpose: `DI_Init_Keyboard()` initializes and acquires the keyboard. This function should always work and return `TRUE`, unless another DirectX application has taken over in a really uncooperative way. Here's an example:

```
if (!DI_Init_Keyboard())
   { /* error */ }
```

DI_Init_Mouse

Function prototype:

```
int DI_Init_Mouse(void);
```

Purpose: `DI_Init_Mouse()` initializes and acquires the mouse. The function takes no parameters and returns `TRUE` if successful and `FALSE` otherwise. But it always works, unless a mouse isn't plugged in or another DirectX application has totally taken over! If everything goes well, then `lpdimouse` becomes the valid interface pointer, as in the following example:

```
if (!DI_Init_Mouse()) { /* error */ }
```

DI_Init_ Joystick

Function prototype:

```
int DI_Init_Joystick(int min_x=-256, // min x range
                     int max_x=256,  // max x range
                     int min_y=-256, // min y range
                     int max_y=256); // max y range
```

Purpose: `DI_Init_Joystick()` initializes the joystick device for use. The function takes four parameters, which define the X–Y range of motion of the data sent back from the joystick. If you want to use the defaults of –256 to 256 for each axis, then you need not send parameters (because they have default values — a C++ thing).

If the call returns a `TRUE`, then a joystick was found and has been set up, initialized, and acquired. After the call, the `lpdijoy2` interface pointer will be valid if you need it for anything. In addition, the string `joyname[]` will contain the "friendly" name of the joystick device, such as Microsoft Sidewinder Pro or whatever.

Here's an example of initializing the joystick and setting its X–Y ranges to –1,024 to 1,024:

```
if (!DI_Init_Joystick(-1024, 1024, -1024, 1024))
   { /* error */ }
```

DI_Release_ Joystick, DI_Release_Mouse, and DI_Release_Keyboard

Function prototypes:

```
void DI_Release_Joystick(void);
void DI_Release_Mouse(void);
void DI_Release_Keyboard(void);
```

Purpose: `DI_Release_Joystick()`, `DI_Release_Mouse()`, and `DI_Release_Keyboard()` release each of the respective input devices after you are done with them. A function can be called even if you haven't initialized the device, so you can just call them all at the end of your application if you want to. Here's a complete example of starting up the DirectInput system, initializing all the devices, and then releasing them and shutting down:

```
// initialize the DirectInput system
DInput_Init();

// initialize all input devices and acquire them
DI_Init_Joystick();
DI_Init_Mouse();
DI_Init_Keyboard();

// input loop, insert program code here

// now's time for your program to end
// first release all devices (order is unimportant)
void DI_Release_Joystick(void);
void DI_Release_Mouse(void);
void DI_Release_Keyboard(void);

// shut down DirectInput
DInput_Shutdown();
```

DI_Read_Keyboard

Function prototype:

```
int DI_Read_Keyboard(void);
```

Purpose: DI_Read_Keyboard() scans the keyboard state and places the data in keyboard_state[], which is an array of 256 BYTES. This is the standard DirectInput keyboard state array, so you must use the DirectInput key constants DIK_* if you want to make sense of it. When a key is pressed, the array value will be 0 x 80. Here's an example of testing whether the right- and left-arrow keys are down using the manifest constants in DirectInput (which you can look up in the DirectX SDK Help file or the abridged table in Chapter 14 on DirectInput):

```
// read the keyboard
if (!DI_Read_Keyboard())
   { /* error */ }

// now test the state data
if (keyboard_state[DIK_RIGHT]
   { /* move ship right */ }
else
if (keyboard_state[DIK_LEFT]
   { /* move ship left */ }
```

DI_Read_Mouse

Function prototype:

```
int DI_Read_Mouse(void);
```

Purpose: DI_Read_Mouse() reads the mouse state and stores the result in mouse_state, which is a DIMOUSESTATE structure. The data is in relative change (delta) mode. In most cases, you only need to look at mouse_state.lX, mouse_state.lY, and rgbButtons[0..2], which are Booleans for the three mouse buttons. Here's an example of reading the mouse and using it to move a cursor around and draw:

```
// read the mouse
if (!DI_Read_Mouse())
   { /* error */ }

// move cursor
cx+=mouse_state.lX;
cy+=mouse_state.lY;

// test whether left button is down
if (mouse_state.rgbButtons[0])
   Draw_Pixel(cx,cy,col,buffer,pitch);
```

DI_Read_Joystick

Function prototype:

```
int DI_Read_Joystick(void);
```

Purpose: DI_Read_Joystick() polls the joystick and then reads the data into joy_state, which is a DIJOYSTATE structure. Of course, if no joystick is plugged in, then the function returns FALSE and joy_state is invalid — but you get the idea. If successful, then joys_state contains the state information of the joystick. The data returned will be in the range you previously set for each axis, and the button values are Booleans in rgbButtons[]. As an example, here's how to use the joystick to move a ship right and left, and move the first button to fire:

```
// read the joystick data
if (!DI_Read_Joystick())
   { /* error */ }
```

(continued)

(continued)

```
// move the ship
ship_x+=joy_state.lX;
ship_y+=joy_state.lY;

// test for trigger
if (joy_state.rgbButtons[0])
   { // fire weapon // }
```

Of course, your joystick may have a lot of buttons and multiple axes. In that case, you can use the other fields of `joy_state` as defined in the `DIJOYSTATE` (defined in Chapter 14) DirectInput structure.

Just a Dash of Graphics

Part I of the GPDUMB engine was pretty darn complete if I say so myself, but it's missing finesse. So I decided to add a few more functions to give it those final, useful touches. Two of the new functions are special-case line-drawing functions, because using a general line-drawing algorithm to draw horizontal and vertical lines (which can be highly optimized) is sacrilege. The last function is a screen-transition system. Screen transitions are cool effects that you can use to start a game, exit a level, change menus, and so forth. So check them out!

HLine

Function prototype:

```
void HLine(int x1, // starting x position of HLine
           int x2, // ending x position of HLine
           int y,  // row or vertical position of HLine
           int color, // color of HLine 0-255
           UCHAR *vbuffer, // destination memory buffer
           int lpitch); // memory pitch of buffer
```

Purpose: `HLine()` draws a horizontal line on the memory surface pointed to by `vbuffer`. The line is drawn using a `memset()` type of function, so it's very fast. In addition, the line is clipped to the clipping area `min_clip_x`, `min_clip_y`, `max_clip_x`, `max_clip_y`. Here's an example of drawing a line from (20,30) to (100,30) on the primary surface:

```
// always make sure to lock and unlock surface
DD_Lock_Primary_Surface();
HLine(20,100,30,color, primary_buffer, primary_lpitch);
DD_Unlock_Primary_Surface();
```

VLine

Function prototype:

```
void VLine(int y1, // starting y position of HLine
           int y2, // ending y position of HLine
           int x,  // column or horizontal pos of VLine
           int color, // color of HLine 0-255
           UCHAR *vbuffer, // destination memory buffer
           int lpitch); // memory pitch of buffer
```

Purpose: VLine() draws a vertical line on the memory surface pointed to by vbuffer. The line is drawn using a for loop, so it's fast, but not as fast as Hline(). In addition, the line is clipped to the clipping area min_clip_x, min_clip_y, max_clip_x, max_clip_y. Here's an example of drawing a line from (100,150) to (100,200) on the primary surface:

```
// make sure to lock and unlock surface
DD_Lock_Primary_Surface();
HLine(150,200,100,color, primary_buffer, primary_lpitch);
DD_Unlock_Primary_Surface();
```

Screen_Transitions

Function prototype:

```
void Screen_Transitions(
           int effect,     // transition to perform
           UCHAR *vbuffer, // destination memory buffer
           int lpitch);    // memory pitch of buffer
```

Purpose: Screen_Transitions() is the coolest new function of the bunch. With a single call to it, along with a couple of parameters, Screen_Transitions() can manipulate and morph the screen image for you in preparation for another level, and so on. The commands are listed in the earlier header section definitions, but in general, you can create three types of effects:

✔ **Color transformations:** The colors of the image are slowly changed to some target color such as black, white, red, green, or blue.

✔ **Dissolves:** The image on the screen is eroded away by a random function.

✔ **Wipes:** The image is wiped away from the top, bottom, left, right, or all at the same time.

You must follow a couple of rules when you use the function:

✔ If you request a color transformation effect, then both the primary and secondary surfaces must be unlocked! This rule means that you need to make a call to DD_Unlock_Primary_Surface() and DD_Unlock_Back_Surface(). And you must save the palette before and restore it after you call the function, because the function will mangle the palette entries.

✔ If you request a dissolve or wipe, make sure that the memory buffer and pitch are valid and correct. Otherwise, you will crash the system, because the transition function will try to write in the region.

To perform a dissolve on the primary buffer, assuming that it's already locked, do this:

```
Screen_Transitions(SCREEN_DISSOLVE,
                    primary_buffer, primary_lpitch);
```

And here's how to fade to black on the primary surface:

```
// make sure primary buffer is unlocked
DD_Unlock_Primary_Surface();

// do the transition; note that the buffer
// and pitch are irrelevant because this is a color effect
Screen_Transitions(SCREEN_BLACKNESS,NULL,0);
```

And here's a swipe like *Star Wars* movies do from location to location:

```
Screen_Transitions(SCREEN_SWIPE_X,
                    primary_buffer,primary_lpitch);
```

The Six Million Dollar BOB

After putting the BOB engine through the ringer on Star Ferret (see Chapter 12 and the code for that chapter on the CD), I wanted to add only one thing to that engine for this chapter: a way to reuse the bitmap imagery loaded into each BOB.

Suppose that you want to have a bunch of objects, such as asteroids or creatures. Also, imagine that they are all the same image, but in different states, positions, and so on. You definitely need a BOB for each, but currently each BOB has its own bitmap imagery. So if you create one BOB with the imagery of an asteroid, and then another, you have to use twice the amount of surface bitmap memory.

The trick is to use a *master-image BOB*. In other words, you create one BOB and load it with the imagery, and then alias all the image pointers of your remaining BOBs, but use the other fields of the BOB structure as you normally would (as shown in Figure 16-3). This technique is called *cloning*.

The only problem with cloning is that you need to be careful about deleting memory and resources of clones. For example, suppose that you create a master-image BOB of an asteroid and then make 100 copies of it. No problem. But then suppose that you make a call to Destroy_BOB() with one of the clones. In that case, whammo! The master BOB and all the clones just had their imagery deleted.

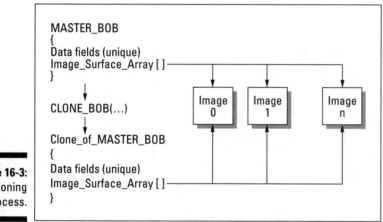

Figure 16-3: The cloning process.

A number of solutions are possible: a more advanced set of creation and deletion functions, reference counting (such as with COM), or just tracking the BOB yourself. I opted to use common sense along with a new deletion function and cloning function to do things in a civilized manner. Therefore, you can clone a BOB and delete a clone, but you must delete the master-image BOB at the very end. The clones are deleted with a new function called Destroy_BOB2(). It can handle both normal BOBs and clones. You just need to make sure that you destroy the master BOB last, and everything will be fine. Take a look at the new cloning and destruction functions.

Clone_BOB

Function prototype:

```
int Clone_BOB(BOB_PTR source, // the source BOB to clone
              BOB_PTR dest);  // the destination BOB
```

Purpose: `Clone_BOB()` creates a memory clone of the source master-image BOB in the destination BOB's memory space. The result is a reuse of the imagery and animations held in the master-image Bob. However, after the cloning process, you must do the following:

✔ Fill all the fields that you want changed, such as position, state, velocity, and so on; they will be the same as the source BOB immediately after the cloning call.

✔ Delete all clones with `Destroy_BOB2()`; otherwise, serious memory problems will result.

Here's an example of creating 64 clones:

```
BOB master_bob,      // the master BOB
    clone_bobs[64]; // the clones of the master

// first create the master BOB (single frame, multi, etc.)
Create_BOB(&master_bob, 0,0,
          64,64,1,BOB_ATTR_SINGLE_FRAME);

// load the image into the BOB
Load_Frame(&master_bob,
          &bitmap8bit,0,0,0,BITMAP_EXTRACT_CELL_MODE);

// create the clones
for (int clone=0; clone<64; clone++)
    {
    // create the clone
    // don't load imagery; just clone it
    Create_BOB(&clone_bobs[clone], 0,0,
              64,64,1,BOB_ATTR_SINGLE_FRAME);

    Clone_BOB(&master_bob, &clone_bobs[clone];
    // reset the fields you want changed (code not shown)

    } // end for clone

// now you can use all the clones
```

Destroy_BOB2

Function prototype:

```
int Destroy_BOB2(BOB_PTR bob); // bob to destroy
```

Purpose: Destroy_BOB2() destroys a normal BOB or a clone. The function can tell the difference based on the internal flag BOB_ATTR_CLONE, which is set during cloning. If the BOB is a clone, then the memory is zeroed out and the imagery links are NULLed, but the original DirectDraw surface bitmaps are not altered. On the other hand, if the BOB is a master BOB and not a clone, then the BOBs are zeroed out, and the DirectDraw surfaces are released. Here's how to destroy all the BOBs from the previous example:

```
// first kill all the clones
for (int clone=0; clone<64; clone++)
    Destroy_BOB2(&clone_bobs[clone]);

// now the master
Destroy_BOB2(&master_bob);
```

When Worlds Collide

Last but not least, I added a couple more collision functions to the library. These functions are the kind that programmers end up rewriting over and over because they're so simple, but I'm tired of rewriting them for all the demos. Therefore, I added two more collision functions to help you detect when two rectangles are overlapping and when a rectangle contains a specific color or colors — a pixel scanner of sorts (as shown in Figure 16-4). Both of these functions will help you immensely when you try to decide whether objects are hitting each other.

Collision_Test

Function prototype:

```
int Collision_Test(
    int x1, int y1, // starting position of test rect 1
    int w1, int h1, // width and height of test rect 1
    int x2, int y2, // starting position of test rect 2
    int w2, int h2);// width and height of test rect 2
```

Purpose: `Collision_Test()` tests whether the sent rectangles overlap in 2D space. This function is useful for crude collision detection when the test objects have relatively rectangular shapes. The function returns TRUE if an overlap or collision occurs, and FALSE otherwise. Actually, `Collision_Test()` was derived from the BOB collision code, but I simply parameterized the rectangles instead of extracting them from the BOBs themselves.

Here's an example of testing whether two objects collide. Both rectangles are 64 x 64, and they are located at (x1,y1) and (x2,y2):

```
if (Collision_Test(x1,y1,64,64,x2,y2,64,64))
   { /* boom */ }
```

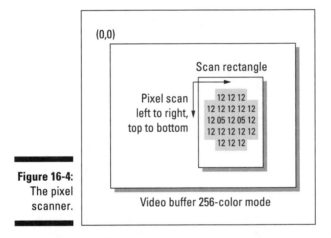

Figure 16-4: The pixel scanner.

The black art of collision detection

In general, collision detection is a black art in game programming. Most game programmers do this detection by using tricks and assumptions, because real pixel-to-pixel collision detection is costly (testing a 64-x-64-pixel bitmap against another 64-x-64-pixel bitmap could take upward of 64^4 or 16.7 million computations). Thus, the rectangular collision method is widely used by game programmers, but instead of using the bounding boxes of each object, programmers usually cut the boxes down by 30 to 50 percent and center them on the mass of the object to make the collisions more realistic in cases of scathing collisions. However, this technique has really upset a lot of players. For example, have you ever thought that you hit the alien with your missile, but you didn't score a hit? Well you did hit the alien, but the bounding box of the alien graphic was shrunk so much that the hit registered as a miss!

Color_Scan

Function prototype:

```
int Color_Scan(
    int x1, int y1,  // upper left-hand corner of rect
    int x2, int y2,  // lower right-hand corner or rect
    UCHAR scan_start,// starting color in range to scan for
    UCHAR scan_end,  // ending color in range to scan for
    UCHAR *scan_buffer, // memory buffer to scan in
    int scan_lpitch);  // memory pitch of buffer
```

Purpose: Color_Scan() scans for a particular color or range of colors in a rectangular region within a 256-color bitmap surface and returns TRUE if it finds one or more of the color. This function is useful for determining collisions with objects that are extremely irregular or very small. For example, I used a technique like this to make the skeleton collide with the walls in the DirectInput keyboard demo (see Chapter 14 for information about this demo).

Alas, the method does have a single flaw — speed. The algorithm scans the rectangular region until it detects one of the colors in the range from scan_start to scan_end. This method is fine if you are only using it for player-to-object collision detection, but if you were to compute object-to-object pixel level scans — such as this one — you would bring your machine to its knees very quickly. Am I depressing you? Well, by the time you finish this chapter, Intel will have released another processor that's two times as fast as today's, so the speed shouldn't matter!

As an example of using color collision detection, here's how to test whether a BOB is touching within its bounding box colors 10 to 20:

```
// perform test on backbuffer surface, so make sure
// it's locked!
if (Color_Scan(master_bob->x, master_bob->y,
              master_bob->x+master_bob->width-1,
              master_bob->y+master_bob->height-1,
              10,20,
              back_buffer, back_lpitch))
{ /* collision true */ }
else
   { /* no collision */ }
```

Collision detection in the worst case is a $O(n^2)$ — pronounced *big-O* — problem. In other words, the amount of computation is bounded by a squared function. For example, if you have 10 objects, you must test each object against every other object. That is 10*10 or 100 comparisons. Of course, you can optimize this task a bit with the observation that you don't need to test every object against every other object per se, but each pair of objects. In this case, you can see that the number of computations is $C(n,2)$ or "n choose 2" which is equal to 10!/(10-2)!*2! = 45.

My friend Richard Benson has converted the graphics portion of the GPDUMB engine to 16-bit color. You can find the code on the CD in WGPDUMB\SOURCE\GPCHAP16. The file is named BOB16BIT.ZIP.

Star Ferret Deluxe

Alrighty, then! As an example of putting all this new technology to use, I have upgraded Star Ferret (originally created using the game engine developed in Chapter 12) to include sound, music, joystick input, and as many of the new library functions as possible. The new source is named STARFER2.CPP and the executable is STARFER2.EXE, both of which are on the CD.

If you want to recompile the program, remember to include the following files in your project:

✔ GPDUMB1.CPP/H
✔ GPDUMB2.CPP/H
✔ DDRAW.LIB
✔ DSOUND.LIB
✔ DINPUT.LIB
✔ WINMM.LIB
✔ STARFER2.CPP

And, of course, you must copy all the bitmaps (including DPAINT.PAL) and sound files from the CD subfolder CHAP16\ for the program to feed from.

The object of the game is simple: Stay alive. To control Star Ferret Deluxe, you can use all the input devices. The mouse and joystick will move Star Ferret, and the buttons will fire the weapons. If you prefer the keyboard, use the arrows to move and the Ctrl key to fire. To exit the program, press Esc.

That's all folks, and may the X be with you!

Part IV
The Glue of Games

"It's been reported that we went a little crazy trying to bring this game to market on time..."

In this part . . .

Finished with the preliminaries of Windows and DirectX? Then you're ready for the main course: game programming. In the following chapters, you discover the many uses of artificial intelligence, or how to make the game characters seem intelligent. You get a crash course in game physics and see how to make objects fall, skid, collide, and more. Next, I cover data structures and the details of putting a whole game together. After reading this part, you will have just about all the knowledge you need to create a complete commercial game!

Chapter 17

What Goes Up Must Come Down: Physics Modeling

• •

• •

*I*n the '70s and '80s, video games didn't have much physics. For the most part, games of that time were shoot-'em-ups, search-and-destroy missions, adventure games, and so on. However, in the current 3D era, physics modeling is much more important. You simply can't get away with making the objects in games move in such a way that the motion isn't consistent with what the player would expect from reality, or at least a reasonable approximation of it. Understanding how to approximate reality is what this chapter is all about.

If the universe is just a simulation in some unbelievably advanced computer, then God is one heck of a programmer! Physical laws work perfectly at all levels, from the cosmological level to the quantum level. The beauty of physics is that just a few laws govern the whole universe. Granted, the collective human knowledge of physics and mathematics is still infantile, but we do know enough to create computer simulations that can fool just about anyone.

Most computer simulations and games that use physics use models that are based on standard *Newtonian physics,* a class of physics that works pretty well on motion and objects within speeds much under the speed of light and sizes much bigger than a single atom but much smaller than a galaxy. However, using even the most basic Newtonian-based physics models to simulate reality takes a great deal of computing power. A simple simulation of real rainfall or a pool table (if done correctly) would cripple a Pentium II.

Nonetheless, games running on anything from an Apple II to a Pentium PC have simulated rainfall and pool games because the programmers of these games understand the physics that they're trying to model. Within their budgets and computing power, they create models that are close to what the player expects in real life. This programming magic consists of tricks, optimizations, and, most of all, assumptions about the systems that are being modeled. For example, figuring out how two spheres will react after a collision is much easier than figuring it out for two irregular asteroids; thus, a programmer might equate the physics calculations of all the asteroids in a game with those of simple spheres.

Now, a course in state-of-the-art game physics would take about 10,000 pages, so I cover just some of the most fundamental physics models, from which you should be able to model everything you need for your first 2D games. Most of this stuff should be familiar from any physics class you may have taken in school.

Note: Any physics gurus among you may quibble with some of the statements in this discussion. Not all these statements are entirely true at the quantum or cosmological level; I simplified them to make them easier to follow, but they're accurate enough for game programming.

Also note that I lean toward the metric system because it's more accurate and easier to use than the English system (which is about 200 years antiquated).

Making physics models that work

The key to physics modeling in your games is to use the concepts and some of the hard math to make working models that look good. Players of your game won't know whether the models are 100-percent correct, nor will they care. If you use approximations, then put some thought into how close to reality your approximations need to be.

For example, if you're trying to make a racing game and you want to race on road, ice, and dirt, you'd better have some frictional effects, or your cars will drive like they're on rails.

On the other hand, if you have an asteroid field that the player blows up, and each asteroid splits into two or more smaller asteroids, I don't think that the player is going to care about or know the exact trajectory that the smaller asteroids would take. So just pick trajectories that look good.

The Fundamental Laws and Concepts

To give you a vocabulary for understanding the more advanced topics that follow, this section covers the fundamental concepts of physics and the properties of time, space, and matter. (The parenthetical text in the following subheadings give you the standard abbreviations that I use throughout the chapter for these terms.)

Mass (m)

Mass is the measure of how much matter an object is made of and is measured in kilograms in the metric system or — ready for this — *slugs* in the English system. All matter has mass; mass is a measure of matter.

Mass has nothing to do with weight, though many people confuse the two. For example, they might say that I weigh 131 kilograms (kg) and I weigh 210 pounds on Earth. Here's what's wrong with that statement: First, kilograms are a metric measure of mass — that is, how much matter — while pounds are a measure of force or, more loosely, weight. Furthermore, matter has no weight per se; it only can be acted upon by a gravitational field to produce what we refer to as *weight*. Hence, the concept of mass is a much purer idea than weight (which changes from planet to planet).

In games, the concept of mass is only used abstractly in most cases, as a relative quantity. For example, you may set a spaceship equal to 100 mass units and an asteroid equal to 10,000. You could use kilograms, but unless you're doing a real physics simulation, you don't need to specify the unit of measure. All you need to know is that an object with 100 mass units has twice as much matter as an object with 50 mass units. "Force (f)" later in this chapter revisits mass.

Time (t)

Time is one of the most abstract concepts to try to explain. Luckily, everyone knows what time is, so I don't have to define it, except in terms of how it relates to games.

In real life, time is usually measured in seconds, minutes, hours, and so forth. Or if you need to be really accurate, you use milliseconds, microseconds, nanoseconds, and so on. Most games don't have a close correlation to real-time. Algorithms are designed more around the frame rate than around real-time. For example, most games consider one frame to be one virtual second — in other words, the smallest amount of time that can transpire.

Thus, most of the time, you don't use *real* seconds in your games and your physics models, but *virtual* seconds based on a single frame as the fundamental time step.

On the other hand, sophisticated 3D games often do use real-time. All the algorithms in the game track real-time and, invariant of the frame rate, adjust the motion of the objects so that, for example, a tank is moving 100 feet per second (ft/s) even if the frame rate slows down to 2 frames per second (fps) or runs at 60 fps. Modeling time at this level of accuracy is challenging but absolutely necessary if you want to have ultrarealistic motion and physical events.

My examples measure time in seconds (s) or in virtual seconds (which simply means a single frame).

Position (s)

Every object has an (x,y,z) position in 3D space, or an (x,y) position in 2D space, or an (x) position in 1D or linear space (linear space is sometimes referred to as *s*). Figure 17-1 shows examples of all these dimensional cases.

However, sometimes the position of an object isn't clear even if you know where the object is. For example, if you have to pick one single point that locates the position of a sphere, you'll probably pick its center, as Figure 17-2 shows. But what about a hammer? A hammer is an irregular shape, so most physicists use its `center of mass`, or balancing point, as the position to locate the hammer; see Figure 17-3.

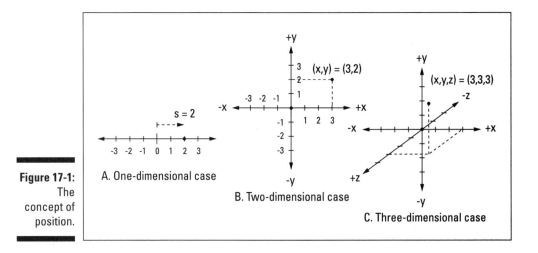

Figure 17-1: The concept of position.

A. One-dimensional case

B. Two-dimensional case

C. Three-dimensional case

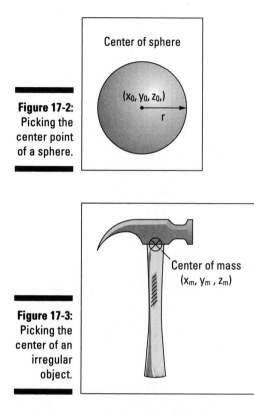

Figure 17-2:
Picking the
center point
of a sphere.

Figure 17-3:
Picking the
center of an
irregular
object.

The concept of position in games is usually rather lax. Most game programmers place a bounding box, circle, or sphere around all the game objects, as Figure 17-4 shows, and simply use the center of the bounding entity as the center of the object. This technique works when most of the object's mass is located at the center of the object; but if that's not the case, any physics calculations that use this artificial center will be incorrect because mass is not distributed evenly.

The only way to solve the problem is to pick a better center — one that takes the virtual mass of the object more into consideration. For example, you can create an algorithm that scans the pixels making up the object and make the center the area with the most pixels.

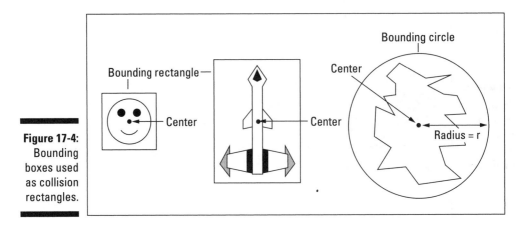

Figure 17-4:
Bounding
boxes used
as collision
rectangles.

Velocity (v)

Velocity is the instantaneous rate of motion of an object and is usually measured in meters per second (m/s) or, in the case of automobiles in the United States and some other countries, miles per hour (mph). Whatever units you prefer, velocity is the change in position (*ds*) per change in time (*dt*). Here's the mathematical expression for a one-dimensional case:

$$v = ds/dt$$

As an example, suppose that you have a race car that's traveled 100 miles in one hour. The velocity is

$$v = ds/dt = 100 \text{ miles}/1 \text{ hour} = 100 \text{ mph}$$

Velocity in game programming

Video games use the concept of velocity all the time, but the units are arbitrary and relative. For example, in a number of the CD demos, I usually move objects at a rate of 4 units in the x-axis (or y-axis) per frame with code that's something like this:

```
x_position = x_position + x_velocity;
y_position = y_position + y_velocity;
```

That translates to 4 pixels per frame. You may be thinking that frames aren't measures of time, but they actually are, as long as the frame rate stays constant. If the frame rate is 30 frames per second (fps), which is equal to $1/30$ second per frame, the 4 pixels/frame translate to

$$\text{virtual velocity} = 4 \text{ pixels} \div 1/30 \text{ second}$$

$$= 120 \text{ pixels/second}$$

Hence, the objects in CD game demos have been moving with velocities measured in pixels per second. If you want to get crazy, you can estimate how many virtual meters are in one pixel in your game world and do the computation in meters per second in cyberspace.

Now you know how to gauge where an object will be at any given time or frame if you know the velocity. For example, if an object is at position x_0, moving at 4 pixels/frame, and 30 frames go by, the object is now at

new position = x_0 + (4 × 30) = x_0 + 120 pixels

Velocity and time

The information in the last section leads to the first important basic law: An object moving with velocity v that starts at location x_0 and moves for t seconds will move to a position equal to its original position plus the velocity multiplied by the time. Figure 17-5 illustrates this concept. Here's the equation:

new position = old position + velocity × time

$$x_t = x_0 + (v \times t)$$

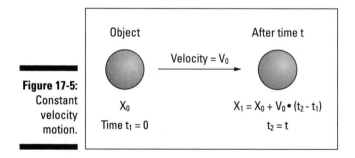

Figure 17-5:
Constant velocity motion.

Object   After time t

Velocity = V_0

X_0 $X_1 = X_0 + V_0 \cdot (t_2 - t_1)$

Time $t_1 = 0$ $t_2 = t$

For an example of constant velocity, I created a demo, PROG17_1.CPP (the executable for which is PROG17_1.EXE), that moves an object from left to right on-screen. The demo displays the virtual velocity in pixels per frame and in pixels per second. Use the ← and → keys to slow down and speed up (respectively) the object. If you want to recompile the demo yourself, you need to include all the files for the GPDUMB game engine (see Chapters 12 and 16).

COOL STUFF

Amaze your friends with physics!

I always amaze my friends by telling them how long before we reach an off ramp or some location when we're in the car. The trick is simple: Just look at the speed and use the fact that when you're driving 60 mph, you go 1 mile in 1 minute. If the off ramp is 2 miles away, you'll reach it in 2 minutes; if it's 3½ miles away, you'll reach it in 3 minutes and 30 seconds. If you aren't driving 60 mph, use the closest plus or minus 30 mph. For example, for 80 mph, do your calculations with 90 mph (1½ miles per minute) and then shrink your answer a bit.

Acceleration (a)

Acceleration is similar to velocity, but it's the measure of the rate of change of velocity rather than the velocity itself. Take a look at Figure 17-6, which illustrates one object moving with a constant velocity and one with a changing velocity. The object moving with a constant velocity has a flat line (slope of 0) for its velocity as a function of time; the accelerating object has a nonzero (positive or negative) slope because its velocity is changing as a function of time.

Figure 17-6 illustrates constant acceleration and nonconstant acceleration. In the latter case, the line is a curve, as shown in Item C of the figure. Pressing the accelerator in your car gives you the feeling of nonconstant acceleration; jumping off a cliff gives you the feeling of constant acceleration.

Mathematically, acceleration (or *a*) is the rate of change of velocity with respect to time:

$$a = dv/dt$$

The units of acceleration are a little weird. Because velocity is already in units of distance per second, acceleration is in units of distance per second × second, or (in the metric system) m/s^2. It makes sense: Acceleration is the change of velocity (m/s) per second.

The second motion law relates the velocity, time, and acceleration: The new velocity at some time *t* in the future equals the starting velocity plus the acceleration multiplied by the amount of time the object has been accelerating. Here's the equation:

new velocity = old velocity + acceleration × time

$$v_t = v_0 + (a \times t)$$

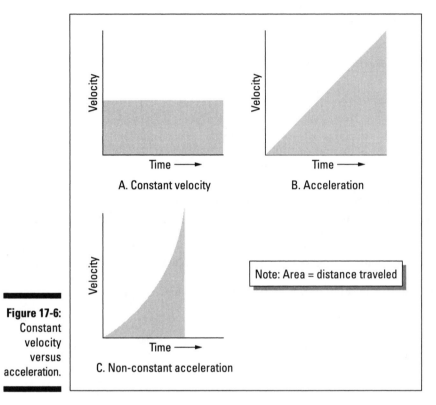

Figure 17-6:
Constant
velocity
versus
acceleration.

Modeling acceleration

Acceleration is a fairly simple concept and can be modeled in a number of
ways. For a simple example, imagine that an object is located at (0,0) and
has a starting velocity of 0. If you accelerate it at a constant velocity of
2 m/s, you can figure out the new velocity each second by adding the
acceleration to the last velocity, as Table 17-1 shows.

Table 17-1	Velocity as a Function of Time for Acceleration 2 m/s^2	
Time (t = s)	Acceleration (a = m/s^2)	Velocity (v = m/s)
0	2	0
1	2	2
2	2	4
3	2	6
4	2	8
5	2	10

Taking the data in the table into consideration, the next step is to figure out the relationship among position, velocity, acceleration, and time. Unfortunately, this calculation takes a bit of calculus. Here's the result in terms of position at some time *t:*

$$x_t = x_0 + v_0 \times t + \frac{1}{2} \times a \times t^2$$

This equation states that the position of an object at some time *t* is equal to the object's initial position plus its initial velocity multiplied by time plus one-half the acceleration multiplied by time squared. The $\frac{1}{2} \times a \times t^2$ term is basically the time integral of the velocity.

Using constant acceleration in your game

See Figure 17-7 for an example of how you can use the equation from the last section in the game world of pixels and frames. Look at the figure, and assume these initial conditions, at frame 0: The object is at *x* = 50 pixels, the initial velocity is 4 pixels/frame, and the acceleration is 2 pixels/frame².

To find the position of the object at any time in C/C++, here's what you use:

```
x = 50 + 4*t + (0.5) *2*t*t
```

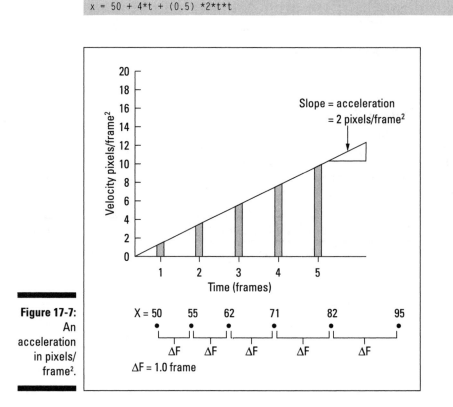

Figure 17-7: An acceleration in pixels/ frame².

In this equation, which is written in the format that C/C++ recognizes, *t* is simply the frame number. Table 17-2 lists some examples for *t*. Note in the table that the change in position each time frame is constant and equal to 2. This doesn't mean that the object moves 2 pixels per frame; it means that the change in motion each frame gets larger by 2 pixels. Thus, on the first frame, the object moves 5 pixels; then on the next frame, the object moves 7, then 9, then 11, then 13, and so on. And the delta between each change in motion is 2 pixels, which is simply the acceleration!

Table 17-2	Object Moving with Constant Acceleration	
Time/Frame (t)	*Position (x)*	$\Delta x = x_t - x_{t-1}$
0	50	0
1	$50 + 4 \times 1 + 0.5 \times 2 \times 1^2 = 55$	5
2	$50 + 4 \times 2 + 0.5 \times 2 \times 2^2 = 62$	7
3	$50 + 4 \times 3 + 0.5 \times 2 \times 3^2 = 71$	9
4	$50 + 4 \times 4 + 0.5 \times 2 \times 4^2 = 82$	11
5	$50 + 4 \times 5 + 0.5 \times 2 \times 5^2 = 95$	13

The next step is to model acceleration with C/C++ code. Basically, here's the trick: You set up an acceleration constant and add it to your velocity for each frame. This way, you don't have to use the long acceleration equation. Then you simply translate your object with the given velocity. Here's an example:

```
int acceleration = 2; // 2 pixels per frame
    velocity     = 0. // start velocity at 0
    x            = 0; // start x position at 0 also
// more game code here...
// then you execute this code each
// cycle to move your object
// with a constant acceleration
// update velocity
velocity+=acceleration;
// update position
x+=velocity;
```

Of course, this example is in one dimension. You can upgrade to two dimensions simply by adding a y position (and y velocity and acceleration, if you want).

To see acceleration in action, I created a demo named `PROG17_2.CPP` (with the executable `PROG17_2.EXE`), which lets you fire a missile that accelerates as it moves forward. Press the spacebar to fire the missile, the ↑ and ↓ keys to increase and decrease (respectively) the acceleration factor, and the A key to toggle the acceleration on and off. Look at how acceleration affects the motion and gives the missile a sense of mass.

Force (F)

Force is very abstract, it is the property that makes a mass accelerate (or decelerate). Figure 17-8 depicts one way to think of force. An object with mass m is sitting on a table with gravity pulling the object toward the center of the Earth, the acceleration equal to gravity $(a = g)$. This gravitational pull gives the mass m weight, and if you try to pick up the object, you feel a pain in your lower back.

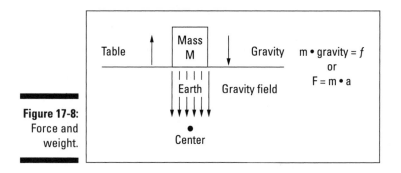

Figure 17-8:
Force and
weight.

The relationship among force, mass, and acceleration is Newton's law: The force exerted on an object is equal to its mass multiplied by the acceleration of the object. Here's the equation:

$$F = m \times a$$

Or if you rearrange terms, an object accelerates an amount equal to the force you place on it divided by its mass:

$$a = F \div m$$

To determine the unit of measure, figure that force is equal to mass multiplied by acceleration, or $kg \times m/s^2$. Hence, a unit of force is

$$F = kg \times m/s^2$$

That's a bit long for a unit of measure, so Newton just called it . . . a *Newton* (N). As an example, imagine that a mass *m* equal to 100 kg is accelerating at a rate of 2 m/s²; the force being applied to the mass is exactly equal to

$$F = m \times a = 160 \text{ kg} \times 2 \text{ m/s}^2 = 320 \text{ N}$$

A 100 kg mass is roughly equivalent to 220 pounds on Earth, and 1 m/s² is a good accelerating run.

A video game uses the concept of force for many reasons. Here are a few:

✔ You want to apply artificial forces, like explosions, to an object and compute the resulting acceleration.

✔ Two objects collide, and you want to compute the forces on each.

✔ A game weapon has only a certain force, but it can fire different virtual mass shells; you want to compute the acceleration the shells would be firing at.

Simple — and I Mean Really Simple — Collisions

The world of physics recognizes two kinds of collisions:

✔ **Elastic collisions:** Both kinetic energy (energy due to motion) and momentum (product of the mass and velocity) are conserved in the colliding objects.

✔ **Non-elastic:** Kinetic energy and momentum are not conserved, and energy is converted to heat and/or used for mechanical deformations.

Most video game programmers don't even try to mess with non-elastic collisions, instead sticking to simplified elastic collisions, which are hard enough to compute. The amount of math you need for those computations is beyond the scope of this book, but game programmers who didn't know anything about elastic or non-elastic collisions have been simulating collisions for years without all that math; you can do the same.

Figure 17-9 depicts a fairly common collision problem in games: bouncing an object off the screen's boundaries. Given that the object has initial velocity in two dimensions (xv,yv), the object can hit any of the four sides of the screen. If one object collides with another object that has mass much greater than the first object, the collision is much simplified because you need to figure out only what happened to the single object that's doing the colliding, rather than two objects.

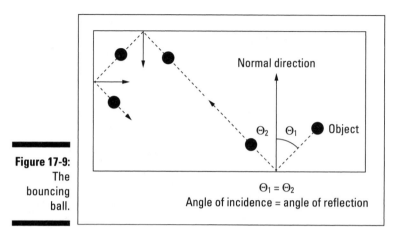

Figure 17-9:
The
bouncing
ball.

A pool table is a good example of this concept. When a ball hits one of the sides, the ball always reflects off the side at an angle equal and opposite to its initial trajectory, as Figure 17-9 shows. Thus, all you need to do to bounce an object off an environment with hard, large-massed edges, such as a pool table, is to compute the normal *vector* direction — the direction that the object struck at — and then reflect the object at the same angle. Figure 17-10 shows that the angle at which an object hits a flat plane (incident angle) is equal to the angle at which the object bounces off (reflectant angle).

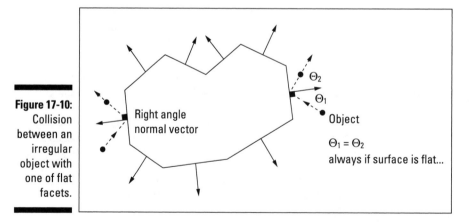

Figure 17-10:
Collision
between an
irregular
object with
one of flat
facets.

Although this situation isn't as complex as the general elastic collision, it still takes a bit of trigonometry. A simpler way involves understanding the physics model. Because you're creating the environment, you have exact knowledge of all the conditions, so the idea is to use that knowledge to solve the problem without using all that math.

Here's the trick: Instead of thinking in terms of angles and all that, think in terms of results. If the object hits a wall to the east or west, you want to reverse the object's x velocity while leaving its y velocity alone. And similarly, on the north and south walls, you want to reverse the y velocity and leave the x velocity alone. Here's the code:

```
// given that the object is at x,y with a velocity of
// xv,yv, test for east and west wall collisions
if (x > EAST_EDGE || x < WEST_EDGE)
    xv=-xv; // reverse x velocity
// now test for north and south wall collisions
if (y > SOUTH_EDGE || y < NORTH_EDGE)
    yv=-yv; // reverse y velocity
```

And amazingly, the object bounces off the walls. Of course, this simplification works well for horizontal and vertical barriers only (side scrolling mountain terrain won't be as easy). You have to use the more general angle calculation for walls or barriers that aren't colinear with the x- and y-axes.

If you want to use the preceding simplified technique to make irregular-shaped game objects bounce off each other, simply assume that, at the moment of impact, each object has a bounding rectangle. Do the collision and then recompute the velocities. Figure 17-11 illustrates this simple trick.

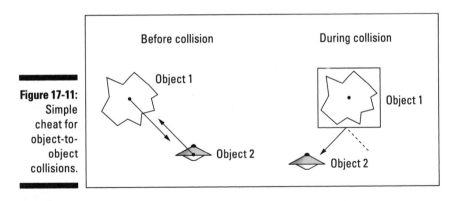

Figure 17-11: Simple cheat for object-to-object collisions.

As an example of using these techniques, I've created a demo named `PROG17_3.CPP` (the executable for which is `PROG17_3.EXE`). The program models a pool table with balls that never stop bouncing around.

Gravity: As Inescapable as Black Holes and the IRS

This section has nothing to do with black holes or the IRS, but they're both things that you can't get away from! One of the most common effects that a game programmer needs to model in a game is *gravity:* the force that attracts every object in the universe to every other object. It's an invisible force and, unlike magnetic fields, can't be blocked.

In reality, gravity isn't really a force. That's simply how we perceive it. Gravity is really caused by the curvature of space. Any object positioned in space creates a bending of the surrounding space, as Figure 17-12 shows. This bending creates a potential energy difference; hence, the objects "fall down" the gravity well toward each other. That's really what gravity is. It's a manifestation of the bending of the space-time fabric.

For the purposes of this book, you don't need to worry about space-time curvature and what gravity really is; you just want to model it. As Figure 17-13 shows, you need to consider two cases when modeling gravity:

- ✔ Case 1: Two or more objects with relatively the same mass
- ✔ Case 2: Two objects where the mass of one object is much greater than the mass of the other

Case 2 is really a subcase of Case 1. For example, you may have learned that if you drop a baseball and a refrigerator off a building, they fall at the same rate. The truth of the matter is that they don't, but the difference is so infinitesimal (on the order of 10^{-24}) that you could never see the difference. Of course, other forces, such as wind shear and friction, may make a difference; hence, a baseball falls faster than a piece of paper because the paper undergoes a lot of wind resistance.

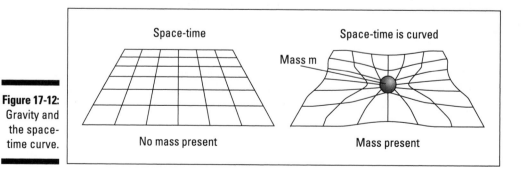

Figure 17-12:
Gravity and the space-time curve.

Space-time

No mass present

Space-time is curved

Mass m

Mass present

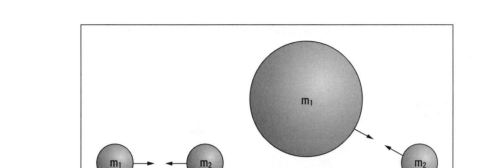

Figure 17-13:
Cases of
gravity.

Case 1

Case 2

$m_1 \approx m_2$

$m_1 \gg m_2$

The math of gravity

Take a look at the math behind gravity. The gravitational force between any two objects with mass *m1* and *m2* is as follows, where G is the gravitational constant of the universe (equal to 6.67×10^{-11} N $\times$ m^2 $\times$ kg^{-2}) and *r* is the distance between the objects:

$$F = (G \times m1 \times m2) \div r^2.$$

For the form of the equation the masses must be in kg and the distance *r* in meters. Also, note that big *G* (gravitational constant of the universe) differs from little *g* (gravitational pull of the Earth). Let's try out an example. Say that you want to compute the gravitational attraction between two average-size teenagers of 155 pounds (70 kg) at a distance of 1 meter:

$$F = 6.67 \times 10^{-11} \times 70 \text{ kg} \times 70 \text{ kg} \div (1 \text{ m})^2 = 3.26 \times 10^{-7} \text{ N}.$$

That's not much force is it? However, let's try the same experiment with a 155-pound (70 kg) person and the planet Earth (5.98×10^{24} kg) at 1 meter:

$$F = 6.67 \times 10^{-11} \times 70 \text{ kg} \times 5.98 \times 10^{24} \text{ kg} \div (1 \text{ m})^2 = 2.79 \times 10^{16} \text{ N}.$$

Obviously, 10^{16} Newtons would crush you into a pancake, so something must be wrong. The problem is that we are assuming that the Earth is a point mass, and the other mass is 1 meter from it. A better approximation would be to use the radius of the Earth, which is 6.38×10^6 m, as the distance. (You may assume that any spherical mass of radius *r* is a point mass as long as the matter the sphere is made of is homogenous, and any calculations must place the other object at a distance greater than or equal to *r*.)

$$F = 6.67 \times 10^{-11} \times 70 \text{ kg} \times 5.98 \times 10^{24} \text{ kg} \div (6.38 \times 10^6 \text{ m})^2 = 685.93 \text{ N}.$$

Now that seems more reasonable. As a sanity check, on Earth, 1 pound is equal to 4.45 N, so converting the force to pounds, you have

685.93 N ÷ (4.45 N ÷ 1 pound) = 155 pounds

Which was the starting weight. Anyway, now that you know how to compute the force between two objects you can use this simple model in games. Of course, you don't have to use the real G constant; the important thing is the form of the equation, which states that the gravity between two objects is proportional to a constant times the product of their masses divided by the square of the distance between the objects' centers.

Using this formulation is how you model a black hole in space game. For example, you have a ship and a black hole on-screen, and you want the ship to get sucked in if it gets too close to the black hole. Using the force equation is a snap. Here's what you do:

1. **Make up an artificial gravity constant G that works well in the virtual game world.**

2. **Assign an arbitrary mass for the ship and a much larger mass for the black hole.**

3. **Compute the force between the ship and black hole and convert it to acceleration with $F = ma$.**

4. **Move the ship directly toward the black hole each frame. As the ship gets closer, the force increases until the player can't get free!**

PROG17_4.CPP (the code for the executable PROG17_4.EXE) gives you an example of a black-hole simulation. You navigate a ship around and have to avoid the black hole in the middle of the screen. To control the ship, use the arrow keys. See if you can get into orbit!

The math of falling objects

"Gravity" in games is also used to simulate how things fall from the sky or off buildings at the proper rate. In this situation, one object has a mass much greater than the other. However, you have one more constraint to deal with: One object is fixed — the ground. Figure 17-14 depicts the situation that I'm describing.

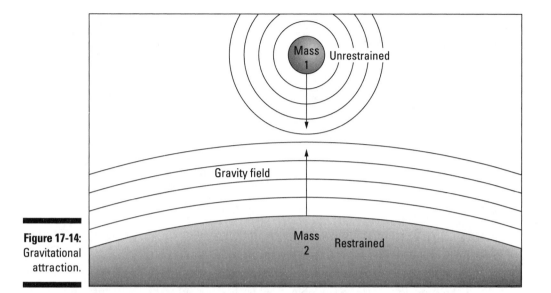

In this case, you can assume several things to simplify the math. The first is that the acceleration due to gravity is constant for the mass that's being dropped, which on Earth is equal to 9.8 m/s² (meters per second) or 32 ft/s² (feet per second). (Of course, that's not really true, but true enough to about 23 decimal places.) Hence, if you know that the acceleration of any falling object is simply 9.8 m/s², you can just plug that into the motion equation for velocity or position. Thus, the formula for velocity of a falling object as a function of time is based on the general acceleration equation with a fixed acceleration constant as shown in the following equation:

$$v(t) = v_0 + 9.8 \text{ m/s}^2 \times t$$

And position is

$$y(t) = y_0 + v_0 \times t + \frac{1}{2} \times 9.8 \text{m/s}^2 \times t^2$$

In the case of a ball falling off a building, you can make the initial position x_0 equal to 0 and the initial velocity v_0 also 0, which simplifies the falling-object model to

$$y(t) = 1/2 \times 9.8 \text{m/s}^2 \times t^2$$

Furthermore, you're free to change the constant of 9.8m/s² to anything you like, and *t* represents the frame number in a game. Taking all that into consideration, here's how you make a ball fall from the top of the screen:

```
int y_pos     = 0, // top of screen
    y_velocity = 0, // initial y velocity
    gravity    = 1, // don't want to fall too fast

// do gravity loop until object hits
// bottom of screen at SCREEN_BOTTOM
while(y_pos < SCREEN_BOTTOM)
    {
    // update position
    y_pos+=y_velocity;
    // update velocity
    y_velocity+=gravity;
    } // end while
```

Note: To simplify things, I used the velocity to modify the position instead of modifying the position directly with the position formula, which is harder to work with because it's a function of time (or frame number in this case).

So how do you make the object fall with a curved trajectory? Just move the x position at a constant rate each cycle, and the object seems as if it were more thrown off than just dropped. The code to do this is

```
int y_pos     = 0, // top of screen
    y_velocity = 0, // initial y velocity
    x_velocity = 2, // constant x velocity
    gravity    = 1, // don't want to fall too fast

// do  gravity loop until object hits
// bottom of screen at SCREEN_BOTTOM
while(y_pos < SCREEN_BOTTOM)
    {
    // update position
    x_pos+=x_velocity;
    y_pos+=y_velocity;

    // update velocity
    y_velocity+=gravity;
    } // end while
```

A falling object is the same as an object accelerating upward, just in the opposite direction. Change the direction in PROG17_2.CPP (executable PROG17_2.EXE) to simulate a falling object by inverting the acceleration constant.

I've been using integers in all the demos thus far to keep things simple. However, you may need to use floating-point values in your code to make things accurate enough. And with Pentium I and II processors, floating-point math is as fast as integer (and faster in some cases).

Putting on the Brakes with Friction

Friction means any force that retards or consumes energy from another system. For example, automobiles use internal combustion to operate; however, a whopping 30 to 40 percent of the energy produced is eaten up by thermal conversion or mechanical friction (in which energy is wasted by parts rubbing and grinding together, for example). On the other hand, a bicycle is about 80 to 90 percent efficient and is probably the most energy-efficient mode of transportation in existence.

Friction is basically a resistance and hence can be modeled with a force usually referred to as the *frictional force.* Figure 17-15 depicts the standard frictional model of a mass *m* on a flat plane.

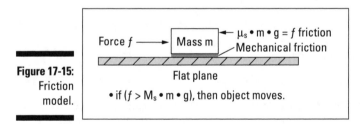

Figure 17-15:
Friction
model.

If you try to push the mass depicted in Figure 17-15 in a direction parallel to the plane, you encounter resistance — frictional force that presses back against you. This force is defined mathematically as F_f shown below, where *m* is the mass of the object, *g* is the Earth's gravitational constant (9.8 m/s²), and μ_s is the static frictional coefficient of the system, which depends on the conditions and materials of the mass and the plane:

$$F_f = m \times g \times \mu_s$$

If the force *F* that you apply to the object is greater than F_f, the object begins to move. Once the object is in motion, its frictional coefficient usually decreases to another value, which is referred to as the *kinetic friction, μ_k.* Then when you release the force, the object slowly decelerates and comes to rest because friction is always present.

To model friction, all you need to do is apply to all your objects a constant negative velocity that's proportional to the friction that you want. Mathematically speaking:

velocity new = velocity old – friction

The results are objects that slow down at a constant rate after you stop moving them. Of course, you have to watch out for letting the sign of the velocity go negative or in the other direction, but that's just a detail. (But it's a detail that's important enough to take into consideration, as I do in the next example.)

Here's an example of an object that's moved to the right with an initial velocity of 16 pixels per frame and then slowed down at a rate of 1 pixel per frame due to virtual friction:

```
int x_pos      = 0,  // starting position
    x_velocity = 16, // starting velocity
    friction   = -1; // frictional value
// move object until velocity <= 0
while(x_velocity > 0)
    {
    // move object
    x_pos+=x_velocity;
    // apply friction
    x_velocity+=friction;
    } // end while
```

The first thing to notice is how similar the model for friction is to gravity. They're almost identical. Gravitational forces and frictional forces act with the same laws. In fact, all forces can be modeled in the exact same way. Also, you can apply as many forces to an object as you want: Just sum them up. That's due to the law of *superposition*.

As an example of friction, I've written a little air-hockey demo named PROG17_5.CPP (or PROG17_5.EXE in executable form). The program fires a hockey puck on a virtual air-hockey table in a random direction every time you press the spacebar. The puck then bounces off the borders of the table until it comes to rest due to friction. If you want to change the frictional coefficient of the table, use the arrow keys. See if you can add a paddle and a computer-controlled opponent to the simulation!

Chapter 18

Putting the Game Engine to Work with Underworld

● ●

In This Chapter

▶ Playing *Underworld*

▶ Exploring the design

▶ Understanding the game elements

▶ Using artwork and sound

▶ Entering the contest

▶ Making changes and recompiling

● ●

*E*ven though *Star Ferret* was a good example of a working game, I wanted to give you another game that is less of a shoot-'em-up and includes a few more elements of a complete game, such as levels and more advanced AI. Hence, I came up with *Underworld,* an underground maze game that uses the GPDUMB game engine I discuss in this book. In this chapter, I cover some of the design issues and point you in the right direction to make your own modifications to the game.

Playing the Game

The goal of *Underworld* is simple: Stay alive as long as possible and rack up as many points as possible.

Underworlder is a miner that tunnels through potential mining sites while ridding the area of aliens and monsters (as shown in Figure 18-1). Underworlder has a single weapon — a grappling pump. The grappling pump fires a projectile that injects a creature with compressed air on impact. If you fire enough of the grappling-pump projectiles into a creature, that creature will explode!

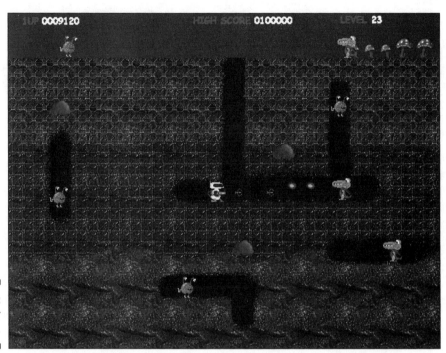

Figure 18-1:
Underworlder
in action.

However, the creatures of the game aren't just going to sit around and let you fire weapons at them. The Puff Dragons are fierce reptilian-based creatures that are not only fast, but can expel fire balls through their nostrils, which, of course, are deadly to Underworlder. The Dyclops are the second foe of Underworlder. These creatures look like they are a genetic experiment gone wrong, but don't let their cute facades fool you; they are deadly. Their touch alone will cause Underworlder to go into anaphylactic shock and die!

Your goal is to run around tunneling and clearing the mining area of all Puff Dragons and Dyclops. However, there's a catch. . . . A number of unstable rock formations are in the area. When you walk under them, they may break loose and crush you — or one of the creatures — so be careful. To clear a level, you must rid it of all unauthorized life. As the game proceeds, you will be transported to different work areas to do your dirty work.

To play the game, run the main executable UNDERWLD.EXE. Here are the controls:

✔ **Arrow keys:** Control direction

✔ **Ctrl:** Fire

✔ **Esc:** Exit game

✔ **P:** Pause

Designing for Fun

I wanted to make an unusual game that had a "maze" format to it, as well as interesting, cartoonish characters and reasonably nonviolent game play. That's how I came up with *Underworld*. The game play involves lots of elements I discuss throughout the book, including: BOBs for graphics (which the characters and weapons utilize heavily), Artificial Intelligence (which motivates the characters), DirectInput (which drives the simple keyboard controls), and DirectSound (which controls all those cool sound effects).

The other reason I decided to do this game instead of another was that *Underworld* is a single-screen game (easier to write and understand) that offers levels. I wanted to show you at least one example of creating a game engine that reads a data file and then uses the file to generate the game level. This capability is a key element of *Underworld*. Moreover, I made the file format ASCII and human readable so that you can add levels and change graphics yourself. The section, "The Level Information File," later in this chapter describes this format.

The 5th Elements of the Game

Underworld includes about five main game elements. I want to briefly explain each in a neo-technical manner, so you can get a grip on how these elements work, and you can make changes yourself later.

✔ **Underworlder:** The main character that you control. Basically, he isn't that smart in terms of functionality, and he depends on you for guidance. The hardest part of writing the character code was making sure that the proper animation was being displayed when he was walking, digging, firing, or dying. This part of the code took a lot of conditional logic to take all the subtle cases into consideration.

✔ **Puff Dragons:** A little more complex than Underworlder because they are controlled by game AI. They use a standard finite state machine (FSM) with tracking logic as the main thinking mode. The firing of the Puff Dragons is controlled by random probability and the distance from the player. (For more on FSMs, check out Chapter 2; tracking logic, Bonus Chapter 23; and using probability and proximity, Bonus Chapter 23.)

- ✔ **Dyclops:** Almost identical to the Puff Dragons, but without the ability to fire. However, because they can't fire, I jacked up their AI a little to make them a bit more aggressive than the Puff Dragons. (I cover AI in detail in Bonus Chapter 23.)

- ✔ **Rocks:** Complicated to implement. I had to write code so that they can fall on any of the game objects and crush them. But they had to act like a magnet when falling on an object; that is, the object has to stick to the rock as the rock falls. My final solution was to write a domino-effect algorithm that stuck the first object to the rock; then other objects can stick to the first object, and so on.

- ✔ **Prizes:** The prizes are the simplest objects of the game. They appear after the player drops two or more rocks. The prize appears for about 10 to 15 seconds and then disappears. If the player touches it, he or she gets a really big bonus.

The Level Information File

The cool thing about *Underworld* is that each level is not defined by hard-coded programming, but by a general-level file that contains the definitions for all the levels in a simple understandable ASCII format. The name of the file that *Underworld* loads is called UNDLEV.DAT. The file format consists of a number indicating the total number of levels followed by each level record. I don't have time to cover the format here, but the header of the file itself contains complete instructions, so simply open the file in your favorite ASCII text editor and read.

Your game of *Underworld* can have up to 64 levels. After you defeat the last level in the game, the program starts selecting levels randomly.

The Artwork and Sound

I drew all the artwork by hand except for the prizes, which were modeled with Caligari TrueSpace III. Other than the prizes, each of the game objects (Underworlder, Puff Dragons, Dyclops, rocks, weapons, and so on) were drawn pixel-by-pixel with Paint Shop Pro 4.0. This goes to show you the power of this paint program. For example, many of the objects are subtly lit, which was accomplished by painting with the light touch-up option. In general, all the art is named UND*.BMP.

The music for _Underworld_ was created by my friend Todd Masten. He is an incredible musician who creates music for games and multimedia titles. He can create any kind of music you like from dark and evil (my favorite) to jazz, rock, and more. If you want to get in touch with him, you can e-mail him at `tmasten@ns.net`.

I made most of the sound effects with my own voice and then post-processed them with Sound Forge. Some of the sounds are from the Sound Ideas General 6000 sound library, which I suggest that you purchase if you are going to do any serious game programming. All the sounds and music are named `UND*.WAV`.

Making Modifications and Recompiling

Underworld is compiled with the same files as _Star Ferret_, so you need all the GPDUMB1,2 library files, the DirectX libraries, and, of course, the main C/C++ source file `UNDERWLD.CPP`. Simply compile as usual, and you shouldn't have a problem.

The Underworld Challenge

As with all my books I like to create some sort of contest or other impetus to get you to write a game from scratch or modify a game that I provide. In keeping with tradition, here's a little contest for you: Improve _Underworld_ as much as you can and send me your game. On January 1 of every year until the year 2005, I will select a winner from all the submissions, send the winner $100 (in US funds), and put the winning game up on my Web site for all to see and download.

If you're interested in participating and want to get more information about the contest, point your browser at the _...For Dummies_ Web site:

`www.dummies.com`

There you'll find the contest rules and a link to my site, as well as more information about other _...For Dummies_ books that you might like.

Chapter 19

Marketing Your Madness

● ●

In This Chapter

▶ Self-publishing

▶ Working with publishers

▶ Making deals

● ●

*I*n the dark ages of game programming — about 10 years ago — you could create nearly any kind of video game and make money from it. Back then, technology wasn't the driving force of games, so the playing field for game developers was relatively even. Sure, some developers had sprite scalers and others knew more about physics modeling, but, really, games were 2D and all you needed to make one was a programmer, an artist, and, maybe, a musician. Typically, one person served as all three!

But the '90s are much tougher. Now, 3D has really taken off, and creating a game that has a chance of making money is difficult because so many people must be involved in its development. The average game development team consists of about 7 people, and many teams include more than 50 members! Nowadays, you just can't just throw a game together and make money.

Even so, millions of people still like 2D games. Those people don't care whether a game is 2D, 3D, or virtual reality; if it's fun, they'll play it. This story's moral: If you want to write serious games and have a chance to market them, know the competition and make sure that you pick a game genre that you have a chance in as a beginning designer. Simply said, don't try to go head-to-head with id Software, Inc. by yourself. Instead, create 2D side-scrolling games or some genre that you can realistically compete in.

This chapter deals with selling your games after you've made them. I talk about three methods of getting your game before the public:

✔ Publishing the game yourself, which means that *you* market it and distribute it.

✔ Using a commercial shareware publisher to market and distribute the game for you.

✔ Selling your game to a professional publisher.

Self-Publishing

All right, you've written your first game, and you want to publish it yourself. The process isn't that complicated. First, make sure that the game is solid (bug-free), and that it has a simple installation and setup. Then compress all the game files into one archive file with WinZip (or a similar product) or self-extracting .EXE. Also, in your game files, include these documents (in simple MS-DOS ASCII format):

- ✔ VENDOR.DOC: This file describes what your terms are for other people to distribute your game. For example, someone in another country may want to put your game on a CD bundle, so use this document to specify the conditions they must agree to.

- ✔ FILEID.DIZ: This file is read by BBSs (bulletin board systems) as a short description of your game. Limit this document to a few lines of information about you and the product.

- ✔ ORDER.DOC: If you want to sell your game and get money for it, use this file to provide ordering information.

- ✔ README.TXT: This standard READ ME file contains information that you want the user to read before using your program. Typically, I include last-minute changes, bug fixes, and other similar notes.

Now that your game is ready to go, the quickest way to get it out there is to upload it to as many BBSs as possible and create a Web page for it (if you have your own Web site). This way, people can get access to your game. In addition, it won't hurt you to buy some shareware CDs and call the producers of the CDs to see if they will put your game on their CD.

Next, you must decide on a price for your game; don't be too expensive, but don't be too cheap. A good price range is usually $30 to $40, and that amount is commensurate with most other games. Don't sell your game for $5.00. I guarantee that everyone will think that it's bad; how could anything be good for $5.00?

Getting the money is the next problem. Of course, at first, you will probably only be able to handle checks or money orders unless you have a credit card merchant account. If you do decide to have people send you checks, get a post office box so that you don't need to divulge your street address.

However, you can contract a company to handle e-commerce for you. The company's staff will take credit card orders, allow people to download your product from their site, and send the money to you once a month. The cost for these services ranges from free to a 50-percent commission on the profits, so shop around! Here are a couple of companies I have used:

- ✔ Get Software: `http://www.getsoftware.com`
- ✔ Maagnum Commerce: `http://www.safesell.com`

If you have an Internet/Web account, create a Web site for your company and place your product on the Web for downloading. Don't worry if you can't afford a full-blown domain name and 50MB Web site with CGI scripts and FrontPage extensions. Most Internet accounts come with a free 3MB to 5MB personal Web site that you can put your game on for free. The address may look something like `www.provider.com/~you`, but that's life.

If you want to do everything by the book, start up a small sole proprietorship and get a business license and bank account. The bank account is usually free to open for sole proprietorships (small fee or initial deposit for some banks), but starting a small company costs anywhere from $30 to hundreds of dollars per year, depending on your state. Call your local county clerk's office or Chamber of Commerce to find out about your local laws. You may want to consult a tax advisor or read a good book on the subject before you do anything. For more guidance contact the Association of Shareware Professionals at:

```
www.asp-shareware.org
```

That's it. Write the game, make a `.ZIP` file with the added information and ordering documents, and then upload your game to every site you can (you can start by searching for game sites on the Web and link from there). Some of my favorite sites are:

- ✔ Happy Puppy: `www.happypuppy.com`
- ✔ C-Net: `www.cnet.com`
- ✔ The Adrenaline Vault: `www.avault.com`

In addition, you may want to download or purchase a Web spider or bot that will upload your information to hundreds of Web sites for you! You can find a number of spiders or bots just by searching the Web using "bot" or "spider" as the keyword, but to start off, check out the shareware sections of the Windows 95 site at: `www.windows95.com`. This is the coolest site for Windows users and programmers — a must-have link!

Commercial Shareware

The next step up from self-publishing is still a shareware method, but instead you go through professional shareware channels such as GT Interactive, Apogee, or Epic Mega Games instead of distributing your game yourself. All these companies started out small with simple 2D games, and now they are just as powerful as commercial publishers. Here are some tips with regard to dealing with shareware publishers:

✔ The best way to try to sell your game to these companies is to call or e-mail them and find out the proper party to send submissions to. The companies will consider completed games and works in progress, but make sure that you make a good impression with your call or e-mail.

✔ Be aware that most of these companies have submission packets that include NDAs (Non-Disclosure Agreements) to protect you and them from trade secrets and technological theft. Also, many publisher NDAs stipulate that you only work with them and not with many companies at once (which they don't like, because you might get a better deal).

✔ If you make a deal with a professional shareware publisher, hire a lawyer (if you can afford one) to review the final contract and help you negotiate a fair deal. Shareware publishers should give from 30 to 50 percent of royalties to the developer (you); if they don't offer such royalties in the contract, then find another publisher!

✔ Most shareware publishers don't give any kind of financial support or advances unless your game is incredibly hot. However, many of them will give you resources such as artists and an extra programmer.

Professional Publishing

The ultimate level of game publishing is, of course, the professional level — selling your game to a company such as Electronic Arts or Lucas Games. This approach is very similar to going through a shareware publisher, but a lot more intense and difficult to consummate a deal. If your game is of such high quality that you're even considering going to a big publisher, be sure to have all the answers about your game, and be ready to spend a lot of time and money on lawyers and negotiations.

I can tell you from experience that you need to negotiate the deal you _really want;_ otherwise, you'll be miserable. Many game developers have a great prototype, and they need some supplementary financing or an advance as part of the deal. Publishers will always try to get the best deal for themselves, which in many cases isn't the best deal for you or the project. You must be very clear to the publisher and explain every detail of the game and the resources you need so that they can better understand your objective.

The development of a game is so unpredictable that you had better demand the time and money you need or simply bite your tongue and don't sign the deal. I know that making demands is difficult, but you can't afford to make a bad game because you didn't get the right money or time.

Part V
The Part of Tens

The 5th Wave — By Rich Tennant

"YOU KNOW THAT GUY WHO BOUGHT ALL THAT SOFTWARE? HIS CHECK HAS A WARRANTY THAT SAYS IT'S TENDERED AS IS AND HAS NO FITNESS FOR ANY PARTICULAR PURPOSE INCLUDING, BUT NOT LIMITED TO, CASHING."

In this part . . .

No *...For Dummies* book would be complete without "The Part of Tens." I open up my most secret Xtreme Games files and give you some of the coolest little game-programming tidbits you could want. You get to uncover the game programming secrets passed down from the masters, the most common mistakes a game programmer makes, and finally, the URLs and information that takes you to the hottest game resources on the Web.

Chapter 20

Ten Basic Rules of Game Design

*W*riting a good game is difficult to do. Face it: Out of the thousands of games that are written each year, only a handful of them are any good. Therefore, it's really hard to say what makes a good game and a bad one. Sure, if a game has good graphics and sound, that's probably a good start. However, plenty of games have good graphics and sound, but they don't sell well. I think that the key to making a good game is a good design, so take a look at some basic rules that work for me and other game developers I know — or at least the ones that I intercept e-mail from.

Start with a Good Story and a Good Idea

Writing a good game is difficult enough with a good idea and story line, but starting a game with a bad idea and story line is certain death. Therefore, think through your game. Brainstorm about it. Even if you are writing a shoot-'em-up or a side scroller and the player isn't going to see a lot of story, make up a story line to help you make the game coherent and logical.

Finally, acid test your idea with a number of game players and see what they think. You may not know that 5,000 *Pac Man* clones exist or that your idea simply stinks! So get a little feedback. Now, don't let other people change your mind about what you want to do, but see if they can give you some ideas or criticisms that help. Remember, everyone is a critic! It's the one thing that everyone is good at.

Write Your Design on Paper

One of the biggest mistakes you can make when you write a game is to write it "on the fly." Even though you may have a great idea and story line, write it down. Make a little script of sorts, with some drawings, some names, key elements of the game, and the overall flow of the game. This written plan (often called a *design document* in the industry) will help you stay on target, and it will help you remember all those cool ideas.

Furthermore, when you write ideas down and read them later, it gives you a better chance to realize whether a concept is good, stupid, of high quality, or generally unbecoming to a game developer. Lastly, if you somehow get lucky enough to get some millionaire friend or big company to help finance your game, they're going to want to see a design document, so recording your ideas is a good habit to get into.

Don't Bite Off More Than You Can Chew!

The biggest mistake I think that "newbie" game developers make is trying to create a game that is too advanced for their current skills. I get mail all the time from people who ask, "How do you make a *Quake* engine? I also want to make the computer think, so can you help me there, too?" Anyone who asks these kinds of questions must be under the assumption that I'm going to send them 5,000 to 10,000 pages of text. Obviously, they don't know what they are asking. The moral of the story is this: If you don't know what you're doing, try a simpler game. Otherwise, you will never finish it.

You'll be better off making a game like *Pong, Asteroids,* or *Centipede* for your first attempt and finishing the project, rather than starting on a game you'll never finish or learn from because your goal was too lofty.

This point brings me to a little story about this guy named Mike. I met Mike when I was about 13 years old. He said he was making a 3D game called *Escundar,* or something like that. I'm not *that* old, but I was 13 a long time ago, and a 3D game was far out of Mike's reach. Instead of choosing a simpler design, he ended up never making any game! But all he *talked* about was making games.

So take my advice: Start with a simple design; otherwise, you'll never finish the game.

Target an Audience and Stick with It

In the age of politically correct everything, don't jump on the bandwagon. We're *not* all alike. Whether I like it or not, I will never be able to play basketball better than Michael Jordan, and likewise, he will never be able to design a RISC processor out of TTL chips. My point: Games are art. If a game's content is going to offend someone, too bad. I'm offended by commercials on TV, pork, salesmen, and a lot of other things, but I like to be offended; it makes me think.

So when you design your game, design it to entertain the people that you know will play it. If your target audience consists of militant teens who want to blow things up, then write the game for them; include lots of explosions, monsters, weapons, antipersonnel devices, and other not-so-politically correct elements. Don't worry about infuriating some game-violence watchdog groups; some of those folks could find fault with *Space Invaders.*

A game is like a piece of music, art, or film. It should be designed to invoke thought, stir up emotions, and in general make you feel something. Hence, don't try to make everyone happy; just write the game you want to write for the market you are targeting. Of course, don't go crazy and be sexist, racist, or otherwise obnoxious in general with your program's elements and game play; just use the right amount of edgy bitmap characters and NC-17 situations to make your game say what you want it to say.

Come Up with a New Idea

When you start on a game design, you can do anything you want. You have no laws, rules, or limits on what you can do. Think about that for a minute — you have the chance to make the next *Tetris, Doom, Quake,* and so on. So don't confine yourself to any preconceived notions; be open-minded about any kind of game. So many games are available that you can't get away with content based on mindless murder and mayhem (but of course, those are always a good start). You need to come up with something — drum roll — *creative!*

Developing a unique idea can be more difficult than you think, but remember that some of the stupidest ideas make the best games. On the other hand, if you just can't seem to get anywhere, examine another game that you like and use it as a model. Take note of all the best elements you like about the game and then add your personal touches.

Using another game as a model does *not* mean duplicating the game elements (such as the characters or background) or the game play (such as the setting or even the plot line). Copyright infringement isn't the same as studying a game and using what you learn from it in your own design.

Be Flexible

When you start writing your game from your initial design, you may realize that there is no way it's going to work. Your graphics engine can't handle it, you don't have enough time, or whatever. This dilemma happens all the time. Don't trip; just take a step back and make changes that reduce your problems. Make sure that your modifications don't destroy the entire theme — or the game itself. I mean, you can't have a graphic adventure without graphics!

Design for the Future

Even the simplest shareware game is going to take 3 to 12 months to create, which means that you should plan ahead a little with your game design and try to take advantage of any technology or trends that will be popular when your game is released.

For example, suppose that you're writing a dinosaur game and you know a dinosaur movie is coming out in 6 months. Releasing your game at the same time is probably a good strategy for boosting sales.

If you know that a new processor is in development and just about everyone is going to get one, don't kill yourself writing your game to run on a 386! For example, the game I am starting on now needs hardware that doesn't exist, but I know the hardware will in two years!

Think Series, Sequels, and Add-Ons

If you happen to be so lucky as to write a really good game, make sure that you save some of your good ideas for a sequel. Or, better yet, design for a whole series. Of course, some games have complete closure, and a sequel may not be possible, but that doesn't stop the creators of *Nightmare on Elm Street* — and it shouldn't stop you! So when you're designing and writing your game, at least think about making another version. This approach will also help you because, hopefully, you can *prepare* to reuse some of the code and tools if you know that you're going to use them again.

Content Is Everything

If I see one more game that provides awesome graphics without good game play, I'm going to throw up! Games are successful for two main reasons: The graphics and technology are just so amazing that everyone has to see them, and the game is fun to play and offers good content. Content is as elusive as your best friend on moving day, but nonetheless, you'll know you have it when you have it. The best way to create content is to do it in layers like a musical track. First, create the main characters, and then the background characters, and so on; build up so that you're not overwhelmed.

For example, the most successful game in history — *Duke Nukem* — is nothing more than content. Sure the graphics are great, but the 3D engine was almost two years old when the game was released. The content made *Duke* a killer game. The designers kept adding little touches that made the game the funniest thing on Earth to play — I mean, the player-character's ability to go to the bathroom is the greatest selling point I can think of. This tuning process went on for almost a year before the game was released!

Give the Player Goals

I hate playing games that have no goals, no conclusion. One of the most important design features of a game is to give the player some sense that he is getting somewhere as he plays. If the player doesn't feel that she is making progress, then what's the point? A great example of goals and progress is *Out Of This World* by Interplay. If you can get a copy of it, be sure to check it out. It's a side-scrolling action/puzzle game that I became addicted to almost as badly as *Doom* when it came out, so *Out Of This World* is worth a look. When the player solves a problem, he is rewarded with the next level, a cool effect, or a piece of the story.

Don't Be Dumb!

Last but not least, make sure that your game design is cool. Don't make a game that only you and two Peruvian terrorists are going to "get." Make your game reasonably accessible to mainstream people and their knowledge banks.

Chapter 21

Ten Biggest Mistakes Game Programmers Make

*Y*ou can make about 10 billion general mistakes when you write a game and another 100 billion technical mistakes. In this chapter, I cover some of my favorites that span the spectrum of game development.

Making a Bad Deal

This mistake is the biggest one. If you're writing, financing, distributing, marketing, selling, and testing your game in-house, this advice won't apply to you. Otherwise, read on. Chances are good that you are going to involve one or more other parties in the development of your game. Maybe another party is going to finance it or distribute it. Regardless, don't let yourself be exploited. I know that this is easier said than done, but in the end a bad deal makes everyone unhappy.

If your game is going to take 15 months to make, then you need 15 months; that's all there is to it. If you need $50,000 or $1.5 million, then that's what you need. If you do the game in a shorter time frame or for less money, then I can guarantee that the game will be awful, it won't sell, and everyone will point their fingers at you! So when you make any kind of financial deal — marketing, sales, or distribution — make a good deal or you'll be sorry!

As a rule, a 2D game takes between six and nine months to complete and costs about $100,000 for commercial-level quality. A 3D game has an unlimited upper boundary, but 15 months and $750,000 is the absolute lower limit for any quality game.

Forgetting to Back Up Your Work

You have 1 million lines of C++ code in 50 modules, and it's all sitting on one hard drive. You worked on it for 6 months and — bang — there's a fire, a robbery, a crazy one-time significant other, or a hard-drive crash that destroys it all. Although the probability of these events happening is slim (except maybe for the one involving the crazy former significant other), one in a million is still too much of a chance for me to sleep peacefully. So make sure that you back up your work daily onto tape, Iomega ZIP disk, CD-ROM, or a remote server. If you lose your work, you are the only one to blame.

Truthfully, I have lost work only once. I lost a 3,500-line, 8-bit game back in the '80s — a 3D chess game. I had just printed it on thermal paper (40 columns) and, all of a sudden, my hard drive crashed and I lost it. I had to type all 3,500 lines of code from the printout! Granted, 3,500 lines isn't that bad, but the fact that I was dumb and didn't back it up made each line torture!

Missing Christmas

If you're going to write a game that is going to be released any time during the latter part of the year, then don't miss Christmas. Your best bet is to have the game finished by October or November at the very latest. If the game is shareware, then the time of release isn't that important. However, people always seem to be in more of a spending mood around the holidays, so don't shoot for Arbor Day or some other less-than-profitable time.

Failing to Test Properly

You've just written a killer game, and it works great on your computer. Well, so what! You had better test it on a number of different machines — and let others test it, as well — because you are probably (unconsciously) too easy on your game when you test it.

If you make a game that has one single problem, people will blow it out of proportion. A single pixel out of place will turn into "a bad video driver" on the Internet within 24 hours. Therefore, make sure that you beta test your game on a number of machines with different configurations. If you don't have access to 20 to 30 computers (like anyone does), then take your game on a disk or CD to the nearest computer store and try the game out on their computers. If someone asks you what you are doing, just tell them that you are thinking of buying some computers, and you want to see if this game is compatible — unless, of course, you want to use my response: "I'm a store shopper. If you play your cards right, I won't write you up."

If you don't like pretending to be James Bond, a local college (or high school) computer science lab will probably allow you to try your game during off-peak hours. But, pretending to be James Bond — or Janice Bond — is more fun.

Using Old Technology

We're not all millionaires, but using old technology and old ways doesn't pay. Try to keep up-to-date as much as possible. Even if you can't afford to get the latest C/C++ compiler or the best 3D modeler, at least you know that they exist. Maybe you can ask the company for a demo version or an evaluation unit. However, all excuses aside, game development is a high-tech business, and you have to be as up-to-date as possible.

Writing for DOS

DOS is *so* dead; it has been dead for 10 years. Game programmers used it only because a better alternative wasn't available. Well, if you're reading this book, you know that Win32 with DirectX is better. If you are making a professional game, don't even entertain the thought of writing for DOS. However, if you're creating a shareware game and you want to use a simple design, then I guess DOS is okay. DOS is good for learning purposes — heck, I used it for all my previous books — but if you can, write for Windows. If you want to make a DOS version for older computers (and stubborn people), then feel free — but Windows is better now that DirectX is in the picture.

Lying to the Public

The public is brutal. One minute they love you and see all your movies; the next, all the work you can get is in an ad for chewing gum. My suggestion: Don't lie — exaggerate, but don't lie. Better to hold back and blow the socks off the public and the critics than to hype your game to the point that everyone's expectations are too high, and they are going to be let down.

Neglecting to Advertise

If you are a former employee of Atari, please read this carefully: Products do *not* sell themselves. I repeat, products do *not* sell themselves. If you want your game to sell, you need to advertise in some fashion. If you're doing the marketing yourself, set up a simple Web site, put up some screen shots during development, and get some interest going. When you are about 1 to 2 months from release, then start sending out betas to game sites. When you're finally ready to release your game, go all out. Upload it to hundreds of sites manually or with an Internet spider or bot to put the game all over the place and at least let people know that it exists.

Allowing Too Many Cooks in the Kitchen

"Too many cooks spoil the broth." This adage applies to video games. For some jobs, more is not better. When you are writing a game and you realize that you need help from others, don't go nuts and involve too many people. Don't add people to the project just because they are friends or they think that game development is cool. Only bring in talented, dedicated people that you can trust and that really want to work on the project. And the fewer people working on game code, the better the game will be — that's a fact.

Omitting Comments in Your Code

Working with code that is insufficiently commented is my worst nightmare (and probably why I hate working as a software engineer at other companies). Please, I beg you, comment your game code with at least one comment per line. Let yourself and others know what the heck is going on. There is no excuse for not commenting the code. I don't know anyone that can program as fast as they can type for any sustained period, which means that you always have time to add comments. Furthermore, if you ever want to license or make a new version of your game, you won't need a Vulcan interpreter to figure out what you were doing!

Chapter 22

Ten Best Game Programming Resources on the Web

*I*n this chapter, which is the last chapter of The Part of Tens, I want to provide you with some information about where to look on the Web for various types of resources.

Game Programming Sites

The Web offers hundreds of cool game programming sites, so I can't list them all here; the following are some of the best ones:

✔ Woj@Moj: www.eating-out.co.nz/wojmoj

✔ Atmospheric Heights Arcade Emulators: www.xs4all.nl/~delite/arcade_mame.html

✔ The Games Domain: www.gamesdomain.com

✔ The Coding Nexus: www.gamesdomain.com/gamedev/gprog.html

✔ The Computer Game Developers' Conference: www.cgdc.com

✔ Game Programming Page: www.geocities.com/SiliconValley/Heights/3013/

Hot Downloads

A game programmer needs to have access to cool games, tools, and utilities. Here's a list of places that I like to download from:

- ✔ GT Interactive: `www.gtgames.com`
- ✔ Apogee: `www.apogee1.com`
- ✔ Epic Megagames: `www.epicgames.com`
- ✔ C-Net: `www.cnet.com`
- ✔ Windows 95.com: `www.windows95.com`

CompuServe Forums

I use CompuServe, and it provides a great number of game-related forums and areas. The best one is called GAMDEV and is designed for developers. You can find code, discussions, industry news, and more. So if you have a connection to CompuServe or access through a friend, check out GAMDEV.

3D Engines

The focal point of all 3D engine development on the Web is The 3D Engine List. This site contains 3D engines of varying levels of technology. The amazing thing is that many of the authors will let you use their engines for free! Here's the address:

`cg.cs.tu-berlin.de/~ki/engines.html`

Cool Books

A lot of books on graphics, sound, multimedia, and game development are available, but buying them to try them is too expensive. Here's a site that reviews game-related books and gives you the lowdown:

`www.gamesdomain.com/gamedev/gdevbook.html`

Microsoft DirectX Multimedia Expo

Microsoft undoubtedly has the biggest Web site in the world. The site has zillions of pages, sections, FTP sites, and so on. For information on DirectX, visit the DirectX Multimedia Expo at

```
www.microsoft.com/directx/default.asp
```

Notice the `default.asp` start-up page. This is an Active Server Page, which means that the page can do cool stuff. On this page, you can find the latest news and download the latest versions of DirectX, DirectMedia, and any patches to previous versions. I like to spend four to eight hours a week locked in my room reading everything on it. It's a good way to keep up with the constantly changing world of DirectX. Also, the Microsoft page has a number of links to DirectX-related sites, so you can get to many other sites from the URL listed here.

Usenet Newsgroups

I've never been interested in Internet newsgroups because they are such a slow way to communicate, but a few newsgroups are worth checking out:

- `alt.games`
- `comp.graphics.algorithms` (my favorite)
- `comp.graphics.animation`
- `comp.ai.games`
- `rec.games.programmer`

If you've never read news before, listen up. You need a news reader that can download the information and allow you to read the threads (that means messages). Most Web browsers (such as Netscape Navigator and Internet Explorer) have a news reader built in. Just look at the Help program and figure out how to set your browser up to read news. Then log on to any of the newsgroups (such as `alt.games`) and download all the messages.

What's Happening — Blue's News

About 99.9 percent of the Internet is a complete waste of bandwidth — mostly a bunch of people talking back and forth and communicating flights of fancy. However, *Blue's News* — a place where various industry icons and posers post their thoughts of the day — is worth checking out. Just visit

```
www.bluesnews.com
```

Game Development Magazines

To my knowledge, only two game development magazines are published in the English language. The first and largest is *Game Developer,* which is published monthly and contains articles on game programming, art, 3D modeling, market trends, and more. Their Web site is at

```
www.gdmag.com
```

Their sister site, *Gamasutra,* is at

```
www.gamasutra.com
```

The second game development magazine is *The Cursor,* a grassroots, back-to-basics magazine that has more of a free form. The Web site is located at

```
www.thecursor.com
```

My Site!

The name of my company is Xtreme Games LLC. We develop and publish 3D games for the PC platform. You can check us out on the Web at

```
www.xgames3d.com
```

You can find articles on 3D graphics, artificial intelligence, physics, DirectX, and a lot more. In addition, I'll post any changes or additions to this book on that site. Xtreme Games LLC publishes games as well as develops them, so if you think that you have a good game, log on and check out the information about authoring games through Xtreme. We also provide technical assistance to developers.

Appendix

About the CD

*H*ere's what you'll find on the *Windows Game Programming For Dummies* CD-ROM:

- ✔ Paint Shop Pro 5.01, one of the best shareware graphics and image processing programs for Windows.

- ✔ Caligari trueSpace 4.2, a state-of-the-art 3D modeler and animator.

- ✔ SoundForge XP, a sound processing and sound generation program.

- ✔ Adobe Acrobat 4.0 Reader, a high-end digital text reader that reads .PDF files such as the bonus chapters on the CD.

- ✔ The complete DirectX 6.1 SDK, including DirectMedia run-time.

- ✔ Source files for the code and sample programs that are discussed in each chapter.

- ✔ Stock graphics and sound effects to use in your own games.

- ✔ A number of 2D and 3D shareware games for your enjoyment during those breaks in your programming duties!

System Requirements

Make sure that your computer meets the minimum system requirements listed below. If your computer doesn't match up to most of these requirements, you may have problems using the contents of the CD.

- ✔ A PC with a Pentium or Pentium II processor.

- ✔ Microsoft Windows 95/98/2000/NT 5.0 or later.

- ✔ At least 16MB of total RAM installed on your computer. For best performance, we recommend that PCs have at least 32MB of RAM installed.

- ✔ At least 25MB of hard drive space available to install all the software from this CD. (You'll need less space if you don't install every program.)

- ✔ A CD-ROM drive — double-speed (2x) or faster.

> ✔ A 16- or 32-bit sound card.
>
> ✔ A monitor capable of displaying at least 256 colors.
>
> ✔ A modem and Internet connection if you want to check out all the online game programming resources.

If you need more information on the basics, check out *PCs For Dummies,* 6th Edition, by Dan Gookin; or *Windows 95 For Dummies,* 2nd Edition by Andy Rathbone (both published by IDG Books Worldwide, Inc.).

Using the CD in Windows

The CD for *Windows Game Programming For Dummies* is set up in a very simple way without a general setup program — such programs usually do more harm than good. Here's the main directory structure:

```
WGPDUMB <DIR> - The main directory
   |
   \DIRECTX    <DIR> - Contains DirectX and DirectMedia
   \APPS       <DIR> - Contains the applications
   \ARTWORK    <DIR> - Contains stock art media for your use
   \SOURCE     <DIR> - Contains the entire source code for the book
   \GAMES      <DIR> - Contains lots of cool games
```

Within each directory folder is a README.TXT file that gives you more information on what's in the folder and how to install each of the programs. However, in general, here's what you should do to get started:

1. **Place the CD in the CD-ROM drive and open it up with either Windows Explorer or My Computer.**

2. **Install the DirectX 6.1 SDK and run-time (if you don't already have them).**

   To install DirectX, navigate to the DIRECTX\ folder on the CD. There you will find the setup/install program for DirectX, which will install both the DirectX SDK and DirectMedia files on your system. Be sure to read the README.TXT file for any last-minute changes.

   After you have the DirectX SDK and run-time installed, you can copy the code and executables referred to in each chapter to your hard drive.

3. **Drag the SOURCE\ directory to your hard drive and your usual work area.**

   You want to drag the SOURCE\ folder to your drive so that you can work with the source files and compile the programs. Note that the demo programs will work running from the CD if you just want to check them out (but the DirectX run-time still must be loaded on your computer for the demos to work).

4. **To install the applications and games, you must either run an install application or a set-up application, or decompress each respective file.**

    Details on these procedures are within the APPS\ and GAMES\ subfolders.

 To help you with all the installation details I wrote a number of README.TXT files and sprinkled them throughout the directories of the CD. Make sure to read them if you get stuck installing a specific piece of software.

What You Find

The CD-ROM contains useful applications for game programming, cool shareware games, the DirectX SDK, stock artwork and sound effects that you can modify and use in your games, and the source code from all the programs and demos in the book. In addition, as a bonus I include two extra chapters (Bonus Chapters 23 and 24) in Adobe Acrobat .PDF format on the CD. To read these, use Adobe Acrobat Reader (which is also on the CD).

Applications

Here's a summary of the application software on this CD within the APPS\ folder:

- ✔ **Paint Shop Pro, from JASC, Inc.:** Paint Shop Pro is a shareware graphics viewing and editing tool. The Windows 95 Version is on the CD. Check out www.jasc.com/pspdl.html on the World Wide Web for a full description of the program.

- ✔ **Caligari trueSpace 4.2:** trueSpace 4.2 is a 3D modeler and animator that you use to create 3D objects and animations for your games. It has one of the easiest user interfaces available, but yet has many of the same features as high-end 3D modelers such as 3D Studio Max or Soft Image.

- ✔ **SoundForge XP:** SoundForge is the premiere sound processing application used by game programmers and musicians around the world. SoundForge has more features that any other sound program available — I still haven't figured out half of them!

- ✔ **Adobe Acrobat 4.0 Reader:** Acrobat Reader is used to read digital text saved in .PDF format. Version 4.0 not only has a standalone application to read .PDF files, but it also adds a plug-in to your Internet browser allowing you to read .PDF files that are on the Web. You need Acrobat Reader to read Bonus Chapters 23 and 24, which are on the CD.

> ✔ **WinZip 7.0:** WinZip is the world-famous compression-decompression program. This version is the very latest and supports all kinds of new features including a browser plug-in for "on the fly" Web decompression. Check out WinZip and install it (if you don't have it), because a number of applications on the CD are compressed and must be decompressed to install.

Finally, each application has its own method of installation, so be sure to read the README.TXT files within the directories to see how each should be installed.

Artwork

Within the ARTWORK\ directory, you find lots of artwork that you can use royalty-free as-is or that you can modify for your own personal use. The directory includes textures, monsters, explosions, mechanisms, backgrounds, and more.

DirectX

This book focuses much attention on DirectX game programming, so to save you about two days of downloading the 35MB DirectX SDK from the Microsoft Web site, the complete DirectX 6.1 SDK and run-time is on the CD! (It's in the DIRECTX\ subfolder.) In addition to DirectX, I include the latest top-secret DirectMedia run-time technology, which allows DirectX to communicate with most current Web browsers. Very cool.

To install DirectX, be sure to read the README.TXT files. They inform you of the installation details and of any last-minute changes to the program.

Games

Within the GAMES\ subfolder, I put some really cool games that you can play. (Call it "research" if anyone asks you what you're doing.) Check out these games, see what other game programmers are doing, and get some ideas. Each game has a particular installation method, so read the README.TXT file within the GAMES\ subfolder for some hints.

Source code

The entire source code for the book, along with all the executables and data, can be found in the SOURCE\ subfolder of the CD. Each chapter in the book is represented by a folder within the main SOURCE\ subfolder. For example, the source code for Chapter 12 is in the subfolder GPCHAP12\.

Also, check out the two Bonus Chapters: Chapter 23, "The Lowdown on Artificial Intelligence;" and Chapter 24, "Game Programming Potpourri." The .PDF files for these chapters are located within GPCHAP23\ and GPCHAP24\, respectively. Just load them into the Acrobat Reader and read them on-screen or print them out.

If You Have Problems (Of the CD Kind)

I tested all the software and programs from this book on a number of different machines and everything worked fine. However, when you are dealing with such complex software as games and DirectX, the possibility exists that some programs may not work properly. The following is a short list to help you if you encounter problems with either the installation or execution of the example programs.

Installation problems

The two likeliest installation problems are that you don't have enough memory (RAM) for the programs you want to use, or you have other programs running that are affecting installation or running of a program. If you get error messages such as Not enough memory or Setup cannot continue, try one or more of these methods and then try using the software again:

✔ Turn off any antivirus software that you have on your computer. Installers sometimes mimic virus activity and may make your computer incorrectly believe that it is being infected by a virus.

✔ Close all running programs. The more programs you're running, the less memory is available to other programs. Installers also typically update files and programs. So if you keep other programs running, installation may not work properly.

✔ Add more RAM to your computer. This is, admittedly, a drastic and somewhat expensive step. However, if you have a Pentium PC, adding more memory can really help the speed of your computer and enable more programs to run at the same time.

General execution problems

✔ **DirectX driver problems:** DirectX may not have a driver for your video or sound card. If this is the case, you will be notified during installation. Go to the manufacturer of your video or sound card and look for DirectX drivers, or keep an eye out at the Microsoft DirectX site for new updates. Don't worry if DirectX doesn't install a driver, however; it will still work, just not as well.

✔ **Compilation problems:** Fully 99 percent of compiler problems are "pilot" errors. So before you think that something is wrong, make sure that you have the DirectX library and your header paths set up in the compiler. Verify that you are creating a standard Win32 .EXE (if you're making a DirectX app). And finally, make sure that you can compile a basic Hello, World program. Don't jump into DirectX Windows programming without properly setting up your compiler and environment.

✔ **Video problems:** Some video cards don't work properly even with a DirectX driver. If you see a sudden flash of black or white video when you try to run some of the demos, click the Display Properties icon in Control Panel and change your video setting to 640 x 480 in 256 colors. This mode is the most common one for the demos and code in the book, and the new setting may solve your problems.

To make switching video modes quick and easy, check your favorite Web search engine for the utility program Quickres.exe (search for Quickres). After you install it, you can use Quickres, which sits in your system tray, to instantly change video modes without rebooting.

✔ **Read-only flag:** This is a very important detail, so read on. When a CD-ROM disk is created, all the files are written with the Read-only flag enabled. This setting is fine in most cases, unless you copy the files to your hard drive, edit them, and then try to write the files back to your drive (which you will do). You get a Read-only protection error. To fix, clear the Read-only flag on any files that you want to modify by choosing one of these methods:

- Use the Windows Explorer or My Computer to navigate into the hard-drive folder that contains the file you want to fix, select the file by right-clicking the mouse, click Properties in the resulting list, clear the Read-only check box in the Attributes section, and click the Apply button. You can do this with more than one file at once by selecting a group of files.

- Use the DOS ATTRIB command at a DOS prompt. Assuming that you have copied the entire SOURCE\ directory on your hard drive to the location C:\SOURCE, you can reset all the Read-Only attributes in one fell swoop by keying this at the DOS prompt:

```
C:\SOURCE\ATTRIB -r *.* /s
```

This instructs DOS to clear the Read-only flag (r) from all files (*.*) and all subfolders of C:\SOURCE (/s).

If you still have trouble installing or running the items from the CD, please call the IDG Books Worldwide Customer Service phone number: 800-762-2974 (outside the U.S.: 317-596-5430) or e-mail me at necron@slip.net.

Index

(continued)

(continued)

• J •

• *X* •

IDG Books Worldwide, Inc., End-User License Agreement

READ THIS. You should carefully read these terms and conditions before opening the software packet(s) included with this book ("Book"). This is a license agreement ("Agreement") between you and IDG Books Worldwide, Inc. ("IDGB"). By opening the accompanying software packet(s), you acknowledge that you have read and accept the following terms and conditions. If you do not agree and do not want to be bound by such terms and conditions, promptly return the Book and the unopened software packet(s) to the place you obtained them for a full refund.

1. **License Grant.** IDGB grants to you (either an individual or entity) a nonexclusive license to use one copy of the enclosed software program(s) (collectively, the "Software") solely for your own personal or business purposes on a single computer (whether a standard computer or a workstation component of a multiuser network). The Software is in use on a computer when it is loaded into temporary memory (RAM) or installed into permanent memory (hard disk, CD-ROM, or other storage device). IDGB reserves all rights not expressly granted herein.

2. **Ownership.** IDGB is the owner of all right, title, and interest, including copyright, in and to the compilation of the Software recorded on the disk(s) or CD-ROM ("Software Media"). Copyright to the individual programs recorded on the Software Media is owned by the author or other authorized copyright owner of each program. Ownership of the Software and all proprietary rights relating thereto remain with IDGB and its licensers.

3. **Restrictions on Use and Transfer.**

   (a) You may only (i) make one copy of the Software for backup or archival purposes, or (ii) transfer the Software to a single hard disk, provided that you keep the original for backup or archival purposes. You may not (i) rent or lease the Software, (ii) copy or reproduce the Software through a LAN or other network system or through any computer subscriber system or bulletin-board system, or (iii) modify, adapt, or create derivative works based on the Software.

   (b) You may not reverse engineer, decompile, or disassemble the Software. You may transfer the Software and user documentation on a permanent basis, provided that the transferee agrees to accept the terms and conditions of this Agreement and you retain no copies. If the Software is an update or has been updated, any transfer must include the most recent update and all prior versions.

4. **Restrictions on Use of Individual Programs.** You must follow the individual requirements and restrictions detailed for each individual program in the "About the CD" appendix of this Book. These limitations are also contained in the individual license agreements recorded on the Software Media. These limitations may include a requirement that after using the program for a specified period of time, the user must pay a registration fee or discontinue use. By opening the Software packet(s), you will be agreeing to abide by the licenses and restrictions for these individual programs that are detailed in the "About the CD" appendix and on the Software Media. None of the material on this Software Media or listed in this Book may ever be redistributed, in original or modified form, for commercial purposes.

5. **Limited Warranty.**

    (a) IDGB warrants that the Software and Software Media are free from defects in materials and workmanship under normal use for a period of sixty (60) days from the date of purchase of this Book. If IDGB receives notification within the warranty period of defects in materials or workmanship, IDGB will replace the defective Software Media.

    (b) IDGB AND THE AUTHOR OF THE BOOK DISCLAIM ALL OTHER WARRANTIES, EXPRESS OR IMPLIED, INCLUDING WITHOUT LIMITATION IMPLIED WARRANTIES OF MERCHANTABILITY AND FITNESS FOR A PARTICULAR PURPOSE, WITH RESPECT TO THE SOFTWARE, THE PROGRAMS, THE SOURCE CODE CONTAINED THEREIN, AND/OR THE TECHNIQUES DESCRIBED IN THIS BOOK. IDGB DOES NOT WARRANT THAT THE FUNCTIONS CONTAINED IN THE SOFTWARE WILL MEET YOUR REQUIREMENTS OR THAT THE OPERATION OF THE SOFTWARE WILL BE ERROR FREE.

    (c) This limited warranty gives you specific legal rights, and you may have other rights that vary from jurisdiction to jurisdiction.

6. **Remedies.**

    (a) IDGB's entire liability and your exclusive remedy for defects in materials and workmanship shall be limited to replacement of the Software Media, which may be returned to IDGB with a copy of your receipt at the following address: Software Media Fulfillment Department, Attn.: *Windows Game Programming For Dummies,* IDG Books Worldwide, Inc., 7260 Shadeland Station, Ste. 100, Indianapolis, IN 46256, or call 800-762-2974. Please allow three to four weeks for delivery. This Limited Warranty is void if failure of the Software Media has resulted from accident, abuse, or misapplication. Any replacement Software Media will be warranted for the remainder of the original warranty period or thirty (30) days, whichever is longer.

    (b) In no event shall IDGB or the author be liable for any damages whatsoever (including without limitation damages for loss of business profits, business interruption, loss of business information, or any other pecuniary loss) arising from the use of or inability to use the Book or the Software, even if IDGB has been advised of the possibility of such damages.

    (c) Because some jurisdictions do not allow the exclusion or limitation of liability for consequential or incidental damages, the above limitation or exclusion may not apply to you.

7. **U.S. Government Restricted Rights.** Use, duplication, or disclosure of the Software by the U.S. Government is subject to restrictions stated in paragraph (c)(1)(ii) of the Rights in Technical Data and Computer Software clause of DFARS 252.227-7013, and in subparagraphs (a) through (d) of the Commercial Computer–Restricted Rights clause at FAR 52.227-19, and in similar clauses in the NASA FAR supplement, when applicable.

8. **General.** This Agreement constitutes the entire understanding of the parties and revokes and supersedes all prior agreements, oral or written, between them and may not be modified or amended except in a writing signed by both parties hereto that specifically refers to this Agreement. This Agreement shall take precedence over any other documents that may be in conflict herewith. If any one or more provisions contained in this Agreement are held by any court or tribunal to be invalid, illegal, or otherwise unenforceable, each and every other provision shall remain in full force and effect.

Installation Instructions

● ●

*T*he *Windows Game Programming For Dummies* CD-ROM contains many cool applications, sample code blocks and programs, and shareware or demo games. To use the CD in Windows 95, Windows 98, or Windows NT, do the following:

1. **Insert the CD into your computer's CD-ROM drive, click Start⇨Programs, and click Windows Explorer.**

2. **In the list box that appears, double-click your CD-ROM drive's icon.**

   If this book's CD is in the drive and is functioning properly, the drive icon is marked *WINGP_FD.*

3. **Double-click the License Agreement text file.**

   Notepad opens with the License Agreement inside. Read the agreement and, if you agree with the terms, nod your head and then exit Notepad.

4. **Double-click the** WPGDUMB **folder.**

   The Windows Explorer list box shows that the CD-ROM is divided into several folders, each with descriptive names about the folder's contents. For example, the Source folder contains even more folders (named by chapters) that hold the code and sample programs referred to in the chapter text.

5. **To get more information about the contents of a folder, click the Readme text file.**

6. **To install a game program, click the program's setup or installation icon; if you want to work with a program or executable that's described in the chapter text, drag the appropriate chapter's folder to your hard drive.**

   After you click an install or setup icon, Windows Explorer drops to the background while the CD begins installation of the program you chose. Copying chapter folders to your hard drive makes it possible for you to recompile and modify source code — or just play around with it.

You can make copies of the sample files and modify them for your use. You may not publish the files in any form or claim copyright to them. If, after following the instructions in the "About the CD" appendix, you still have problems using the CD, please call the IDG Books Worldwide Customer Service phone number at 800-762-2974 (outside the U.S.: 317-596-5261).

Special note about the DirectX SDK on the CD: This program was reproduced by IDG Books Worldwide, Inc. under a special arrangement with Microsoft Corporation. If your diskette is defective, please return it to IDG Books Worldwide, Inc., which will arrange for its replacement. PLEASE DO NOT RETURN IT TO MICROSOFT CORPORATION. PLEASE DO NOT CONTACT MICROSOFT CORPORATION FOR PRODUCT SUPPORT. End users of this Microsoft program shall not be considered "registered owners" of a Microsoft product and therefore shall not be eligible for upgrades, promotions or other benefits available to "registered owners" of Microsoft products.

Notes

Notes

Notes

Notes

Notes

Notes

IDG BOOKS WORLDWIDE BOOK REGISTRATION

We want to hear from you!

Visit **http://my2cents.dummies.com** to register this book and tell us how you liked it!

- Get entered in our monthly prize giveaway.

- Give us feedback about this book — tell us what you like best, what you like least, or maybe what you'd like to ask the author and us to change!

- Let us know any other *...For Dummies*® topics that interest you.

Your feedback helps us determine what books to publish, tells us what coverage to add as we revise our books, and lets us know whether we're meeting your needs as a *...For Dummies* reader. You're our most valuable resource, and what you have to say is important to us!

Not on the Web yet? It's easy to get started with *Dummies 101*®: *The Internet For Windows*® *98* or *The Internet For Dummies*®, 5th Edition, at local retailers everywhere.

Or let us know what you think by sending us a letter at the following address:

...For Dummies Book Registration
Dummies Press
7260 Shadeland Station, Suite 100
Indianapolis, IN 46256-3917
Fax 317-596-5498

BESTSELLING
BOOK SERIES